Praise for *A Few Days of Trouble*

"The murder of Emmett Till is an inflection point in the story of America—a moment of particular and of universal significance. In this moving and important book, the Reverend Wheeler Parker Jr. and Christopher Benson give us a unique window onto the anguished search for justice in a case whose implications shape us still. . . . A vital and absorbing book."

—Jon Meacham,
Pulitzer Prize–winning author of *And There Was Light*

"Everyone should read this compelling account to understand why we must continue to fight for justice on all levels."

—Carlotta Walls LaNier,
author of *A Mighty Long Way: My Journey
to Justie at Little Rock Central High School*

"Emmett Till's murder changed the course of American history. Like so much of our history, the truth of it has been shrouded and distorted, but Reverend Parker's riveting book reveals new details about Till's life and community, as well as shocking twists in the decades-long quest for justice. It's a precious contribution to our shared history, and I am grateful for it."

—Heather McGhee,
New York Times bestselling author of *The Sum of Us*

"A critical piece of a story that has haunted America for more than sixty-five years is finally revealed—it is in this book that we begin to understand the core components of the movement we know as Black Lives Matter."

—ALICIA GARZA,
author of *The Purpose of Power* and
co-creator of #BlackLivesMatter

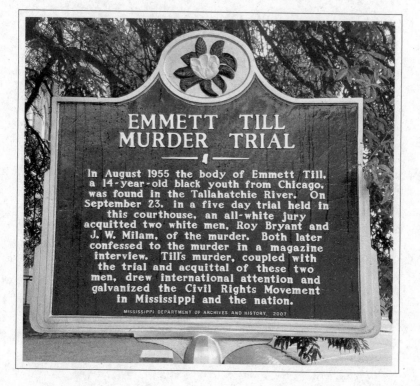

A Few Days Full of Trouble

*Revelations on the Journey
to Justice for My Cousin and
Best Friend, Emmett Till*

Reverend Wheeler Parker Jr.
and Christopher Benson

ONE WORLD
New York

LIBRARY OF CONGRESS CATALOGING-IN-PUBLICATION DATA
Names: Parker, Wheeler, author. | Benson, Chris, author.
Title: A few days full of trouble: revelations on the journey to justice
for my cousin and best friend, Emmett Till /
Reverend Wheeler Parker Jr. and Christopher Benson.
Description: New York: One World, [2023] | Includes bibliographical
references and index.
Identifiers: LCCN 2022022035 (print) | LCCN 2022022036 (ebook) |
ISBN 9780593134269 (hardcover) | ISBN 9780593134283 (trade) |
ISBN 9780593134276 (ebook)
Subjects: LCSH: Till, Emmett, 1941–1955. | Lynching—Mississippi—History—
20th century, | African Americans—Crimes against—Mississippi—History—20th
century, | Murder—Investigation—Mississippi—History—20th century, | Racism—
Mississippi—History—20th century, | Civil rights movement—Mississippi—
History—20th century
Classification: LCC HV6465.M7 P37 2023 (print) | LCC HV6465.M7 (ebook) |
DDC 364.1/34—dc23/eng/20221123
LC record available at https://lccn.loc.gov/2022022035
LC ebook record available at https://lccn.loc.gov/2022022036

Printed in the United States of America on acid-free paper

oneworldlit.com

2 4 6 8 9 7 5 3 1

To my lovely wife of fifty-five years,
Marvel McCain Parker

"And ye shall know the truth,
and the truth shall make you free."

—JOHN 8:32

Contents

Contents

Introduction

J ULY 12, 2018. Breaking news. The Associated Press was first with the story, which moved across the media and into public attention like wildfire. "US Reopens Emmett Till Investigation, Almost 63 Years After His Murder."[1]

According to this story and the others that followed, the FBI had reopened the Emmett Till murder investigation—an investigation conducted between 2004 and 2006 looking into a grisly lynching that had occurred in 1955. There was no conviction in the 1955 murder trial. No indictments handed down by a Mississippi grand jury in 2007, after that part of the FBI investigation. No more hope for justice. The cold case had grown even colder, and it seemed like nobody ever would answer for Emmett.

Now in July 2018, according to the news, things were heating up all over again. Reportedly, renewed government interest in the case was connected to new information, most likely a revelation published in a book by Duke University senior scholar Timothy Tyson.

The book claimed that Carolyn Bryant Donham now admitted she told a lie on Emmett Till—a lie that had cost him his life on August 28, 1955.[2]

The quality of the reporting now was different from the reporting I had endured for nearly sixty-three years—reporting that had carried mistakes, misinterpretation, misrepresentation, and very often seemed to validate her lie if only by repeating so much of it. The horrible loss of my cousin, my best friend, had been made all the more painful because of the distorted narratives I had been forced to read and hear over the course of three generations. Now there would be new action, according to stories reported with greater care and context by the AP, *The Washington Post, The New York Times,* and echoed by so many other conversations. And we, the family of Emmett Till, responded for the record.

"It's a prayer come true for her to recant," I told *The Washington Post.*[3]

What I knew at the time of the July 2018 reports, however, was what only a few other people knew. Four things, really. First, the Emmett Till case launched by the federal government in 2004 never had been closed—not completely, anyway. Several years of research, interviews, document analysis, an autopsy, and a grand jury inquiry, and no conclusion. So the dormant case—at least the FBI investigation—really hadn't been reopened in 2018 as reported. Maybe just reawakened, nudged a little.

Second, while this latest phase of the investigation was news in the summer of 2018, the information presented by the stories actually had been revealed in a federal report earlier and published on the US Department of Justice website that year, in March, four months before the media reports were published. There it was on page 17 in part 2 of the DOJ report following references to two other cases the department had opened: "The Department has re-opened In re Emmett Till, a case which had been listed as closed on prior Reports, after receiving new information."[4] This boring bureaucratic blurb had gone unnoticed at first, as it was just a routine checklist item resting there in a quiet space halfway through the report. Now, four months later, it was reported as breaking news. But even more, that March announcement came a year after several surviving Till family members and I had attended a meeting with government officials in Oxford, Mississippi—a meeting to discuss the case, to consider a way forward. And in that meeting, federal and state officials told the family elders what they planned to do, after hearing what we wanted them to do. So, this was hardly news to us. "This came as no surprise to members of the family," cousin Airickca Gordon-Taylor told *The Washington Post.*

Third, the July 2018 media reports pointed to the investigation's potential focus on Carolyn Bryant Donham, who, years earlier as Carolyn Bryant, had been at the center of it all—the lies that led to Emmett's brutal lynching, the lies that framed him and provided the justification for his murder in the racist culture of the Mississippi Delta. Still, she only represented half of the equation. For quite some time, I had known about the other half—a revelation hidden inside a revelation—and had promised to keep quiet while the government investigators and lawyers looked into every aspect of it. Not even all our family members could know that other part, given concerns that any leak could affect the outcome.

Fourth, the way forward in this latest phase of the investigation—the reawakening, the nudging—was what some people might call ironic. I prefer to call it divine intervention. You see, in a very important way, it all was made possible by Emmett Till. His death inspired the law that gave new life to the murder investigation—the Emmett Till Unsolved Civil Rights Crime Act.

This book is about all that—all that and then some. It presents a multidimensional search for justice stretching back to Emmett's murder. It presents my personal story, that of a survivor of the night of terror—August 28, 1955—when Emmett Till, our beloved "Bobo," was taken from us. It presents an emotional experience, one I've spent sixty-seven years suppressing. And it presents a process toward healing, one I share with so many family survivors of horrific spectacles—the photographed lynchings of the last century by criminals in hoods, and today's video-recorded murders executed by criminals with badges.

I have come to recognize that the story of Emmett Till is larger than Emmett Till himself. Larger and longer lasting than even our family's cries for justice. It is the story of power, and the way that power is used to put Black people in our place in society. The way it is used to keep us there. The way it is used to punish us when we step out of our assigned place. Bird-watching in Central Park.[5] Jogging in Georgia.[6] Standing our ground, protecting our home, our castle, in Louisville.[7] Playing with a toy gun in a public park in Cleveland.[8] Walking through a gated community at night.[9] Or yes, this too, pulling a childish prank at a tiny store in Money, Mississippi.

The story of Emmett Till, today, is also about power over the story itself—the way the story is told and who gets to tell it. Sadly, so many storytellers have seemed more interested in appropriating the story, making it their own, and elevating themselves as heroes somehow just for telling it. I am taking back the power to define it, to tell it, to preserve it as best I can. After all these years, Bobo's truth has not been told—not completely, anyway. This book is an attempt to accomplish that. And in that, to achieve some measure of justice, if only because we clear the record of so many errors and out-and-out lies in a number of the stories about Bobo—the Emmett Till I knew so well.

His mother tried to take back his story, just before she died in 2003. She wrote in her book published after her death that when many people wanted to tell the story, they would use her name, Emmett's name, and then write about themselves. She wanted us to know her son. She wanted us to know what was taken from her with his murder and what was taken from all of us in the absence of justice for his murder. She remembered her son in loving ways. Of course a mother is going to see her child in that way—a good way, the best way. That's her job. That's the truth that beats in the heart of a mother. I want the same thing she wanted. And maybe even more. While I feel like I was handed the baton in this long-distance journey to justice, there are parts of this story Mamie couldn't possibly know because, sadly, she didn't live long enough to experience them. And then, too, there are parts of Bobo's story she lived and didn't know. Let's just say that, as one of the boys on the block, I might have a unique perspective on Bobo. In that way, I might have known him— a big part of him—even better than his mama did. At least I knew him differently. After all, his mama knew the Emmett who wanted to go out and play. I knew the Bobo who played his mama. But that is all part of showing the fully developed person, the human being who wasn't recognized or respected as a human being by the men who took his life, and so much of our lives, too. In a way, it is that humanity that has been missed over the years by writers who really don't realize how their race affects their view of the world and the people in it. They are not racists. But they have biases they don't even see. And that's a problem. A big one when it comes to seeking and telling the truth. Especially our truth.

There is more still. Recent protests against abuse of power and demands for action show that America is getting awakened—once again. But this national conversation is only just beginning. There still is a need to put it all in context—historical context, as well as social context. Emmett Till should have been the beginning and the end of this conversation on racism and racial violence. But we still are talking about it. We still are experiencing it. That is why we see the resurrection of Emmett Till—at least his name—every time another African American life is taken by someone whose power over the Black body seems to include the power to destroy it, and to get away with it. We saw it in 2012 with the slaying of Trayvon Martin and the beginning of the Black Lives Matter Movement. To know Emmett Till is to know Trayvon Martin. And Michael Brown. And Tamir Rice. And Eric Garner. And Philando Castile, Laquan McDonald, Ahmaud Arbery, Breonna Taylor, and George Floyd. And on and on and on. Emmett Till was the first Black Lives Matter story.

That is the story I live every day. The story I tell here in this book. You see, I was there at the house, the house of my grandparents, my uncles, their house on the plantation in the Mississippi Delta, on that night of terror when White supremacists exerted their power over us—their power to take one of us away. I have been carried back to that house repeatedly over the past sixty-seven years, carried back by the memory of something I once wanted so much to forget. I am a witness, a truth-bearer, the last authentic voice on this story.

And now you will be there with me as it all unfolds—bearing witness to the witnessing. Everything I learned over the years since we lost Bobo: the things I learned about racism, about politics, about all the people who wanted to own the memory of Emmett Till or make themselves *part* of this powerful story, if only because they were *retelling* the story. Sad to say that, in too many cases, people obviously were retelling the story for the wrong reasons. To make money, yes, but also to *remake* themselves.

For so many years, I never really wanted any part of it. There was no reason for me to try to elbow everybody out of the way, like too many other people have done, to take exclusive ownership of the memory of Emmett Till in public. I was content to remember Bobo in my own way, until one headline after another kept turning up the volume in the quiet space of my memories. One after another, the news stories were heating up this cold-case story, people began to ask questions, and other people began to speak to those questions. With all the wrong answers.

I have known the truth; I was there back in Argo, Illinois, where I met Bobo when he was only five years old. Back on those Southside streets of Chicago where we hung out. Back at that store in Money, Mississippi, one fateful summer evening. Back at our family home. In the Delta. In the dead of night.

I have known the truth. I became a minister in the years after they took Bobo away from us, a pastor of the very church that had been built by his grandmother Alma. I have known the truth. The wonderful truth you enjoy with your closest friend. The horrible truth you endure when that friend is taken from you in the most vicious, violent way.

I have known the truth, all right. When you quietly say your prayers, you hear the truth. When you fulfill your ministry, you live the truth. When you stand at the pulpit, you speak the truth. And, when you are a man of the cloth—as I am—you always stand in the pulpit, no matter where you are.

So, finally, I had to stand up for the truth I knew, whenever the Emmett Till story started churning again. Beginning in 1985 with the thirtieth anniversary of Bobo's lynching, when Rich Samuels of the Chicago NBC station, WMAQ, came calling. And I've been standing up every time a new story would break since then and many times in between: at conferences and commemorations and colleges, talking to young people all across the country, helping them understand their debt to our history, urging them to affirm their dedication to our future.

That is why I decided to tell the story. The whole story. The true story. Here, in this book, where I can share with you how a personal tragedy can lead to a great public responsibility—a duty, an obligation to make a difference. I survived a night of terror for a reason, a purpose. I feel blessed that my purpose was revealed to me, even as it was through the pain and suffering of tragic loss. Now I feel challenged by that purpose every waking moment of my life. And I am determined to live on purpose.

This work did not come easily and I did not come easily to it. Much of the credit is due to my wife of more than fifty-five years, Dr. Marvel Parker, a member of the Summit, Illinois, Board of Trustees. A super-talented grant writer, who contributed mightily to the development of our community, she has had the discipline to keep me focused on sitting down to tell this story even while managing our hectic professional and personal lives. We were joined by Chris Benson, a journalist and lawyer I met in 2002 when he was working with Mamie on her book. We have kept in touch over the years and even participated in a number of public events together. He agreed to help us put this book together and even to serve as our attorney in navigating the bumpy road we have traveled in making it happen.

What you will read here is one part personal memoir and one part FBI investigation. They are connected, these two things. The investigation drives the memory; the memory informs the investigation—two themes that play out on parallel tracks. On one level of this journey, you are in the "room" where it happens—sometimes in meetings, sometimes by way of phone and email briefings—as I do my best to assist the FBI, the Department of Justice, the US attorney for the Northern District of Mississippi and the district attorney for the Fourth Circuit Court of Mississippi. You'll get an insider's view of the process of FBI cold-case investigations—what crime reporters taking overnight notes from the back seat of a police squad car like to call a ride-along. On the second level of this journey, you are there in the intimate space of my own reflections, as I am compelled to relive my personal experience hanging out with Bobo—doing what boys do when their mamas aren't looking—even while I resurrect the trauma. Emmett Till's fateful kidnapping. The sight of his mutilated remains. Called upon now by government investigators and lawyers to reexamine the circumstances surrounding Bobo's death, a painful drilling of traumatic memory for anything that might be used to move a case.

There also is a tension that quickens the pulse—as well as the pace—of this narrative. A political drama playing out in today's Washington, DC, that in some ways echoes the politics of 1955 and raises concerns about whether the current investigation might be limited somehow by a racial project that has moved from the indifference of the administration of Dwight D. Eisenhower to the outright hostility of the administration of Donald J. Trump. This concern becomes all the more compelling with personnel shifts in the nation's capital and beyond, the people we come to trust with the course of this probe— the career people—who wind up leaving the government, leaving us to worry about the course of events to follow. What meaning can we draw from these departures? Will the conclusions of this investigation be left at the mercy of the politicians at the top, as we have seen in other cases? Even as I began to write this, there was uncertainty about who ultimately might be in power to draw it all to a conclusion. Just what might that conclusion be? What might the motivation be? Legal? Social? Political? At the beginning of the journey that unfolds here, these were the kinds of questions that could keep you up at night.

They also are the compelling questions that have driven my journey: Ultimately, what does justice mean in the resolution of a sixty-seven-year-old cold case? What does justice require? In the end, what do we take from this story that might move us forward through protest and policy?

As we consider answers, we have to recognize that the story of Emmett Till is not just an African American story. It is an American story. You cannot begin to understand the history of the United States in the last half of the twentieth century without understanding the Civil Rights Movement. You can't understand the Civil Rights Movement without understanding the story of Emmett Till—the way we were, the way we are, the way we need to be in order to move forward into a new experience of shared power. And if we have observed anything in recent years, it is that Black people are not the only ones who experience abuse of power. We truly are all in this together now.

Following the 2020 killings of Ahmaud Arbery and Breonna Taylor and George Floyd, some young activists were heard saying, "This is our Emmett Till moment."[10] In his last essay published in *The New York Times* after his death, Representative John Lewis flipped the script when he wrote that Emmett Till was his George Floyd.[11] Many other civil rights and Black Power activists have said that the slaying of Emmett Till marked the beginning of their activism. But what does all this mean? We can't even begin to answer that question without setting the record straight, and taking away a deeper understanding of the Emmett Till moment I lived through and continue to live through every day I live.

This is my story. The story of an investigation that was reawakened in 2017. The story of my participation and my process in that participation. Raising questions. Answering the questions. Questioning the answers. This is the story of my search for answers and the revelations along the way of a nearly four-year journey that took a lifetime to understand.

A Few Days
Full of Trouble

I

White Lies

The year 2017 started off with a lie and a confession.

First, the lie. It was told by Donald Trump—a small thing, really, but a big deal to him. He claimed that the crowd attending his January 20 presidential inauguration was the biggest ever, even though the entire nation saw a different picture in an aerial photo showing vast empty spaces on the Capitol Mall where the inaugural crowd stood. That was just the first of more than thirty thousand false or misleading statements by Trump that would be documented by *The Washington Post* over the next four years.[1]

It was the confession revealed that January, though, that wound up dominating the attention of so many of us. At the center of it was a much bigger lie than the one Trump told. It was the lie that had cost the life of Emmett Till in August 1955, the lie that forever changed the lives of all the rest of us: Bobo's family, friends, other African Americans, people all across the country who were not related but were connected anyway by race and the threat of racial violence. This lie changed the course of our history.

The confession was published in news stories about the soon-to-be-released book *The Blood of Emmett Till*, written by Duke University senior scholar Timothy Tyson. Right there in chapter 1, on page 6, first paragraph, last line, was a four-word revelation by Carolyn Bryant Donham: "That part's not true."[2]

The part that's "not true," Tyson told us in the book, is the part a twenty-one-year-old Carolyn Bryant testified to under oath in the 1955 murder trial of her husband, Roy Bryant, and her brother-in-law J. W. Milam. The part about how she claimed Bobo accosted her in Bryant's Grocery and Meat Market in Money, Mississippi, how she swore he grabbed her and propositioned her.[3] The story she must have practiced for several weeks before she told it and acted it out in a white-hot Tallahatchie County courtroom in the Mississippi Delta on September 22, 1955.

"This nigger man came in the store and he stopped there at the candy case," she said from the wicker witness chair back then. With coaxing by Sidney Carlton, one of the five defense attorneys representing her husband and his half brother, nudging her through her story, she went on from there. After this "man" picked out his candy, she said, she held out her hand for the money. "He caught my hand," she said, with a "strong grip." While he was holding on to her hand and before she "jerked it loose," he said, "How about a date, baby?" Frightened, she swore in her courtroom testimony that she ran toward the back of the store and "he caught me at the cash register" where "he put his left hand on my waist, and he put his other hand over on the other side." That's when she claimed he spoke again. "What's the matter, baby. Can't you take it?" And, after freeing herself, "You needn't be afraid of me." And then, he boasted to her that he had had sex "with white women before," although she claimed he used an unprintable word to describe "sex." That's when "this other nigger came in the store and got him by the arm." He turned around and said, "Goodbye." She said she ran from the store to get her pistol from the car outside.

That's when it happened. The one thing all the stories about this moment have in common. Emmett Till whistled. The wolf whistle that echoed for years in the many stories that were told about her story and about Bobo.

Hers was a lie that was meant to justify the brutal ritualistic torture and lynching of a fourteen-year-old—as if anything possibly could justify that. Fortunately, Judge Curtis Swango dismissed the jury before she told this story. Unfortunately, he did not dismiss the angry capacity crowd of White spectators, who got the word to the jurors. According to the Tyson book, what she was saying now was that what she said back then in a court of law was "not true."[4]

That revelation came as a shock, but not as a surprise. The shock was that she finally was telling the truth. But we were not surprised by the truth she told. We'd all known it to be true for so many years—those of us who were there standing around on the porch outside the store, who knew what didn't happen in that store on that day or any other day. Those of us who knew Bobo had a severe stutter and couldn't say all those words. And yet even though we always believed the truth would be told one day, we still were shocked by the telling on the day it finally *was* told.

The public reaction was exactly what you might expect. And what you might never expect.

For my part, there was great joy, satisfaction that the true story finally was being told, that Emmett Till had been exonerated. He had done no wrong. From then on, when I would go out to tell the story, I would not be confronted by people suggesting that my cousin got what he deserved. Yeah, people actually have said that, or suggested it with their skeptical expressions. One such experience happened at my own high school when I was invited to talk about the story and my personal connection to it. One male student asked, "Why are we here? Till misbehaved." That kind of reaction is so disturbing to me, for obvious reasons that go beyond my own personal relationship. First, the facts had been distorted. Second, even if you believed that Bobo had been out of line, what about due process? Some process that might investigate claims and decide on the appropriate punishment. Instead, dismissing Bobo as a wrongdoer who deserved what he got basically is a way of supporting people who take the law into their own hands. In my experience as a public speaker, there are many people out there who seem to accept that idea.

That is part of the reason why I had been suffering on multiple levels for so long, trying to convince people that *I* was the one telling the truth. That even though the media kept repeating the story Carolyn Bryant had told, that didn't mean it was true. So I felt a deep sense of relief that Timothy Tyson finally had gotten this woman to admit that she had lied. Even so, while there was great joy in the revelation, there was great sorrow just because of the reminder of the injustice. The reaction to that injustice is what led to the position taken by so many others after hearing the news, including members of our extended family. As you might expect, there were calls to go after Carolyn. Investigate. Prosecute. Lock her up. No doubt about it, I definitely wanted justice, too. I mean, no one should get away with murder, or with playing a role in a murder. Any role at all. Anybody at all. No matter how old they might have become. But what did justice require at that point in 2017, some sixty-two years after Emmett Till was murdered? What did justice mean for the survivors, the family members, who have lived with the unbearable grief of loss every day since? How does our system compensate for something like that?

What about others who have come to learn about their own place in our society—their lower status—by way of the Emmett Till story? So many others over the years limited their options for fear they'd be punished for stepping out of their assigned place, for simply trying to behave as equals.

Would locking up Carolyn Bryant Donham—in the court of public opinion, if not a court of law—balance the scales, make it all even out somehow? As far as I was concerned, there was a certain amount of justice even in that.

The full spectrum of these views was covered by the news media. As you might expect, members of my family were asked for our reaction. "I was hoping that one day she would admit it, so it matters to me that she did, and it gives me some satisfaction," I told *The New York Times*.[5] My interview with WTTW, the PBS station in Chicago, went even further. Brandis Friedman, host and correspondent for the station's *Chicago Tonight*, spent quite a bit of time going deeper with our family, as she had a couple of years earlier during her coverage of the sixtieth anniversary of Bobo's lynching.

Among other things, I talked about the power of the lie that gave Bobo's killers "the justification" to do what they did, since that lie fed into the racist narrative of African American men "portrayed as rapists," I said. "So now my cousin can be painted in a different light."[6]

Cousin Ollie Gordon talked about how the enduring pain of our family mirrors the pain of so many other Black families. "Each time a book comes out, or the story of a movie comes out, wounds are reopened in our family," she said, fighting back the tears. "Subconscious grief comes back. Sure his mother's gone, but her spirit lives within me," she continued, referring to Emmett's late mother, Mamie Till-Mobley. "I don't think a day went by that she didn't cry."[7]

That last point really hit me. It resurrected so much of what had been buried deep inside me. You see, for so many years, I couldn't cry. But in recent years, it seemed, I couldn't stop crying. Clearly, the pressure had been mounting—the pressure of convincing people of the truth when they had been so influenced by the lies, the pressure now to see where this revelation might lead us. Was legal justice even a possibility?

Chris Benson talked about that in his interview with Brandis Friedman. What might the authorities make of this new information? Carolyn had been interviewed by the FBI in 2005 during a two-year-long investigation into Bobo's murder. During several sessions, she pretty much stuck to the original story she told in court fifty years earlier.[8] So if she was saying now that the courtroom testimony was "not true," then she had committed perjury in 1955. If she repeated that lie to the FBI in 2005, it was another act of something like perjury; giving false information to the FBI is its own crime. In each case, though, the statute of limitations had expired by the time the Tyson book was published in 2017. If the FBI had been provided information earlier, information about what Tyson included in his book, information he got back in 2008 when he interviewed Donham, the government could have pursued a federal case in time for Carolyn to face some punishment for lying. Sadly, now it was too late. But there was another possibility for the federal government to step in on the basis of this recantation and investigate to see if there were other things that might be revealed—other things that connected Carolyn as an accomplice to some aspect of the murder of Emmett Till. And since murder has no statute of limitations, there could be action taken by the State of Mississippi.

"To have someone convicted at this point would send a message to the larger population that, no matter how long it takes, no matter how old you get, if you've committed a horrible crime, or participated in a horrible crime like this, you will pay eventually," Chris told Brandis.[9]

The calls for a new investigation started right away. Congressman Bobby Rush of Illinois and Congressman Bennie Thompson of Mississippi sent letters to US Attorney General Jeff Sessions calling for the Department of Justice to step in.

While I supported the call for a new probe, and really appreciated that Tyson had made the call for an investigation possible, something else was troubling me, deeply. And it began to surface with the increasing revelations about Carolyn's confession in this new book, *The Blood of Emmett Till*. First, the interviews Tyson had with Carolyn reportedly had occurred nearly ten years before the book was published. That would mean most likely 2008. If what was reported was true, that would mean Tyson had Carolyn Bryant's confession no more than three years after she had repeated her lies to the FBI in 2005—within the five-year statute of limitations on perjury, the deadline for her to be charged.

"What really angered me was that this man, Timothy Tyson, received this confession of sorts ten years ago, and he had just now released it," cousin Airickca Gordon-Taylor told Brandis Friedman in that WTTW interview. Airickca, Ollie's daughter, was an activist and the founder and executive director of the Mamie Till Mobley Memorial Foundation. "And it could have been very essential to the reopening of the case at the time he received the information. It could have helped our family with our plight to get justice for Emmett."[10]

She was right about all of that. I had to put aside my gratitude for Tyson's revelation about Carolyn to consider the value of the published confession now as opposed to its higher value at the time it was made. What was the purpose of holding it for nearly ten years for his book when it might have made an important *historical* difference to reveal the recantation to the public when she made it? A partial answer already had landed in the in-box.

On February 22, 2017, the day before the WTTW segment aired, we got an email. Actually, it was my wife, Dr. Marvel Parker, who got the email. She'll tell you in a minute that I don't do email, don't do text messages, don't do tweets—don't know how to do any of those things. I was still using a flip phone when all this news was breaking. That should tell you everything you need to know about my technical skills. That's why Marvel takes the important calls and makes the important appointments for me to speak, or preach, or travel. And that's why she gets all the emails, like the one that came that day in February from Timothy Tyson. It actually was a short 184-word note greeting me as "Reverend Wheeler" and transmitting a much longer 2,325-word note he had sent to Brandis Friedman the day before, on February 21.

That note to Brandis was a response to harsh criticism he had received from other members of our family whose basic message was that *The Blood of Emmett Till* represented more than just the title of Tyson's book since, it was argued, he and Carolyn Bryant Donham now were profiting off the blood of Emmett Till. In his note—the one to Brandis, not the one to me—he went to great lengths to clarify that Carolyn did not get paid for her interviews (interviews she and her daughter-in-law Marsha Bryant had requested of him, he wrote), and she did not earn anything from the proceeds of the book. In fact, he wrote, "a good deal of the profits are going to the North

Carolina NAACP," since he is a member of the state executive board, works closely with Bishop William Barber, and has lived "a life in the struggle."[11]

While it was curious to me that he was quite concerned about his public profile, it was even more striking to me that he didn't see the Carolyn Bryant Donham confession quote as all that important. "Did anyone with any relationship to or familiarity with this story actually believe that Carolyn Bryant told the truth in court? I did not consider this a big revelation," he wrote to Brandis. "I am a historian and I do not operate in the 24-hour cable news cycle or the popular press, and so the news value of the interview was not my concern."[12]

As I read these words, I kept thinking about the fact that all the promotion for the book, all the headlines caused by that promotion, all the buzz of people reading those headlines focused on that one line, that one revelation by Carolyn Bryant Donham that he now was dismissing as unimportant.

"I regret that the interview with Carolyn is all that the sensationalist media has chosen to report, since they are interested only in titillating stories that focus on the drama of the white conscience, which is not the object of my historical interest nor the subject of my book," he wrote.[13]

There was even more that I found concerning about this note. It was Tyson's explanation about why he had not contacted a single Till family member in the course of the ten years of research he claimed he had done for the book. "I did not bother Emmett Till's family for interviews because many others have already done so and repeated versions of their accounts were available to me in many other ways."[14]

Early on, when the news broke, I had great respect for what Tyson had accomplished and deep gratitude for his work in getting the confession of Carolyn Bryant Donham. While I still appreciated that fact because of the path it had created for me to continue telling the Emmett Till truth, I was becoming concerned with what I was learning about Tyson's approach to the whole thing. He wrote that he didn't want to bother us—never considering that we, too (not just

Carolyn), might have new information, or a fresh perspective to provide, after living with this story and its pain for all these years. It troubled me to think that the pain and suffering of the Black survivors, the victims of a horrendous act of White racial violence and terror, were not worth as much as the time he had spent on capturing the story of a White woman—one of the persons involved in that victimization. Interestingly, while he criticized the "sensationalist press," he also relied on it heavily for his research, the "other ways" he had gotten our family stories, or what the press had claimed were our stories.

It seems to me that this is a critical part of the problem we are facing in struggling against the weight of historical racism in this country. Too often, the media have been complicit in storytelling that tends to value White over Black, even if only subconsciously in the way the stories are framed. Until recently, there has been an assumption that the White person, whether a cop or civilian, is telling the truth and the Black person, whether a victim or suspect, is not telling the truth.

I have something to say about this story, whether Tyson relied on my truth or not. After all, I lived through it. There is not a day that has gone by over the past sixty-seven years when I haven't relived some portion of this experience, starting with the day Bobo walked into that store.

IT WAS WEDNESDAY, August 24, 1955, and just as we had done since that Monday—the beginning of cotton-picking season—we had been picking cotton all morning on the Grover Frederick Plantation. Just half a day. That's all anybody could take no matter how much money we might stand to make. It had been in the nineties all afternoon. Somehow, nineties in Mississippi is a whole lot hotter than nineties just about anywhere else. Much hotter than Chicago, where I had been living for the past eight years. Bobo couldn't take it, even for half a day. He had thought it was going to be fun and found out it was work. Work was not fun, and fun was about all he was used to having.

Never a dull moment in his life, except for picking cotton, row after row, boll after boll. Backbreaking, hand-blistering, sun-burning work—not much breeze to speak of and a ton of humidity weighing you down. For my part, it had all been good since my nine-foot sack weighed in heavy enough to mean a pretty decent payday. Bobo's, not so much, actually only about half as much. My little twelve-year-old uncle Simeon even shamed me, pulling in just about twice as much as I did. Yeah, well, he was used to it and I had lost my touch.

About midday, my uncles, Maurice, Robert, Simmie, my grandfather Moses Wright ("Papa"), and I joined Gramma in the house for dinner. Bobo already was there, had been for quite a bit. He preferred chores inside the house. After dinner (what we called lunch), we all had gone swimming in the lake across the road. Darfield Road. I thought that's what it was called, although up to this point, we called it Dark Ferry Road just as much. In the future, I would hear another name that fit even more than the others did, one that would tell more about this story than the others could.

Later that day, my uncle Maurice drove my grandparents to service at the tiny cinder-block East Money Church of God in Christ, the church where Papa used to preach, when he still was preaching. We were going to keep the car and drive around for a while. But since Maurice didn't have his license, Gramma told him not to drive too far. I only wish we had listened. Instead, we all piled into the car—Bobo, Simmie, Roosevelt Crawford, his niece Ruth, and me—and we went too far, definitely too far: three miles into Money.

Uptown is what we called it. We parked at Bryant's Grocery and Meat Market, where mostly Black croppers came to buy everything from shoes to fatback. And there was other stuff inside—soda pop, candy, and ice cream—that could attract a car full of teenagers on a hot, muggy Mississippi evening. What got Maurice's attention, though, was not inside the store, but outside on the porch. A game. Seemed like there always was a game on the porch. Somebody always playing something: dominoes, checkers. No checker pieces, though.

Just bottle caps: Coca-Cola, Orange Crush. In the Delta, folks made do, made a way. Maurice sat down to the checker game. The rest of us just stood around for a while, playing a different game. Trash talking with the other kids who were there before we arrived. Somebody always playing something on the porch. Bobo played center in this game. Somehow, he always wound up in that position, the center of attention, bragging about something or other. This evening, it was how different things were in Chicago: big city, big deal, different from here. He even went to school with White kids in Argo. That sure got everybody's attention. After all, this was the summer *Brown v. Board of Education* was decided—the second *Brown* decision, the one that picked up on the first one (the one that had declared "separate but equal" was unconstitutional) and ordered an end to racial segregation in schools "with all deliberate speed." White folks in the South were up in arms about that. The kids on the porch knew that even *talking* about it could mean trouble. In fact, Black kids from Chicago could mean trouble. Black kids who talked about going to school with White kids. That might encourage Black kids here in the Delta to want to do the same thing. The thing the Supreme Court said they finally could do and White folks warned they would fight to the death to keep them from doing.

I took a break and went into the store to get some soda pop. The woman inside didn't look too much older than me. She was a White woman, though, so I knew to be careful with what I said, what I did, and even how I looked at her. In fact, I knew not to look at her—not directly, anyway. I knew this place and my place in this place. I had lived near this place, first seven years of my life. I knew that a sixteen-year-old Black boy like me could get lynched just for reckless eyeballing. So I didn't look at her. More like looking in her general direction but not exactly at her when I was paying for my soft drink, wondering how much of the porch talk she could hear through the screen door. That's when Bobo came in. It made me nervous, him being there. Nervous about him having his "Yes ma'ams" and "No ma'ams" in order. If he didn't, there could be trouble. I reacted without thinking much about it, knowing how rambunctious he could be. I left with my bottle of soda pop.

As soon as I came out, Maurice sent Simmie in to be with Bobo because, despite the drill his mother had taken him through before he left Chicago, Bobo still didn't seem to know the ways of the South. We were relieved when it didn't take too long before they came out. Bobo hadn't been in there nearly long enough to have said all that Carolyn said he did, even in a normal conversation let alone with his severe stutter. The way he got stuck on the kind of words she swore he said, we would still be waiting for him right now to finish saying all that. So Simmie and Bobo came out and we were relieved. Then Carolyn came to the door. She stepped outside and was looking around at us, like she was curious about all the talking and laughing. Almost like she didn't want to be left out. Nothing unusual about something like that back in Chicago, or even Argo, I guess. But I was on edge here in the Delta. For some reason, it seemed like something was about to happen, the way everything gets real calm just before a big storm hits. So I was waiting. And that's when everything happened. Bobo whistled. That wolf whistle that we all heard.

Carolyn started moving toward a car parked alongside the store. It was a determined move, an aggressive one. Somebody said she was going for a gun. That's when we all broke and ran to our car. Now Bobo knew he had done something wrong—very wrong. Inside the car, he kept shouting at Maurice to get moving. But somebody had dropped a cigarette on the floor and Maurice was not about to drive off until we found it. Bobo kept shouting at him until finally, we found the cigarette and took off down Darfield or Dark Ferry—or whatever it was called—to make the three-mile drive back home.

A short way down the road, just as we were starting to breathe easy thinking we had made a clean getaway, somebody spotted some headlights trailing us. Panic set in. We were sure they were coming after us. We all shouted at Maurice to pick up speed. But that old '49 Ford was doing the best it could just holding it together. It had no first gear, and the rest of the gears seemed to be ready to give out on us. Meanwhile, the headlights on the dark road behind us kept getting closer and closer, gaining on us, until Maurice decided to pull over to the side of the road. Now we were really scared. What was he doing that for? Didn't take long for us to get the answer, as he jumped out and started running into the deep cover of the cotton field next to the road. Right away, the rest of us jumped out after him. Except for little Simmie, who just lay down across the back seat.

As we ran, the ripe cotton bolls knocked against our legs so hard that Bobo finally fell down. All at once, we fell to the ground with him, to protect him against whatever was about to happen. From that position, we watched that mysterious car get closer and closer and closer to our car until we realized that it was not slowing down. It just kept on going down Darfield Road, a road that was beginning to take on its new frightening identity. One that would seem to change with the telling of the many stories people recalled in that place. Stories that might have started out like this one did, but ended up differently. Stories about Black people who were driven down that road before they were killed and dumped in the river.

In the deep Delta drawl, Darfield Road easily slid on the tongue to sound more like Dark Ferry Road and ultimately like what we would hear later. Dark Fear Road.

AFTER READING THE February 22, 2017, email from Timothy Tyson, I was left to puzzle over the truth he had revealed, over the lie that we always had said was a lie but now was validated only because a White researcher had revealed it. I considered what that original lie had cost us and whether the value of the long-overdue confession was enough to compensate for that.

Over my eighty-three years, I have learned a lot about lies. White lies, we're told as kids, are the little ones, the harmless ones. Because of what I have experienced in my time on this planet, I know now that the White lies are the big ones, the ones that do the most harm. I'm talking about the lies that support Whiteness, like the one told by the Trump administration, about the "largest audience ever to witness a presidential inaugural, period."[15] Much bigger, much better than the Black predecessor's inauguration turnout. White lies can look like truth beyond a reasonable doubt. A White lie can set a 911 call from Central Park far past the nearest New York police precinct to orbit around the world. "I'm going to tell them there's an African American man threatening me."[16] A White lie can send an innocent Black man to prison and set a killer cop free. A White lie can set a lynch mob on an innocent Black man. Or a Black boy. A fourteen-year-old Black boy. Barely fourteen. Just three weeks fourteen. A White lie can turn a murderer into a victim and a childish prank—a whistle—into a capital offense.

I don't accept that lie.

In his note to me, Timothy Tyson suggested that we perhaps meet on a trip to the Chicago area he might be able to arrange in promoting his new book. He wanted to talk.

At this point, I had no interest in talking to him about why he had no interest in talking to me all the years he had been working on his book. I didn't accept the invitation.

2

What Is Life?

WHEN THE CAROLYN Bryant Donham confession story broke in January 2017, FBI Special Agent Walter Henry knew what he had to do. In his twenty-three years with the bureau, his natural curiosity had been refined and focused into sharp investigative skills. They had served him well in his work—not only in important civil rights investigations in Mississippi from his post at the bureau's state field office in Oxford, but also in federal civil rights investigations halfway across the country.

Special Agent Henry had been assigned to investigate the choke-hold death of Eric Garner, working with DOJ civil rights attorney Kristy Parker and others from "Main Justice" out of Washington, DC. The 2014 case first came to national attention with the viral video of Garner being restrained in a choke hold by New York police officer Daniel Pantaleo. As just about everybody knows by now, Garner was heard on the video saying eleven times "I can't breathe," before he finally died in what the medical examiner ruled a homicide. A homicide caused by a choke hold.

In October 2016, US Attorney General Loretta Lynch had shaken up the federal civil rights investigation into Garner's death.[1] The case against Pantaleo had been stalled. There had been no local grand jury indictment. There was a dispute between the US Attorney's Office of the Eastern District of New York and the Civil Rights Division of the Department of Justice on whether a federal civil rights case should be filed.[2] It seems that Attorney General Lynch felt a case could be made. After all, she had been US attorney in the Eastern District of New York before becoming attorney general and was there in New York when Garner was killed.[3] The decision was made to bring in an experienced civil rights team from outside New York. That is why Henry and Parker got the nod.

Now, even with the Garner investigation still under way, it seemed that Henry would have another high-profile matter to consider with the published recantation of Carolyn Bryant Donham.

He definitely had his work cut out for him. Just reviewing the Emmett Till file was a huge undertaking. Some eight thousand pages of documents had been put together between 2004 and 2006 and reviewed by the Mississippi district attorney and grand jury for another year. Among these documents was the transcript of the murder trial of J. W. Milam and Roy Bryant, along with extensive research and interviews.

I know something about the challenge he faced, since I am one of the twenty-four "Persons Involved" listed in the report. Some living, some dead. Some witnesses, some victims. Some named, some redacted. I was positioned to watch it all unfold in 2004, nearly fifty years after the crime was committed and two killers were acquitted. It'd been nearly fifty years since President Dwight D. Eisenhower ignored the pleas of Emmett's mother, Mamie, to intervene. It'd been nearly fifty years since FBI Director J. Edgar Hoover questioned whether Mamie was being influenced by Communists in seeking justice for the death of her son.

When this massive file was compiled in 2004, a federal investigation was stepping up—a little over fourteen months after Mamie's death, five months after the publication of her book, *Death of Innocence: The Story of the Hate Crime That Changed America,* three months after her congressman, Chicago Democrat Bobby Rush, became the first member of Congress to call for a federal investigation by way of a congressional resolution he introduced,[4] and just a week before Mamie's book was honored with a Robert F. Kennedy Book Award. Finally, it came. A federal investigation into the 1955 murder of Emmett Till.

"The Emmett Till case stands at the heart of the American civil rights movement," according to a May 10, 2004, statement released by R. Alexander Acosta, assistant attorney general for the Civil Rights Division at DOJ in announcing the national government intervention.[5] "This brutal murder and grotesque miscarriage of justice outraged a nation and helped galvanize support for the modern American civil rights movement. We owe it to Emmett Till, and we owe it to ourselves, to see whether after all these years, some additional measure of justice remains possible."[6]

Of course, *any* measure of justice at all would have been "additional" at that point, since there never had been any justice for Bobo in the first place. After all, his killers had gotten away with it and his family was left to endure the lies about him that were repeated each time his story was told.

Acosta's statement made it clear that, if any justice would come from this federal investigation, it would not be from a federal indictment. The five-year statute of limitations on any possible federal claim on a civil rights violation had passed years earlier. Instead, the federal government would put its resources to work searching for evidence that could be used by the State of Mississippi in handing down murder indictments against anyone who might have been involved in Emmett's death.[7] There is no statute of limitations on state murder charges, or on manslaughter charges.

We all were excited about this news, even though some skeptics in the family wondered whether this action by Acosta and the DOJ might just be a ploy by the George W. Bush administration to divert the country's attention. (There had been a great deal of media coverage of the Abu Ghraib scandal involving allegations of abuse of Iraqi prisoners by US forces in the Middle East.[8]) So, even as we all rejoiced in the announcement, some family members continued to keep a watchful eye on the developments—developments that would lead to rising tensions and factionalism in the family.

On the positive side, at least things were starting off a whole lot differently than they had back in 1955. In 2004, there seemed to be a spirit of cooperation between the state and the feds, between Democrats and Republicans, between the office of District Attorney Joyce Chiles (a Democrat and the first African American elected to serve as prosecutor for the Fourth Judicial District of Mississippi) and Jim M. Greenlee, US attorney for the Northern District of Mississippi (a Republican and a Bush appointee). Greenlee's office would preside over the FBI investigation and then hand over the file to Chiles for a Mississippi grand jury to consider.

As Special Agent Henry worked his way through the case file in January 2017, it was clear this 2004 collaboration was not the beginning of the story, and the latest revelation by Carolyn Bryant Donham meant that it would continue. There was plenty to go through—much more than you ever will find in an FBI case file. Even one as extensive as this one.

DURING THE 2002 holiday season after Christmas, just before the New Year, Mamie Till-Mobley got a call from somebody she had never heard of. Getting a call from a stranger was no big deal—her number was listed, she was easy to find. But what the caller said to her was a big deal—a very big deal. He wanted to help start an investigation into the death of her son.

At eighty-one, Mamie had been hit with quite a few offers, pitches, assurances, and scams. People would say just about anything to get close to her and her story. As she said once, people suggested producing versions of her story that would use her name, use Emmett's name, and then make up the rest. One celebrated Black journalist, the late George Curry, had helped to get a book contract with her and then never wrote a single chapter. (She had to return the book advance to keep from getting sued by the publisher, according to her attorney, Lester Barclay.) Some people would promise to help her seek justice, only to help themselves to her files and keepsakes—things that never were returned. By this time, she felt a certain urgency about everything, about clearing up the loose ends of her life, much closer now to her death. She was in desperately poor health. Failing eyesight, heart problems, kidney failure. She was on dialysis three times a week. The clock was ticking on what would wind up being the last two weeks of her life. She seemed to know she would not have much time left to set things in motion. To finish the book she had been working on for the six months leading up to this moment. To seek justice for her son after nearly fifty years. So, even though she was wary at first of this mystery call, she was moved by the passion she heard coming through the phone and the vital need she felt to get something started, something she most likely would wind up leaving behind. Emmett was an only child. She was an only child. What else did she have to leave the world but her story and some sense of triumph over racial injustice? She agreed to meet with the mystery caller and learned that he already was on his way, driving to Chicago from Kansas City, Missouri.

Immediately, Mamie called Chris Benson, who had been working with her on her book and running interference during moments like this one. Chris would be there to meet this person, to ask the questions Mamie might not consider, to calm her anxiety, help her evaluate. Help her avoid another scam. This was important. There was no time to waste. The clock was still ticking.

After that intense moment of soul searching, the appearance of the man on her doorstep was not a great confidence-builder. Alvin Sykes, an activist from Kansas City, was threadbare, unpolished, unschooled. But as he and his professional partner, Don Burger, sat with Mamie in her dining room, photos of Bobo looking over her shoulder, Chris taking copious notes, there was a special quality that emerged. It was spiritual. Sykes was a Buddhist, with an aura that connected with Mamie, a devout Christian. It set a context for the credentials he laid out for her in explaining how he, along with Burger, would develop a plan for an investigation into Bobo's murder.

Sykes had a record of success in reaching just outcomes in other matters, campaigning in Kansas City to desegregate schools, lobbying lawmakers to lower the age of jurors serving in Missouri from twenty-one to eighteen, and getting the Justice Department involved in a couple of civil rights cases. His most celebrated case rose from the beating death of musician Steve Harvey in a public park restroom. Laying the groundwork in that case involved an intense period of study at the public library for Sykes, a high school dropout. He found a federal law that protected people's use of public spaces, and the Justice Department was able to use that research to help mount a successful case in convicting Harvey's killer.[9]

What she heard, what she observed was how Sykes would turn his energy, his Zen-like focus to the Till case. Sykes wanted to contact both the federal and state authorities to share with them his proposal to open an investigation. And he wanted to be sure he had Mamie's blessing before attempting to convince the authorities that there still were issues to be investigated in connection with Bobo's lynching. If nothing else came from his efforts, she reasoned, it would at least serve as another chapter—likely the final chapter—of the book she was writing. Along with her blessing, Mamie gave him a contact: Keith Beauchamp.

A little more than three years earlier, she had welcomed Beauchamp, a young amateur filmmaker, into her home because he had provided a very persuasive and unique reference letter—from his mother. In her letter, according to attorney Barclay, Beauchamp's mother asked Mamie to give her son a chance—a chance he had not been given by others due to his youth and inexperience. Mamie was moved by another mother's plea, and she gave him that chance— sitting for video-recorded interviews with him. Beauchamp had talked about turning his recordings into a documentary and submitted a detailed, structured contract to Barclay for Mamie to sign. The contract with Beauchamp's Big Baby Films provided for various uses of those recordings—television, cable, movie theaters—at various levels of compensation. But rather than sign this exclusive contract with Beauchamp—concerned it would have kept her from making other deals—she wound up signing with acclaimed documentarian Stanley Nelson for an *American Experience* documentary to air on PBS stations. Even so, she continued to talk with Beauchamp, who had told Mamie about the sources he had developed in his work.

There had been all kinds of stories and names floating around the Delta for years after Bobo's death. In Mississippi, tales could grow tall in the summer heat and the fertile ground of people's imagination—just like cotton, spun into narrative yarn. Whether legend, or lore, or lies, Beauchamp took note of these tales, and somehow they got repeated and reported, but never proven.

His first sources were University of Alabama history professor David Beito and his wife, Stillman College associate professor Linda Royster Beito, chair of Stillman's Department of Social Sciences. The Beitos had collected a great deal of documented facts about Bobo's murder during their years of research on the work of Mississippi civil rights activist Dr. T.R.M. Howard, who, along with Medgar Evers, had taken an active role in the Emmett Till murder case.[10] The Beitos' research was not based on legend or lore or lies, but on documentation, and it included at least two key witnesses in the case.

On January 6, 2003, Mamie was supposed to talk with Keith Beauchamp and Alvin Sykes. She was anxious at the time, preparing for an accelerated dialysis session so that she could travel to Atlanta the following day. It was the beginning of the extended celebration of Dr. Martin Luther King Jr.'s birthday, and she was scheduled to deliver a keynote address at King's Ebenezer Baptist Church. Apparently, Alvin had convinced Beauchamp that he could build a case, and the two of them had convinced Mamie to support Sykes in forming the Emmett Till Justice Campaign.[11] That January 6 follow-up call never took place. Mamie suffered a massive heart attack. She died that day.[12]

Following Mamie's death, Alvin continued to work to fulfill the commitment he had made to her. To keep the promise he had made in that first conversation he had in her home, and the last call he ever would have with her on the phone after that. Known for his tenacity, he somehow was able to arrange a meeting with US Attorney Jim Greenlee and others in the Oxford, Mississippi, office. He shared a copy of Stanley Nelson's powerful documentary, which had aired on PBS stations that January before going on to win Peabody, Emmy, and Sundance awards. Alvin also would introduce authorities in Oxford to my uncle Simeon Wright, whose personal story was gripping. Simmie's narrative was emotional. It was powerful. He humanized the story about the kidnapping and murder of our cousin, and the acquittal of the confessed murderers. And yet Simmie's impassioned plea and the scope of injustice set out in Nelson's documentary would not amount to much if there was no legal basis to investigate. And there could be no investigation if there was no chance of prosecuting somebody. The feds were not going to investigate just for the sake of doing it, no matter how moving the story might be.

Alvin had an answer for that. It was one that had emerged in his hours and days in the Kansas City Public Library, his careful reading of law books, and his persistent follow-up questioning of lawyers. One of those lawyers was Richard Roberts, a former DOJ Civil Rights Division attorney, who went on to become chief judge of the federal district court for the District of Columbia, and a mentor of Sykes.[13] For Sykes, this intensive research was like digging for something precious. Finally, he hit it—struck gold with a big assist from Judge Roberts. And he explained it all to Chris Benson for a *Chicago Tribune* commentary.

In 1976, Antonin Scalia was an assistant attorney general in the Office of Legal Counsel at the Department of Justice when he was given a special assignment. He was challenged to find a legal justification for the FBI to reopen the investigation into the assassination of President John F. Kennedy.[14] There was a big problem, and Scalia was assigned to find a way around it. When Kennedy was assassinated on November 22, 1963, there was no law making it a federal crime to assassinate the president. If there was no law, the federal government had no power to step in—no jurisdiction. And if there was no jurisdiction, then there could be no federal investigation, the very thing Scalia was supposed to justify. Even when there is a federal law, the only way the federal government can investigate is when there is probable cause to believe the investigation might reveal evidence of a federal crime leading to an indictment. Without a specific law setting out a federal crime, then a murder—even the murder of the president—was a state crime and had to be investigated in the state where the crime was committed.[15] Worse, even if there *had* been a federal cause of action (like conspiracy, or civil rights violation, or perjury), by 1976 the statute of limitations would have run out and there would have been no time left to file a charge or issue an indictment.

Scalia was able to see a way through all of that, and this is what drew Alvin in. Scalia was able to weave together different federal provisions to come up with a solution.[16] And Alvin was practically looking over the shoulder of this future Supreme Court justice, absorbing every ounce of legal reasoning he could from Scalia's seven-page memorandum to the attorney general's special assistant Jack Fuller.[17]

First, Scalia determined there was government authority to investigate in order to "detect and prosecute crimes against the United States." He saw this language in a number of federal laws, and he fixed on the word "detect."[18] Second, he argued that statutes of limitations only affected the government's ability to *bring* cases.[19] So, just because the time had run out to *charge* somebody with a crime didn't mean that the crime had not been committed. That crime had not been erased, whether or not the government could bring a case. And there still could be a public interest in pursuing an investigation to resolve unanswered questions—to "detect" whether a crime had been committed.[20] Finally, in the case where "the original matter was under the control of the government"—no matter how long ago it occurred—a reexamination could be justified even "to review and evaluate" the earlier decisions.[21]

The Scalia analysis wound up being used successfully to reopen the Kennedy case. And it would be used again in an April 20, 1998, memorandum by Beth Nolan, deputy assistant attorney general in the DOJ Office of Legal Counsel, in support of a reexamination of the assassination of Dr. Martin Luther King Jr.[22] All of this was made to order for Alvin, who put it together in his yearlong meetings with the DOJ and the FBI officials beginning in 2003. Just as Scalia had done with the JFK issue, Alvin fixed on the word "detect."

He proposed to officials in Oxford, Mississippi, that the government could open the door to a federal investigation into the murder of Emmett Till in 2004 even if only to "detect" whether a federal crime had been committed in 1955. The statute of limitations on any potential federal crime wouldn't matter so long as the federal government had exercised any "control over the matter" back in 1955. When then-Acting FBI Director J. Edgar Hoover determined that there was no federal crime committed in the death of Emmett Till back in 1955, there had been no federal investigation.[23] But Alvin reasoned that, in order for Hoover to decide there was no federal crime to investigate, he had, indeed, exercised "control over the matter." By dismissing the whole thing, the 1955 FBI set the hook for the 2004 DOJ. Despite the fact that the statute of limitations had run on potential federal charges like violation of civil rights in the murder of Emmett Till, the federal government in 2004 could step in to "detect" whether a federal crime had been committed in a case the federal government had taken control over just by rejecting it in 1955. Alvin's well-reasoned argument served its purpose: Assistant Attorney General Alexander Acosta announced the opening of the federal investigation on May 10, 2004.

The objective in 2004 was to reexamine what happened in 1955, when Hoover basically shuffled paper, in order to "detect" whether anybody else had helped Milam and Bryant with kidnapping, murder, and other related crimes. Even if no one could be prosecuted under *federal* law at that point, there might be other people who could be indicted under *state* law. At the end of the federal investigation, the entire FBI file could be turned over to the State of Mississippi as evidence against any person who still could be prosecuted under

Mississippi law for the murder of Emmett Till—anyone, including Carolyn Bryant Donham.[24] And that's how Alvin Sykes—a self-educated high school dropout—was able to set up a case that moved the federal government to investigate the lynching of Emmett Till. Finally.

"With all honesty, had it not been for the Department of Justice and the FBI, this investigation could not and would not have taken place on the local level," DA Chiles told Chris for a *Chicago Sun-Times* article.[25] "Locally, we do not have the resources necessary to conduct an investigation of this nature."[26]

Those resources made a huge difference. The point person on the investigation was Special Supervisory Agent Dale Killinger, working out of the FBI's Oxford office. He quickly read up on the Emmett Till story. That would be very important in meeting the serious challenges of investigating this cold case—figuring out where to look for answers. By this time, Milam and Bryant were dead. Milam had died of cancer in 1980. He was sixty-one. Bryant had died of cancer in 1994. He was sixty-three.

As DA Chiles told NPR, the first problem in the investigation was piecing together all the aging elements of it. "A second problem would be whether or not some of the main participants, other than the two that were tried, are still alive," she said. "Third, if there are others who are alive, who participated in the murder of Till, was their participation willing?"[27]

Through his relentless search for answers, Special Agent Killinger made a key discovery: a copy of the transcript of the murder trial of Milam and Bryant. It had been missing for years, and many thought it would go missing forever. Apart from the recordings of memories of the people who took part in the trial, the only record had been the many newspaper accounts that had to be pieced together to make sense of it all, as in the collection of stories edited by Christopher Metress in *The Lynching of Emmett Till: A Documentary Narrative*.[28] Now, with the trial transcript, there would be a road map to help chart a course forward, identify additional witnesses who were still alive, compare the testimony of record with the testimony of memory. Killinger also was able to find an aerial map of the three Mississippi counties involved in Emmett's night of terror and torture. And with a key witness, Willie Reed, who had been located by the Beitos and referred to Beauchamp, Killinger visited the seed barn, the shed near Drew in Sunflower County where Emmett had been taken and beaten and killed. He even took Willie Reed with him and noted the nervous reaction Willie had as they approached the shed where he had heard the sounds of beating and cries for help. So many years later, and Willie still seemed terrified by the memory. A forensic examination of the shed was done to find any traces of Emmett's blood that might still be there. But the building had been cleaned over the years, and floorboards replaced.[29]

As with Milam and Bryant, others who had been witnessed or even rumored to have taken part in the abduction, murder, and cover-up had already died. There were at least two exceptions. One was Carolyn Bryant Donham. The other was Henry Loggins.

Carolyn was interviewed by Killinger five times during the course of his investigation. She was just seventy-one years old at the time, but couldn't seem to remember a lot about the circumstances surrounding her encounter with Bobo, except for the part she told in court. In a couple of the sessions, Killinger pressed her to get more information about a situation that arose after Carolyn's husband, Roy Bryant, talked to her about the night Emmett was at the store. There had been a confrontation at the Bryant store between Roy Bryant and a young Black kid he thought might be the boy from Chicago. On October 2, 2005, Carolyn said, "I vaguely remember something happening in the store with the young Black boy and his mother, but I don't remember the details of it."[30]

On October 19, 2005, Killinger came back to it to follow up. This is how it went:

KILLINGER: "The other thing that happened? A little while later I guess, is that right? Where the boy came in the store . . ."

CAROLYN: "Yeah."

KILLINGER: ". . . with his mother?"

CAROLYN: "Seems like it was like mid-afternoon or something like
that. And I, I don't know what happened. I can't remember what
was said or what, uh, anything, I just remember that they did
come in. They were in there."

KILLINGER: "Do you remember anything happening at all that day?"

CAROLYN: "Yeah, I do remember something happened, but I, but it's
not, but it doesn't come clear to me, except I know that there
was a lady and her little boy or her grandson or somebody was in
the store and, I don't know, Roy said something to 'em and I
remember telling him to leave him alone that, you know, that
wasn't him."

KILLINGER: "Meaning it wasn't Emmett?"

CAROLYN: "Yeah."[31]

Henry Loggins was another key person of interest, a Black man
who had worked for J. W. Milam. Loggins's name was revealed to
journalist Jimmy Hicks in one of the intriguing stories surrounding
the 1955 murder trial of Milam and Bryant.

A number of celebrated Black journalists covered the trial of
Bobo's murderers in September 1955 and would go on to cover the
most significant events of the entire Civil Rights Movement. Included
among them was Simeon Booker, the *Jet* magazine Washington
bureau chief, who had been the first Black reporter hired by *The
Washington Post* and a Nieman Fellow. There was L. Alex Wilson, who
was an enterprising reporter for *The Chicago Defender* chain. And there
was Jimmy Hicks of *The Afro-American* chain and the Washington
bureau chief of the National Negro Press Association. Hicks had
gone undercover to find witnesses in the case. That led him to King's
Place, a popular juke joint in the Delta, where he met a young woman
and, in a round of flirtation and dancing, learned the names of Loggins and Levi "Too Tight" Collins, another Black man who worked
for Milam. There had been rumors that these two had been involved

in Bobo's murder, but they had disappeared and stayed disappeared during the entire trial in 1955. The *Defender* later found Collins and got him up to Chicago, where he sat for an interview and denied everything. Linda and David Beito later found Loggins and gave his contact information to Keith Beauchamp, who gave it to the FBI for Killinger to pursue.

I also was interviewed by Killinger. A few times. On September 28, 2004, in a session at my barbershop, Simmie was there. So was my cousin Crosby Smith Jr., "Sonny." It started off in a very jovial way. Killinger had me draw a floor plan of the Wright family home where we were staying in Mississippi. Simmie had to step in to get it right. It was his house, after all. We all were joking around for a bit, about street hustles and the like, and slowly moved into the stories Killinger really had come for. This was our third session together and I had learned this was his way: loosen you up, make you comfortable, ease you into it. We talked about the train ride down to Mississippi, about Bobo running all over the train, rambunctious—couldn't sit still. We talked about picking cotton, about how much we got paid for picking: two dollars for every hundred pounds. My grandfather Moses Wright had me tallying up everybody each day—made me feel important. Every now and then Killinger would drop in another funny line, like how some people picked cotton like champs, like Michael Jordan racked up points. That was Killinger's way, put you at ease like that. I was no Michael Jordan, but I would make seven dollars that week—close enough to being a champ. It was a good week for me. Until it wasn't.

Eventually, Killinger steered us to the night at the store, our scare on the road, that near miss with the mystery car. He just kind of eased into it. That night of terror. The night that has haunted me every day since that night. The night I knew I was going to die.

AUGUST 28, 1955. The night I knew I had to get right with God, I began to pray. I prayed hard. I was only sixteen—too young to think about dying, yet somehow old enough to figure I was close to doing it. It sounded like death was at the door—knocking, pounding to the beat of my heart. Does death really knock first, though? Does it call you out?

"Preacher. Preacher. This is Mr. Bryant."

Did anyone hear it—besides me? It was loud enough. Determined. Threatening. And getting louder. The house—the whole house—was asleep except for me. We had been to Greenwood earlier that night and had a few drinks—my uncles, even Bobo. All of us—all teenagers—drinking white lightning. Were we going to pay now? For our sins?

It was the dead of night—the night I knew I was going to die. It was morning, really, two-thirty in the morning, but darker than any night I could remember, darker than a thousand midnights. And it was about to get darker still. Couldn't tell for a moment—just a moment—whether I was awake or asleep. Images from Greenwood ran through my mind like a dream—the "stroll," all those fine Black folks passing by, floating on a cloud as we left the 4/5 Plantation juke joint. But these pleasant moments in my mind were quickly erased by echoes of Ruthie Mae's words from Wednesday night: "This is not over."

I could hear the voices in the other room talking about something that had happened Uptown.

That's when I knew, not just who they were, but why they had come, what they had come for. I knew it even before Papa heard the question.

"You got a boy from Chicago in here?" This was no dream; this was my worst nightmare. After all, I was a boy from Chicago. And I was running out of time to get right with God.

They must have just pushed past Papa, because the next thing I knew, they were rushing into the room where Maurice and I were. Gun. Flashlight. This was J. W. Milam and Roy Bryant, who looked even more sinister with the light coming from that flashlight down low. And I hadn't finished my prayer. Was I going to die before I could finish my prayer, get right with God?

Finally, they realized that I was not the "fat" boy from Chicago and moved down to the room where Bobo and Simmie were sleeping. They got Bobo up, made him get dressed. At one point as Milam was barking orders, Bobo answered just by saying, "Yeah," and Milam exploded.

"Don't you yeah me, nigger. I'll blow your head off! You say, 'Yes, sir,'" he yelled, and told Bobo to put on his shoes, not to worry about socks. This had to be when it got very serious for Bobo—the anger, the power these two had over our entire family that night. Even so, he insisted on taking a moment to put on his socks before he put on his shoes. He said he didn't wear shoes without socks. As they marched Bobo out, Papa pleaded with them to leave his nephew with him. He would see to his punishment—send him back to Chicago. Grandma even offered to pay them some money if they would leave Bobo. Milam just yelled at her. "Get back in that bed, woman. And I better hear them springs."

Maurice stayed asleep. I stayed awake the rest of that night. Paralyzed by fear, I couldn't move. Kept thinking that there was something we should do, but I couldn't move. They could kill us all. What was to stop them? What could we do? How could we just let Bobo go like that? What my grandparents had offered to do obviously was not enough. What more? And why couldn't I move? It was all happening so fast. And while I was thinking about what we couldn't do, what was Bobo thinking? As they marched him out and we did nothing to stop it, what was he thinking? Suddenly, all by himself—helpless. Why didn't I move? Why didn't I force myself to move?

Papa followed in their wake, out to the porch. They headed to some vehicle he couldn't quite recognize in the pitch-black darkness. He did see that somebody was standing there waiting to take hold of Bobo—appeared to be a Black man, though he could barely make it out. There was somebody else in the vehicle, too, but Papa couldn't see that person, either. Milam spoke to the person in the truck. "Is this the boy?"

That's when Papa heard the voice in the dark, the voice from inside the vehicle, a voice that was lighter than a man's voice. A woman's voice that said simply, "Yes."

THERE CAME A point in the 2004 investigation when family tensions began to bubble up. As long as Mamie was still alive, we always had maintained at least the appearance of family unity. What can I tell you? We respect our elders and she had risen to that status in our family. She was a church mother—a prominent role in the church—and she was the matriarch of our family. With her passing, though, it was not clear who should be the center of gravity. And there were a bunch of people who were stepping into the spotlight. The younger family members were activists with their own followings. And the elders—like Simmie, Sonny, and me—well, we were the torchbearers, the storytellers. Sonny had been named to head up Mamie's estate. Cousin Airickca Gordon-Taylor became quite active organizing anniversary events and responding to breaking news with other national activists. Two other cousins were in the picture: Bertha Thomas, a paralegal, had helped in handling a lot of Mamie's business affairs when she was alive, and Abe Thomas, Bertha's brother, had been Mamie's caregiver. They were Sonny's niece and nephew and still were being contacted by media for comments, as was cousin Ollie Gordon, Airickca's mother, who had known Emmett as a child, when they lived together.

But as we got closer to June 1, 2005, when the FBI planned to exhume Emmett's body and perform an autopsy, cracks in our family unity were exposed. There were two important considerations for an autopsy. First, the FBI had to confirm that the remains that had been returned to Mamie in September 1955 were, in fact, the remains of her son. An autopsy and DNA testing would settle that. Second, an autopsy would verify the cause of death, which would help connect to a person or multiple persons who caused the death. And no autopsy had been performed before Emmett was buried.

The media was right there, ready to cover the family uproar. The very idea of digging up Emmett, of disturbing his resting place just across the cemetery from where his mama was entombed, was hard for the family to process. Yet some family members supported it. Simmie was a leading voice on that side. He had been convinced that the autopsy and identity process would be critical to moving the case forward. I was uncertain about it, believing that somehow digging up Bobo's remains was a violation of the sanctity of his resting place, but said I would go along if the government compelled this action in order to complete its work. If this could lead to justice, then I would support it, however reluctantly. But the family would not voluntarily consent to an exhumation and autopsy.

Bertha in particular believed that this was not something Mamie would have wanted. It was unsettling. Besides, Mamie had examined Emmett's remains when they were returned to her. She had confirmed "beyond the shadow of a doubt" that the body she had examined was her son. The Reverend Jesse Jackson stood with Bertha and supported the objection to the proposed government action. He had been a longtime friend of Mamie and the family, had been at Mamie's house to comfort the family later on the evening when she passed, and had eulogized her at one of her two homegoing services.

Alvin Sykes and Keith Beauchamp supported the government move. In fact, Alvin had been talking it up for a while and even enlisted Charles Evers, Medgar's brother, to support it. This only seemed to make matters worse for a moment. Some family members were suspicious of the motivations of Alvin Sykes and Keith Beauchamp, let alone the government. That had started at Mamie's second homegoing service on January 11, 2003, when the two of them took to the stage to talk about the investigation that would be launched. No one really knew Alvin at that point. And some family members had heard Mamie say that she had decided to work with Stanley Nelson and not Beauchamp on a documentary. What was this really all about? I had worked with Nelson, and Simmie would work with Beauchamp.

Finally, things got resolved when the family dissenters were persuaded that they should not stand in the way of the investigation. We put aside the dissension. We agreed to the government process.

The glass top that Mamie had placed on the casket had done a good job of preserving the remains for testing. As a result, the autopsy, which included a match of DNA between Simmie and Bobo's remains, proved the truth of what we always had believed to be true. This was Emmett Till. There also was useful evidence confirming death by gunshot and something else that had been the subject of Delta rumors. Bobo had not been castrated, as Beauchamp still included in his documentary.

Now we could move forward. Hopefully, this evidence would help the investigation. Hopefully, there would be some measure of justice. But first, we had to put Bobo back in the ground. And that became yet another moment for me.

WHEN EMMETT TILL's mutilated remains were returned from Mississippi in September 1955, I refused to accept that it was my cousin. I refused to accept that he had left us—refused to accept that I had left him. Left him in the store in Money, left him back in Mississippi the night they came to get him. Now in 2005, I was being asked to deliver the eulogy and I was refusing once again. I couldn't do that. Instead, I agreed to deliver a recommittal sermon. The theme I set for the sermon was "What Is Life?" I had put it off until late the night before we would return Bobo to his resting place at Burr Oak Cemetery, a traditional Black burial ground where people like singer Dinah Washington and bluesman Willie Dixon were laid to rest— segregated even in death.

At the funeral in 1955, I had been numb. No sorrow, really. No sadness. I hadn't cried back then. But I cried this time as I thought through the lines I was writing and wondered how I would hold it together during the service.

The day of the re-entombment was a beautiful, sunny early-June day. But it wasn't quiet. The news had gone out that Emmett Till would be reinterred June 4, three days after his exhumation. And it seemed every media organization in town had a helicopter to try to capture the private family gathering that had been closed to the press. In a way, that overhead noise quieted me, calmed my anxiety as I watched the new casket brought forward by the pallbearers. Included in this special group were Simmie; playwright David Barr, who had written a dramatic version of the Emmett Till story with Mamie; Odell Sterling, a former gang member, now a motivational speaker, whose life had been turned around by Mamie, his favorite teacher; Chris Benson; and Alvin Sykes and Donald Burger, who quickly had gained family acceptance after the earlier family tension eased. Urging government action that led to a positive identification of Emmett Till did a lot to raise Alvin's standing among family members.

Through the helicopter noise, I found my voice. And I posed the provocative question that had been inspired by Bobo.

"What is life? As we come today to this solemn occasion, we are reminded again that our burial services are not for the dead, but for the living."

As a minister, of course, I had long been in touch with serving God. That certainly is my purpose. But as I delivered the sermon, emphasizing the need to connect with our purpose and to live a committed life, I could see God's work in the pursuit of justice and my role in that process as a servant of God on earth.

"Till's voice has been crying out to us. Rosa Parks heard his cry, and wouldn't give up her seat. Martin Luther King Jr. heard his cry when he gave that great speech in Washington. Acosta of the Justice Department, he heard his cry and said, I am going to open up the investigation. We all hear the voice of Emmett Till crying out for justice."

That is our purpose, I told those who had gathered under the tent. It is to be of service. I was telling them and I was reminding myself.

WHEN HANDING OVER the investigative file to Mississippi District Attorney Joyce Chiles, FBI Special Agent Killinger believed that

Carolyn Bryant Donham should be indicted. It seems that he had seen enough circumstantial evidence to justify that belief. There had been a question about whether there was enough evidence to justify an indictment of Henry Lee Loggins, one of the two Black men who had been implicated. The other, Levi "Too Tight" Collins, had died some time earlier. Some people expressed concern about indicting Loggins—feeling it would have been tragically ironic if the person ultimately made to pay for Bobo's murder was a Black man who might have been forced to participate.

That wasn't Simmie's feeling at all. As far as he was concerned, Loggins had the power to say no, and beyond that, he "had almost 50 years to come forward," to provide evidence against those who had committed this horrible hate crime. "He didn't do it. He could have cleared the air, gotten those who were involved while they were alive," Simmie said at the time. "As the saying goes, it's on him now. I would like to see him talk. And if he doesn't talk, throw the book at him."[32]

As for the other unnamed persons Beauchamp had been saying were involved—fourteen in total, and some still alive—no credible evidence had been produced to support his claims. Jerry Mitchell, an investigative reporter for the *Mississippi Clarion-Ledger* who has reported on the Emmett Till case for years, asserted that Beauchamp's claim of a huge lynch mob was a "legend."[33]

We did not get the answer we had been hoping for. Marvel got the call from Killinger. The grand jury did not hand down an indictment against Carolyn or anybody else. No reason was given. The grand jury operates in secret and doesn't have to explain. He had believed in the case so strongly that Killinger was quite upset about the outcome. I was, too. After three years of hard work, we had come to believe that justice finally would be done. No one, though, was as angry about it as Simmie.

"You're looking at Mississippi," he said in a February 27, 2007, CBS interview. "I guess it's about the same way it was fifty years ago. We had overwhelming evidence, and they came back with the same decision" as with the acquittal in 1955, he felt. "I don't know how many years I have left on this Earth. We can leave this world and say, 'Hey, we tried. We tried to get some justice in this, and we failed.'"

FOLLOWING HIS REVIEW of the Emmett Till file in January 2017 and with clearance from his supervisor, Special Agent Henry began the next phase of his inquiry from his home base in Oxford, Mississippi. After the decision by the Mississippi grand jury not to hand down indictments in the Emmett Till case, a December 28, 2007, DOJ "Notice to Close File" had been issued by DOJ attorney Karla Dobinski, but it did not get implemented at the FBI field office in Oxford. That's because, after Special Agent Killinger retired, the responsibility to close the file had been passed along to Special Agent Henry, who had just transferred into the Mississippi office from the bureau's San Antonio office. There were questions about how to handle certain sensitive items in the FBI file, like Emmett's bone fragments that had been examined during the DNA testing. Because Henry became busy with other matters, he never actually closed the Emmett Till case. Instead, he marked it as "Inactive," which kept it open in case something else might turn up. Now, in 2017, Henry was free to look into that quote, that recantation by Carolyn, in Tyson's book, without jumping through all the bureaucratic hoops in Washington for permission to reopen the case. He could get started even before any public outcry for reopening the investigation surfaced—no more procedure than just routine pursuit of leads, requiring approval only by his supervisor.

By March 2017, preliminary interviews with Carolyn Bryant Donham and Timothy Tyson had been completed. That's when Henry contacted Marvel and me. He invited us to travel to Oxford to meet with the FBI and other government officials.

We accepted the invitation, even though we had no idea what lay ahead of us.

3

"What Does Justice Look Like?"

MARCH 2017. THE meeting had been set—all travel arrangements made, all plans worked out and organized. We knew everything about our estimated time of arrival in Memphis from our Chicago-area home, the government official who would meet us at Memphis International, drive us into Mississippi, the hotel where we would stay in Oxford, and the official departments and agencies that would be represented at the meeting the morning of March 22, after we had a good night's sleep. All the details . . . except for one: What were we supposed to *accomplish* in Mississippi?

Marvel would be with me on this journey, just as she had been with me at all the most important moments along the way. For nearly fifty years of marriage, she had been by my side, and had been supportive at every turn. So she would be there at this time, standing by me, on this journey to seek justice for Bobo. At least that's what I hoped we would be doing down there.

By necessity, it also would be a journey of remembrance, reflection, and redemption. Remembrance: a night of terror and the days and weeks and months and years that followed, haunted by the memory. Reflection: what it all meant to my family, what it has meant to so many others in the extended family that is Black America, and what we all have needed in order to find peace. (That is, if peace ever even is possible for the victims of terror—the immediate victims—and all the others continually terrorized by the threat, the fear, the expectation of becoming victims themselves.) Redemption: finding a path to reconciliation, finding forgiveness for those who trespass against us. And this, too, finding forgiveness for ourselves—permission to ease the guilt we all have carried, survivor's guilt.

Marvel knew better than most about that particular lifelong burden I'd shouldered—despite the invitations of my faith to lay it all down at the Lord's feet. And she knew the weight of it even after years of healing—a weight that connected me and preserved my compassion for people I'd meet along the way. People I'd reached through my ministry, people I'd counseled in troubled times of loss, people who also were forced to ask themselves, as we all did: Was there something we *could* have done—*should* have done—that would have kept our loved ones alive? Should I have forced myself to get up that night when Bobo was taken? What was he thinking? Did he think about me, wondering why I hadn't forced myself to get up, forced those racists to let him go? As he was forced along his death march, did he think it would all turn out okay, that somehow, some way, his cousin would come after him?

The questions always were there, in those dark, lonely spaces between other thoughts, demanding answers that never came. This is what victimization is all about. You might survive, but you are never really whole again.

We had been waiting for nearly sixty-two years. Suddenly now, despite all that, I wasn't sure I was ready yet to hear the answer that would come from the people we were trusting to give it to us straight. Why was Carolyn confessing now? Was she motivated by poor health, close to death, wanting to get right with God as I had wanted to do when her husband and brother-in-law busted into my grandparents' home? When I thought they were going to kill me? If so, how much more would she tell us, and what could we do with that information? Was there a chance now that someone would be made to answer for Emmett Till? What would that answer be? What *should* it be? What measure of justice could we even achieve in 2017 for a brutal lynching that occurred in August 1955?

For so many years, I had avoided being at the center of it all, avoided being the person telling the story. As I have said before, there was no reason for me to take exclusive ownership of the memory of Emmett Till. Being able to remember Bobo was a gift in itself—a unique and cherished gift that could be claimed only by the few of us to whom it had been given. But, as they say, to whom much is given, much is expected. Very much.

So, in 1985, when Mamie asked Simmie and me to take part in the Rich Samuels documentary on Emmett Till, I began to realize my responsibility. And each subsequent television, radio, and newspaper interview was another reminder of my duty to Bobo and the preservation of his truth. That had become even more clear to me as I struggled to find comfort in conceiving and writing and delivering that recommittal address when we laid Bobo to rest once again, following the exhumation and autopsy. Being that close to the body of Emmett Till—hearing him speak to us once again, the living part of him, through his DNA, telling us he was still with us, calling on us to be with him, as he must have on that dark lonely night, his very last night—my strength had been renewed. I knew the truth. And I was determined that everyone would come to know it. Everyone.

So that was a critical part of my purpose in traveling to Oxford, Mississippi, in March 2017. By telling my story, I hoped the truth would be confirmed, be validated, and serve as a transformative force for the others involved. As a minister, I know one thing is certain: Ask and ye shall receive. As I had persisted in asking questions of a lifetime in pursuit of the truth, it seemed that I finally would receive. Whatever I could offer the government officials I would meet in Oxford could help them with whatever they decided to do. Whatever they could offer me would help me with what I needed to do. And, with that, I was resolved. My uncertainty about what lay ahead had disappeared. It was empowering. Here in Mississippi, we would prepare to write the final chapter in a story that began here. Closure.

The echoes of that revelation in Timothy Tyson's *The Blood of Emmett Till* still were reverberating by the time of our arrival in Mississippi on March 21. As so many times before, the headlines had started heating up the Emmett Till story, the cold case. People had begun calling for an investigation to be reopened and for Carolyn Bryant Donham to be charged as an accessory to something: kidnapping, battery, manslaughter, murder, conspiracy, obstruction, perjury, something. *Anything.* And things already were in motion.

Even we—the family members who were being called upon to help set the course—even we had not agreed on the best way forward. My uncle Simeon Wright had been one of those people calling for this woman to be arrested, charged, convicted. Like me, Simmie had lain awake that night, so many nights ago. All the other boys had slept through it back then. While Marvel and I were working in the background, other family members were more vocal about the way Bobo's story serves, again and again, as tragic proof that there is no equal justice in America. Some people actually can get away with murder—especially when it's White people killing Black people. Whether it's unprosecuted lynchings in the 1950s or unjust prosecution in the 2000s, what Michelle Alexander calls "The New Jim Crow," there seems to be no fairness as far as Black people are concerned. There is a heavy weight on the scales, pushing down hard against fairness for us, against justice for us, like a knee on the neck.

That's why we agreed to a meeting with authorities in Oxford, Mississippi. In a way, Special Agent Henry and the folks on the front lines of law enforcement had feelings that were not unlike those shared by the family and by the activists: a dedication to justice, an uneasiness with the denial of justice. And when it comes to denial of justice, the Emmett Till case was the one everyone pointed to. The unfinished business of that lynching was scratching at our collective consciousness like fingernails on a chalkboard.

The family agreed that only the elders would participate in the meeting, which made sense. Simmie and I had been in the house with Emmett the night of his kidnapping. My aunt Thelma Wright Edwards, Simmie's sister, had lived with Emmett and his mother, Mamie, just before the time of his Mississippi visit. Crosby Smith Jr. ("Sonny") was Mamie's first cousin and the executor of her estate. His father, Mamie's uncle, Crosby Smith Sr., had brought Emmett's body back to Chicago. Marvel and I would attend the Oxford meeting in person. So would my aunt Thelma. Simmie was terribly ill by this time, suffering from cancer, and would have to call in on the conference line. Sonny also would listen in on Simmie's end of the line. Also there with us in Oxford would be Chris Benson. Marvel and I asked Chris to attend as our representative, our lawyer, to take notes and to help us focus in on questions that should be raised, and to explore the possibilities that might arise. The authorities approved. And so it was done.

My thoughts on that flight down to Memphis were focused on what lay ahead of me, but also on what lay behind, if only because I would need to remember all that had happened in order to help the authorities consider the direction ahead. The possibility that there might be a future in the case was opened up once again by the Tyson book. Clearly, the federal and state authorities were taking that possibility very seriously. Now the question was whether that admission by Carolyn Bryant Donham had opened the door to an examination of her guilt on some charge related to Emmett's death.

Finally, there might be some answers, some justice. Even though Bobo had been taken from us, gone for several generations, he had never been silenced, as I had said in my sermon at his recommittal. Clearly, people were still hearing his cries for justice. The public anger was growing. No one really had believed the initial story Carolyn Bryant had told in court back in 1955. No one but the jury that acquitted Emmett's murderers—her husband, Roy Bryant, and his half brother J. W. Milam. But, even though we knew from the very beginning that she had lied, reading that she was admitting it now only reminded everyone of the injustice Black people have suffered in the justice system.

As it turned out, though, after traveling to Mississippi on a hope and a prayer, we were about to get whiplashed again.

On Tuesday, March 21, 2017, we were greeted by our government escort at the Memphis International Airport for the drive to Oxford, Mississippi. The eighty-six miles between Memphis and Oxford had become so familiar to me. My family had left Mississippi during the second wave of the Great Migration in the 1940s, but I had returned countless times like a migratory bird, drawn back to the familiar and the memories it conjured up. Just a few blocks away from Oxford's Graduate Hotel where we would stay, a memory was stirred. We passed the historic home of Nobel laureate William Faulkner and we were reminded of the Mississippi native son's warning about what might be in store for the state following the murder of Emmett Till. The whole world was changing in the 1950s as people of color were pushing hard for their independence in the global south, just as they were pushing for equal rights in the American South. From Rome, Faulkner wrote a warning to his fellow White Mississippians and, in fact, to all of America after Bobo's death. "If we as Americans have reached that point in our desperate culture when we must murder children, no matter for what reason or what color, we don't deserve to survive, and probably won't."[1]

Agent Henry stopped by the Oxford Graduate Hotel to speak with us after we arrived. We met in the lobby of the hotel. The atmosphere of that lobby reminded me of the kind of conflict Faulkner suggested in writing about Bobo. Without a doubt, the hotel was a charming place, where Ole Miss students took advantage of free off-campus Wi-Fi to surf the internet. It definitely welcomed us with cultivated southern charm on the warm Mississippi evening we were there. I couldn't help but think, though, about how hostile such a setting might have been to us back in the day. After all, we were only a few blocks from the town square where the historic courthouse still waved the Mississippi state flag with its Confederate stars-and-bars symbol—a symbol of White supremacy. Neither we, nor Agent Henry, a tall and powerful-looking Black man—a former offensive lineman for Wisconsin—none of us would have been allowed to sit in a hotel lobby in the central business district of Oxford, Mississippi, back in the 1950s. We certainly would not have been among the Ole Miss students congregating there. The school wasn't desegregated until October 1, 1962, when James Meredith was enrolled, followed by bloody riots by White students, who eventually were confronted by thirty-one thousand federal troops.[2]

That is the history that frames our awareness. The fact that we have to think like this is part of the burden African Americans carry with them at all times. We might be able to look White people in the eye now in the "Magnolia State," but it is not just an expression of our hard-won legal equality. It also is a deep soul-searching scan to see how each person is going to step to us. Each person who might not have forgotten that history, and might not have moved beyond it. Friend, or foe? "The past is never dead," Faulkner wrote. As he concluded and as we would be reminded in the course of our nearly four-year ride-along with the FBI investigation into Bobo's death, the past "is not even past."[3]

Henry briefed us on who would attend the meeting and what we might want to offer in terms of background and information that might be helpful to authorities looking for anything they could use to bring someone to justice. Somewhere in this conversation, though, he laid something on us that I didn't expect. The hype might have outstripped our hope. Our hope—at least my hope—was that, after so many years, we finally would have the truth told about that encounter at the store. The revelation in the Tyson book had brought us that much closer to it. Now this meeting would set the stage for the final act. That's when we heard the words from Special Agent Henry and observed his expression just before he spoke them. It was a thoughtful pause. A fraction of a second, but still detectable.

The revelation in the Tyson book had been called into question, he told us. In a follow-up interview with the FBI, Carolyn Bryant Donham denied that she had spoken the words attributed to her by Tyson. We would hear more about it all in the meeting.

*   *   *

THAT NEXT MORNING, Wednesday, March 22, 2017, with all the new uncertainty surrounding us, we arrived at the offices of the US attorney for the Northern District of Mississippi to attend the high-powered meeting with government officials. There had been a shake-up in federal law enforcement. Attorney General Jeff Sessions had requested and received the resignations of all US attorneys in the country, so that he could have a hand in appointing all federal prosecutors and reshaping the system.[4] That meant that the two US attorneys for Mississippi—the first Black appointees—were gone now and the person in charge of the Northern District of Mississippi was Acting US Attorney Bob Norman, along with Deputy US Attorney William Chad Lamar, two White men. Acting US Attorney Norman had only been appointed on March 10, just under a week and a half before we arrived. It was not clear what impact the Jeff Sessions Department of Justice in the administration of Donald Trump would have on this matter. Would it be snuffed out—a change of course from what would've been possible under the leadership of Felicia C. Adams? She had made history as the first Black woman to serve as US attorney in Mississippi, when she was appointed by President Barack Obama to replace Jim Greenlee in 2011. Before she was confirmed as US attorney, she had served as an assistant US attorney in Mississippi for twenty-two years.[5] So she had been there when the original Till investigation was launched and had a real interest in what we were going to take up on this trip. We were told she had wanted to sit in on the meeting, before the politics set in and she was asked to resign. It was no comfort to realize that, after all these years, the investigation of Emmett Till's murder still might be as political as it was legal. No wonder, then, that we were sensitive to every detail that might reveal the level of commitment in moving forward. How things would get interpreted just might be influenced by who was doing the interpreting.

As it turned out, our introduction to Acting US Attorney Norman was quite comforting. Norman quickly waved us through security—

a gesture of trust—and we were ushered into a conference room with a table that looked like it could stretch across two rooms. Something about the way we were greeted by everyone made us begin to feel more comfortable. The big guns were drawn. And they weren't aimed at us. This was going to be a significant meeting in Oxford, a meeting of people who seemed like they could make a difference, if nothing or no one got in their way. Special Agent Henry was very supportive. We knew that from the night before. On this morning, he took charge of opening the meeting, making all the introductions.

People participating from the government side included Norman and Lamar; Dewayne Richardson, who had succeeded Joyce Chiles as the district attorney for the Mississippi Fourth Circuit Court District; Tamicko Ransome Fair, district manager for the Mississippi Fourth Circuit Court District; Kristy Parker, deputy chief, Criminal Section, Civil Rights Division of the US Department of Justice, who flew in from Washington, DC, for the meeting; and Special FBI Agent Shannon Wright, among other local staff. On the phone were Simmie and Sonny talking to us from back home in Countryside, a Chicago suburb. Marvel and I were in the meeting room, along with my aunt Thelma Wright Edwards, her son Ozzie, and Chris Benson, who sat at the end of the table taking notes.

Before anyone even said a word on the briefing part, you could feel the energy in the room. This US Attorney's Office for the Northern District of Mississippi had a reputation and one of the most active dockets on civil rights investigations. No wonder Henry had been called in to work on the Eric Garner investigation in New York. The lawyer assigned to the Garner case out of the Civil Rights Division of the Department of Justice in Washington also was seated right there at the table with us. Kristy Parker had a reputation for toughness and determination with fifteen years of experience prosecuting hate crimes.

Henry began by delivering a summary of the history of the case and the latest development that brought us all to that conference room. It was clear from his thorough summation that he had spent a great deal of time absorbing everything—not just because he had come to *know* it all, but because he had come to *feel* it all. In fact, the energy around that conference table was very strong, very positive, very supportive from everyone there. This definitely was not the federal government of 1955: a White House that ignored the murder of Emmett Till, never even answered Mamie's telegram to President Eisenhower, crying out for a federal investigation. This was not the FBI of 1955: an agency led by longtime director J. Edgar Hoover, who saw no reason for the federal government to enter into the case. Clearly, there was a commitment around that table in Oxford that day in March 2017—a commitment to doing anything possible within the bounds of federal and state authority to reach a just end. But there were a lot of conditions wrapped up in that last point. What was in the bounds of the law? What would it take to reach a just end?

Special Agent Shannon Wright had interviewed Carolyn Bryant Donham after the Tyson book was promoted, and so we were eager to hear what she might have to reveal to us. According to Agent Wright, she was turned away at the door when she first tried to visit with Carolyn at the Raleigh, North Carolina, home of her son Tom Bryant and daughter-in-law Marsha Bryant. Agent Wright was asked to come back an hour later. The Bryants wanted the local police to be there when she returned to check out her credentials, make sure she was legitimate. They had been receiving more threats than usual after the Tyson book was published and felt a need to make sure Agent Wright wasn't somebody just trying to get in their house to attack the Bryant family. Apparently, they live with the anxiety that somebody is out to get them. The anxiety of guilty knowledge. After Agent Wright was cleared to come in, a strange thing happened. Carolyn came into the room carrying her medications, and she handed them to her daughter-in-law. It was as if she thought she was being taken into custody. It was as if she knew there was some reason that she might be arrested. At least that's the way we saw it when we heard the story.

Agent Wright went on to explain to us what was said in that conversation. Carolyn denied that she had told Tyson what he published in the book. She had not confessed to lying about Bobo. She claimed Tyson misrepresented what she said and that she was standing by her statements to the FBI during her questioning in 2005. Then, if Tyson published something that was false, something that harmed her, why hadn't she sued him for libel? She and her daughter-in-law explained that they didn't want to have to talk about the matter again, as Carolyn would have to do in a lawsuit.

According to Agent Wright, Carolyn did stick with the part about how Emmett didn't do anything to deserve what was done to him. She had said that before, during the FBI investigation that started in 2004. So she wasn't giving up anything new. After all that, what were we left with? Another lie, on top of a lie, wrapped inside a lie? What had started out as a new take on a he-said-she-said story had become a mess of a she-said-she-never-said-what-he-said-she-said kind of a story.

Mess or no mess, the conversation turned to what steps might be taken from that point. That conversation was impacted by everything that our family offered. The pain we had suffered. "I lost ten pounds, couldn't eat for a week," Aunt Thelma recalled about that period after Bobo's body was found.

Simmie talked about his father, my grandfather, who had to make a tough choice to stand up, testify at the murder trial, "and risk losing our whole family. He lost his job, but wanted to see justice done. Now, sixty-two years later, the motive is the same. We seek justice and truth."

Marvel spoke up, pointing in my direction. "This Tyson book is opening a wound with this man I've lived with for fifty years," she said. "We're going to just let her get away with it again?"

The conversation weighed heavily on me. "You really can't understand it if you haven't lived it," I said, finally. "I am literally in tears every time I have to speak about it. Kids feel Emmett must have done something. They ask whether I could have done something. People say he got what he deserved."

That clearly moved something in the room. As if our hearts had stimulated the minds, the talk shifted from that emotional moment to strategy. Would there be enough in the Tyson book to justify an indictment? The grand jury had determined that there was not enough evidence to indict in 2007. One member of that grand jury panel had said recently that the Tyson revelation probably wouldn't make a difference. But was that true? I noted that there were other potential grand jurors who might see things differently. The question for this group was whether the book added anything now that had not been known back then. Clearly, since that published recantation was being denied, more would be needed. Could that "confession" lead to other information that might justify an indictment? Was there anything else in Tyson's notes that might add to a circumstantial case against Carolyn? Had she done anything to set it all in motion? Maybe there was a cause of action in that, like manslaughter, something that survived the statute of limitations. Did she play a role in the kidnapping? There was that voice in the truck, the one Papa had heard. Simmie reminded everybody of that. It was a voice that was lighter than a man's voice. It was a woman's voice, he said. But Papa had died in 1977. Who was around now who might testify, verify? What about perjury, lying to the FBI? No. The five-year statute of limitations on lying to the FBI had expired in 2010. Tyson had conducted two interviews with Donham within three years of her five FBI interviews in 2005. Maybe, if he had revealed the information back then, Carolyn could have been brought in and charged with something. But it was too late now, unless there was some proof that she had just lied to the FBI about what she said in the Tyson book. The Tyson interviews had been recorded. Maybe the first step would be to go after those recordings. But even that would have to be handled carefully. Would Tyson give up the material voluntarily, or would he have to be compelled by another grand jury? Could he be compelled? Could a writer be forced to give up his source materials?

At this point in the conversation, Tamicko Fair, District Attorney Richardson's district director, asked the family a critical question:

"What would be a just outcome for you all now? What does justice look like?"

Simmie was quick to speak up on the phone. He was adamant. He did not waver. He said he wanted an indictment. He wanted someone sent to prison.

I certainly wanted justice, but had been struggling with this very question for so long. Even before that question had been put to us at that meeting. What would that mean in a case like this? Based on everything that was being said, I wasn't sure whether there would be enough to send Carolyn or anybody else to prison. As I had learned in the 2004 investigation, you can have a feeling in your gut, a certainty in your head, you can know something is wrong, that something wrong has been done, but can you prove it? That was the issue former Special Agent Dale Killinger had faced back in 2007 when the grand jury handed down a no true bill—refusing to indict Carolyn Bryant Donham.

"It's been sixty-some years that we have lived with this idea that Emmett Till got what he deserved," I finally said to the group. "I want to see that get straight. I want to get as much information as we can, by any means necessary."

There was a question of whether immunity might be offered in exchange for full disclosure—to get a complete and truthful story, a confession, out of Carolyn.

Simmie was opposed to anything other than a criminal prosecution. "No immunity. No deal. I will do nothing to dishonor my father by giving immunity to hear her talk."

Acting US Attorney Norman was moved by the personal reflections of our family. He thought about how he would feel if his own fourteen-year-old son was attacked. He talked about the possibility that correcting history—at least that—would be a form of justice. But he soon was reminded that correcting history was not something the criminal law was designed to do. Only bringing charges and prosecuting. There had to be probable cause to believe that an investigation would lead to a prosecution. If there were no charges for the Department of Justice, or for the State of Mississippi, then maybe there was nothing to be done. And now we were entering a strange place where the very *rules* of justice might just *deny* us justice—even the smallest measure of it.

I just shook my head. "So we're actually back where we were."

Finally, Chris looked up from his note taking at the end of the conference table and spoke up. There was an exception to the rule. Ironically, that exception had been inspired by Emmett Till and created in his memory: the Emmett Till Unsolved Civil Rights Crime Act, which had just been reauthorized by Congress the year before and signed into law by President Barack Obama.

For a fraction of a second, everything in that room seemed to go into freeze frame—as everyone who knew anything about that law processed the point. They nodded as Chris reminded us all of the provision in that law that might open the door, nodded in recognition of the fact that a path forward just might have been cleared by the very person at the center of our attention and the focus of the investigation.

Emmett Till.

4

"Investigate and Legislate"

As we sorted the pros and cons of the different paths forward at the March 2017 meeting in Oxford, I was reminded of what I had seen ten years earlier. In 2007, we were all disappointed when the Mississippi grand jury handed down a no true bill, meaning no indictment, against Carolyn Bryant Donham and Henry Loggins. There were limits on the amount of time you had to charge or indict somebody, even when the wrongdoing was obvious. There were limits on the range of charges that could be brought if the wrongdoing in question didn't fit the way the law was framed. There were limits on the life spans of perpetrators, on the memories of the witnesses against them. There were limits on the willingness of prosecutors even to try a case, or a grand jury to approve a case for trial, it seemed, unless it looked like a winnable case to begin with. In the end, that meant there were limits to justice.

Unlike the rest of us, though, Alvin Sykes, the Kansas City activist, had a vision of a second path forward. Even when getting the federal investigation started in 2004, Alvin had been determined to continue fighting on the national level no matter what happened, no matter how long it took. Alvin's plan had called for a two-pronged assault on injustice in the case of Emmett Till—actually, in the name of Emmett Till. Investigate *and* legislate. And when the investigation produced so much for the historical record, even without an indictment, his legislative strategy kicked in: introducing a bill in Congress, getting it passed, having it signed into law and enforced, not just for Emmett Till but for many other victims of injustice across the nation.

What Alvin had in mind was to use the public attention that had been drawn to the Emmett Till investigation to push for the opening of investigations into a number of unsolved murders that had taken place during the civil rights years. He got his chance within months of the launch of the FBI investigation of Emmett's lynching. As we would see, that investigation was only part 1 of his plan.

On November 19, 2004, four national lawmakers issued a joint, bipartisan resolution urging the federal government to expedite its investigation into Emmett's lynching, the one that had been announced that May. *Hurry it up* was the message.[1] Senator Chuck Schumer of New York, Senator Jim Talent of Missouri, Representative Charles Rangel of New York, and Representative Bobby Rush of Illinois were concerned that, according to a release by Representative Rush, the "nominal" opening of the investigation that May was not moving swiftly enough "to interview elderly witnesses."[2] Representative Rangel warned that the commitment to investigate could wind up looking like "an empty promise" to the family of Emmett Till if the government didn't proceed quickly.[3] The need for a "speedy" investigation was clear, according to Senator Schumer. "Time is of the essence," he wrote, "because of the advanced age of many of the potential witnesses, and we haven't a day to spare."[4]

The resolution wound up having no impact on speeding up the investigation. It wouldn't go before District Attorney Joyce Chiles and the Mississippi grand jury until 2007, and Special Agent Dale Killinger was going to take the time he needed to build the case by building the evidence. But, recognizing that some of the facts cited by the senators and congressmen were based on the unverified (and what Alvin considered unpersuasive) information Keith Beauchamp had provided, Alvin decided to intervene. He reached out to the member of this group many would feel was the least likely to support progressive change: conservative Republican Senator Jim Talent, from Missouri, Alvin's home state.

There was something Alvin had recognized in Talent that caused him to believe he could connect with his senator on this effort. Senator Talent had made a statement in connection with that joint resolution calling the failure to bring anybody to answer for Bobo "a stain on our country's judicial record." Talent went on, "Emmett Till was murdered because he was black and his murderers were acquitted because they are white. No matter how much time has passed, if there are still people out there who were responsible for the brutal murder of Emmett Till, they should be brought to justice."[5] That last line was the key: "They should be brought to justice."

"If you want to do something meaningful," Alvin recalled saying to Talent, "then go after all these other unsolved civil rights cases."

"I had never met him before," Alvin wrote in his unpublished manuscript, *Show Me Justice*. "I told him that the FBI was not going to speed up the investigation just because some members of Congress say so."[6] Talent listened as Alvin shared his deep concern that the congressional resolution "was at best symbolic involvement and at worst interfering with an ongoing criminal investigation."[7] So, committed to furthering federal–state action in the case, Alvin shared with Talent a new suggestion, one that would realize the senator's commitment to justice in something concrete.

Among the top graduates in his class at the University of Chicago Law School, and a clerk for the ultra-conservative Judge Richard Posner of the US Court of Appeals for the Seventh Circuit in Chicago, Talent was true to his family name in responding to Alvin. He definitely was a *talent*, a politician with the ability to see the social and personal value in Alvin's plan and the skills to persuade his colleagues. Alvin wanted a law that would create an unsolved crimes section in the Civil Rights Division of the Justice Department, and an unsolved civil rights crime investigation office in the FBI. "There needs to be a centralized place in the Justice Department and the

FBI that would have the funding and the means to focus in on the cases," Alvin recalled telling Talent.[8] That centralized place would adopt the model Alvin had urged officials to follow in launching the Emmett Till murder investigation. A partnership between the national government and states, it would rely on federal money and staff to help state prosecutors move cases forward—cases that might be too complicated and costly for the states to pursue on their own.[9] It would be based on legislation drafted by the staffs of members on both sides of the aisle and in both houses of Congress, with input and influence from the high school dropout who had conceived of the whole thing. For Alvin, this was a continuation of his bipartisan approach to cutting through political distractions in order to reach his goals. Surely, the words of twelve-term Missouri Congressman William Clay must have echoed in the head of this Kansas City activist. "No permanent friends, no permanent enemies, just permanent interests."[10]

Apparently, according to Alvin's recollection, Talent agreed with his argument and wound up assigning his staff to work with Alvin in developing the language for the Senate bill. Ordinarily, legislative support in the Senate would be important in getting support in the House of Representatives. In this case, though, Alvin was already approaching key figures who would simultaneously jump-start a separate bill in the other chamber.

Like so many civil rights activists, the late Congressman John Lewis had grown up with the Emmett Till story in his Troy, Alabama, hometown, about 345 miles away from Tallahatchie County, Mississippi. Bobo's lynching had a deep effect on Lewis, who was just a year older than Bobo in August 1955. "I was fifteen, Black, at the edge of my own manhood, just like him," Lewis wrote in his memoir, *Walking with the Wind*. "He could have been me. That could have been me."[11] Quite a few civil rights activists were inspired by the events surrounding the death of Emmett Till. Now Representative Lewis, a Georgia Democrat, was able to bring his activism to the legislative process in honor of that inspirational moment, the moment when news of Bobo's lynching was reported throughout the South, across the nation, halfway around the world.

As things go too often in Congress, this legislative effort moved very slowly—despite Alvin's maneuvering in both chambers. Senator Talent introduced the Unsolved Civil Rights Murders bill in the Senate Judiciary Committee on July 1, 2005, but it never made it out of the committee.[12] And, though reintroducing the bill in the next session of Congress won more support—at least in the House—Talent didn't make it back to the Senate in 2006. He was unseated by Claire McCaskill, a Democrat, who also would become a supporter and co-sponsor of the bill. Still, not until 2007, when Representative Lewis retitled the bill as the Emmett Till Unsolved Civil Rights Crime Bill, was it able to pass the House, with a vote of 442 to 2. Although Talent had managed to get bipartisan support for the Senate bill before his departure, McCaskill was unable to hold on to that leverage. The late Senator Tom Coburn, a Republican from Oklahoma, had become an obstacle. A physician, Coburn was known as Dr. No in the Senate because of his opposition to any spending bill that did not provide for equal spending *cuts* somewhere else in the budget.[13] The challenges kept growing. By this time, Alvin was homeless, living in the W.E.B. DuBois Learning Center in Kansas City. He kept fighting for the law that was so close to passing, but not close enough. He fought hard. With a flip phone, calling cards, and air travel paid for by business leaders in Kansas City, he hung out in Coburn's office until he finally spoke with the senator and convinced him to lift his hold on the bill and allow for a unanimous consent vote, with no roll call needed to move forward.[14]

Alvin wrote, "The next day, September 24, 2008, I turned on C-SPAN. There was Harry Reid, the majority leader of the Senate, talking about these various amendments and one is the Till Bill. He said he was going to introduce it for unanimous consent and the senator who was acting as president of the Senate said, 'Without objection, so ordered,' and that was it."[15] The Emmett Till Unsolved Civil Rights Crime Act was signed into law by President George W. Bush on October 7, 2008. It set up the two cold-case units and authorized up to $13.5 million a year to investigate crimes committed before 1970.[16]

It is an amazing story of the determination of Alvin Sykes, who was as "poor as a church mouse," Coburn had said when he took to the Senate floor to sing the praises of the activist he finally had bonded with, the one he credited with changing his position on the passage of the bill.[17] Alvin watched on television as Coburn spoke.

"We have wrangled a lot over this bill, because of the financial problem we find ourselves in today. But the greater call was to allow this bill to pass. One person has truly made a difference and that one person is Alvin Sykes. I can't say enough about his stamina, his integrity, his forthrightness, his determination."[18]

Even with all those qualities, the ones we all came to recognize and admire in Alvin Sykes, there would still be hurdles to clear. Just as with the investigation of Emmett Till's murder, there were problems opening the cold cases, mostly because so many witnesses had gotten old enough to have forgotten key facts, or because some had died, or because some still feared reprisal. Other problems centered on earlier jury verdicts, like the one in the Emmett Till murder case against Milam and Bryant. If an all-White jury had let killers off—as we know they *routinely* did—then those killers couldn't be tried again under the double jeopardy protection of the Fifth Amendment. At least 122 cases were investigated under the Till Act, and the Syracuse University Cold Case Justice Initiative (an organization of law school faculty and students) provided documentation of hundreds more cases to congressional leaders in working on the reauthorization bill over the next eight years. Of course, a number of cases were also closed because of the act, since information was revealed by investigators that allowed the government at least to answer the unanswered questions.[19]

One important case did end in a conviction.

On February 26, 1965, Jimmie Lee Jackson, a twenty-six-year-old church deacon, was beaten by Alabama state troopers in Marion, Alabama, during a peaceful march in support of voting rights. Finally, he was shot to death by State Trooper James Bonard Fowler. A state grand jury refused to indict Fowler in 1965, and no federal authorities investigated.[20] One month after killing Jimmie Lee Jackson, Fowler went on to stand with his fellow troopers on the Edmund Pettus Bridge in nearby Selma, during the police riot on "Bloody Sunday." Forty years later, Fowler admitted shooting Jackson, falsely claiming self-defense.[21] In a 2005 interview with John Fleming published in *The Anniston Star,* Fowler claimed Jackson was going for the trooper's gun. "That's why my conscience is clear," he said.[22] In a demonstration of the arrogance of White supremacy, he told Fleming why he was not afraid he would be indicted. "I don't think legally I could get convicted for murder now no matter how much politics they got 'cause after 40 years they ain't no telling how many people is dead," he said, referring to the belief that there would be no witnesses left to testify against him. Fowler wound up being indicted in 2007 and, with evidence produced by the FBI following passage of the Till Act, he wound up pleading guilty to manslaughter in 2010 and was imprisoned for six months.[23]

The death of Jimmie Lee Jackson was a source of inspiration for the Selma-to-Montgomery march in March 1965 and was featured in the award-winning film *Selma*.

The Emmett Till Unsolved Civil Rights Crime Act has served as a warning that, no matter how old you get, if you have committed murder, or participated in any aspect of a murder, conspiracy, or cover-up, there will be consequences. This is why Alvin Sykes knew it would be important to have the initial law reauthorized before its ten-year life span expired in 2018. And knowing how much time it had taken to get the law passed in the first place, Alvin began preparing in 2015 for a renewal. Once again, he engaged a bipartisan and bicameral strategy, reaching out again to Representative Lewis and this time to Senator Richard Burr, a Republican from North Carolina. His goals for the new measure were even more ambitious. It would not have a "sunset," which is to say, it should never expire; it would extend the coverage period by an extra ten years to include any crimes committed up through 1979; and it would provide for financial support for community groups and universities engaged in public education, research, and investigations into civil rights cold cases. Alvin wanted it signed into law by the first African American president, Barack Obama, who was going to leave office at the end of his second term on January 20, 2017. That desire would become even more critical set against the rising racial tensions during the 2016 presidential campaigns. And, with a divided Congress, there was a great deal of concern that elected officials might not be able to come together to renew the commitment to racial justice that the Till Act was designed to fulfill.

Of course Congressman Lewis would be a natural ally once again, and the congressman was able to pull together the support needed in the House, starting with Democratic Representative John Conyers of Michigan and Republican Representative Jim Sensenbrenner of Wisconsin. Lewis introduced the bill in April 2016. "We can never heal from the injuries of the past by sweeping hundreds of crimes under the rug," he noted in a statement. "We have an obligation, a mission, and a mandate to continue the effort required to wash away these stains on our democracy."[24]

As it turned out, Senator Burr became an important supporter, too, largely as a result of the many conversations Alvin had with him and his staff. Burr was joined by Senate co-sponsors Missouri Democrat Claire McCaskill, Missouri Republican Roy Blunt, and Vermont Democrat Patrick Leahy.[25] As he introduced the bill on the Senate floor that April, Senator Burr, just like Senator Coburn ten years earlier, sang the praises of Alvin Sykes, "a person that taught himself how to do these investigations in the civil rights cases, a guy that is passionate about trying to bring justice to individuals that are no longer here," and he said he hoped he had made Alvin Sykes proud. By July, on the eve of the national political conventions, the Senate passed the bill by unanimous consent.[26] The House would follow in September.[27] And President Obama signed the bill into law on

December 16, 2016, just a little more than one month before he would leave office.[28]

That was a great relief to Alvin, and to all of us, increasingly concerned about political obstacles to getting the law through in a new administration. To say the least, Donald Trump and Jeff Sessions, his nominee for attorney general, were not seen as friends of civil rights.

BY THE TIME we got to that meeting in Oxford in March 2017, we all were heartened by the provisions of the act reauthorized a few months before as we talked about what justice might look like for Emmett Till—for him and for the family left behind, those of us seated around that long conference table trying to figure out how to make the law work for us. And the moment Chris brought it up, we saw how the Till law opened the door to what we needed to do. Even if it did not lead to an indictment—which is the only thing that might move a prosecutor to consider a case—it could yield answers to critical questions that had been floating out there for years. That is the power of the Emmett Till Act. It allows the government to pursue an investigation even if it is only going to provide answers to open questions, and not lead to a court case. That is a big deal and something I really wanted. Answers. The truth.

Would all this give us leverage to get Carolyn Bryant Donham to talk—perhaps revealing more information about lies told again and again over the years? Carolyn seemed to think she was being taken into custody when Agent Shannon Wright came to visit her after the Tyson book was published. Did she think she was being arrested because she knew there was a reason she *should* be arrested? She had no idea whether a case against her even existed, let alone whether it was a strong case. Maybe she would be motivated to cooperate with a grant of immunity, an assurance that no charges—real or imagined— would be brought. But Simmie already had taken a strong position against that move.

No matter what course was taken, though, the next step would be to try to see what was in the files of Timothy Tyson. Unless Tyson voluntarily released the material, the authorities would have to seek authorization for a subpoena and court order. I thought it odd that a historian wouldn't want to show that his writing was accurate, to show the integrity of his work rather than forcing a subpoena. But time would tell how far this process would have to go and whether Tyson would try to argue that he had a right to protect the confidentiality of his work and keep it from going public. Given the significance of this particular historical event, there was an even stronger argument on the other side.

In addition to providing answers to our family and to the public, the federal and state authorities would determine if any charges might be filed based on potential revelations in any of three areas. First, whether any new information might be produced showing that Carolyn Bryant Donham had participated in Emmett Till's murder on any level. Second, whether any previously unknown living suspects might be identified. Third, whether evidence might reveal that Carolyn Bryant Donham had lied to FBI agents during their February 2017 interview with her.

While the federal resources were needed to pursue the investigation, we knew that, if anything would happen as a result of that work, it would happen because of the district attorney's office. Only the State of Mississippi could bring charges. The time had run out on any potential federal charges, unless there was a new charge of lying to the feds during that February 2017 interview. Otherwise, District Attorney Richardson would pore over the eight-thousand-page file of the 2004 FBI investigation and would be ready to consider any new evidence produced by the federal agents. With Donham aging and claiming more and more that her memory was fading, the pressure was growing to do something before it simply was too late to do anything.

DOJ attorney Kristy Parker was reassuring. "We will look at everything," she said, at the same time urging us to "keep expectations reasonable," given all the variables.

Special Agent Henry agreed. "We all wish that we were superheroes." But, clearly, there were uncertainties. Then he added a personal note that was very moving. "We would not have a cold-case law if not for the sacrifice that you all made with the loss of Emmett Till and your willingness to come forward. I wouldn't be here if not for the sacrifice of your family. It's an ongoing motivation. Emmett Till didn't die in vain." Through the newly reauthorized cold-case law, Bobo had made it possible for us to move forward in this next phase.

Over the speakerphone, we all heard a much calmer Simmie respond to the personal assurances. "All we ask is that you do your best."

There were promises from all around the table to keep us in the loop on developments. Of course, this is one of the requirements of the Till Act: The government was obligated to keep us informed of the ongoing status of the investigation, especially since Simmie and I were witnesses as well as victims and survivors. Even so, I was feeling uneasy. I had come to Oxford believing Carolyn Bryant Donham had confessed and we only had to decide how to bring closure to this case at long last. Maybe with her arrest. Conviction. Something. Now things were back up in the air. The title of her unpublished manuscript also disturbed me: *I Am More Than a Wolf Whistle*. What did she mean by that? Also, she and her daughter-in-law had told the FBI that they were working with Tyson on this book. So how did he wind up writing his *own* book? And how did these two books fit together?

Clearly, this was a continuing story, and while there was a part of me that was wishing we had reached the dramatic conclusion, another part of me was eager simply to get to the next chapter. And it looked like this matter just might proceed without what we most wanted to avoid: interference from Washington, from a president who was dismissive at best and distrustful at worst. As I finally was relaxing into these thoughts, someone in the room spoke up, with a casual comment—just matter-of-fact—that shook that calm.

Someone in Attorney General Jeff Sessions's office had asked for a briefing on the Emmett Till case.

5

Unreasonable Doubt

THE STORY OF Emmett Till refuses to fade into the background. We—Bobo's family and everyone who comes to know his story—refuse to let him go. Right after his lynching, "Emmett Till" became a rallying cry. People would say his name as his mother wanted them to do. People would see his mutilated remains, as she wanted them to do. "Let the world see." So many young people—people like the late congressman and civil rights hero John Lewis—became activists in large part because of Emmett Till. And for a couple of generations after his murder, Bobo's story was told by so many Black parents to so many Black children—a rite of passage, a cautionary tale. In a way, it was their stranger-danger story—a graphic illustration of why you had to be careful dealing with White folks and what could happen to you if you weren't. If you didn't understand race and place in America, they would remind you about the worst that could happen: "You don't want to end up like Emmett Till."

Yet even after parents stopped showing their tattered old copies of *Jet* magazine or *The Chicago Defender* with the screaming headlines and horrifying photographs of Bobo's mutilated body, stuffing them away in boxes and drawers and steamer trunks, the name of Emmett Till continued to echo across the years. The name of Emmett Till was repeated almost every time a young Black male was killed by a White person who got away with it.

So, in a strange kind of way, the name Emmett Till has represented two distinct things to people. To some, he is an example of a kid who did something wrong and suffered the worst possible penalty; to others, he is an example of a system that punishes innocent young Black males. And while on one hand Emmett Till has represented racial division, on the other, he has become a great unifier. As in the earliest days of the Civil Rights Movement, we are now brought together by the challenge embedded in the Emmett Till narrative. For those of us who have accepted and believed in the founding principles of America—freedom, justice, equality—the unresolved case of Emmett Till is a violation of the very things that make us whole. And we should be joined in the pain of that violation, no matter what our political leanings or racial identity might be, just as we should be unified by the values of a democratic society.

This is why I was concerned when learning that Attorney General Jeff Sessions wanted to be briefed on the case. It was not an unreasonable assumption that he might be preparing to interfere with the investigation. Instead, as it turned out, he was preparing for a meeting of his own one week following ours—a meeting with Alvin Sykes.

It seems that Alvin never rested, not even with the reauthorization of the Emmett Till Unsolved Civil Rights Crime Act. He knew that the law on the books still needed to be matched with a commitment to enforcing it. And that commitment to enforce the law had to be matched with money to pay for that enforcement. Even with *authorized funds* up to $13.5 million, there would have to be an *appropriation* of the money—somebody within the Department of Justice would have to ask for that money . . . and get it approved by the leadership there. That meant convincing Sessions to follow through. So Alvin arranged a meeting through Senator Richard Burr. And that was why Sessions wanted to be briefed. We were relieved.

During the meeting with Sessions, Alvin made the case for enforcement of the Till Act and seemed to get a commitment for that, so that the many unsolved civil rights era murder cases could be revealed and investigated.

Just as the horrible injustice of the Emmett Till case unified and motivated government law professionals and investigators back in Oxford, it also continues to bring together young people who want to take action to set it all right. You could see it, hear it in the chants of "Black Lives Matter" following the 2012 killing of Trayvon Martin (and the acquittal of his killer) in Florida. You could see it, hear it, in the protests that sprang up after Michael Brown was killed in Ferguson in 2014 and Tamir Rice in Cleveland only a few months later that year. Such protests have brought all kinds of people together—across racial, ethnic, religious, geographic, and generational lines—because they see that we're all connected in this pursuit of those American ideals. That's what Emmett Till represents.

During the month of April 2017, just one month after our meeting with officials in Oxford, Mississippi, we would return to that state—to the Delta—to experience that connection with a group of North Marion High School students who had traveled thirteen hours and 865 miles from their hometown in Farmington, West Virginia. They came to the Delta to reenact the Emmett Till murder trial in the restored Tallahatchie County Courthouse in Sumner, Mississippi, where it all took place between September 19 and 23, 1955.

The idea for this event started with one of the presentations I have made for a number of years during The Most Southern Place on Earth Institute sponsored by the Delta Center for Culture and Learning at Delta State University. Schoolteachers from all across the country participate in the weeklong summer institute that includes a presentation on the Emmett Till case inside the very courtroom where the case was tried. One year, Bill Stalnaker, a journalism teacher at North Marion High, was there to see it. He was so moved by the Emmett Till experience in that courtroom that he decided to make the trial reenactment a learning experience for his students back in West Virginia. Tall in stature with a beard and ponytail, Stalnaker looks very much like the musician he has been. He has worked to harmonize his diverse classes of students by allowing them to immerse themselves in controversial stories. He has guided and engaged his students to elevate their understanding of what it takes for reporters to cover live events, like criminal trials. To enrich this experience, he has included reenactments in his curriculum.

Stalnaker had started this process with Watergate hearings and wound up focusing on Emmett Till. Back in Farmington, and armed with the trial transcript that Special Agent Dale Killinger had dug up, Stalnaker led his students on a moving reenactment of the trial, a presentation that I was invited to attend at the West Virginia high school—an experience that took Marvel and me down some rather scary dark roads in that rural space. The reenactment affected me much more deeply. It brought me to tears. I had not attended the 1955 trial, nor had I read the trial transcript before then. Immediately, we agreed that the next reenactment should be done back in Sumner at the county courthouse, where the students could experience the trial, bring it to life once again. I wanted to share this event with people back in the Delta, but I think a big part of me also wanted to re-create it for myself: to be in that space and hear the words and feel the tension of the trial and the spectators, set in the middle of a town without pity. Maybe I would find something in that performance that I might not see otherwise, something in that old courtroom that would add to my search for justice.

In April 2017, during their spring break, the North Marion students re-created the moment over the course of two days. They were very impressive. They didn't just read the edited trial record, they absorbed it. They threw themselves into the characters they would portray without regard for traditional roles: Black students playing the roles of White people, White students playing the roles of Black people, teenage girls playing the roles of old men. Even beyond the immersion into the storytelling, this act of stripping away their own identity helped them develop a deeper understanding of the experiences of others. They began to see the world differently.

As it turns out, they immediately would be confronted by the persistence of racial resentment in the Delta. Stalnaker attempted to find a cotton gin fan to display in court, like the one that had been there on display in the courtroom during the original trial: the seventy-five-pound gin fan that had been tied to Bobo's neck with barbed wire to weigh his body down in the Tallahatchie River. Stalnaker had planned to bring a fan on the trip with the group, but somehow it got left behind in West Virginia.

"And I thought, 'Oh, that's not really a big deal. We can find one there,' 'cause we were gonna be in cotton country," he recalled. He finally found someone who might be able to provide one as a prop and called the man. "He said, 'I hope this isn't about that thing that's goin' on over in Sumner.'" That's when Stalnaker realized that news of "that thing," *our* thing, was getting mixed reviews even before it began—reviews based on attitudes that threatened to carry us back to the Delta of 1955 as effectively as the reenactment itself. When Stalnaker confirmed that the fan would be used as "a stage prop," the man shook Stalnaker with his response. "I'll tell you what, you can go straight to hell."

The next call was even worse. A woman answered the call, and Stalnaker could hear a man's voice in the background when he asked about a fan. "And this woman was laughin'," Stalnaker recalled. "And she said, 'D'you hear what he said?'" He thought he did, but wanted her to repeat it. She obliged, repeating the words from the background that had made her laugh. "She said, 'The last one of those we had they tied it around some nigger's neck and threw him in the river.'"

Attitudes, anxiety, anger were all deeply rooted in the culture of this place. Maybe that was why, despite the promotion, the public turnout for the student reenactment was light. Just as there was such intense hostility among some folks who didn't want us in this place, there clearly was concern—if not fear—among the folks who still were the targets of all that. Or believed they could be. Just being seen coming to this event might be viewed as a challenge of some kind—defiance, troublemaking. And even the courtroom setting would not provide a sense of safety or sanctuary from that suspicion. After all, the Confederate statue still stood out front as it did when Papa and Mamie walked into the courthouse building back in 1955. A symbol of protection for some, threat to others. What was protected was a culture of White supremacy. What was threatened was a guarantee of equal justice in the courtroom the soldier was watching over, as if to ensure that the threat would be carried out. And across from the courthouse, right there on the town square, were the law offices of the county's leading attorneys back in the 1950s: Breland & Whitten Lawyers, the ones who had defended White supremacy as much as they defended two killers, the enforcers of that way of life.

There were echoes of a distant trial that had taken place in that courthouse building, but it really had shaped up as a morality play. Good against evil. Heroes against villains. Truth against lies.

Papa was there to take a stand. Simmie was there, just in case they needed him as a backup witness to the kidnapping. Mamie would come down from Chicago. They were joined in a courtroom challenge here in the Delta by people we would come to recognize as the beginnings of the Civil Rights Movement. Medgar Evers had just been appointed as Mississippi field secretary for the NAACP; the Emmett Till lynching was his first investigation. Ruby Hurley was there; a sharp lawyer, she was the head of the NAACP's operations in the entire Southeast region. Dr. T.R.M. Howard was there; he was the founder and head of the Regional Council of Negro Leadership, which at that time was bigger than the NAACP in Mississippi. Congressman Charles Diggs of Detroit was there to observe. And, of course, there were celebrated Black journalists who all would go on to cover some of the most important developments of the coming years. At this point in 1955, though, for their own protection they all stayed in all-Black Mound Bayou, where there was some measure of safety. At his estate, Dr. Howard maintained guards—armed with shotguns and Tommy guns.

Although I wasn't there in the courtroom during the 1955 trial, or even in Mississippi for that matter, I had seen some of what happened back then in the pages of the newspapers I delivered on my route back in Argo/Summit. Now, in a 2017 presentation directed by Stalnaker with his wife, Cathy O'Dell, a theater instructor at West Virginia University who served in the role of Judge Curtis Swango, I sat there in the front row of what once had been the Whites-only spectator section, with Marvel next to me, just behind the bar and the defense table, the jury box off to the left, the witness chair close to the judge's bench dominating center stage, the vacant space off to the right where the Black press and Black dignitaries once sat at a rickety, splintered Jim Crow card table. Now I would see it all unfold, see the truth told by heroes on the one side, and the lies told by the villains on the other, living it all through the work of these amazing kids who were reenacting a pivotal moment in time and, in the process, resurrecting so many historical moments, conjuring up so many ghosts.

SEPTEMBER 19, 1955, the first day of the trial, was just routine—setting up jury selection, establishing the rules of the trial, like the judge's order that there would be no photography during the proceedings. Tallahatchie County Sheriff H. C. Strider was there to lend his support . . . to the defendants, the murderers. J. W. Milam and Roy Bryant hugged their wives and played with their sons and got *attaboys* from the good ol' boys during part of the proceedings. Why wouldn't they be relaxed, at ease? They had every reason to take it all in stride since Strider had been taking care of them. First, this Tallahatchie County sheriff from central casting already had set the stage for what was to come. He had told the press that he couldn't be sure the body that was retrieved from the river really was Emmett Till. Second, he had helped the defense attorneys—all five lawyers practicing in the county at the time—make the right decisions in picking jurors. As the county sheriff, he knew the folks most likely to let the killers off. Third, he helped to set the "us-against-them" tone for the five-day trial, a power struggle, set out in his famous comment to the press: "We never have any trouble until some of our Southern niggers go up

North and the NAACP talks to 'em and they come back home. If they would keep their nose and mouths out of our business we would be able to do more when enforcing the laws of Tallahatchie County and Mississippi."[1]

During the questioning of the jury pool, the three prosecutors, District Attorney Gerald Chatham, Special Assistant to the District Attorney Robert Smith III, and County Attorney Hamilton Caldwell, wanted to know whether anybody under consideration had contributed—or even *thought* about contributing—to the defense fund, the jars that had appeared at shops all over the town square. Defense attorney J. J. Breland asked generally whether potential jurors would require the state prosecutors to prove guilt beyond a reasonable doubt—the standard for a criminal conviction. As the trial would reveal, he wanted to challenge any reasonable person unwilling to find *un*reasonable doubt.

Those three prosecutors were outgunned by the five defense attorneys, and not just because the killers were the hometown favorites. There was no real investigation of the murder, so the case really didn't have any evidence except for what happened at the house when Bobo was taken.[2] Papa and Simmie could testify to the kidnapping, since they were eyewitnesses to that. But the murder? There had been rumors—always rumors in the Delta—that there were witnesses who were keeping low, or that two Black men who might have participated in Bobo's kidnapping, death, and cover-up were being hidden away by Strider in the county jail at Charleston.[3]

That's what had led *The Afro-American* newspaper reporter Jimmy Hicks to go undercover at that popular juke joint, King's Place, in search of Levi "Too Tight" Collins and Henry Loggins, the two Black men who had worked for J. W. Milam. Meanwhile, Dr. Howard had learned about Willie Reed, the eighteen-year-old sharecropper who was believed to have seen something. This all led to a search party headed by Leflore County Sheriff George Smith that included Black reporters like Simeon Booker and Moses Newson, and White reporters Clark Porteus of the *Memphis Press-Scimitar*, and W. C. Shoemaker and Jim Featherstone of the *Jackson Daily News*.[4] As a result, Willie Reed, his grandfather Add Reed, and neighbor Amanda Bradley all were convinced to come forward to testify under the protection of Dr. Howard, who, among other things, would get the witnesses safely out of town after their testimony. Even so, it was a tremendous act of courage since testifying against a White person in Mississippi at the time could be considered a capital offense for a Black person. Like whistling at a White woman.

As a result of the work by the team of reporters, civil rights activists, and one halfway decent county sheriff, the witness list for the state grew to twelve with the addition of these three surprise witnesses. For the defense, there would be ten witnesses.

Of the people who testified for the prosecution, three were the most important. First was Papa, Moses Wright—or "Uncle Mose," as District Attorney Gerald Chatham called him.

As the North Marion students re-created Papa's testimony, I could hear distant sounds, starting with that banging on the front door, and my prayer, and my promise to God. And that devil's voice on the other side.

"Preacher . . . Preacher."

It was around two in the morning, Papa testified. "And then I said, 'Who is it?'"[5]

"This is Mr. Bryant. I want to talk to you and that boy."[6] Papa got out of bed.

Chatham: "And what did you see when you opened the door?"

Mose: "Well, Mr. Milam was standing there at the door with a pistol in his right hand and he had a flashlight in his left hand."

Then, just minutes into this testimony, the most dramatic moment in the entire state case.

Chatham: "Now stop there a minute, Uncle Mose. I want you to point out Mr. Milam if you see him here."[7]

As Papa rose from the wicker witness chair, the only sound in the courtroom came from the whirring ceiling fans. Across the room at the Black press table, photographer Ernest Withers slowly angled his camera up from the tabletop, aiming it toward the witness. As Papa looked directly at Milam and raised his hand to point Milam out, Withers looked directly at Papa and hoped he was in frame of the camera lens. Papa pointed. Withers popped off a shot.[8]

Mose: "There he is."

One moment, two acts of defiance. Withers defied the judge who had ordered people not to do what Withers had just done, take photos in his courtroom during the proceedings. Papa did a whole lot more as he defied the social order. As I said, reckless eyeballing could get you lynched. He confronted two White men at a time when Black folks weren't even supposed to look White folks in the eye, let alone point at them—point and accuse. He had been warned by Milam at the house.

Mose: ". . . they started out, then he asked me if I know anybody there and I told him, 'No, Sir. I don't know you.' And then he said to me, 'How old are you?' And then I said, 'Sixty four.' And then he said, 'Well, if you know any of us here tonight, then you will never live to get to be sixty five.'"[9]

Despite that threat, Papa went on to point out Bryant, as the prosecutor asked him to do.

They had made it clear what they were there for. Just before these terrorists pushed into the house, Milam said, "I want that boy that done the talking down in Money."[10]

Papa told the truth—the whole truth, step by step. The abduction. How Milam and Bryant roused Bobo from his sleep, marched him out to the truck. About the Black man he thought he saw outside in the darkness. And then there was that voice. At the truck as Milam and Bryant held Bobo in front, someone else spoke from inside the cab.

Mose: "They asked if this was the boy, and someone said, 'Yes.'"

Chatham: "Was that a man's voice or a lady's voice you heard?"

Mose: "It seemed like it was a lighter voice than a man's."[11]

They drove off into the darkness. Papa stood there on the porch and watched.

In her sworn testimony, Mamie told how just about three weeks earlier she had positively identified her son's horribly mutilated remains at the A. A. Rayner Funeral Home in Chicago.

"I looked at the face very carefully. I looked at the ears, and the forehead, and the hairline, and also the hair; and I looked at the nose and the lips, and the chin." Clearly, she had been told that there was a question about Bobo's identity and that would be the one point she needed to nail for the jury. "And I knew definitely that it was my boy beyond a shadow of a doubt."[12]

In her book, Mamie gave a much more detailed description of the horror she saw on a slab in a funeral home in Chicago.

"When I got to his chin, I saw his tongue resting there. It was huge. . . . I couldn't help but think that it had been choked out of his mouth. I forced myself to go on . . . Step by step, as methodically as his killers had mutilated my baby, I was putting him back together again . . . From the chin I moved up to his right cheek. There was an eyeball hanging down, resting on that cheek. It looked like it was still attached by the optic nerve . . . Right away, I looked to the other eye. But it wasn't there."[13] And she went on, she wrote, as a "forensic doctor" might do, despite her mother's anguish.

If the testimony of Papa had identified the men who took Emmett away, and Mamie positively identified his body, the question for a jury was whether the two men who kidnapped Emmett had anything to do with his death. That's where Willie Reed came in.

Between six and seven in the morning, Sunday, August 28, 1955, Reed was headed to Glenn Patterson's store and took a shortcut from his home on the Shurden Plantation across the Sturdivant Plantation managed by Leslie Milam, J. W. Milam's brother, Roy Bryant's half brother. He saw a green-and-white '55 Chevrolet truck with four White men in the cab, and three Black men in the back, on the side of the cargo area. He saw a boy sitting on the bottom of that cargo area. When he came back from the store, he passed a barn, a seed shed, on the Sturdivant Plantation. That truck was parked in front and something was happening inside the barn.

"I heard somebody hollering, and I heard some licks like some-body was whipping somebody," he testified.[14] He also saw J. W. Milam come out of the barn, wearing a pistol "on his belt"; he drank water from the well before going back inside the barn.[15]

The defense attorneys seemed to want to throw everything against the wall to see what might stick. Of course, they raised questions about the testimony of all of these witnesses. It was too dark for Papa to recognize the defendants, who were lit only by flashlights.[16] Reed might have heard sounds coming from the Sturdivant Plantation barn, but the pounding could have been someone working on a car, they suggested.[17] Reed hadn't identified Roy Bryant, and hadn't he only connected Emmett to the boy on the truck days later when he saw Bobo's photo in a newspaper story?[18] Mamie might have been born in nearby Webb, Mississippi, but she had lived in Chicago just about all her life—one of those uppity Negroes from the North.[19] And she read *The Chicago Defender*,[20] which was seen by many south-ern White people as radical and hostile to their way of life.

Attempting to further muddy the water, the defense lawyers tried to discredit Mamie to cast doubt on whether Emmett Till was the victim pulled from the Tallahatchie River. They played to the fears of White people in the area—their fear of change, change threatened by the Supreme Court ruling in *Brown v. Board of Education* and pro-moted by the Black press, papers like *The Chicago Defender* read by people like Mamie, the kind of people Sheriff Strider had in mind when he had said, "We never have any trouble until our Southern niggers go up North . . ."[21]

After the state rested its case, the defense lawyers moved for a "jus-tifiable homicide defense," a term coined by Davis Houck, Fannie Lou Hamer Professor of Rhetoric at Florida State University.[22] Enter "Mrs. Roy Bryant," as she identified herself on the record after "being first duly sworn"—proudly aligning with one of the murderers on trial.[23] As defense attorney Sidney Carlton began asking about her encounter with Emmett that Wednesday evening, August 24, Robert Smith, the special assistant to District Attorney Chatham, jumped in.

"If the Court please, we object to anything that happened on Wednesday evening unless it connects up," he argued.[24]

The judge dismissed the jury to hear the lawyers' arguments on both sides—one argument legal, and one factual. The legal argument was based on the state supreme court ruling on whether something that happened one day could justify something that happened on a later day. The factual argument was based on whose story was going to drive this case. The prosecutors wanted to start the story at the Wright family home at 2:30 A.M. on August 28. The defense lawyers wanted to start the story at the store on August 24, arguing that the murder was one "entire transaction" set in motion at the store.[25] That way, they could introduce into the record that racist narrative that a Black kid somehow did something so offensive to a White woman that her husband had to protect her honor. They argued further that the state had opened the door to this connection by allowing Papa to testify that Milam had said he and Bryant had come for the "boy who done the talking down at Money."[26] That left open two questions: What talking? And what happened at the store that made them come for Bobo? Finally, the judge allowed Carolyn Bryant to provide her ugly claims for the record.[27]

Even though the jury would remain out of the courtroom during her testimony, all of the spectators were riveted, as if they needed to hear her story, to hear the justification for a lynching. The jurors might not have heard it directly, but they surely heard it—reportedly leaked to them by White Citizens' Council members while they were "sequestered" in the Delta Hotel across the town square from the county courthouse. Everything Carolyn Bryant was about to say under oath was a lie aimed at providing what Professor Houck has described as that "justifiable homicide defense" in the minds of the jurors, even if not in the record they could review.[28]

The defense was taking no chances. In addition to character witnesses they put on the stand, there were three "experts" who would provide testimony that would raise doubts about whether Bobo was even killed. Seriously.

First, Sheriff Strider—who was supposed to be on the side of the state prosecutors—offered the sort of testimony that a forensic expert might provide, despite the fact that he wasn't a forensic expert and his opinion had no scientific basis. At one point, he testified that he examined a hole in Bobo's head (probably the bullet hole) at Graball Landing, the site where the body was retrieved. "I cut a stick about the size of a pencil and tried to find if it penetrated through the skull or not . . ."[29] And when questioned by defense attorney John Whitten Jr., he made ridiculous statements about the length of time the body had been in the water. "I would say at least ten days, if not fifteen."[30] Bobo had been missing for only three days before he was found. So, if you believed him, then the body couldn't have been Emmett Till. Then, about the condition of the body, Whitten asked, "Could you tell whether it was a White person or a colored person?" Strider basically shrugged. "The only way you could tell it was a colored person and I wouldn't swear to it then was just his hair. And I have seen white people that have kinky hair."[31] Whitten then asked whether the body was recognizable as "any particular person's."[32] And here Strider aimed to contradict Mamie's positive identification. "Well, if one of my own boys had been missing, I couldn't really say if it was my own son or not, or anybody else's. I couldn't tell that. All I could tell, it was a human being."[33]

On cross-examination by prosecutor Smith, Strider admitted that he signed a death certificate, but denied that he had identified the victim as Emmett Till.[34] "I said it was a dead body. I had never seen Emmett Till before, and I couldn't swear it was Emmett Till because I didn't know Emmett Till or what he looked like."[35] In her testimony a day earlier, answering a question about whether she had filed a life insurance claim, Mamie testified that she had not because she had not received a death certificate.[36] She did receive it later and learned that Strider's September 22 testimony—under oath—had been a lie. On September 1, the day after the body was retrieved, Strider signed the death certificate identifying the homicide victim of a "gun shot or axe" as Emmett Louis Till, a Negro from Chicago.[37]

That was twenty-one days before he swore he had not identified the body as Emmett Till.

Strider's testimony was bolstered by the next witness for the defense.

Dr. L. B. Otken testified that he had viewed the body, but had not done a pathological examination.[38] As for the condition of the body, like Strider, he testified that it looked like it had been in the river for at least eight to ten days and that neither the victim's brother nor parent could have identified him.[39]

Harry Malone was the embalmer at the Nelson Funeral Home in Tutwiler, "a negro funeral home" where Bobo's body wound up to be prepared for the journey back to Chicago.[40] Malone testified that he had examined the body and described the condition it was in, concluding "that the body had been dead possibly ten days or longer."[41] Under further questioning, he lengthened that time, clarifying what "longer" meant. "Somewhere between ten and twenty, or maybe ten and twenty five days, perhaps."[42]

If Malone was right in his assessment, reinforcing the testimony of Strider and Otken, then the body he examined could not have been Emmett Till. Again, Bobo had been missing for only three days. As with Strider, though, this testimony was not true. Prosecutor Smith stated in his closing argument that Malone had not embalmed Emmett Till. In recent years, historians have come to agree that Woodrow Jackson, Malone's Black assistant, had prepared Emmett's body, which means Malone could not have determined how long Bobo had been dead nor how long his body had been in the river.[43]

Two of the three prosecuting attorneys and four of the five defense attorneys made closing arguments. And there was a lot said on both sides about the identity of Bobo's body. Was it proved? Was it not proved? Lawyers call this sort of thing the corpus delicti. Basically, no body, no crime. No crime, no conviction. But this case was about more than the crime of murder.

District Attorney Gerald Chatham was first to present, reiterating the positive identification of Emmett Till's body before going on to address the issue that had put all the White folks in the Delta on the defensive. He called Emmett's murder "a cowardly act,"[44] apparently pulling on the traditional southern male identification with courage, and then he framed his argument around southern values. "I say to you, unless you judge this case on its merits it will endanger the precepts and examples which we hold dear here in the South."[45]

The most blatant appeal to racism came from two of the defense lawyers, starting with J. W. Kellum, who equated an acquittal of Emmett's murderers with an act of patriotism. "I want you to tell me where under God's shining sun is the land of the free and the home of the brave if you don't turn these boys loose; your forefathers will absolutely turn over in their graves."[46] Bringing it all to a close, defense attorney John Whitten faced the jury, confronted what was foretold here in Tallahatchie County—confronting the beginning of a movement, laying out the issues of the struggle ahead, as he saw them. "There are people in the United States who want to destroy the way of life of the Southern people," he said, obviously referring to the NAACP. People who would "go as far as necessary to commit any crime known to man to widen the gap between the white and colored people of the United States."[47] He was stressing the theme that the lawyers—the power elite of the county—wanted the jury to take away when he called for the jurors to acquit and told them he was confident that "every last Anglo-Saxon one of you has the courage to do it."[48]

After "deliberating" for only sixty-seven minutes (including a Coke break to stretch it out, make it look good for the national press), the jurors were ready to render judgment on September 23, 1955. They faced the judge.

Judge Swango: ". . . have you gentlemen reached a verdict?"

J. A. Shaw Jr. (jury foreman): "Yes, Sir, we have."[49]

And, with that, the verdict was handed to the clerk to be read to the court . . .

"GUILTY," THE STUDENT jurors declared in the 2017 reenactment, finding against the defendants—the racist killers—who, in real life, were acquitted by that 1955 jury of their peers. The students had given us the decision we deserved and had been denied so many years earlier, ruling in favor of justice—racial justice as well as justice for Bobo—which is to say they ruled against the historical record, as much as the original jury had ruled against the weight of the evidence in favor of White supremacy.

In the single-minded view of that 1955 Mississippi Delta jury—those twelve angry White men—the state had failed to prove its case beyond their unreasonable doubt. It seems they didn't believe the body pulled from the Tallahatchie River was Emmett Till—at least that was the story they could tell any reporters who asked.

The five defense lawyers—the entire bar of Sumner, Mississippi—had protected much more than two murderers. They had protected a way of life—American apartheid—against the looming threat they feared the most: equal justice. They had defended a way of life, in which White people could get away with murdering Black people they believed had stepped out of line, forgotten their place. And no one was going to judge them, or question that belief. The belief was their bond.

As we entered and left the courthouse during the two-day reenactment in April 2017, I gazed up at that Confederate statue that still stands guard over the town square. I considered what it represented to the community, what the engraved dedication—TO THE TALLA-HATCHIE RIFLES AND ALL WHO SERVED FROM THIS COUNTY—meant when it was unveiled in 1913, a gift by the United Daughters of the Confederacy. I thought about what it meant to the White folks who remained dedicated to what the statue stood for over the years, the people who stood in its shadow in 1955 when they couldn't get into the overcrowded courtroom it guarded. I read the inscription, an excerpt from the poem "The Apotheosis of War" by Virginia Fraser Boyle, who as a young girl had been anointed by Confederate States President Jefferson Davis as the "Poet Laureate of the Confederacy."

> *For truth dies not, and by her light they raise*
> *The flag whose starry folds have never trailed;*

And by the low tents of the deathless dead
They lift the cause that never yet has failed!

Haunting words: "the low tents." The foot soldiers, like the jury and the community that supported them, battled on the front lines of that "cause that never yet has failed!" And that inscription served as a reminder, a challenge. The "Lost Cause." From 1861 to 1913 and 1955 and yet still today.

The 2017 student panel, brought together in the same space as the 1955 jury, absorbing all the energy that still filled that space, was able to transform it, rededicating it as a true place of justice. And that renewed my belief in the possibility.

When media folks and university scholars talk about systemic racism, they don't always break it down so the public really can understand what it means, where it starts, how it ends. This is where it starts—with people whose beliefs, attitudes, behaviors laid the foundation for the entire structure of our society, top to bottom. The 1955 jury was told to find that the prosecutors had proven guilt beyond a reasonable doubt, based on the evidence. But they viewed the evidence the same way they saw their world, seizing on the White lies of defense witnesses, that the mutilated remains dragged out of the Tallahatchie River were not really what was left of Emmett Till. No. It was some "rotting, stinking body" that had been thrown in the river with Emmett's ring to fake his death, Whitten had claimed in his closing.[50]

It's called jury nullification—a judgment against the weight of the evidence, the unreasonable doubt that attorney J. J. Breland and the other defense lawyers had sought to create. In the case of Emmett Till, a jury of their peers remained doubtful that J. W. Milam and Roy Bryant had committed murder. Or, at least, they acted like it. Either the body wasn't Emmett Till, or, even if it was, Milam and Bryant could not be found guilty of killing Emmett Till and everything he represented—given the findings of a corrupt county sheriff, a local legal establishment, and even a US senator, as we soon would learn.

*   *   *

FOR THE HIGH school students in April 2017, reliving such an important time in history and having the chance to rewrite the outcome definitely amounted to a growth experience. It reinforced the idea that each one of us can effect change. They had thrown themselves into the preparation for this moment. They pored over written narratives and documentary films. "The research these guys did was phenomenal," Stalnaker said over breakfast the next day after the presentation and just before leaving for West Virginia. "I mean they, they were totally absorbed by it. Our prosecutor was comin' in like every class period, she'd pop by my room and say, 'Hey, I found out somethin' else.' She said, 'Did you know about this?'" Hunter Fluharty, a senior, a White student, said now she wanted to become a civil rights lawyer after playing the role of District Attorney Gerald Chatham. She felt ready to apply the lessons of this trial reenactment to play an even more important role. "I don't judge," she said. "Now I take others' views into consideration." She paused to gather her next thoughts. "I have come to hate my color." We all knew what she really meant. She hated the abuse of power associated with race. She had learned just how race, gender, and social status all can be weaponized.

I had been talking to young people for years, but this was the first moment I could see just how impactful the Emmett Till story could be in helping young people teach themselves. When reasonable people begin doing the math and see how it just doesn't add up, they recalculate. This kind of educational work would become a central focus for my ministry. "I came here to teach your students," I told Stalnaker in our post-trial discussion. "They taught me."

THE MISSISSIPPI DELTA is my neighborhood. I know it well. And I wanted to share it with the students, to give them a basis for understanding everything else they had considered. The remains of Bryant's Grocery and Meat Market and the vandalized Emmett Till historical marker out in front of the store. We talked about that, and the Black Bayou Bridge, where we believe Bobo's body was thrown into the tributary that carried it to the Tallahatchie River. We followed the river and stood for a moment on the Tallahatchie Bridge, the site made famous by Bobbie Gentry in "Ode to Billie Joe," a song that drew some inspiration from the Emmett Till story. There were other stops on our historical tour, including the East Money Church of God in Christ, where Papa was preparing to bury Bobo's body before Mamie stopped it all and ordered his remains returned to Chicago. There was the town of Glendora where J. W. Milam once lived, where King's Place once stood and provided that important lead for Jimmy Hicks. It was also the site of the former cotton mill, where the murderers stole the gin fan they used to weigh Bobo down in the river. The building has been rededicated as the Emmett Till Historic Intrepid Center (ETHIC), a museum now dedicated to history, operated by Glendora's mayor Johnny B. Thomas, who happens to be the son of Henry Loggins.

We wound up at the grave site of Robert Johnson, the famed blues artist who inspired generations with his music and his dreams. While we were there at that shrine of a tombstone with offerings of guitar picks and other memorabilia left behind by pilgrims, a woman rode up on the back of a motorcycle. Her name was Francesca, a blues singer from Italy, and she had come to this place with her guitar to sing praises. As she sang "Sweet Home, Chicago," first recorded by Johnson in 1936, just three years before I was born—it all came full circle for me. Johnson's driving desire to leave this place in search of the Promised Land had brought him to the crossroads, where legend has it he sold his soul, a legend that now brought a European woman to that land in his honor. And I had a fresh appreciation for the ways our lives are interconnected. How White students from West Virginia had come here to learn about justice and their role in the process of making it real. How music and storytelling and justice are all wound up together. How we can find harmony and unity of purpose through it all. Here, on this fertile ground, is where it all began for me.

6

A Place Called Slaughter

I WAS BORN IN a place called Slaughter.

There's a lot packed into that short line that says a lot about me—my lived experience and my consciousness, as much as where I've come from. "A place called Slaughter." Wasn't exactly a city. It was barely a town. More like an area in the Mississippi Delta, between the Quiver River and Highway 442. A community, which is to say a frame of mind. A sense of belonging. And not. In Slaughter, everybody knew their place, whether we were told where we stood—that is, where we were *supposed* to stand—or whether we just kind of understood it, took it in with the water, or with our food—our cultural nourishment. The knowledge, the awareness, the alertness that sustained us.

Maybe it came up through our roots, planted deep in that fertile Delta soil, like the generations of cotton there. Maybe it was branded onto us by the blistering summer sun as we picked our way through a living. Through life, really—a life of hand-me-down expectations balanced against limitations based on our place. And we definitely understood our place in that place that wasn't exactly a city, barely a town. That place called Slaughter.

In my early days, I had no idea just how Slaughter would serve as a kind of prediction, a prophecy, a warning. I didn't know that when

I would say where I came from, in a way, I also was saying just as much about where I was headed.

There is something else, though. Something very interesting about this place is that, even though we called it Slaughter, that really wasn't the name at all. I only recently learned that the name of the place actually is Schlater; the fact that we called it what we called it says more about where I come from than any name possibly could reveal.

Most of what we—Black folks—came to understand about our world, and our place in it, came by word of mouth. So, what we said and how we said it became our truth. That would mean more to me as we sifted through what so many people said and how they said it about Bobo in our search for the truth.

My truth? I was born in a place *named* Schlater. But it was a place we *called* Slaughter.

My mother, Hallie, and father, Wheeler Sr., had five children. And I spent my first six years in Slaughter, or Schlater. The little bit of direct contact I had with White people was all the contact I needed to reinforce the things I had been told to watch out for. Six years is plenty of time to see that White people were always the ones giving the orders and Black people were the ones taking them. There were rules that guided these relationships. Don't talk to White people unless they speak to you first. Always address them as "sir" or "ma'am" and never look them in the eye. For little Black boys, there was yet another lesson. Stay away from White women. Or, at least, make those contacts as short as possible. And respectful. And non-threatening. But mostly just stay away and there will be no eye contact or disrespect or threat.

Those were the most basic lessons we learned. But those lessons came to life when I realized just how willing my people were to accept the harsh way they were treated. At home, we were all laughter and love, and we were rich with the things that mattered the most in a family, even if we were far from rich in worldly things we saw in the lives of the White people who were so distant and so frighteningly close to us. But, despite the joy of our own community, when we were around White people, it was clear that we were less than equal, less than loving family members, less than human, really. In those first six years, you learn a lot by imitating the grown-ups around you. So the things they told us to watch out for, those things were important. But it was nothing like watching how they acted, and acting the same way when we were around White folks. You could feel the tension in those moments. Even in my young mind, I could process how important it was to walk that fine line, careful not to step too far this way, or even a little bit that way. The White folks were quick to put you back in your place in the most humiliating way. Sometimes, even when you stayed in line, they would feel a need to put you back in the place you thought you already were in, or some other spot they said you *should* have been in. Just to make a point. That they could do that—move things around like that. We were pieces on a game board. They played us for their sport.

By 1945, the year I turned six, my grandfather Moses Wright moved his family to Money, Mississippi. My mother and father decided to move from Schlater to Money that same year with my sisters, Elayne and Patricia, and brothers, Milton and William, and me. We would live with Papa, my grandmother Elizabeth ("Lizzy"), and five of their children on the Grover Frederick Plantation—Thelma, Loretha, Maurice, Robert, and Simeon.

Plantation life had not changed much since slavery ended. The shacks for the enslaved evolved into the living quarters for sharecroppers, like us. These *quarters* remained the homes for the Black 'croppers, and the living conditions pretty much remained the same. We were indentured servants and had only slightly better chances than our enslaved ancestors of running away from it all. It seems that we were as valuable a commodity as the cotton we were there to pick. The big house, where the master once lived, now was the home of the plantation owner.

Frederick Plantation was connected to the town of Money, an unincorporated Mississippi Delta community in Leflore County,

Mississippi. It is near Greenwood, which was the big city as far as we were concerned. Money sits along railroad tracks and is located next to the Tallahatchie River. Money Road is the main street, cutting through town and connecting several communities. Somewhere along the way, once you cross the river and the railroad tracks, Money Road runs to Grand Boulevard through the "Beverly Hills" of Greenwood. The contrasts along this road are striking—cotton fields that dominate the landscape as far as the eye can see, and on the beautiful Grand Boulevard in downtown Greenwood the houses spring up as mansions, each more impressive than the one before. This boulevard was one of the locations where *The Help* was filmed, and it still reminds us of the rigid caste system that has existed in the South for so many years.

Back in Money, there is a gravel road veering off Money Road. This road—the road where Papa's house was located, about three and a half miles from uptown Money—was called different things by different people at different times, kind of like Schlater and Slaughter. Apparently, its official name has always been Darfield Road. But what we called it had some meaning, too: Dark Ferry Road, a name along the way, transporting us to what was next. And to some of us, it was Dark Fear Road, which would take on a whole new meaning for me later.

Nobody lived on the north side of the road, for good reason. During the rainy season every year the area would flood and the water would wash out the bridges. Our house sat on concrete pillars to raise it up above the floodwaters. I remember the water running under the house all day during this season. It was so clear, so inviting as we watched it run past. Of course, we wanted to play in it, but our folks knew better—didn't allow it. Currents, tree branches, snakes: At this time of year, the only safe way into the water was with a boat, for those who had one. We weren't those folks.

That's not to say we didn't have fun. We were kids, after all. And we had quite a crew. My younger brothers, William and Milton, were now joined by my uncles Maurice and Robert. Simeon, the third boy in the Wright home, was still a toddler at this point. The river nearby was a huge attraction, our playground. We would fish by tying our lines around glass jars and digging the jars into the mud to anchor them. We could leave them overnight and come back the next day to see what we caught. Swimming in the river was a lot more challenging. We'd have to beat the shoreline with sticks to drive out the water moccasins on the other side. We made a game out of it, diving in to see who could go the deepest, using our hands to pull up mud from the bottom to prove who won.

It was my dad, Wheeler Sr., who had taught me how to swim. He did it by swimming with me on his back. He was a great swimmer. He could swim across the river with one hand holding his clothes up in the air to keep them from getting wet. Being with him taught me more than just how to swim across a river. It taught me to have the confidence that I could.

That house on the concrete pillars—the home of Papa and the Wright family, our home—had been the manager's house. So it was pretty nice, actually. Not a shack, as it was described in so many media reports on the Emmett Till story. Not like the homes of so many other sharecroppers. It was a large four-bedroom house with a screened-in porch across the front. The same house I would come back to visit in August 1955. The same house that would be terrorized in the pitch black of night. The same house where Bobo would sleep, until he was woken and taken, and all the rest of us threatened. The house on Darfield Road, or Dark Ferry Road, or Dark Fear Road. What it was called can only begin to express what it recalls.

We lived in the house with my grandfather's family for a short while, before a new house was built for us, separated from Papa Moses's house by a fruit orchard. An artesian well was at the back of our house, so we had running water all the time. On the other side of our house was a sawmill. Lumber was the second biggest commodity after cotton in the Mississippi Delta when I was a kid there. And I still can hear the grinding noise of the saws and the crashing sounds of logs that once were trees and soon would become lumber and eventually homes, like ours. Transformation was all around us back then.

All the sounds of that place come back to me and calm me from time to time, even though some of them might have been startling once upon a time. Like the night we all were sitting out by a wood-pile, the moon shining brightly over the fields on one side, into the woods on the other. Dead quiet when all of a sudden we were rushed by the screech of an owl somewhere beyond the light. We broke and ran. My path took me straight into a barbed-wire fence. This was the country—no doubt about it. Even though I was bleeding and crying, my face cut (a permanent scar), thumb almost severed, there was no professional medical attention to speak of, just home remedies like coal oil and meat fat to draw out the impurities. Obviously, I lived to tell about it. So did my sister, Pat, after I once spilled boiling water on her arm, water from the kitchen stove that I was trying to carry to the Number 7 washtub—scarred her for life, despite our family's healing powers. In a way, though, that is the real story in all this. We did what we had to do to survive. We used what we could find to do what we had to do. We made do with our ingenuity. Hot water on the stove. Medicine out of the earth. Food from the field to the table. It was a life that made us strong—physically, mentally, emotionally. The misfortunes of life itself made us tougher, able to withstand the pain that life can bring. They made us aware of the great inner strength we had that made endurance possible. We came to believe in our ability to overcome. We constantly were reminded of our ability to control our lives, within the small space we were allowed by the folks who controlled all the spaces surrounding us and every other aspect of our lives. That's why moving beyond physical pain was just the beginning of something driving us. Moving beyond our physical boundaries soon would become a goal.

None of this would have been possible without a strong belief system, our spirituality. Church was at the core of our family. Cotton might have been the focus of our earthly life, but faith in God was the core of our spiritual life. Our deep faith, the belief in something larger than the entire Delta, dominated every aspect of our lives. The second school I attended in Mississippi was at the East Money Church of God in Christ—the church where Papa once preached, where Papa later would prepare to bury Bobo, after Sheriff H. C. Strider gave the order and before Mamie vetoed that order with her own demand that the body be returned to Chicago. The East Money Church of God in Christ was the church where Papa would park his car at night during the murder trial to sleep near the small cemetery, where he might have slept eternally if he had dared to go back to his house after accusing two White men of kidnapping his nephew. It was said that a mob of White men came to that house on Dark Fear Road looking for him. In that church, we prayed for everything—crops, animals, even our enemies (well, those were a different kind of prayer). You name it, we prayed for it—"No hate, just appreciate," we'd say. But with everything going on all around us in the Delta, we also prayed for deliverance. Sometimes, it seemed we prayed for that most of all.

It made sense that the one-room, cinder-block church would double as a schoolhouse for all ages. In so many ways, after all, this was a learning space, where we would master the most important lessons we would need to succeed in life. The four r's: reading, 'riting, 'rithmetic, and religion. Most of all, I learned discipline—no choice about that. One thing I remember most was the threat that loomed over that place during school hours: switches to keep us in line stood at attention in the corner of the room, a constant warning. The threat of punishment was punishment enough for us in that small space and, it seemed, in the larger world outside. I was spared the switches, but I would always be mindful of the threats that existed all around me in the Delta.

Among those threats is what could happen to you if you didn't stay busy during harvesttime, keep your head down, keep moving. Black folks caught relaxing in the Delta could wind up getting arrested and charged with vagrancy or some other minor, trumped-up offense. That meant going to prison, most likely Parchman Farm. This prison was established in 1901 as a way of keeping many of the formerly enslaved people in bondage.[1] It was part of what Pulitzer Prize–winning writer Douglas A. Blackmon called "slavery by another name."[2] Black people picked up on phony charges were forced to work Parchman Farm, tending crops or sewing cotton garments. Parchman's chain gangs and work gangs paved roads that farmers used to get their crops to market more easily. Parchman made money for the state but not for the inmates,[3] who were treated severely and beaten on a regular basis.[4] Although this threat made us much more wary of contact with White folks, we really didn't need it to motivate us to work. We had a deep devotion to hard work as part of our Christian upbringing.

Good thing we did. There was plenty of backbreaking and hand-cutting work to do in the cotton fields. Actually, I was pretty good at it and could meet my quota and then some. After picking the cotton on our plantation, we would be hired out by the day to pick at other plantations, riding together on wooden benches in the back of a big truck, stopping at different plantations to pick up more workers. There was one good thing about this extra hard work: We actually got paid. Money, on the spot, same day, no wait. That was a big deal because sharecroppers would have to work our plantations all year before settling up at the end of picking season in the late fall. And settling up was, well, unsettling, to say the least. The owner always tallied up what you were owed for the cotton you picked, and then deducted money for everything you had gotten from the plantation store: the seeds he had given you to plant for yourself; the food you had gotten from the store on credit. Somehow, after all this adding and subtracting, many sharecroppers were told at the end of the harvest, "You broke even." Some tell of never receiving any money, only credit. There was a joke that went around the Delta, about a sharecropper who tried to game the system by holding back a few bales of cotton until the landowner finished the tally. After breaking even once again, the sharecropper presented all that extra cotton he thought would put him over the top. That's when the landowner said, "Now I got to add it up all over again . . . to make it come out even."

The joke was on us. White folks kept the records—and the profits. There was no such thing as disputing the tally, not if you wanted to live. One of my uncles, Elbert Parker, made the mistake of questioning the boss man at the end of his tally. The man told my uncle that his daughter had worked out the tally. If my uncle didn't want to have his tongue cut out, he better not challenge again. Black folks had been lynched just for complaining about the tally, and not just to punish them for speaking up. It was to warn all the rest of us not to do the same thing. That is what a lynching is all about: punish the immediate victim and, just as important, send a message to everybody else. Stay in your place, a place where the value of your life was so limited that White folks could take it from you—*murder you*—and get away with it.

Our value in those days was measured by the pound. In that sense, I guess I had great value since I could pick a hundred pounds of cotton when I was only six years old. People would brag on me, saying I would make a good husband. That's why I found myself wanting to be a man even at six. Sometimes incentives were given to those who picked the most cotton. I wanted to be that person. On the other hand, for those children who were lazy, or simply did not work hard enough, whippings were the incentive to do better. No foolishness was tolerated.

Even putting food on the table was a chore. It took work. Canning season came first and it was the hardest for me. I would have to help peel peaches, a job I did not like. Cooking and sealing jars felt like too much work, even if those canned goods were delicious later on. I also didn't like churning the milk for the butter that would rise to the top. Then there was the meat, the main course for our mealtime at the church schoolroom: sausage, biscuits, and molasses in a small pail. But the sausages in those biscuits we ate during our dinner (lunch, really) didn't come from a store. They came from our smokehouse. I remember the noisy squeal of the pigs at hog-killing time in the fall. I watched it all in amazement, the sacrifice of one life to sustain others'. I helped make the sausage, grinding the meat, putting in the spices, packing it in the casings, and hanging it in the smokehouse. All this extra work in the fall is what it took to make sure we would have plenty to eat during the colder winter months: hams, hocks, salt pork, chitterlings. Despite the hard work, the thing I took away from all this was just how self-reliant and industrious we were. And then there was our creativity. Sometimes I realize just how much we survived by our wits.

As it turned out, we wound up living in Money at Papa's and then at our new house only a little under a year, until January 1947. Everything was changing in the 1940s—a push and pull. We were pushed out by the brutal oppression from White people who were determined to keep us down, keep us from ever doing better than just breaking even. And we were pushed out by the development of new machinery that put many field hands out of work.

And thanks to the war in the 1940s, we were pulled by a demand for labor in the factories of the North, drawn away from the farms and plantations of the South. Many African Americans moved up north for work. Some went west to California. Black newspapers like *The Chicago Defender* had been publishing stories about the "Promised Land" in places like Chicago—stories about Black people doing important things, successful things, living happy lives as lawyers and doctors and teachers and entertainers. The "Double V" campaign of papers like the *Pittsburgh Courier* called for victory in the war effort overseas, followed by victory against racial discrimination back home. I can remember when World War II was over, there was the spirit of celebration all around. In the end, this country had defeated authoritarianism abroad. So why were we still accepting it in the South? The answer was that we wouldn't accept it any longer. You could feel it in the air down there. The beginning of the fight for social change on the battlefields of our own country.

It was clear in the way my uncles James and Cornelius Wright looked and acted and talked after they were honorably discharged from the military in 1945. A kid could notice this sort of thing— a whole new attitude. Like so many other Black enlisted people, they saw the larger world outside the limited world of places like the Mississippi Delta and felt a new drive for basic rights and liberties. My uncles set this new vision in motion. They relocated to Illinois where their oldest sister, Willie Mae Jones, already was living.

They were two of the approximately five million people who moved to the North as part of the Great Migration. Picking up and leaving the South was a significant act of defiance for Black people. It was saying, "We no longer accept the limitations you imposed on us, the limited opportunities you have afforded us." And we purposefully sought out opportunities for a better life, opportunities to occupy a better place.

Even with new machines, though, White landowners in the South still needed cheap labor and wanted to keep Black folks in their place, physically and socially. Black folks were arrested at train stations, charged with vagrancy, and thrown in jails and prisons, places like Parchman. As a result, many families moved during the night, packing up cars and trucks to slip away. They were determined, and in that determination, there was something else, something that would become stronger in the coming years. A belief in the endless possibilities of life in the "Promised Land."

In making a quick getaway, some families headed north with very little money and were forced to squeeze into homes and apartments with family members who had migrated earlier. This gave them a jump start on finding a job and sufficient lodging. My aunt Willie Mae was one of those early pioneers, and her door was always open to help new arrivals. She was a beautiful person. So was Mamie's mother, Alma Spearman. She was the sister of Elizabeth Wright, the wife of my grandfather Moses. But Alma wound up with that name herself, my grandfather's name. She was like "Grandma Moses" to so many folks from the Delta. Harriet Tubman to those who were convinced by her to come up to Illinois, to Argo/Summit, and start a new life with jobs that she would help them find right there in the community, just outside Chicago. My family got that message and quietly started putting our plan in place.

It is amazing what an active young imagination can conjure. Seven going on eight years old by this time, I was both active and imaginative. For my part, the dreams came in pictures. Vivid images. "Up north." When I first heard that term, I took it literally. I saw my family climbing a ladder, carrying all our personal things—going *up*. And in a community of devout Christians, going up a ladder had special biblical meaning. When I think about it now, there is no way we could have carried everything up that ladder. Without truly understanding all that was involved in real life, I saw in my childlike way what so many Black people would discover during those Great Migration years—sometimes our dreams of a better life did not match the reality of the life we found waiting for us in a strange new place.

My father left first and was waiting for us in January 1947 when we arrived in Argo, home of the Argo Starch Company (also known as the Corn Products Refining Company), makers of Argo Corn Starch, Mazola Oil, and Karo Syrup, among other products. It was a factory town. To my young mind it was sort of the urban version of the plantation we left behind. The Argo Starch Company owned the surrounding land, which was called the Argo Sub-Division. And many of our neighbors were the family members and friends we had known back in Mississippi. The Argo Starch Company managers seemed to like our folks, employing many from the South because of the work ethic we had rolled into the very fabric of our being. For all those Black transplants from the South, this was a great job. The workers arrived at the plant from the nearby community on the streetcar. Not many people owned automobiles. Over forty thousand people worked in the Clearing Industrial District, where companies such as Continental Can, Johnson & Johnson, 3M, Nalco, Cracker Jack, Viskase, the Belt Railway, and Inland Steel were hiring Black folks, providing good salaries and benefits. No more just breaking even, and never quite getting ahead, and remaining stuck in the post-slavery Jim Crow society of the South. My father, and my mother's older brothers James and Cornelius, were employed at Corn Products Refining until they retired. We now have third-generation Parkers who work for the company.

Even though we felt we were freed from the bondage of the southern plantation system, there still were reminders of the control White folks can maintain over Black life. At the time when we arrived, companies like Corn Products could own banks. The company bank was named Argo State Bank, where workers kept their savings and where it always seemed like company officials could keep an eye on how well we were doing. Even the schools built for us served as reminders of who was in charge. There was the Argo Elementary School and the Argo High School. The US Post Office branch was the Argo Post Office, where the mail was flown in by helicopter. Many businesses were named after the Argo Plant, even our church, the Argo Temple Church of God in Christ. The subdivision bordering Argo, where the Corn Products executives lived, was named Bedford Park, after Mr. E. T. Bedford, the president of the company.

We moved into a house that had been left vacant by Crosby Smith Sr., Aunt Alma's brother, who decided—for reasons no one ever really understood—to move back to the Delta. That house was a great new living space, modern by our standards, with a big school building right across the street. We were in a wonderful new community, warmed with familiar faces. It was called Little Mississippi by all of us who had escaped the South. And to add emphasis to the point, we even held on to a lot of our Mississippi. We would continue to plant crops in a nearby field, tend to them and harvest them. It was embarrassing to me to continue doing what I saw as "country" in what I was beginning to see as "big city." At least we were eating with knives and forks by this time, something we never did back in the Delta. In fact, I am not sure I even knew what silverware was back then.

The most significant thing about that house we moved into—at least for me—was where it was located: right next door to Aunt Alma, her daughter, her daughter's husband, and her grandson, Emmett Till. They had called him Bobo or Bo from the time he was born. By the time I met him, he was five and I was seven—basically only two years apart but practically dog years at that point in a boy's life. Somehow, though, we connected, partly because of his mother, I think.

Mamie saw me as a big brother for Bobo; he was an only child and since she had been an only child, she knew what it was like to be alone. With my family living next door now, he had an instant crew of playmates and he made the most of it. He started out competing with my brother Milton to see who got to push my new baby sister, Alma, in her stroller.

One of the first things I noticed about Bobo is that he had everything. By comparison, I realized how little we had. But it didn't matter, because Bobo was very generous. He was spoiled, to be sure, but he shared his toys and especially his money.

At this point, Mamie was married to Lemorse Mallory, her second husband. Her first husband, Louis Till, had died during the war. That's about all I knew about Louis Till at the time. He had been abusive to Mamie and was given the chance to avoid jail time by going to war. Lemorse had served with Louis, since they both came from the same town, and he commanded respect from everybody. Even Aunt Alma, who was always aspiring to rise above her share-cropping roots, would address him by his title: "Sergeant Mallory." Aunt Alma was big on status, and Lemorse had that. He came from a prominent family, and it was clear that Mamie had married well. That is, until she found out that Lemorse was cheating on her, with the woman who lived right downstairs. So, as far as Mamie was concerned, he had to go.

Although Bobo was a very active kid, something happened to him during his sixth year, within a year after we met: He developed polio. At that time, before a vaccine was developed, polio was about the worst thing that could happen to a child. It was caused by a virus that spread from one person to another mostly by coughing or sneezing, and it destroyed nerves and took away muscle control. You could die from it. Thankfully, Bobo didn't die, but he didn't fully recover, either. He could rip and run again, but he developed a severe stutter—so bad that he often got so caught up on the words he wanted to utter that he would have to pump the words out of his mouth, mostly by punching the arm of the person next to him.

They say that when one of your senses is taken away, your other senses get even stronger. I have wondered over the years whether something like that happened to Bobo and his ability to speak. It had become limited because of the lack of control over his vocal cords. But he became one of the most active kids in the neighborhood. His very life had been at risk from a terrible disease and for all his years after that, he was the liveliest boy around. His was a life in constant motion. We played war games in the field, near where my family grew our vegetable crops. We hopped freight trains that ran at the edge of that field and down a slope. We would ride for about half a mile before jumping off to walk back home. We would play Superman jumping from his front porch onto mine, before we got caught. Later, in Chicago where he and his family moved, Bobo would climb the back porch stairs with his cat and drop it to watch it turn over and land on its feet. We went with the boys in the neighborhood to the beaches in Chicago. We fished nearby in the Des Plaines River, with his grandmother Alma. One time, I remember, he actually caught a pretty decent-sized fish, but dropped it on the riverbank as he struggled with it. He held it in the water to wash off the mud. Well, in the water is exactly where a fish wants to be and Bobo lost his grip as the fish wriggled its way back into the deep river. It was a funny moment. Our lives back then were filled with funny moments. In fact, Bobo would pay our friend Donnie Taylor to tell him jokes he could retell. He lived to laugh. And he loved the life we lived back then.

That's why we were inseparable—even after Mamie took him away, moved to Detroit. He begged to come back to our community in Argo, and he did. He lived with his grandmother until Mamie came back to town with a new husband, Pink Bradley. That's when they all moved to Chicago, but Bobo kept coming back to our stomping grounds in Argo. He would spend hours on the streetcar going to and fro—worth every second for the good times we had growing up together.

IN AUGUST 1955, Papa came to Chicago for a family funeral. It was a special moment for me to see him again, and I wanted to hold on to that moment. Somewhere along the way, we agreed that I would return to Mississippi with him for the couple of weeks before I would have to start school again. Like all migratory birds, eventually I had to return home. It wasn't long before Bobo found out. Of course, he wanted to go, too. No, he *had* to go. He insisted on going. From the time we had become close friends a little more than eight years earlier, except for the short time he was in Detroit, we had never been apart for two whole weeks. As far as he was concerned, that would be unthinkable.

At first, there was resistance from our families. All of the Mississippi transplants had felt the hostile energy in the air, especially my folks when we left Mississippi in 1947. The new sense of our ability to control our lives was met with a White rage now coming out of the South. The Supreme Court had decided the *Brown v. Board of Education* case in 1954, the year before, declaring that "separate but equal" was unconstitutional. It was a death sentence for Jim Crow, the end of a way of life. That following year, 1955, the year Papa came to Chicago, the year I planned to go back with him, the year Bobo pleaded with everyone to let him go, too, that year, the Supreme Court handed down its second ruling in *Brown*, ordering schools to be desegregated "with all deliberate speed." The pushback was intense and violent. That May, Reverend George Lee, a leader of the local NAACP and Dr. T.R.M. Howard's Regional Council of Negro Leadership in Belzoni, Mississippi, was shot in the face while driving on the road, causing his car to crash. The sheriff, Ike Shelton, ruled the death an accident and said the lead shotgun pellets removed from Reverend Lee's face were dental fillings. Just under a week before we were planning to travel to Money, Lamar Smith, a Black farmer and World War I veteran, was shot and killed on the courthouse lawn in Brookhaven, Mississippi, at ten in the morning in front of about thirty witnesses who never saw a thing. Both Reverend Lee and Smith were advocating Black voting rights and participation. Stepping out of their assigned place. Threatening a way of life. Both were killed in Delta towns near Money. Both served as warnings to other African

Americans to stay in *their* place. Don't even think about trying to carry out the Supreme Court rulings. Don't even think about freedom, justice, equality. It was that serious.

So, in a way, the possibility of that night of terror at my grandfather's home, the Wright home—that house on Darfield Road, or Dark Ferry Road, or Dark Fear Road—the possibility had always existed in our worst fears about what lay in wait for Bobo in the Mississippi Delta. A place of deceptively wide-open spaces that had real limitations for a particularly energetic boy. We had let our desires overtake our fears in giving in to Bobo. He was strong-willed. He knew what he wanted and didn't give up until he got what he wanted, did what he wanted to do. It was one of his greatest strengths. Ultimately, it would be his downfall.

Something happens to you when you come from a place called Slaughter. When you live close to nature, feel the flow of things, learn how to survive, you can sense danger well before you see it. I knew what to expect. It was in me. In my roots. Was it in Bobo? He really didn't know need. He didn't know struggle. He didn't know racism. My family had been survivors in a hostile land where everything was a challenge. We ate what we killed. Bobo ate what was provided to him—store-bought, packaged. In his world, the cotton was high. His living was easy. In our world, cotton meant hard work and barely breaking even.

This would not be the best time to return to Mississippi. In fact, it would be the worst time to go back with a cousin who never learned all that I had learned by living it. Mamie said she gave him the talk. The talk that Black parents in the North always gave little Black kids before sending them to the South for vacations with relatives. Over the years, I have wondered about that. Was it enough? I had nearly eight years to learn what I had learned. Could eight days possibly have been enough, as Mamie drilled Bobo on the things we had grown up knowing? Was there something else? Something maybe I could have shared with him, told him, warned him about? I was his cousin, his best friend, and in a way his big brother. What did he really know about what lay ahead? All he really knew was that I was going to Mississippi, so he was going to Mississippi. All he knew was that he wanted to be with me. That thought, that realization, has stalked me over the years.

I was his reason for going.

August is seared into my memory—the whole month. It burns there, white hot—white hate. And while I don't need reminders of the explosion of fear and anger and brutality in the lynching of Emmett Till, I am reminded by events of the present moment, events that show us over and over again just how destructive it all can be.

August 11 and 12, 2017. Charlottesville, Virginia. A rally to Unite the Right against pretty much everybody else, in a city named in honor of a Black queen of England. Fear, anger, and brutality spun out of control and so much damage was done and so many people were hurt and Heather Heyer was killed. And something else— White power, a reappearance of elected officials who incite when they should inspire. Like Mississippi Senator James Eastland, who once encouraged people to "fight to the death" against change. Donald Trump. "Very fine people, on both sides." In Charlottesville, there were White supremacists, racists on one side, people opposed to White supremacy and racism on the other. In saying what he said, the president of the United States gave his approval to people who wore the emblems of Nazis, the Ku Klux Klan, and other White nationalists we would come to know in the years that followed.

So what would happen when the case of Emmett Till worked its way up to him, as I was sure it would—from the special FBI agents to the Department of Justice attorneys to the segregationist attorney general and finally to the White House? It would have to go that far, wouldn't it? Just because Jeff Sessions would think that Donald Trump should know about such a high-profile case.

Would Trump look at Carolyn Bryant Donham and call her "very fine people"?

7

Broken Promises

Throughout my life, I have known death. I've come to know it well, to live with it. Early on—way too early—there was tragic death: Bobo's lynching, cruel, vicious, inhumane. I had lived such a short while—only sixteen years, just two years longer than Bobo— already having to face the horrible reality that I might be living on borrowed time back in 1955. It was overwhelming, as I joined the long lines of people who viewed Bobo's mutilated remains in that glass-topped casket as a dignitary might lie in state in Roberts Temple Church of God in Christ. From the funeral service on Saturday, September 3, until the Tuesday, September 6, burial, more than one hundred thousand people, according to reports at the time, attended what the Reverend Jesse Jackson years later would call the first big civil rights demonstration. Mamie had been determined to "let the world see" what had happened to Bobo. Her son. My cousin. And it seemed like the whole world had come to bear witness.

Even while I had to accept the fact that he was gone—even gazed through the glass upon the remains in that casket—I refused to recognize the friend I had loved and lost. It wasn't just because Emmett Till was disfigured beyond recognition. It was mostly because the possibility of such a horror was beyond my recognition, beyond my understanding, beyond my imagination of the worst things that could happen. To a kid. But those things *had* happened. And I would have to live with that reality forever—the reality that survivors could be victims, too.

On that night of terror, the night when I thought I was going to die and knew I had to get right with God, on that night I had made a solemn promise through prayer. I would get my life right if I was spared. And I was. But what about Bobo? Should I have included him in that prayer for deliverance? Now, at such a young age, not only would I deal with death as a real part of life—an immediate possibility, in fact—but I also would be troubled by something else: guilt. Of course, I didn't kill Emmett Till, but I didn't save him, either.

As a Christian minister, I preach about death, teach about it as a sacrifice for eternal life—a transition. A key part of my calling—one of the reasons I get called so often—is to deliver eulogies for people I have come to know and love, and to provide comfort for the living, the survivors. I know about the survivors, what they are going through. After all, I am one of them. I can minister to them with a special connection, a deep understanding of the meaning of each particular life, and the continuation of it, even after death. My eulogies often touch on the importance of celebrating memories—as much as celebrating our loved ones' passage into a blessed afterlife—about our duty to continue honoring them, being inspired by them, motivated by them to do good works. I had been inspired by the life of service of Mamie Till-Mobley. When I eulogized her on January 10, 2003—the first of two days of services—I challenged all those gathered to celebrate her homegoing.

"Mamie died with her boots on. How do you plan to die?"

In a way, I was asking myself that question as much as I was asking that massive crowd. It was not unlike when Mamie asked me back in 1985 to lace up my boots and get into the battle. "His truth is marching on." As the thirtieth anniversary of the lynching approached, she had asked me to participate with her in the first television documentary on Emmett Till, the one on Chicago's WMAQ. She also had asked Simmie. For good reasons, he and I had not been out there talking about Emmett Till before then. But there was something wrapped inside Mamie's request. It was sort of an embrace of us with her as the only survivors who could provide testimony. And Simmie and I had been out there talking about Emmett Till since then. Together. A lot. We had strengthened our special bond—the bond of the survivors—from the moments of August 1955 through the moments of 1985 and beyond, becoming more public storytellers and celebrants of our cousin's legacy. We were bonded by Bobo—the memory of him, the memory of what happened to him.

Even though I have known death throughout my life, even though I have been there to comfort so many people in their period of grieving, it isn't any easier for me to face losing someone I have known and loved, a fellow traveler on a journey to justice.

On September 4, 2017, Simeon Wright died. He was seventy-four.

We knew he was going to leave us someday. We had known it for a while. He had cancer. It was just a matter of time. But we didn't realize time would run out so quickly. It hadn't been quite six months since the meeting in Oxford with those federal officials and the ones from the State of Mississippi. Little did I know that within six months of that meeting, even with the promise of another gain, we would suffer yet another terrible loss. Simmie had succumbed just one week to the day following the sixty-second anniversary of Emmett's kidnapping, a night Simmie had recalled so many times in interviews and with me in public appearances, as well as in his book.

We just didn't accept that Simmie might not be there with us to see it through. As much as we might expect death, we still want to hold on to life, much longer than we ever can.

Now I would have to let go, even as I was called upon once again to deliver a eulogy. I had known Simmie pretty much all his life. I thought about that as I considered what words I would speak at his funeral service. And I thought about that dreadful night, the night in East Money, Mississippi, when Simmie and I lay awake after Emmett Till was taken from the Wright family home. The house on Dark Fear Road.

* * *

IN THE DARKNESS all alone that August 28 night, Papa waited on the porch for twenty minutes after the truck rolled out of the lane and onto the road. He waited to see if Bobo would be brought back after his kidnappers figured he wasn't "the one" or gave him a whooping if he was. Maybe that's all they would do. Maybe that's all he *hoped* they would do. My grandmother, Simmie's mother, had run to the house next door—the house I lived in before we moved to Chicago—to beg for help. The people in that house now were White. Surely, they could do something. But they didn't want to get involved. They were White. Somehow without knowing any of the details, they must have known how this story would end—the way it always ends when they come for you in the dead of night and carry you down Dark Fear Road. They were White. And because of that, they had the privilege of choice, the freedom of choice and the power that comes with it. They could choose to be involved in the atrocities, forcing Black folks back in their place and raising themselves up in the process. They could choose to stand up to all that. Or they could choose to just stand back and let it all happen, choosing to take comfort in the belief that they were not involved. But, you see, they *were* involved. Standing back, letting it happen, benefiting from the advantages that a system of racial atrocities had given them—they were not innocent bystanders. Refusing to act is itself an act.

After the neighbors denied her request to intervene, Grandma insisted that Papa take her from their home in Money, Leflore County, to the home of her brother Crosby Smith Sr. in Sumner, over in Tallahatchie County, roughly thirty miles away. She didn't want to be around if those men came back. Like her White neighbors, she knew how this story could end . . . for the witnesses. I didn't want to be there, either. So, I got dressed and got ready to run out the back door if I needed to escape across the field and into the woods. Hadn't really thought much past that, but it seemed like a good start.

Besides Papa, Grandma, and Bobo, Simmie and I were the only ones who had woken during all the ruckus in the house. Simmie's brothers Maurice and Robert slept through it all—probably due to the 'shine we all had been drinking at 4/5 Plantation, the juke joint in Greenwood, earlier that night, what seemed at this point like a lifetime ago. Our cousin from Chicago, Curtis Jones, had arrived at the house while we were out having fun, hanging out in the big city, and he was asleep when we got back around midnight. Slept through the whole thing. When he finally woke up and found out from Simmie and me what had happened, he ran to the Fredericks', the White landowners, and somehow got them to let him make a long-distance phone call. Curtis called his mother, my aunt Willie Mae, in Chicago. She called Mamie and told her what no mother ever wants to tell another mother—what no mother wants to hear from anybody.

Meanwhile, Papa reached out to John Crawford, whose family also lived on the Frederick Plantation. Papa got John to drive him uptown to the Bryant store. Roy Bryant had given up his name, identified himself, when he was pounding on the door. So Papa knew who took Bobo—at least one of the men—figured he would go there, to the Bryant store, find Bryant, bring Bobo back home. That's what he figured, hanging all his hope on that figuring, that this story would not wind up the way stories like this always had wound up in the past. It was just after daybreak when they got uptown to Bryant's Grocery and Meat Market, and Papa knocked on the back door of the store. There was no answer—just an eerie kind of presence, like somebody might be there. It was that hope—that somebody might be there—that had led Papa to this place, the only place he could figure they might come, knowing that the alternative places were as unthinkable as they were undiscoverable. It was that hope that held him there for just one more heartbeat of a moment, one more knock on the door, one last chance to find Bobo, take him home.

"They're not here," he finally said to John Crawford as they turned to leave. Without Bobo. And with quickly dwindling hope that he ever would be brought back alive.

Papa and John spent a little time checking in vain under bridges and along rivers, those unthinkable alternative places, the typical places where Black bodies might be left.

Meanwhile, over in Greenwood, Crosby Smith reported the kidnapping to Leflore County Sheriff George Smith, based on what he'd been told by his sister, my grandmother Elizabeth Wright.

While all this was going on, I was able to get out, too. After my aunt Willie Mae broke the news to Mamie, she called her sister—my mother, Hallie—and my father, Wheeler Parker Sr. My parents contacted my father's brother, my uncle Elbert Parker, the one who had challenged the boss man on his tally, the one the boss man had threatened to cut out his tongue for speaking up. Uncle Elbert lived on the Carter Plantation right next to the Frederick place. It was still early that Sunday morning when Uncle Elbert walked over to the Wright home to ride along as Maurice drove us to my uncle William Parker's place in Duck Hill. Uncle William would then put me on the next train at the Winona station five miles from his house. Simmie had stayed behind with his other brother Robert, waiting for Papa to get back, take them to a safe place.

By the time I had escaped from Mississippi that Monday night, August 29, Leflore County Sheriff Smith already had arrested Roy Bryant, who admitted he had taken Bobo from the Wright home.[1] J. W. Milam was arrested later after he voluntarily visited the county jail in Greenwood where Bryant was being held.[2] Even though both Bryant and Milam admitted they had taken Bobo out of the Wright home, and they had brought him up to the store in Money, the outcome was different in each story, according to the trial testimonies Sheriff Smith and Deputy Sheriff John Ed Cothran would give about three weeks later.

Bryant said Bobo "wasn't the right one so then he turned him loose."[3] According to Cothran's testimony, Milam said "they had got the boy and then turned him loose at the store afterwards; at Mr. Bryant's store," never mentioning anything about identifying Bobo. "He just said that they brought him up there and talked to him, and then they turned him loose."[4] Only Roy Bryant even mentioned his wife, claiming she did not identify Bobo. In the story they told and what they left out of what they told, Carolyn Bryant wasn't implicated in the kidnapping and murder.

SOON AFTER I got back to Chicago, Grandma arrived, too. Papa, Simmie, and the boys would stay down in East Money. In the Delta there still was a lot of work to be done—it was still cotton-picking season. In Chicago there was a lot of organizing to be done—activists, labor leaders, politicians—to put political pressure on Mississippi. In Argo there was a lot of praying to be done. Pressure or blessing, in both cases folks definitely—desperately—were appealing to higher authority. At a prayer vigil at the Argo Temple Church of God in Christ the day they got the news of the kidnapping, someone had a premonition—a premonition that Bobo would be found, but not alive, that Wednesday, August 31. After all the prayers and pleas and pleadings, that's just how it turned out.

Now the kidnapping arrest against Milam and Bryant in Leflore County, where Bobo had been taken from the house, would be raised to a murder indictment in Tallahatchie County, where his body was found. Somehow, even what looked like justice was not enough to make up for the damage—the emotional devastation—all around us at the time. At Mamie's home, where everybody collapsed in despair, and throughout Argo, where an entire community mourned the loss of its native son. Eventually, the horror of it all would ripple out across the entire country.

Simmie would have to stay down there with Papa, since they both would be called as witnesses in the trial. Papa had to be there since he had seen the men and talked to them. Simmie had to be there, not only because he and Bobo had been asleep in the same bed that night, but because he also knew the ring that had been pulled off Bobo's body at the river. Papa hadn't been sure when it was handed to him at the river, as he stood over the boat with Bobo's mutilated remains lying there. Bobo had been beaten beyond recognition even by his great-uncle. But Bobo had let Simmie wear his ring for a while. If this was that ring, well, Papa took it back to show Simmie, who recognized it right away. That's how they were able to make a positive identification of the remains of Emmett Till. And now Simmie would be called to establish Bobo's identity in court.

For most of the time during the trial, Simmie was held in the witness room, no locks, no guards, no protection—no immediate help if somebody rushed in to grab him. This was not a safe place to be, not if you were a Black person accusing a White person of a crime. Black folks were even afraid of getting killed right there in the courtroom. In fact, the Black reporters had devised an escape plan, since their Jim Crow–segregated press table was surrounded by the angry White spectators. The journalists had decided that a nearby window was going to be the way out. Two stories up from ground level.[5] But Simmie was even more vulnerable in that lonely witness holding room where nobody could bear witness to any crimes committed against a witness—him.[6] Even if they could, it was not likely that they would.

Overnight during the trial, Papa would pack up the boys to stay with friends while he camped out near the cemetery at the East Money Church of God in Christ. It must have been a frightening time for all of them. Papa. The boys. This was the place where they came close to laying Bobo to rest under orders of Tallahatchie County Sheriff H. C. Strider, just before Leflore County Sheriff George Smith stopped them. On Mamie's orders, the sheriff reported.

"I want the body here. I'll bury Bo," she recalled, insisting that the body be returned to Chicago.[7]

As it turned out, even though Papa wound up being a crucial witness in the murder trial, Simmie was never called. Not that it would have made a difference. Seems like the only thing that made a difference was Carolyn Bryant's testimony.

After the not-guilty verdict, Papa had a family meeting with the boys and told them they had to leave Mississippi. For Simmie and the Wright family, this move was not nearly as easy as ours had been. Like millions of other Black folks, my family had thought it through when we made that move North in 1947 to seek more opportunities. My father found work right away. Not so for Papa. First, while our family had made the choice, the Wright family had no choice. It was made for them. And there was no time for them to plan the family move. Papa knew he had just a couple of days after the trial—if that long—to get away. He and the boys were not alone. Willie Reed quickly relocated to Chicago. He suffered a nervous breakdown shortly after he got there. Mamie also suffered a nervous breakdown the same day. Just like eighteen-year-old Willie, Papa knew there was no more life for him in Mississippi, only certain death. So he had to sell what he could, give away the rest. The family dog, Dallas, was left behind. The family car, too. Papa never even got paid for the bales of cotton he and the boys had picked.[8] But they made it out.

Several back-to-back events added even more to the injustice we experienced—injustice that would shape our lives forever.

Not long after his move to Argo, Papa was asked to return to Mississippi to testify at a grand jury proceeding for the kidnapping case against Milam and Bryant. It would take place in Leflore County, since that's where Bobo had been taken out of his bed and driven away into the pitch-black night.

According to Simmie, Leflore County Sheriff George Smith had told Papa that things would be different this time. Different county, different White folks, and, of course, different sheriff. These were reasons for Papa—for all of us, really—to hold out hope that the men who had terrorized our family, tortured Bobo, and finally killed him would have to pay at least for some of that. So, on a hope and a prayer, Papa went back to Mississippi in November 1955. Just a little over a month earlier, he had pointed a finger at two White men accusing them of a horrible crime, and in the process indicting a whole system of White supremacy—a system that let them get away with it. Papa had risked it all back then. What was left to risk now?

Whatever was being put on the line, it was worth it. This seemed like an open-and-shut case, since Milam and Bryant admitted to dragging Bobo off. Seemed that way, open and shut. But the way it seemed and the way it was were two entirely different ways.

In the short time between the not-guilty verdict in Tallahatchie County and the grand jury findings in Leflore County, a blockbuster story appeared in the *Jackson Daily News*.⁹ It was about Louis Till, Bobo's daddy, whose ring was used at the edge of the Tallahatchie River to identify Bobo as Louis's and Mamie's son. The story got picked up all over the country. According to the report, while he was stationed in Italy during World War II, Louis Till had been charged with raping two women and murdering another. He was court-martialed, found guilty, and hanged to death.

Back in Argo, we were all shocked when this news came out after the Milam-Bryant murder trial. Nothing had ever been said about any of this back in Argo. Nothing from Mamie. Not even from Lemorse Mallory—Sergeant Mallory—who had served with Louis Till in Italy. It didn't come up during the murder trial, even though Mamie was asked about Louis Till and the ring that had been sent to her after his death. Nobody asked how he died, and Mamie never said one way or the other. The only thing that had been revealed to Mamie was that he had died out of combat for "willful misconduct."¹⁰

Court-martial records tend to be classified as felonies. Whoever leaked that court-martial record must have had the power and access to do all that, and a strong reason for doing so. That reason became apparent when the Leflore County grand jury refused to indict Milam and Bryant for kidnapping, despite the fact that the brothers already had confessed to that crime.

It seemed clear that this was the second phase in the demonizing of Emmett Till. The first phase had been rolled out with Carolyn Bryant's testimony, the one that probably had made the most difference at trial, her claim that Bobo had assaulted her. Now it was continuing with the conclusion—against the weight of Scripture—that the son actually *shall* "suffer for the iniquities of the father." That was the point of declassifying and leaking the court-martial record. Mak-

ing sure the public—especially the Leflore County grand jury—
would see Emmett Till as a Black beast, a rapist who was determined
to attack a White woman, just as his father had done, just as all Black
men might do if given half a chance. But there would be one last act
in this tragic, dehumanizing three-act narrative that was developed at
the time. The White lie.

The January 24, 1956, edition of *Look* magazine carried an article
titled "The Shocking Story of Approved Killing in Mississippi," by
William Bradford Huie. The article was a national sensation because
it presented an exclusive interview with Bobo's killers—at least the
two who were accused, tried, and acquitted. They are referred to as
"killers" here in my story because the *Look* magazine article included
a confession, quoting J. W. Milam extensively recounting how he and
Roy Bryant had pistol-whipped Bobo, finally shot him at the edge of
the river, tied a seventy-five-pound gin fan around his neck, and
rolled his naked body into the water. Milam could speak freely at this
point, because he never again could be tried for murdering Emmett
Till. It's a constitutional thing—Fifth Amendment, double jeopardy.
The story was horrifying to read, not just because of the description
of what these murderers did to Bobo in taking his life, but because of
the distressing, offensive way they were distorting Bobo's memory,
basing it all, it seems, on their own warped view of Black boys and
men.

If there is any truth presented by Huie in the *Look* magazine article, it is that Bobo was in the store, he whistled at Carolyn Bryant, and
he was kidnapped and killed by White supremacists. That's about
the extent of it. But people got so caught up in the admission by
Milam—the confession—that he had murdered Emmett Till
(because who admits to something like that?), they didn't notice all
the flaws, misrepresentation, and dehumanization in the story. Or
maybe they were just conditioned to accept threatening images of
Black boys. The editors at *Look* and the public seemed quite willing
to accept the negative portrayal of Emmett Till that fit their stereo-
type of the young Black thug from Chicago, however untrue.

For years afterward, researchers cited the Huie story as the authoritative Emmett Till source mostly because of the confession. Timothy Tyson summarized the Huie account without fully critiquing it, including the lie that Bobo "boasted to his young cousins about having had sex with a white girl."[11] I am one of those cousins who was there—in the Delta at the store where Huie was not. At the store with Bobo and our cousins. I am one of those cousins who never heard him say any such thing. I am one of those cousins Huie never bothered to interview for his magazine story and Tyson never bothered to interview for his book.

Inadvertently, though, Huie might have revealed a truth Tyson does not appear to recognize. You have to read between the lines of the Huie story to see it. Bobo's mother did in her 2003 book. Mamie noted that the Huie account failed to acknowledge a key Black witness who saw and heard quite a bit. Willie Reed testified about hearing the "moans" and what he called the "licks"—sounds of the violent beating—bleeding through the walls of the shed on the Sturdivant Plantation as he walked by.[12] Huie wrote Reed's testimony out of the story, just presented the Milam account that Bobo never even cried out as he was getting beaten to death. Instead, Huie painted Bobo as a tough Chicago Black kid who stood up to the torture, the pain, the agonizing slow-motion death, defying his killers with his last breath.

Huie also ignored other important information revealed during the murder trial. One example of this is the testimony by Leflore County Sheriff George Smith and that of his deputy John Ed Cothran implicating Carolyn Bryant. These law enforcement officers testified that they were told by Milam and Bryant that they had taken Bobo back to Bryant's store to have Carolyn Bryant identify him, even though they claimed to have let Bobo go at the store without ever mentioning exactly what Carolyn said.[13] In his piece, Huie wrote that Bobo had admitted to being the kid they were looking for—at the house before they took him. "Had there been any doubt as to the identity of the 'Chicago boy who done the talkin',' Milam and Bryant would have stopped at the store for Carolyn to identify him. But there had been no denial. So they didn't stop at the store."[14] And, if they "didn't stop at the store," then Carolyn was not involved in what might have earned her at least a manslaughter charge. In the end, what was considered to be a revealing account seems more like a cover-up—collusion, maybe, between Huie and the defense lawyers who set up the interview with Milam and Bryant and sat in on it.

Apart from all the false statements, Huie's characterization of the killers—especially Milam—always seemed more positive than the depiction of the Black people in the story, whose words are often printed in Black dialect or crude representations of it. Milam is described as "an extrovert" whose boots "accentuate his height," a man who is "dark-visaged" with lips that "curl when he chuckles."[15] He is practically heroic in Huie's eye. "Big Milam soldiered in the Patton manner. With a ninth-grade education, he was commissioned in battle by the 75th Division. He was an expert platoon leader, expert street fighter, expert in night patrol, expert with the 'grease gun,' with every device for close-range killing. A German bullet tore clear through his chest; his body bears 'multiple shrapnel wounds.'"[16] In this same vein, Huie compares the pistol-whipping of Emmett Till by Milam and Bryant to the way "Milam got information out of German prisoners."[17] In other words, Emmett Till was treated the same way Milam treated enemies of this country—the kind of action that earned Milam a field promotion and medals. An American hero.

Bobo was presented as a threat because he didn't respect them and "wasn't afraid of them! He was tough as they were. He didn't think they had the guts to kill him."[18] The threat was all the more grave because this kid, described by Huie as "stocky, muscular, weighing about 160, five feet four or five," a fourteen-year-old kid who "looked like a man," represented danger to White women. Danger that Huie, a White Alabama writer, appeared to validate. "When her husband was away, Carolyn Bryant never slept in the store, never stayed there alone after dark. Moreover, in the Delta, no white woman or group of white women ever travels country roads after dark unattended by a man."[19] Notice that he didn't write that no *woman* traveled the Delta roads after dark. He wrote that "no *white* woman" did. The suggestion really wasn't all that subtle. Apparently, there was no concern about Black women traveling alone after dark. And, with everything else presented in this story, the threat to White women clearly was posed by Black men.

So, even while the Huie story revealed some of the brutality Bobo suffered—not all of it, not the worst parts of it, but some of it—the story also created the impression that this defiant Black boy from Chicago was asking for it. Like the murder trial itself, the Huie story indicted Milam and Bryant and then acquitted them. Bobo deserved what he got. He, the victim, should have known better. His behavior was indefensible. His death was inevitable. His killing justifiable.[20]

In the end, Milam and Bryant are centered in the Huie story. They are humanized. They are developed as people, while the "Negroes" in the story are marginalized. And "Negroes" is the reference used for the group of kids, flesh-and-blood individuals with lives and life stories—individual stories—that never are given the personal attention, the detailing Huie gives to the murderers.

For so long, we were disturbed by the Huie article, so much so that we were embarrassed even to talk about it. It was painful every time to read Milam's quotes presented by Huie (and interpreted here, by Tyson) that Emmett Till "virtually committed suicide."[21] Seriously? Huie put Emmett Till in such a bad light that we didn't even recognize him. It kind of seemed at the time that Huie must have talked to somebody, because he wrote his claims with such confidence. We just couldn't figure out at that time who would say such things about Bobo, about us. Who would tell Huie stories about Bobo showing off a photo of a White girl? Huie claimed that girl was Bobo's girlfriend. I never saw such a picture, I never knew Bobo to have a White girlfriend. And I would know. There was one girl in Argo he was sweet on right up to the Mississippi trip. Her name was Ducie and she was Black. As for the photograph, Mamie wrote that there was a photograph in Bobo's wallet when she bought it for him. It was a photo of an actress, Hedy Lamarr, she said.[22] But I can't say.

Huie also wrote about a dare, claiming that somebody caused Bobo to do something he might not have done on his own. Well, I never heard a dare. Neither did Simmie. There certainly were rumors like that going around in the weeks and months following the lynching and then after the trial. In fact, they circulated for years afterward—growing with each telling, with each television or newspaper report. The Chicago press published several stories with quotes that were supposed to be from me, which was so strange to me. Not strange because I saw my name in print, but strange because I never had talked to any of the reporters printing it. A lot of people were getting the story wrong. There was one case where my father was quoted and erroneously identified as me. We do have the same name. Except for the "senior" and the "junior" parts.

Even David Halberstam, the celebrated journalist who contacted me when his book, *The Fifties*, was being produced as a documentary, even he got it wrong. In his book, he wrote that Emmett Till was preparing to travel to Mississippi with his cousin Curtis Jones to stay with Curtis's great-uncle, and never mentioned that Bobo actually traveled with me and Papa, *my* grandfather.[23] And Halberstam actually covered the murder trial in Sumner. He would write that it was "the first great media event of the civil rights movement,"[24] but he didn't check the facts on the Curtis story. Neither did the producers of *Eyes on the Prize*, who featured Curtis in the PBS series segment dealing with the Emmett Till story. Curtis tells the story about the whistle, but also talks about a dare and the photo of the White girl as if he was there that fateful night the rest of us went to the Bryant store. But he wasn't there. As I said, Curtis didn't get down to Mississippi until Saturday—nearly a week after Bobo and I got there, several days after the whistle at the store. The one thing he might have been able to talk about as an eyewitness was Bobo's kidnapping—but he slept through it.

Huie also is featured in the PBS series, but no one from the documentary contacted Simmie or me to participate in the 1989 production, even though we had been out speaking in public about the case since 1985. Curtis later apologized to the family for misrepresenting the story. Can't really say whether Huie might have based his story about the dare and the photo on misinformation he got from Curtis Jones, or whether he fed it to Curtis. Can't say whether Huie is the person who recommended Curtis to the *Eyes on the Prize* producers. But it always was curious to me that the producers included the one person who was not there the night Bobo whistled, and failed to include those of us who were.

We had to live for years with a story we had no power to correct. Timothy Tyson wrote in his January 2017 note to *Chicago Tonight*'s Brandis Friedman that he really didn't need to talk to us. It was as if two White southerners had collaborated across so many years in perpetuating a narrative that denied justice to Bobo, to all the rest of us who survived, and to all the folks in Black communities across the country who constantly are reminded of what Emmett Till has come to represent: the denial of equal justice under law.

We just couldn't shake the falsehoods the Huie story set in place. For years. Simmie took it hard, too. "For us, it was like running salt in a raw, open wound," he would later write, referring to the injustices in his memoir, *Simeon's Story: An Eyewitness Account of the Kidnapping of Emmett Till*, co-authored with journalist Herb Boyd.[25] Like so many Black survivors of White supremacist terror in the South, we just accepted that this was what White folks down there referred to as "a way of life." It was the way of our world. Our understanding of this reality was part of an unspoken agreement we had forged—Simmie and I—an agreement simply never to talk about it again, try to move on, have a normal life. Whatever we might have thought that meant— a normal life—it sadly wasn't to be for us in those early days.

ARGO WAS NOT an easy transition for the Wright family back in 1955. As Simmie recalled in our later conversations and as he writes in his memoir, Papa had lived his life as a farmer and now "had to start all over again" in his mid-sixties, an age that made it impossible for him to get a factory job.[26] The NAACP sent him out on a speaking tour for a short time after the trial. They had sent Mamie, too. "But for all their hard work and success on the organization's behalf, Dad and Mamie received little compensation."[27] Papa wound up working as a custodian in a nightclub.

Simmie found people in the North less friendly than people had been in the South. And going to the store for eggs, meat, fish, and milk took some getting used to by a family that had always gotten everything they needed to survive right off the yard, and out of the smokehouse, and from the nearby waterways.[28]

Simmie and I would grow closer over the years. He and his family had moved into the house where we lived, which was right next door to the house where Bobo and Mamie and Sergeant Mallory had lived. At first, I was like a big brother to him, "babysitting" and always making sure he stayed in line while I was in charge. True to his hardworking farm experience, Simmie always was industrious. He definitely wanted to make some money, whether that was from delivering the *Chicago Sun-Times* or shining shoes in the streets around Argo with a shoeshine box he bought with that newspaper delivery money. Years later, after I became a barber, he would set up a shoeshine stand in my shop in Argo.[29] Later still, Simmie received a certification in pipe fitting, through a correspondence course offered by his job, and became the best in his trade.

For my part, after the trial, the kidnapping grand jury, the Huie article, I wound up returning to my old ways: hanging out, betting on dice. Despite it being against the law—and against my religion—gambling was all around us in Argo. Even the place where I worked for a while—the Terminal Liquors and Newsstand—had slot machines. In fact, one of my jobs was to move the machines into a back room just before the police would raid the place. I had time to do that because the owner always got tipped off ahead of the raids. He was White. White people had it going on like that back in the day.

The owners of the Black joints weren't so lucky. They weren't connected, so they didn't get tipped off. They got busted. Somebody had to go to jail—make it look good. You know, law and order. But it was clear to me back then as a teenager just how unbalanced everything was. The law seemed to only work for White people, even when they were breaking it. A confidential tip right before a police raid. A get-out-of-jail-free card. A get-away-with-murder verdict. A cover-up story in a national magazine. As far as I could tell, I was living in a lawless society. So why should I be the only one to obey the law?

It wasn't long before I got an answer to that last question.

You see, I had made that promise to God on that horrible night in the Mississippi Delta—that night I thought I was going to die. I had promised to change my ways, and I had broken that promise. Didn't change my ways at all. Well, you don't break promises to God. You can't get away with that. My first revelation came when my father caught me gambling. He gave me a surprising good talk. You would think I wouldn't need another sign. But I was damaged, badly in need of repair. Badly in need of more revelations.

Back on the street, I got one when I started gambling again and this time got busted by the police chief. I was not going for a third strike. God was talking to me and I got that message—finally. I kept my promise and started down a different path—a path that eventually would bring me back to the doorstep of the church, back to the congregation, and eventually up to the pulpit.

Later, after Simmie and his wife, Annie, moved to suburban Countryside, a south Chicago suburb, he would continue to travel about four miles every Sunday to pray with us in the Argo Temple Church of God in Christ, the church built by Emmett Till's grandmother. Simmie served as a deacon and trustee there, saving us quite a bit of money with his management skills. And following his lead, I would spend more and more time there—time that later would prove to have been well spent.

In addition to the family connection, in addition to a love for the Lord, there was something else that always bonded us: the memory, the injustice, the compelling need to get the truth out. A big part of the truth was revealed during the 2004 FBI investigation and its immediate aftermath. Among the many other discoveries made by Special Agent Dale Killinger was a collection of confidential documents in the archives of William Bradford Huie held by The Ohio State University. Those documents revealed the story behind the *Look* magazine story—one more shocking than the article itself. These documents—letters and publishing agreements—showed how Huie had negotiated a deal to tell the story of the lynching of Emmett Till and ultimately worked with a couple of the attorneys of Milam and Bryant, the murderers, to tell it their way.

Huie first tried to sell his story idea to Roy Wilkins, the president of the NAACP. He proposed a book that would expose White southern racism. In a letter to Wilkins sent just after the murder trial, Huie boasted that he had exclusive access to the killers and their lawyers. He even quoted defense attorney J. J. Breland saying Milam had "a chip on his shoulder," that "he likes to kill folks." Breland's writing made it clear, the murder of Emmett Till wasn't just about two White racists, or even a group of racists in a lynch mob. It was about the enforcement of racism itself, protecting White supremacy. "But hell, we've got to have our Milams to fight our wars and keep the niggahs in line."[30] Huie promised Wilkins that he would be able to "dramatize the abduction, torture, and murder of that boy in a way that will be more explosive than Uncle Tom's Cabin—and a lot more honest."[31]

When Wilkins didn't respond to the book idea, Huie pitched the story as a magazine article to *Look* magazine. The editors went for it based on what Huie promised to deliver: a revelation that there were four men involved in the lynching of Emmett Till, not just two. And to make sure he had access to the killers, Huie promised Bryant and Milam's attorneys that he would deliver a story that would be "a bitter dose to the NAACP." The NAACP headed by Roy Wilkins, to whom he had promised the exact opposite, an exposé on White racism.

In a letter to defense attorney John Whitten, Huie also promised to write about the court-martial and execution of Louis Till.[32] Despite Huie's earlier promise to Roy Wilkins that his story would be "a lot more honest" than *Uncle Tom's Cabin*, Loyola University Chicago professor Elliott Gorn has written that Huie "conspired with the attorneys on the story he wrote," and they all got money out of the deal.[33]

According to his archived documents evaluated by Professor Gorn, Huie was paid $7,500 from *Look* for the first publication and another $5,000 for second rights. He also was paid $25,000 by United Artists for a screenplay that never was made into a movie. He paid Milam and Bryant a total of $3,000 and their lawyers, Breland and Whitten, a total of $1,260.[34] The money reportedly paid to Milam and Bryant in 1955 amounts to a little more than $29,000 in today's dollars.

Once we learned about the collusion between Huie and the lawyers, everything fit into place. It had been puzzling to match some things in the story with the reality we knew. But after reading the words Huie put into the mouth of J. W. Milam and the words of White supremacist lawyer J. J. Breland, it all became very clear. A long speech by Milam in the *Look* article didn't really sound like words he would speak or thoughts he would put together.

"Well, what else could we do? He was hopeless," Huie quoted Milam as saying in the article. "I'm no bully; I never hurt a nigger in my life. I like niggers—in their place—I know how to work 'em. But I just decided it was time a few people got put on notice. As long as I live and I can do anything about it, niggers are gonna stay in their place. Niggers ain't gonna vote where I live. If they did, they'd control the government. They ain't gonna go to school with my kids. And when a nigger even gets close to mentioning sex with a white woman, he's tired o' livin'. I'm likely to kill him. Me and my folks fought for this country, and we've got some rights. I stood there in that shed and listened to that nigger throw that poison at me, and I just made up my mind. 'Chicago boy,' I said, 'I'm tired of 'em sending your kind down here to stir up trouble. Goddam you, I'm going to make an example of you—just so everybody can know how me and my folks stand.'"[35] When compared with a Breland letter, it appears more likely that these words are his, not Milam's. A member of the White supremacist Citizens' Council, Breland wrote:

"The whites own all the property in Tallahatchie County. We don't need the niggers no more. There ain't gonna be no integration. There ain't gonna be no nigger votin'. And the sooner everybody in this country realizes it the better. If any more pressure is put on us, the Tallahatchie River won't hold all the niggers that'll be thrown into it."[36]

The story of Emmett Till is about racism, and it's about racist atrocity. No doubt about it. But what all this shows is that it mostly is about power—White power in America and the desperate need to hold on to it, by lynching anybody who stepped out of their place.

William Bradford Huie had shifted gears from the story he proposed to Roy Wilkins, but he ended up exposing the racist abuse of power anyway. He did it, though, by tipping the scales toward the racists and the power elite. In other words, it was not balanced. This is not intended to suggest that the Huie story is bad journalism. It is meant to say out loud that it is not journalism at all. Journalism is about presenting facts in a fair, accurate, and balanced way. In a word, it is about truth. In large measure, the Huie piece in *Look* was a work of fiction.

MAMIE TILL-MOBLEY ALWAYS wanted the truth to be told about the death of her son—what it meant, what it still means. She had passed the baton to Uncle Simmie and me. He and I had not spoken about Bobo for thirty years after he was killed and before she asked us to step up and agree to be interviewed for the WMAQ documentary in 1985. For another thirty years after that, it was always Simmie who had been out front. Even though I would step up for interviews, I always deferred to him, just as he and I had always deferred to Mamie before that. Now I would be the only one left to carry on.

"There's a way people *want* to see you," I said in eulogizing Simmie. "There's a way you want to *be* seen. And there's the way you *are* seen." I spoke about the person I knew, the person I had known just about all his life. The person who had dedicated the last half of his life to seeking justice for Emmett Till. The person I had joined on that journey. He was one of a kind, a role model. And I realized as I spoke about him just how greatly I missed my uncle. I miss him still.

In our fight for justice for Emmett Till, Simeon Wright was a true champion. That is the way he was seen. It was the way he wanted to be seen. Not because of any ego gratification, but because it would serve as an inspiration to others to step up. And the memory of his determination and his advocacy would become a big part of my charge to keep moving forward. While I always felt like I was a step behind Mamie and Simmie—conscientiously deferring to them— now they both were gone and I was the last man standing, the last person who could take a stand. On that night of terror back in Money in 1955, I had made my promise to God that if I got through that night, I would turn my life around. Then I turned around on that promise and went back to my old ways, got busted, and then turned around again. Got right with God, got right with myself. Finally, I kept my promise.

Over the years, I have learned a lot about keeping promises. I learned a lot about the importance of keeping them by seeing the damage done when promises are broken. We saw it very clearly in the aftermath of Bobo's lynching. Elected officials make a promise to serve the public interest. They swear to it when they take the oath of office. Journalists make a promise to the public to tell the truth so people can make sure elected officials are keeping their promises. Elected officials like Mississippi Senator James O. Eastland broke that promise, the promise they made to the public. So did journalists like William Bradford Huie. There would be others I would learn about over time, others who broke their promises to serve the public good.

Following Simmie's transition, I would be charged more and more each day to set it all right. The folks we had met with in Oxford earlier that year—the lawyers, the investigators, the alphabet of justice, the AUSA, DOJ, FBI, DA—they had made a promise to us: to see it through, to do right by Bobo. We decided to rely on their promises, and to make sure they were kept.

8

Law and Order

I ONCE BAPTIZED IN the River Jordan, not far from Galilee, half a world away from Mississippi. The River Jordan—the water of reflection, the water of repentance. The water that once washed over Jesus Christ and still washes away our sins. The River Jordan—the place where John the Baptist started this process of cleansing and rebirth for the rest of us, those who would become the faithful, the followers. It all started right there at that place, in that water: baptism—the process of transformation through immersion in the Holy Spirit.

The River Jordan is the place where Jesus began His ministry. And it is the place where I renewed mine.

It was 1985: eight years after I heard the call . . . and answered it. In 1977, some thirty years after I made that solemn promise on the night (that terrifying night) when Bobo was taken from us—the night I knew I was going to die, the night I knew I had to get right with God—I had dedicated my life to Jesus Christ as a minister. By the time I waded into the River Jordan in 1985, I had become assistant pastor of the Argo Temple Church of God in Christ, that small church (only about a hundred members) in our small town just outside Chicago. Argo/Summit was where Bobo and I had become the best of friends—hung out together, laughed together, got into mischief together. I mean, boys, right? Argo/Summit is the town where I still live with my wife of more than fifty-five years, Marvel—*Doctor* Parker—a trustee of the township.

So, Argo Temple, my pastorate, might be a small church, but in that place, with all that personal history, it is overflowing with the spirit that established it and has sustained it for nearly a hundred years. You see, this little church began in the home of Emmett Till's grandmother (who was then Alma Carthan) in 1926. While offering sanctuary for all the Mississippi "immigrants" (like my family)—seeking asylum and refuge—she also offered us a place to renew our faith, a place to give thanks to God for delivering us . . . from evil.

The first building of that little church was funded partially by fish dinners hosted by Aunt Alma, a fisher of men if ever there was one. And, in performing her own miracle of multiplication, Aunt Alma and others contributed to the construction of that little church—I mean, the actual brick-by-brick building of it—with bricks she and the other faithful collected from the streets when they were dug up around town to make way for new surfaces transporting us into the twentieth century and beyond. She and her crew provided an after-life for those bricks—bricks from the street that would become a church, and ultimately a new path for our spiritual journey. Nothing wasted, everything gained.

My family joined that church as soon as we arrived from Mississippi in 1947, twenty-one years after it had been built. And between then and 1985, Lord knows how often the path I had been walking seemed more like a road to perdition than to the ministry. But what I hadn't yet realized before I answered the call was that it was my destiny—something that was present before I even was born, which is true of all of us. It is written, look it up: Jeremiah 1:5 says, "Before I formed thee in the belly I knew thee; and before thou camest out of the womb I sanctified thee, and ordained thee prophet unto the nation."[1]

So, despite my unknowing, my life's work was all preordained, long before *I* was even ordained. Predestined, and the destination has meant so much more to me because of the road I took in getting here, the twists, the turns, the things I saw and lessons I learned along the way. We may believe we have created our ideas, our visions, but we really are merely the recipients of them. My calling to the ministry was inside me all along, waiting for me to become aware, conscious, ready to accept. And the preparation is the whole reason for the journey.

In a way, a very important way, Emmett Till has become a central part of it all. My ministry. That certainly became clear to me back in September 1985 when I entered the water of the River Jordan, just two months after the July broadcast of the Rich Samuels documentary *The Murder and the Movement*, featuring the interviews with Mamie, Simmie, and me.

A group of about fifty of us from the Church of God in Christ—the denomination of our Argo Temple—made a stopover in Israel. It was a pilgrimage of sorts—on our way to a world Pentecostal conference in Switzerland. It was the thirtieth anniversary year of Bobo's lynching, and it seemed fitting for me to find myself in the Holy Land— the land of rivers: the Tigris, the Euphrates, the Nile, and, of course, the River Jordan. On that trip we saw Jerusalem, Bethlehem, Jericho, Tel Aviv, and, of course, Galilee. It was an overwhelmingly elevating experience to be there, to feel the place as much as to see it. This is the place where everything we believe in was revealed to us. I reflected on that in the spaces between the places and on my journey—half a lifetime up to that point—from the Mississippi Delta to the fertile delta. I considered the beginning of things, the connection of things. How was a Civil Rights Movement inspired by Emmett Till woven into this world of religions inspired by Abraham? How could those of us calling ourselves practitioners of Judaism, Christianity, and Islam be so consumed by Abrahamic sibling rivalry that we failed to recognize—let alone celebrate—our commonality, our connections? How might I talk about Emmett Till and help people understand the unity of spirit that is the bedrock of my faith?

As I say, preparation is the whole reason for the journey—our purpose. This thirtieth-anniversary year, 1985, was when I would begin to talk publicly about the death of Emmett Till and the meaning of it all, starting with that documentary for Channel 5, NBC in Chicago. It was the beginning of a heightened awareness that clarified for me that—much as with three of the world's leading religions—there are points of connection among people, connections we might never have imagined before they were revealed to us.

One seemed *so* unlikely—one between a White public historian from Utah who had been working for quite a while to document the story of Bobo's murder.

Before coming to the Emmett Till story quite by accident, Devery Anderson had written about the history of Mormons and his Church of Jesus Christ of Latter-day Saints. Over the years, he had developed a website on Emmett Till listing a timeline of events in the murder and its aftermath. That timeline kept growing as Devery added information he was researching, until it eventually became a book-length treatment of the story. Although Devery had never met Mamie, he seemed to be captivated by her story for quite a while before he finally made his first trip to Chicago in 2007, four years after her death and the publication of her book. That February, he came to Chicago and visited the Burr Oak Cemetery where Bobo is buried and Mamie is entombed. He also came to see Simmie and me in my office at the church. Knowing what we have known about the history of Mormons and Black people, their long-standing belief that we were inferior to White people and cursed by God, well, let me put it this way: *Apprehensive* doesn't have quite enough syllables to describe just how apprehensive we really were at first. But we also were impressed by Devery's interest in certain parts of our story—the parts he never could have gotten from any amount of cold research and dusty archival documents and website timelines. The parts that can establish connections between disconnected folks, like a Black preacher from Illinois by way of Mississippi and a White Mormon from Utah by way of Washington State. The parts that set out universal themes, the stuff we all can relate to, like love and tragic loss and pain that can last half a lifetime. Longer, even.

So we talked with him, answered his questions, told our story. I believed we had done a good thing. After all, it had become central to my ministry to do this thing: to tell the story of Emmett Till, making sure to correct the lies and set the record straight. Simmie and I hoped we had made a difference. We hoped we had made connections: between Bobo and racial violence and White supremacy and injustice and power; between our experience and a White audience in need of the understanding our experience could provide. That's what we hoped, and we relied on that hope because, well, we—Black folks—are nothing if not a hopeful people. Despite the fact that hope too often has been used against us, left us hanging, disappointed.

Devery's book was published in 2015, some eight years after the session Simmie and I had with him. It was published by the University Press of Mississippi, the academic publishing arm of the flagship university of the state that denied justice—denied even an apology—to Mamie Till-Mobley. For the rest of her life—up to the very last day of her life—Mamie desperately wanted that apology. She knew an apology would carry with it an admission of wrongdoing, and with that admission, some measure of justice. But Mamie never got justice, or an apology, or an admission from the State of Mississippi or from the White men running it. And I never received a copy of the Devery Anderson book published by the University Press of Mississippi. So I was left with only the hope that he had gotten it right.

By November 2017, still mourning Simmie, we were getting anxious—impatient, really—for the result of the investigation, which was the last major mission Simmie and I had undertaken together. The FBI investigation seemed to be lagging. We had left our meeting in Oxford eight months earlier believing things would move pretty quickly. But quickly is not how things move in cases like this one. All the moving documents, moving dialogue—back and forth between Mississippi and North Carolina, between the state and federal justice authorities—there were so many *t*'s to cross, and *i*'s to dot, and dots to connect, it was all taking more time. What would Timothy Tyson reveal? Would his research materials offer insights into the quote by Carolyn Bryant Donham that he wrote into his book? Would they lead to any new evidence in the kidnapping, lynching, and cover-up of the murder of Emmett Till? Would there be new issues to investigate, new suspects to interrogate? Would there be any charges against Carolyn? What more would be needed? Well, I guess, evidence, for one thing. Evidence would be needed—that's what we were told by the government authorities.

Special Agent Walter Henry updated us, confirming that he and the other authorities believed they had finally collected enough information to review the matter based on the subpoena that had been issued and the North Carolina court's release of certain Tyson documents to federal officials in Mississippi. They were bringing in retired Special Agent Dale Killinger to help with the review, since he had been the person leading the FBI investigation between 2004 and 2006. "He has the most historical knowledge of the case and presented it to the grand jury," Henry said. After everything was reviewed, they would decide whether they wanted to contact Carolyn again. "Another conversation could take place," Henry said. "Definitely after review, that might be considered. We won't take anything off the table right now."

Chris Benson raised the possibility that the authorities might arrange for Carolyn to sit down and talk with our family—face us, look us in the eye, tell her story. This could be a significant part of the resolution, a form of restorative justice. And Henry had said, they weren't taking "anything off the table," but making that happen would depend first on our family—on how we felt about it. I wasn't really sure; did I really want to sit across from her, look at her and listen to her speak? Then again, there was one question I did want to ask her: "Why did you lie on my cousin?" And I did want to hear her admit to me what I had read in Timothy Tyson's book—what we all had read, what we all *knew* even without reading, but still wanted to hear her say the words. I wanted to hear her admit she had lied to the lawyers, lied to the court, lied to the FBI and then tell me—tell our family, tell the world—why she did that. Why she lied. I wanted her to face up to just how much her lies had cost us and how little they gained her. In fact, I wanted her to face up to the fact that they had cost her much more than she gained. In the highest possible court. For what shall it profit a *woman*, if *she* shall gain the whole world, and lose *her* own soul (Mark 8:36)? So, you see, there would have been at least some measure of justice in the admission. But it wasn't just about getting a confession from her. It also was about clearing Bobo, finally, clearing him of the belief so many people had that he had done something wrong, that he deserved what he got. That belief had been encouraged by the lies she had told.

Even though getting her to talk to us depended in part on how we felt, it also would depend on what kind of leverage we might have in order to get her to talk about anything. The investigators would decide whether there would be anything to charge her with— a potential charge we could use to get her to reveal more, in exchange for immunity, a possibility that had been suggested back in the Oxford meeting. Simmie had been opposed to anything like that. He wanted a pound of flesh, and an eye for an eye. It was Simmie's Old Testament approach up against my New Testament approach— retribution versus forgiveness. While the decision would be mine—as the family lead in this investigation process—I still faced the internal conflict between my uncle's voice and my own.

I struggled to consider with Marvel what justice required. Would there be justice in a conviction, in prison time, or in just an indict- ment of Carolyn Bryant Donham even if she wasn't convicted? I had come to understand that a charge or an indictment did not mean that there *would* be a conviction. There still was a missing link, the one that would connect her to the kidnapping and murder—still missing evidence, perhaps a witness, perhaps something else. After all this time, she still could get off, just like her husband, like his half brother had. A missing link raises doubt, reasonable doubt. And reasonable doubt means acquittal. And acquittal means she would be exonerated—at least in the public mind—and that would be worse than never putting her on trial in the first place. So then what? At least immunity—protection from prosecution—might lead her to offer a full and complete confession—about everything that happened, and any people who had made it happen. Everything that Timothy Tyson had failed to explore in his book about why she told that lie, about how she lived with herself knowing that her words had set in motion the brutal murder of a child: That would have to be part of the offer. No talk, no deal.

The weight of this decision about opening to a conversation with her was firmly on my shoulders—a burden I carried for Bobo, for the rest of the family I represented, now as the elder for the larger Black community our family represented. Thankfully, I did not have to decide right at that point since nothing had been uncovered that could be used as leverage. No hard evidence, no proof, or at least not enough to convince a jury.

Agent Henry would keep us apprised of everything along the way—a requirement set out in the Emmett Till Unsolved Civil Rights Crime Act—and he probably would want us to come back to Oxford for a follow-up meeting, likely in about two months, after the first of the year. But he was not sure we could see any of the materials they collected. The North Carolina federal judge's subpoena only authorized release of the files to the US attorney in the Northern District of Mississippi and the FBI, not to us, not even to Mississippi District Attorney Dewayne Richardson. So, it seemed we might wind up getting a report on what they saw in the documents, how they interpreted what they saw, without the benefit of what we might see or interpret if given a chance.

As distressing as that may have been, we also understood that the authorities had to be careful to make sure nothing leaked, which would have violated the grand jury process. Simply put, the grand jury process is confidential. Even more, though, a leak leading to public disclosure could tip off any potential targets of the investigation. So authorities were keeping everything tight back in Oxford,

Mississippi. And we just had to sit tight back in Summit, Illinois. Sit tight, and wait—despite our growing impatience.

It was starting to get chilly in Chicago by early that November 2017. So Marvel and I were happy to have the chance to get out of town for a quick trip to Southern California. I was invited to partici-pate in an event with Devery Anderson to promote his book *Emmett Till: The Murder That Shocked the World and Propelled the Civil Rights Movement*. Shortly after its publication in August 2015, the book was picked up by a production company that had wound up with a deal to turn Devery's version of the Emmett Till story into a series for HBO. One of the producers, Rosanna Grace, invited Marvel and me to come to California and share my story about Bobo as part of a panel discussion. The event date moved a couple of times from August to November and finally to December, because of the busy schedule Marvel and I were keeping back then. But, it seems, the producers were willing to change the Devery book event schedule to make sure I could take part and talk about Emmett Till. And yes, talking about Emmett Till is what I do—part of my ministry. Still, it was kind of curious that they were holding up an event for Devery's book— delaying it—to make sure I could be there. I hadn't read the book, but I did understand that it was long—560 pages long. Seemed like that would be plenty for Devery to talk about all by himself. So, won-dering why they wanted me present was one of a few questions I had about the whole thing.

As we talked about upcoming schedules one day in Marvel's office, we considered in passing why a producer of a TV series was the person contacting me about taking part in a *book* event. This was not a movie event, not a cable TV event. Marvel and I talked with Chris Benson about it, and he said they might want to invite me to participate in the production of that HBO series. Two other video projects had been announced, one involving Keith Beauchamp and Whoopi Goldberg, and another involving Taraji Henson and John Singleton. Simmie had been cooperating with the Keith and Whoopi piece, but he wasn't here anymore. So maybe the Devery/HBO people wanted to include an authentic voice to validate what they were producing in comparison with the other projects. That could mean bringing me on as a consultant or even as a producer. Chris said that if that was the case, I would have an important decision to make, and I might have to make it quickly. "If you don't want to do it, you should tell them right then and there in California—don't string them along," he said. "If you do want to do it, you should not tell them—at least not right away. Just listen to what they have to say and tell them you need some time to consider it." Chris would help me think it through after we got back home. After all, he had been involved in many contract negotiations as a lawyer for Johnson Publishing Company—working out publishing rights for *Ebony* magazine. And he had worked with his agents at the William Morris Agency and later at the Endeavor Agency on a two-year HBO option for Mamie's book and for a screenplay adaptation of the book. Whatever we decided to do, we should not look eager, he advised. "Hold out for some say-so over the story that they are telling," he said. "Make sure they do more than just spell Emmett's name right. Make sure they get the story right."

Not looking eager was the easy part. After all, I was working on my own book, and that's all that really mattered to me. I never had much interest in a movie or television production. So, if it came up, I would be cool—definitely would not look eager. Got it.

A bigger question, though, was even more puzzling to us. Why was this event to promote Devery's book on Emmett Till being held at the Richard Nixon Presidential Library and Museum in Yorba Linda, California?

ONE OF THE things that has driven my journey to justice in the lynching of Emmett Till over the years has been the need to reveal the truth to the public. I have experienced so much frustration with all the people who want to spin the story—spin it so hard it leaves you dizzy and makes the truth unrecognizable. That happens a lot when our story—the African American story—becomes a political project of distortion. After all, politics is all about the spin.

As it turns out, the Devery Anderson book event at the Nixon Presidential Library involved some spin. The folks at the Nixon Library had been trying to promote Nixon as a big supporter of civil rights. Seriously. In fact, one year earlier in 2016, the Nixon Library had organized an event celebrating Nixon as a friend of civil rights because his presidential administration started affirmative action, supported Black-owned businesses with set-asides (the guaranteed percentage of government contracts), and enforced desegregation of public schools in the South. While that was historical record, it wasn't the way I *remembered* Nixon. It wasn't the way *anybody I knew* remembered Nixon.

The first thing that comes to my mind when Nixon's name is mentioned is his so-called Southern Strategy in the 1968 presidential campaign. The second thing is his push for "law and order" during that same time. Both initiatives played on the prejudices of White folks against Black folks. One of Nixon's White House officials even admitted it. An article in *Harper's Magazine* published in 2016 included quotes by Nixon domestic policy aide John Ehrlichman, saying Nixon's "war on drugs" was all about attacking Black people and antiwar activists. The Nixon White House saw both groups as "enemies" who needed to be put down.[2] This way of framing Black people as criminals would continue as a hallmark of Republican presidential campaigns all the way through Ronald Reagan in 1980 and up to Donald Trump in 2016, the same year the Nixon Library seemed to be trying to rewrite history.[3]

Even the school desegregation action that the Nixon Library folks wanted to brag about came because the Supreme Court ordered it.[4] It doesn't look like Nixon's heart was really in it, especially if it would potentially cost him White votes in the South.[5] The Nixon Library site has a two-minute video that shows Nixon basically complying with a 1969 ruling on the issue—in other words, following orders, not showing moral leadership.[6]

Marvel and I discussed all this with Chris at one of our meetings in her office as we tried to wrap our heads around how Nixon connected to Bobo, why this book event was being held at the Nixon Library, and why they wanted me there. Chris had done some research on the whole thing before the trip, pulling documents from the Dwight D. Eisenhower Presidential Library and Museum, since Nixon served as Eisenhower's vice president when Bobo was lynched. Maybe Nixon had gotten involved. Maybe he had spoken up. Memos in the Eisenhower archives written by J. Edgar Hoover, director of the FBI, showed *he* sure was watching the Emmett Till matter—and especially Mamie—very closely. But there was nothing about Nixon in that connection. Instead, Chris confirmed there were boxes upon boxes of revealing memos written by E. Frederic Morrow, an administrative officer for special projects in the Eisenhower administration. Many of his memos were later published in a rare book Chris was able to buy: *Black Man at the White House*. Chris also pulled materials from the Nixon Library, and articles written by university scholars But still, none of this helped us understand what Nixon had to do with Bobo. As it turned out, nothing really. Neither did Eisenhower, for that matter, although Bobo wound up being part of the inspiration for a new federal law in 1957 that ultimately would help set in motion the very case that we were cooperating with the FBI on in 2017— some sixty years later.

NOVEMBER 22, 1955. "Because of many years of investigating lynchings, mob violence, and various forms of terrorism in the country, I am able to spot signs that indicate that we are on the verge of a dangerous racial conflagration in the Southern section of the country."[7] This was a warning written two years into the Eisenhower administration, a warning of what was to come. It was written by a special assistant to President Eisenhower: E. Frederic Morrow, the first Black man in history to fill an executive position at the White House. Morrow was plugged in to Black America through his long-standing connections to Black newspaper editors and others who were contacting him about Black Americans' angry reaction to the lynching of Emmett Till, the acquittal of his killers, and the lack of any response from the federal government.

In July 1955, Morrow had been appointed the White House administrative officer for special projects. "Special projects": That meant *Negroes*, and not much more, as Morrow found out shortly after he left his job as public affairs director at CBS in New York to join the White House staff. It wasn't an easy move. Even after Eisenhower desegregated federal facilities in Washington, DC, Morrow, a lawyer and former New York field secretary for the NAACP, couldn't find a decent place for a Black man to live in the nation's capital.[8] And on top of that, White House staff had threatened to walk out when he arrived.[9] For a while, even secretaries in the White House typing pool refused to work for him. "So I have been sitting alone in the office, bewildered as how to get things going, how to staff, how to find furnishings, and how to make reports," Morrow wrote ten days after arriving at the White House.[10]

Morrow was a Republican, but so were a lot of Black people in the 1950s—still loyal to the party of Lincoln even after President Franklin D. Roosevelt's New Deal pulled many Black people out of the depths of the Great Depression. In fact, Eisenhower would get more than 40 percent of the Black vote in his 1956 reelection on the Republican ticket. But in 1955, the year before that reelection, people around Eisenhower were still concerned about how to hold on to Black support—increase it even—at the same time they were trying to appeal to Whites, southern Democrats interested in conserving racial discrimination. Even so, Morrow kept pushing for the Eisenhower people to speak out on the Emmett Till matter—framing it as a political strategy to secure the Black vote.[11] But that never happened. Nobody in the administration made a public statement about Bobo and his brutal lynching. In fact, Eisenhower never even answered the desperate plea Mamie set out in her September 2, 1955, telegram to him. As the mother of Emmett Till, she wrote, she was pleading with Eisenhower to "personally see that justice is meted out to all persons involved in the beastly lynching of my son in Money, Miss. Awaiting a direct reply from you."[12]

Morrow was unable to get any of the Eisenhower people to make a public statement about Bobo: not Eisenhower, not Nixon, not the attorney general. It looks like Morrow didn't realize what he was up against—at least not at the time. What he was up against was J. Edgar Hoover. The FBI director was sending his own memos to top White House officials at the same time Morrow was trying to make his case. Hoover had a completely different message and a nasty way of looking at Black people. He was suggesting growing Communist influence—on the NAACP and the people protesting the acquittal of Bobo's killers. Even on Mamie.

In Hoover's September 13, 1955, memorandum to White House Special Assistant Dillon Anderson, he pointed to "agitational activity." Typical of the messages he sent during this time (based on a "confidential source who has furnished reliable information in the past"), this one pointed to efforts by activists to organize protests and publish articles that were critical of racism and the lack of any government action to end it.[13] By tying civil rights leaders and labor leaders and Mamie to Communist agitators, the message seemed pretty clear: Protesting racial oppression was un-American. If that was true, then the opposite had to be true: racial oppression was *very much* American—as American as apple pie and fried chicken lunches in picnic baskets. With the kids . . . at public spectacle lynchings.

By November 1955, Hoover was referring to Emmett Louis Till as "the fourteen-year-old Negro Chicago boy" who "allegedly" was murdered. Wait, was he questioning the brutal killing of my cousin? That line in his memo suggested that, at least at that point, he seemed to be accepting all the lies told at the trial that acquitted Milam and Bryant, including the biggest lie, of course, that the body that was pulled from the Tallahatchie River at Graball Landing was not Bobo's at all. In fact, Bobo was not even dead, according to the White supremacist conspiracy theory of the moment. Or maybe Hoover was suggesting that somehow Bobo died of natural causes and not homicide? No, Bobo wasn't "*allegedly*" murdered. He was *definitely* murdered. Murdered and tortured before that. And tormented before he was tortured. But with a single word, Hoover seemed to be supporting the big lie, and sending a copy to the attorney general and to "the intelligence agencies of the Armed Forces."[14]

It didn't stop there, though. It seemed like everybody was out speaking those days. Mamie and Papa were sponsored by the NAACP. Dr. T.R.M. Howard, too. They were drawing huge crowds—tens of thousands of people demanding change—and drawing attention from people in high places.

Morrow's pleas on behalf of Bobo—racial justice, really—did not get the response he wanted. At one point, as Morrow recalled in his book, he got a reprimand from Maxwell Rabb, a special assistant to the president and Morrow's immediate boss. "Max gave me a tongue-lashing on the Negro's attitude on securing his civil rights. He felt that despite what the Administration had done in this area, Negroes had not demonstrated any kind of gratitude, and that most of the responsible officials in the White House had become completely disgusted with the whole matter. He said that there was a feeling that Negroes were being too aggressive in their demands; that an ugliness and surliness in manner was beginning to show through."[15] Even though Rabb had been an ally for Morrow and had supported his efforts, he was pulling back. "In effect, he was telling me that I should walk softly from then on and ask fewer questions of the members of the Administration on this matter."[16]

Morrow didn't accept Rabb's advice and kept pushing for the White House to meet with Black leaders and make public statements in support of civil rights. But he was not getting anywhere, since Hoover's memos—brimming with threats and fear—appeared to be having more impact on the White House, as he expressed much more concern about Communism than civil rights.

One of Hoover's main targets back then was not the scores of White supremacists administering true terror on the bodies of Black folks across the South, but a lone Black man who dared to fight back against it all. Dr. T.R.M. Howard, the man who had sheltered Mamie and others during the Milam and Bryant murder trial, had taken to the national stage talking about Bobo and the lack of justice coming out of Washington. A big part of the problem, he said, was that so many FBI agents were White southerners.[17] Howard wrote to a number of people in the White House, including Nixon, but with no response.[18] Howard's speeches about Bobo's murder, according to research by David and Linda Royster Beito, "invariably moved crowds to 'open weeping' and occasional 'screams.'"[19] One of these events took place before an overflow crowd on November 27, 1955, at the Dexter Avenue Baptist Church in Montgomery, Alabama, just down the street from the Alabama State Capitol and just two months after the acquittal of Milam and Bryant.

"Sitting in the audience was Rosa Parks, a seamstress and NAACP official in Montgomery. Many years later, she singled out Howard's appearance as the 'first mass meeting that we had in Montgomery' after Till's death. She particularly remembered his detailed description of the crime. Only four days after his speech, Parks made history by refusing to give her seat on a city bus to a White man in violation of a segregation ordinance. She later emphasized that Till's murder was central to her thinking at the time of her arrest."[20]

Within a year of Howard's Dexter Avenue speech, Hoover launched his infamous Counter Intelligence Program— "COINTELPRO." The program was supposed to investigate and fight against Communists by building cases against them. But considering how Hoover mixed up Communists and civil rights leaders, well, it didn't take long for the FBI to start setting its sights on Black folks who were pushing for equal rights. Howard was one of the first to get targeted, starting with a campaign in the press to discredit Howard and putting him under surveillance.[21] As we know now, COINTELPRO eventually zeroed in on so many others Hoover wanted to destroy, including somebody else who was at that November 1957 Dexter Avenue Baptist Church speech by Howard: the young pastor of the church, the leader of the bus boycott, the Reverend Dr. Martin Luther King Jr.

It all started, though, with Hoover's reaction to public protests. And the early protests were about Bobo. Just before that Dexter Avenue Baptist Church speech by Howard, in a November 22, 1955, "Personal and Confidential FBI Letter" marked "Racial Situation," Hoover warned Dillon Anderson, special assistant to the president, "of an attempt by the Communist Party to 'exert pressures against the Eisenhower administration and Attorney General Brownell to intervene in the Emmett Louis Till lynching.'"[22] Now, Howard and the event organizers simply wanted the federal government to step up and step in, to investigate a crime that the State of Mississippi just wanted to bury. But Hoover thought that was worth a memo, a warning, more federal spying rather than doing something—*anything*—to protect people's rights.

No wonder, then, that when Hoover was asked to report to the Eisenhower cabinet on racial tension, his summary presented on January 8, 1956, seemed almost sympathetic to White southern racists. He downplayed their reign of terror and seemed to blame the victims—Black people who had begun that mass movement in Montgomery—for the violence they were suffering. There still were ill feelings, he wrote, "among some cultured and educated Southerners" due to their unfair treatment under the rule of "blacks," "carpetbaggers," and "scalawags" during Reconstruction.[23] He reported a feeling among White southerners that Black folks weren't intelligent, not ready to share power and social standing because it "would take a generation to bring the races to parity." And, of course, there was the belief that Black people were criminals. He explained that "maintaining order is a primary concern among Southerners and they point to the higher prevalence of crime among Negroes than among whites." Maintaining order—as in "a way of life," as in Jim Crow, as in Nixon's coded "law and order" language a decade later. And the press, Hoover wrote, had not treated the South fairly in clarifying all this.[24]

Hoover's efforts paid off—at least for a while.

In an October 23, 1956, memo to White House Press Secretary James Hagerty, Maxwell Rabb explained the reason Eisenhower never responded to the pleadings of Mamie—that telegram she sent about the "beastly lynching." Rabb wrote that she had "permitted herself to be an instrument of the Communist party, which seized upon the case as a cause celebre and upon her as the means of making the race question a burning issue." Rabb wrote that Mamie had been taken around the country "as a prize exhibit," and he described her as a "phoney" (sic) who was "discredited for using her son's death as a means of making a living."[25] He added, almost as an afterthought, "The boy's father, incidentally, was executed by the Army in Italy on a sex charge. For these reasons, it was felt inadvisable to make a courteous reply."[26]

As it turned out, even though Hoover was determined to claim civil rights demonstrations were covers for Communist conspiracies, and other White House officials were buying it, the threat of a "conflagration" Morrow had warned about was becoming hard for people in the White House to ignore by the end of 1956. President Eisenhower came out in support of desegregation in his State of the Union address in January 1957. He had been reelected, so it was safe to do that. He had gotten a 5 percent increase in the Black vote over 1952, so it was only fair to do that.[27]

Words are fine. They sound good. They can make folks feel good. But action speaks louder than words. And it was the action that was taken later that year that would make all the difference in what we would be dealing with exactly sixty years later.

The process for what would become a historic event—passage of a new civil rights bill—started in the White House, partly because of all those memos and hallway discussions prompted by Morrow. He had run into a brick wall trying to get the Eisenhower people to step in on the Emmett Till case. And he even failed to get a meeting set with the president and civil rights leaders like Dr. Martin Luther King Jr. But he kept needling and nudging and nagging people about the racial tensions mounting in the country.[28] And he constantly reminded people about what had happened to Bobo and what didn't happen to his killers. "It certainly strengthened my hand in the day-to-day effort to get the Administration to speak out and do something on civil rights," he said. "I can still see the sacks and sacks of mail the White House received about Emmett Till."[29]

For his part, Nixon had suggested that the administration let Congress take up the civil rights bill and take the responsibility—or the blame—for whatever happened to it. The administration didn't exactly take his advice. On April 9, 1956, Attorney General Herbert Brownell Jr. sent to Congress a four-point plan for a new civil rights act—the first one to come to Congress since Reconstruction. The proposed law would create: a US commission on civil rights to investigate claims; a civil rights division in the Department of Justice with a new assistant attorney general for civil rights; and voting rights protections. And it would give the federal government power to file civil suits in civil rights cases. To his credit, according to all accounts Nixon took his duty as president of the Senate to heart and worked to get the bill passed. But in the upside-down world of the 1950s, it was the southern Democrats who rose up against civil rights progress, like today's Republicans. The bill was sent to the Senate Judiciary Committee chaired by Mississippi's own James Eastland and blocked, temporarily, by South Carolina's Strom Thurmond, who staged the longest filibuster in Senate history—more than twenty-four hours, beginning on August 28, 1957, two years to the day after Bobo was lynched. The bill wound up getting watered down by Senate Majority Leader Lyndon Johnson and supported by Senator John Kennedy. They both wanted to be president, and the South was still solidly Democratic. So, this was their own southern strategy—to support a weaker bill that might get support from southern Democrats without costing them votes in their political campaigns.[30]

Nixon did the right thing by representing the administration's effort to have the bill passed. But he dropped the ball when he had a choice to make on his own. Just before the end of the 1960 presidential campaign, Dr. King famously was arrested at a civil rights demonstration in Georgia and hauled away in the middle of the night. His wife, Coretta, was afraid he would be murdered. She called on Nixon for help, aware that Nixon and King had developed a friendly relationship when they met on March 5, 1957, at the independence ceremonies in Ghana. Reportedly, though, Nixon didn't want to lose the support of southern White voters by getting involved. Senator Kennedy made a different decision and called Mrs. King to express his sympathy. And while Kennedy's brother, Bobby, quietly worked behind the scenes to get King released, the Kennedys made sure Black folks knew what they had done.[31] Although, as we know, Nixon lost this race to Kennedy, he would win eight years later with southern votes on his mind.

It's hard to know what was in Nixon's heart when it came to Black people and civil rights. If you take a close look at the record, it sure looks like nothing was as important to him as winning. If this was all a game to them, the stakes were a whole lot higher than they were with the slots we would hide in the backrooms of Argo restaurants just ahead of the police raids, or the dice we would roll on the street for nickels and dimes. In Washington, they were rolling the dice for votes. But while Morrow was trying to show that protecting Black rights could mean more Black votes for Republicans, other Republicans were ready to trade away Black rights for more southern White votes. Some people, like Nixon, it seems, were trying to have it both ways. And, again, though he lost his bet in 1960, he raised the stakes later in the decade, in a game he was determined to win by any means necessary.

The Civil Rights Division of the Department of Justice would continue to get more effective over the years. It wound up being the unit that launched the investigation into Bobo's murder in 2004, and brought us in to assist in 2017. During the congressional debate over passage of the Civil Rights Act of 1957, a number of witnesses testified about the case of Emmett Till. Like Congressman Charles Diggs, who had been there at the trial, they spoke of the injustice of the Till case and the need for a new law to protect against such injustice.[32]

So, in a big way, it seems Bobo inspired the enactment of the law that would create the arm of the government—the long arm of the law—that would reach out over great distances and reach back over many years in the search for justice in the horrible lynching of my cousin. In the end, the murder of Emmett Till inspired the passage of the very laws that would empower the federal government to investigate his death.

As I reflect on this realization, this reality, I am strengthened in my resolve to continue doing what I have to do. Clearly, it all has been preordained.

THE TURNOUT FOR Devery's November 2, 2017, book event at the Nixon Presidential Library and Museum was pretty impressive—at least a hundred people, mostly White. I chuckled with Chris later when I told him that it looked like the handful of Black folks who showed up were the ones we had invited. But that was okay. I think it's important to tell Bobo's story to White folks as well as Black folks. As I sat there on the stage looking out at the crowd in the auditorium, I thought it was especially important to reach the kind of White folks who come to Nixon Library events. But even though I am always clear on my purpose, on my mission, my reason for being there, I still wasn't sure about their reason for having me there. Hadn't figured out how this Emmett Till book event tied to anything related to Nixon after we had considered the limited connection of Nixon to anything related to Bobo. In fact, if you Google "Richard Nixon and Emmett Till," you do wind up getting a link: to this event.

Onstage, one additional panelist joined Devery and me: Alex Foster, the vice president of production for Middleton Media Group, one of the executive producers of the series based on Devery's book. The actor Casey Affleck and Middleton have hooked up in the Affleck/Middleton Project. The panel was moderated by Frank Gannon, who was an aide to Nixon in the White House and continued working with Nixon after he resigned the presidency. We were all introduced to the audience by Bill Baribault, the Nixon Foundation CEO, who also wanted "to salute" the other TV series producers in attendance: David Clark of Aptitude Entertainment, and Rosanna Grace and Nicole Tabs of the Serendipity Group, who all "were especially helpful in making tonight possible." That acknowledgment reignited my suspicion: that the producers had planned to connect Emmett Till to Nixon somehow. And Baribault's continued remarks only reinforced it without a doubt. "The issue of civil rights was central to Richard Nixon's life and times," he said. "It was something he thought about and cared about deeply."

For his part, Devery only mentioned Nixon a couple of times and essentially acknowledged that Nixon's work on the Civil Rights Act was at the direction of the Eisenhower administration. Rather, Devery talked in great detail about the story he presented in his book. In fact, the entire presentation was an hour and six minutes long. My part was six minutes. The last six minutes—in the question-and-answer period. Even so, I felt a connection with the audience. As I shared my personal connection to Bobo, I could see many people there leaning in, more compelled by the human story than the political story, or the legal story, or even the history of it all. All the fine details Devery was discussing. I could tell by the questions I got.

As expected, when we chatted with Rosanna Grace and others after the program, talk turned to the possibility of having me work with the TV series production. Marvel quickly nixed that, not convinced my authentic contribution would have a meaningful impact on a version of the story they had already set in motion. Even though I had been moved by Devery's summary of the whole thing—and I told him as much during the event—we still were concerned about the integrity of the story that would move forward in the TV series. Were these people, the ones who seemed to us to be connected to the people who seemed intent on rewriting Nixon's story, were these people the best people to render the story of Emmett Till, a story that represented the opposite of what Nixon represented in terms of racial justice? What was the story (and subtext) being presented at the Nixon Library? Was this event about a man who was totally committed to civil rights? Or was it the story of people trying to rewrite the story to create a new reality, using Bobo to do it? If that was the case, what were they prepared to do with the story of Emmett Till?

WE LEARNED LATER that prior to the Nixon Library event, there had been a book event for Devery at Eso Won Books, a celebrated Black bookstore in the Crenshaw District of Los Angeles. Based on what we heard, Devery explained that he accidentally happened onto the story of Emmett Till when he was working on something else—making some bookstore attendees uneasy. That discomfort only deepened as the issue of appropriation surfaced, with at least one man questioning Devery's ability as a White man to tell a story that had such deep meaning to Black people, such significance to a community still experiencing systemic injustice. Apparently, this exchange in the crowd grew quite hostile before the man who raised the volume on it all was asked to leave. I couldn't help but wonder if this incident drove the decision makers to schedule the Nixon Library event—in front of a much friendlier audience—and to invite Marvel and me to participate—as validation.

To be clear, I really don't have a problem with people telling the Emmett Till story through the lens of their own lived experience. But not everybody can be the authoritative voice on a story that might be shaped by their own perspective. In the end, we couldn't take a chance on being used. After all, I had been on a journey to truth and justice. After the public event, over dinner, the topic turned to the video series the Devery folks were planning. We just said no.

LAW AND ORDER. After reviewing the report Hoover had given to the Eisenhower cabinet—the one that included a profile of southern racists who wanted to maintain order—meaning White supremacy—I better understood Nixon's use of the term *law and order* in the 1960s. The real meaning transmitted in the coded language of racism was *order and law:* maintaining a social order through the use of the law—law that either intentionally discriminated or simply wound up discriminating because of how it was enforced.

Law and order. I have learned a thing or two about law and order in my lifelong journey in my ministry as well as my pursuit of justice. There are the laws of God and there are the laws of man. The laws of God are based on a deep sense of morality. They are all about love and forgiveness and balance and fairness and equality and justice. And in morality, there is divine order. In contrast, the laws of man are imperfect. I've learned, just as Frederic Morrow learned back in the day, that without a constant moral foundation, the laws of man can be subject to the politics of the moment, which is to say they are constantly changing. Like the flow of a river—never the same from one moment to the next—the laws of man are different somehow when we, Black people, step into the current, the present, the moment.

I know a thing or two about rivers. Like the one just outside Chicago where Bobo and I used to fish. Like the one down in the Delta where my family and I used to fish, the one that would overflow in the rainy season and wash past our house. Connecting with the natural flow of things. Like the one where Bobo's battered body was found. On the third day following his murder—when he rose again.

Yeah, I know a thing or two about rivers—after all, I once baptized in the River Jordan, in waters of redemption and revelation, of rebirth and resurrection. Over the past two thousand years that river has become polluted, yet it still cleanses us believers, those of us who have faith in things unseen. For hundreds of years, Black people have been propelled forward by a deep faith in things unseen—like justice.

I once baptized in the River Jordan, true believers who had made the pilgrimage to be redeemed, saved in holy water. For my part, as John the Baptist foresaw, I have been baptized by fire as well as water (Matthew 3:11). There remains to this day a burning desire deep in my soul to rise above the pollution of racism, as well as the politics of race, and finally see a moral outcome, when justice is done, when divine order is restored and upheld.

9

Tale of the Tape

ON JANUARY 29, 2018, dignitaries—elected officials, journalists, activists, clergy—all came together at the Washington National Cathedral to honor the life of Simeon Booker, the longtime Washington bureau chief of *Ebony* and *Jet* magazines. He had died on December 10, 2017, at the age of ninety-nine. The late John Lewis was there to remind everyone about the amazing work Booker had done covering the Civil Rights Movement. Donald Graham, former publisher of *The Washington Post*, talked about Booker as a trailblazer, a Nieman Fellow, who in 1952 became the first Black reporter hired by the *Post*, or any major newspaper in the country for that matter.

Chris Benson also was among those who climbed the winding stairs to the pulpit where Dr. Martin Luther King Jr. and Nelson Mandela once stood, and he talked about his years working as a journalist with Booker, his mentor, in Washington and the stories Booker would share with him about Emmett Till. You see, among the many award-winning accomplishments of Simeon Booker was Bobo's story—a story that, in a sense, Booker broke for a national audience, making sure that Mamie could, in fact, let the world see what had happened to her son. Booker is the person who arranged with Mamie to have *Jet* photographer David Jackson photograph Bobo's mutilated remains on that slab at the Rayner Funeral Home, turning what had been a local story in Chicago and in Mississippi into a national story and then an international one. *Jet* sold out the issue with Bobo's photos and then printed a second run. That one sold out, too.

As a journalist, Booker documented Morrow's work during the 1950s. Both men were committed advocates for the truth and for a reckoning they saw out there on the horizon. And Booker's experience at the *Post,* much like Morrow's experience at the White House, showed the extremes of the challenge we faced. Morrow, who couldn't find a decent place to live as a Black man in 1950s Washington, DC, was marginalized in the Eisenhower administration. Booker, who was advised to use only one specific restroom at the Washington Post building to avoid racial problems—at *The Washington Post*!—found those problems followed him into the newsroom despite his best efforts. They persisted and he wound up leaving the paper to write for *Ebony* and *Jet.*

Thanks to Booker's dedication to the story—and Mamie's transformative moment—the photos of Bobo published in *Jet* flipped the script on lynching narratives. The photos we have seen of Black people strung up in trees or on lampposts or hanging from bridges, sometimes with thousands of White folks gleefully looking on, those photos often were used as postcards and sent to faraway friends and relatives to demonstrate White power over the Black body. But with the gruesome Emmett Till photos, Black people took control over the narrative to show what can result from the abuse of power. They laid bare the horrible truth about the extremes of racial oppression. In that way, Black people assumed an awesome power that fueled a mass movement for racial justice. Committed advocates for truth like Mamie and Booker, and even insiders like Morrow, used their platforms to promote a reckoning—a reckoning we still are struggling to reach. I am fueled by that same power.

On February 28, 2018, nearly a year after our first meeting with authorities in Oxford, Mississippi, Marvel and I were there again, in Oxford, for a status meeting. Chris had a travel conflict and wound up participating by telephone. The folks around the table there in Mississippi included Chad Lamar, who was at the first meeting as deputy US attorney for the Northern District of Mississippi, and had been named by the Trump administration as US attorney for that region. Dewayne Richardson, the district attorney for the Mississippi Fourth Circuit Court, was there again. Of course, Special FBI Agent Walter Henry was there, as were a few others, including Dana Mulhauser, DOJ Civil Rights Division attorney, who came in from Washington. She replaced Kristy Parker, the DOJ attorney who had been at the first meeting. Mulhauser was a tough litigator whose commitment to civil rights and justice started with her experience as a student at Harvard Law School, where she was a member of the editorial board of the *Harvard Law Review* and one of the founders of the Harvard Project on Wrongful Convictions.

Special Agent Henry started the meeting with the ongoing question of whether we—Marvel, Chris, and I—were going to have access to the documents and recording that had been produced by Timothy Tyson and the library at Chapel Hill under subpoena. US Attorney Lamar first had to get authorization from the federal court in North Carolina to release the materials to DA Richardson, but they still didn't have permission from the North Carolina judge to show the documents to us, to let us read them, evaluate them. But the authorities were allowed to summarize the significant points, as they saw them. That's what they were doing here.

DA Richardson made two very surprising points in this briefing. The first related to the book manuscript Carolyn Bryant Donham was developing, titled *I Am More Than a Wolf Whistle*. We had learned about the book in our first meeting with this group a year earlier. She and her daughter-in-law Marsha Bryant, who was co-writing the project with her, had asked Tyson to help them edit the manuscript and prepare it for a publisher to consider. So, as it came time for him to write his own book, Tyson had access not only to his two interviews with Carolyn Bryant Donham for reference, but also to whatever revelations she'd made in her own manuscript. However, instead of backing up Tyson's claims about her recanting—quoting her as saying, "That part's not true"—Carolyn's manuscript shows she was sticking to her original story about Bobo.

That information was bad enough.

Then there was DA Richardson's second revelation. Tyson said he had recorded both of his interviews with Carolyn Bryant Donham. But he'd turned over tape recordings of only one of the two meetings. He said he couldn't find the other one, although he and the Chapel Hill library had produced typed transcripts of both interviews. And in the materials they had received, the authorities found no trace of the quote that appeared in Tyson's book—it was not in the transcripts, not in the one recording.

"Nothing to indicate the recantation," Lamar offered. "Nothing to support what is quoted in the Tyson book."

"Nothing," Henry confirmed.

"I can concur," Richardson said.

"We agree. Not much there," Mulhauser said in buttoning it all up.

Wait. Seriously? I could only shake my head on hearing this. That Carolyn Bryant Donham quote had made headlines a year earlier. It was the one thing people remembered from Tyson's book, the one thing they talked about, the one thing that made the book worth reading, let alone buying. That quote had caused pain to those reminded of the gross injustice the lie had set in motion. And that quote had provided a measure of relief to us, believing that justice—not complete justice, but at least *some* justice—was achieved in the form of this confession, finally, of the *truth*. The empowering truth. I even had done interviews with reporters who seemed to be excited just to be part of this moment correcting the historical record. Could it be that the quote about lying was itself a lie?

As of that moment, the government officials in the room weren't prepared to say Tyson falsified the quote—only that they couldn't prove Carolyn said those words. Couldn't prove it beyond a reasonable doubt. Not yet.

It seemed like I missed a couple of beats in the conversation, like I had been transported from the room. I was so caught up in what had been revealed. I struggled to understand. If Tyson didn't make it up, what else would explain the contradiction between his book and hers, between his story about her and her story about all that happened? Did he get Carolyn to confess after she'd finished writing what these authorities said was in her manuscript? And if so, why didn't Tyson edit this in her book—after all, he *was* editing it, right? And he had sent the manuscript to the UNC archives to keep it for future historians in search of the truth. What kind of historian would submit a known lie to the place of record, forcing future researchers to try to figure out whether his version of her story was more reliable than the one she wrote herself?

I was in denial of even the possibility that a historian might just make up something. After all, I wanted her confession to be real. I knew what she had said about Bobo was a lie. I was there at the store. But I wanted her to tell the world that she had lied.

That would be a challenge, since her daughter-in-law was pushing back. When FBI Special Agent Shannon Wright interviewed her right after the book came out in February 2017, Marsha Bryant said the recantation never had been uttered. And she was there and said she would have known if anything like an admission had been expressed. So why didn't she sue Tyson? She told Special Agent Wright that she thought about it. But then decided that it was not in her family's best interest, as she believed it would only attract more attention to them.

So, just as in 1955, the Bryant family certainly wasn't ready to give Carolyn up in 2017 or 2018, or ever, and I wasn't ready to give up on the possibility of getting at the truth. There had to be some record to prove that she said what we read—something *somewhere*. Then again, maybe not.

I had to ask the question. "Is he a credible person?"

They answered by confirming the facts that Tyson is an instructor, a research scholar at Duke with a joint appointment at UNC. And it would seem foolish for someone with such gravitas in the academic world to risk that reputation by making up something as important as the confession of a potential co-conspirator in one of the most notorious murders in American history.

But the people in that room were seasoned investigators and lawyers, and they clearly were not ready to give the benefit of the doubt based solely on Tyson's reputation. At the same time, that reputation kept me believing that there still might be something out there. Even though authorities have to see proof of everything they are investigating, they read the deep concern on my face and started talking about possibilities, as if to assure us that it was not over, that there still might be something out there to be discovered—something to show that Carolyn had spoken the words Tyson wrote in his book.

Tyson had said he couldn't locate the missing recording and, we were told, the US Attorney's Office was at a disadvantage to challenge him on that claim. But there was another step to be taken.

"We can subpoena his computer, his laptop," Lamar said.

The justification for a subpoena would be whether Tyson had provided everything the grand jury subpoena had demanded. If he hadn't, that would be a problem for him. Also, if anything Tyson produced had been altered, again, that would be a problem. And these kinds of problems at this level of a federal investigation could mean charges.

That was the decision: to go after more evidence and have Special Agent Henry visit Tyson. We were told, though, that, given the Department of Justice rule protecting journalists from what might be seen as harassment by federal agents, DOJ might have to grant Henry special permission, or a subpoena to testify would have to be issued by the North Carolina federal judge. There also was a good side and a not-so-good side of seeking a new subpoena. If Tyson was ordered to testify before a grand jury, he would be given "use immunity," which means that nothing he revealed in his testimony could be used against him. It's a constitutional thing. But that might not be such a big deal since the focus of the investigation was not Tyson. It was Carolyn Bryant Donham. The authorities really didn't want to go after Tyson so much as they wanted to go after his information.

That's when Chris chimed in on the phone to urge that we be allowed to review the documents that had been collected. All of them. The transcripts, the recordings, even Carolyn's manuscript. He said that I was both a victim and a witness, a survivor of a night of terror who had seen things one long-ago August week that might be helpful in seeing things in the documents that even the authorities had not seen.

They all agreed—just like that.

"You deserve and should be able to review these materials," Lamar said.

The North Carolina court's order releasing the documents to the US attorney and FBI in Mississippi would first be modified to fully release the materials to DA Richardson for review, and he would seek permission for Marvel, Chris, and me to review as well. It was suggested that a federal judge in Mississippi might be contacted to grant us access—with conditions, of course. We would agree not to divulge whatever we saw in the materials until the investigation was concluded. We were fine with this because we saw the value in protecting the investigation. After all, we wanted to get to the truth and we didn't want to say too much too soon and stop anybody from coming forward.

The authorities also wanted to make sure there were no other family members with direct information who should be included in the investigation. We assured them that there already had been an understanding by the family elders that Simeon and I would be the ones directly involved from start to finish. Now that Simmie was gone, it was all left to me. While I agree that news coverage is important to expose what we need to see, I shared the authorities' concerns that Tyson, who had spoken freely up to that point, might shut down if anything leaked publicly before our work was complete. So I decided not to tell anybody else in the family until the time was right.

The most important thing now would be to get to the bottom of what Carolyn said or didn't say to Tyson. If she could be charged with lying to the FBI, great. But I also wanted to clear Bobo's name and wipe away the stain that woman had put on it with her claims. In that regard, DA Richardson agreed and gave one last assurance before we ended. "Every day is too long to have this lie hanging out there," he said.

Before we left, the authorities said they could try to help set up a meeting with Carolyn, if we still wanted to. Marsha Bryant, the daughter-in-law, already had said her family was not interested in doing that.

Frankly, neither were we.

Following our February meeting in Oxford, Special Agent Henry continued to press on with two US attorney's offices in the Eastern District of North Carolina and in the Northern District of Mississippi, his home base, negotiating for clearance to modify the order releasing the Tyson documents to Richardson and to us. During the next few months, you could almost hear the clock ticking as things developed on this issue and several others.

MARCH 27, 2018. Good news, Special Agent Henry reported. US District Judge Mike Mills in Mississippi approved the motion to allow Marvel and me to have access to the Tyson documents, with Chris being permitted as our attorney to assist us in reviewing and analyzing the materials. Our access would have to be monitored in a government office in Oxford or in Chicago. Most likely, he said, a meeting would be organized with DOJ attorney Mulhauser, DA Richardson, and him, to discuss what would be included in the document submission and what would be excluded, before we would be scheduled to review the materials. But, as with everything else over that past year, the encouraging news about moving forward came with more information that caused us to slow down.

The authorities planned to check the documents against the demands listed in the North Carolina grand jury subpoena and a list compiled by the FBI in the course of its ongoing investigation. Again, even though he wasn't the focus of the investigation, there could be a question of legal jeopardy for Tyson if he withheld any subpoenaed documents, or altered any of them. As I understood it, this concern arose from that missing audio recording, which would be the only place where investigators might find the Carolyn Bryant Donham "confession." Since neither of the recording transcripts reviewed by the investigators included the quote, it raised a question about whether any transcript pages might be missing. We were told that Tyson made an excuse about the missing materials. He claimed that his assistant, who transcribed for him, lost that part of the transcript. So, before we would meet again, the FBI wanted to follow up with Tyson's assistant and with Tyson to confirm that they had turned over all the documents demanded by the grand jury subpoena.

APRIL 27, 2018. Special Agent Henry briefed us on progress. The review of the Tyson documents by investigators was complete. It appeared that original material from Carolyn's manuscripts and from the interviews was used in the Tyson book, despite the fact that there was no evidence that they had a contract, or that he had paid for the rights. The investigators still were considering a follow-up with Tyson. Special Agent Henry informed us that a meeting would be set up for authorities to review the documents with us. That meeting likely would take place at the FBI field office in Chicago. They were shooting for July.

MAY 22, 2018. Timothy Tyson was awarded the prestigious Robert F. Kennedy Book Award, an honor that some consider to be as significant as the Pulitzer Prize. Each year, among its other awards for excellence in journalism, the award seeks to recognize a book that "most faithfully and forcefully reflects Robert Kennedy's purposes," including "his struggle for honest and evenhanded justice." An announcement of Tyson's honor was posted at the Duke University Center for Documentary Studies, which included a statement written by Tyson referring to his "astonishment" at winning. He generally gushed about being included among such highly regarded authors who had been honored over the years. He wrote 410 words, and not a single one of them was about how his work might have contributed to the pursuit of "justice," as recognized by the award. He wrote 410 words, and not a single one of them was about Emmett Till.[1]

JUNE 19, 2018. Special Agent Henry briefed us on the newest development. Investigators had confirmed that no recording existed of the critical Carolyn Bryant Donham passage published in the Tyson book. At least none had turned up. Even more, it looked like the transcript might have been altered, but they still hadn't yet followed up with Tyson and Tyson's assistant, the person who transcribed the audio recording. But was the assistant subject to the same limitation on questioning journalists about their work, their sources and methods? Yes, Henry said, if Tyson was considered a journalist. "The department is very cautious in this area." Okay. Another question then. Was Tyson, a research scholar, a historian, even considered to be a journalist?

JULY 12, 2018. I had made my second trip to Mississippi in a month to make my annual presentation at Delta State University's summer institute for teachers. This time, I had decided to present with Alvin Sykes, who always put Bobo at the center of it all, rather than centering himself, as others had been doing—making themselves the story. Alvin was the person responsible for getting the 2004 federal–state investigation launched. He was the person responsible for getting bipartisan support for the Emmett Till Unsolved Civil Rights Crime Act passed and then reauthorized—the very law that kept the FBI on the case.

Alvin and I had presented together several times and he had included me in meetings with public officials as he was maneuvering like a pro through the halls of power in Washington, DC. In all his work as an activist, a social justice advocate, a lobbyist, he never seemed to want to elbow other people out of the way to step into the spotlight. So Alvin and I were a good truth squad there in Mississippi on this date when the story broke. The FBI had reopened its investigation into the murder of Emmett Till.

Marvel was back home and got the news first. She was shocked since it looked like the federal authorities had reneged on their promise to keep everything under wraps. We had kept our promise in exchange for their promise to tell us everything before they told the public anything. Marvel was receiving a flood of media interview requests and felt a rush of emotions as she began to believe we had been betrayed. She called me and emailed Chris—and though we were all in separate locations, all with a variety of questions, we worked together to get in touch with, of course, Special Agent Henry.

Henry assured us that nothing had been divulged by him or any other authorities in the chain of the investigation.

"Then, was there a leak?" Chris asked, when they spoke by phone. No, it looked like a news outlet just caught wind of a brief mention about our investigation in the middle of a routine activities report by the Department of Justice. Each year in February and September, an activities report is posted on the DOJ website. It is likely the mention was little more than a summary of the internal report compiled after our meeting in Oxford the year before.

Back in Mississippi, Alvin calmed the waters by explaining to all the teachers that the case was not reopened, because it never had been closed. It technically was only inactive, which allowed it to be reactivated whenever new information came to light. He was right on the money, as Henry set out to Chris. I was able to respond to media questions saying just that much and not more. Our cousin Airickca Gordon-Taylor said pretty much the same thing when she was called.[2]

Chris got calls from the Chicago PBS-TV journalist Brandis Friedman and from CBS2 anchor Jim Williams. Friedman had interviewed him several times so she still had his cell number. One of Chris's former journalism students, Maggie Huynh, was a producer for Williams and also still had his cell number. Chris was able to explain to them that the stories were not entirely accurate. The investigation had not been reopened. It was simply continuing, and he would update them at the appropriate time.

While we were relieved that this event did not amount to anything, we still were slightly on edge, realizing just how quickly things could change, demanding we be ready for any potential press with explanations of how we had become so deeply involved in this matter and what we hoped we would gain—not for ourselves, but for Bobo. For justice. Alvin had made sure that one of the key purposes of the Emmett Till Act had been to clear the record for the families of victims, the survivors of racial atrocities, and for the sake of preserving history for future generations. So it was in the name of Emmett Till—his legacy—that the investigation into the lynching of Emmett Till could continue. Again, he was the beneficiary of his own law.

JULY 13, 2018. *The Charlotte Observer* published an Associated Press story on the renewed FBI investigation referring to Timothy Tyson's support for the effort, even though he didn't think "his research alone will provide enough evidence for new charges."[3]

JULY 14–15, 2018. The day after the AP story appeared in *The Charlotte Observer*, it looked like Timothy Tyson was changing his tune. Only one day after he seemed to welcome the investigation, he took a much less supportive tone. In a July 14 interview on MSNBC, it appeared that he was beginning to lay the groundwork for a counter-narrative. He said he had devoted eight years to writing his book.[4] Even though he had been quoted the day before expressing his doubt that his work would contribute anything to the investigation, he said, "I fully support the reopening of the investigation and I shared all my research materials with the FBI happily and if there were justice for Emmett Till available, I would be all for that." He also downplayed the significance of the revelation in his book, stating that "the virtue or lack thereof of Carolyn Bryant seems a minor matter to an historian, but I understand people's interest in it."[5]

And this was all said with a straight face.

On top of it all, I was sickened to see him dismiss the importance of what now was a questionable recantation by Carolyn Bryant Donham. That was the only thing that was important about his book, that and what the FBI said he appeared to reproduce from her manuscript—the personal background from her own family and the family of Roy Bryant and J. W. Milam.

The next day, Tyson appeared even more forceful in his pushback. In a July 15 interview with the Reverend Al Sharpton on MSNBC, Tyson referred to the "breathtaking hypocrisy that Jefferson Beauregard Sessions III and Donald Trump should present themselves as defenders of civil rights and racial justice . . ."[6] He seemed to purposely drag out each syllable of each one of Sessions's three names as if they were slurs, apparently to stress his distaste for the obvious connections to Confederate President *Jefferson* Davis and General P.G.T. *Beauregard*, who led the Confederate victories at Fort Sumter and Bull Run. In support of Tyson, Reverend Sharpton added that the Department of Justice was doing nothing to pursue the Eric Garner civil rights case. But while he might have won over Reverend Sharpton, I certainly knew better. The public announcement of the Till investigation was not news to Tyson; he had been contacted by Special Agent Henry a year and a half earlier. Henry was not a member of the Trump administration. Tyson had to know that. In fact, his earlier correspondence with Henry told a different story than the one he was telling at this point on television. The earlier correspondence had been cordial, if not extremely supportive. What's more, he was the one who had insisted that he should produce his documents under subpoena, for a matter that was set in motion by the "revelation" of his book.

In complying with the grand jury subpoena, Tyson sent an email to Special Agent Henry at 2:16 A.M., September 21, 2017. He discussed his own "due diligence" in making sure there was no ethical breach in releasing the materials in light of what he claimed were the assurances he had given to Carolyn Bryant Donham. "In order to get her to let me take charge of the interviews and documents, as you know, I had agreed to place these materials in the Southern Historical Collection at the University of North Carolina under a 30-year hold." He went on to say that he had been advised by colleagues and senior staff at the American Historical Association that there were no ethical concerns and no breach of his archival agreement in responding to the subpoena. "This was a relief because I have no inclination or obligation to protect anyone from equal justice before the law, and particularly anyone complicit with this horrendous crime. *I am also pleased because I am a great admirer of the FBI's 'Cold Case Initiative' under the Emmett Till Unsolved Civil rights [sic] Crime Act and also have a high opinion of the good folks in the Civil Rights Division*" (emphasis added).[7]

Tyson clearly knew he was working with "the good folks" in the DOJ Civil Rights Division and not under orders from Trump or Sessions. There was nothing anywhere to indicate that Trump and Sessions were trying to "present themselves as defenders of civil rights and racial justice," as Tyson had claimed. Luckily, they were not even involved. But this flip seemed to me like the investigation might be turning in his direction—pressing him to prove that Carolyn actually said what he published in his book.

JULY 17, 2018. New York City announced that it was moving forward in considering whether to hold police officers responsible for the 2014 choke-hold death of Eric Garner. There had been no indictment, the Eastern District of the US Attorney's Office of New York had not pursued the matter, so the Department of Justice had stepped in to consider a civil rights case. Special Agent Henry had been brought in during the Obama administration to investigate. Former DOJ attorney Kristy Parker also had been involved before she left the government. Even though there reportedly was strong support among some DOJ lawyers and FBI investigators for an indictment against NYPD officer Daniel Pantaleo, the Sessions DOJ was not moving aggressively on the case. So the family of Eric Garner was not encouraged by the local news of a personnel action. "I'm tired of the [city's] delays and playing politics with the murder of my son . . ." said Gwen Carr, the mother of Eric Garner.[8]

We had to consider that case in connection with our case. It was something that kept coming up with us. What would happen when the final report on our investigation finally hit the desk of the attorney general, Jeff Sessions? Would they slow-walk it? Would they kill it? Would Trump find a way to politicize it, use it against justice advocates? Tyson's public comments had seemed awfully self-serving. But there might have been something to them.

In any event, we were pleased that we would get our next meeting with the authorities at the FBI offices in Chicago. It was decided. Two days. August 14 and 15. We would have access to all documents: the transcripts of interviews between Timothy Tyson and Carolyn Bryant Donham, at least one recording, and all sorts of memoranda.

Even with all this, though, we knew that among the most revealing documents we would be able to examine was Carolyn's manuscript, *I Am More Than a Wolf Whistle.*

10

Reading Between the Lies

IT SEEMED LIKE we all got there at the same time on the morning of August 14, 2018. Marvel and I were getting cleared at the guard station just inside the security gate of the small public parking lot at the FBI Chicago field office. Chris was parking, Special Agent Henry directing him to one of the few spots that remained open. The others waited inside, where we had to get screened again. Photo ID, pre-clearance checklist, metal detectors. Full security for the secrets that would be shared with us under the watchful eye of people with guns, badges, and the authority that comes with guns and badges.

DOJ attorney Dana Mulhauser had flown in from Washington. Mississippi District Attorney Dewayne Richardson and his district manager, Tamicko Fair, had come up from Mississippi. It was a beautiful, sunny Chicago day as we entered the building. But that was about the most we would see of it for nearly eight hours—except for a quick break to the food truck for lunch. For the most part, we would hole up in a windowless conference room with the authorities and a couple of boxes stuffed with documents. I wondered at first if they had to buy a plane ticket for those boxes. After all, they couldn't have trusted all that sensitive confidential material to baggage handlers. Might have wound up in Cheyenne rather than Chicago. As it turned out, Henry drove from Oxford to Chicago with that precious cargo.

Once we settled into the conference room, Henry opened with a review. The delay in reporting back to us had been helpful to investigators, he said, since additional information was revealed during that period. We heard more about the process involved in getting to this point. The North Carolina grand jury subpoenaed the documents from the Southern Historical Collection at the Wilson Library at the University of North Carolina–Chapel Hill. The archived documents had been held by the library "under lock and key" with a directive that they not be made available until 2038—no public access, not even to us, at first, anyway. A federal judge in North Carolina authorized release of the documents to the Department of Justice and the FBI, and then granted permission to release them to Mississippi District Attorney Richardson. Finally, permission was granted in a Mississippi federal court by Senior US District Judge Michael Mills for the district attorney to share the documents with us in response to the request made by Chris to aid the investigation. As it turned out, the investigators had received three sets of documents. Under the subpoena, they had gotten one set from the UNC library, and one set (which included one of two audio recordings) from Tyson. They also had received copies of the transcripts and the manuscript voluntarily from Marsha Bryant. That meant we might not have even needed court permission to read those since they technically had not been subpoenaed by the grand jury.

Henry stressed to us that having this access was highly unusual. Typically, these kinds of materials are not shared with victims until the conclusion of an investigation. But, apparently, we had persuaded them that, as the last victim in this matter, I was in a unique position to help with the interpretation of the factual evidence. Besides, we had kept our promise not to run to the newspapers and television cameras every time we learned something new, so the authorities kept granting us exclusive access to files under that honor system.

This exclusive access was especially important to me, given how Bobo's story had been distorted so often over the years. I wanted to make sure we got any new information first so that everybody else

room. We would have to leave our written notes in the files—though Chris later told me that once he wrote something down, he could easily remember it and would be able to reconstruct the notes later for reference in our own review outside the FBI conference room. That would help us ask follow-up questions as things moved along.

Before we began to review the materials, we were brought up to speed by Special Agent Henry on what the investigation had produced so far. Among other things, we learned that J. W. Milam and Roy Bryant were allowed to have guns in their jail cells and the cells were not locked. They also were allowed out for family visits while being held in jail for trial. That information might have been shocking but it was not surprising based on all the things we had learned over the years. Henry confirmed that what we were about to learn from the record they would open up to us was only made possible because Timothy Tyson had been contacted by Marsha Bryant (Carolyn Bryant Donham's daughter-in-law) to help with Donham's memoir after they'd heard of an earlier Tyson book, *Blood Done Sign My Name*, about the brutal 1970 racial killing of twenty-three-year-old Henry "Dickey" Marrow in Oxford, North Carolina. Marrow, a veteran, reportedly had made a remark to a couple of Black women standing near a White woman outside a store. The White woman was offended, and Marrow was eventually chased down, shot, beaten, kicked, and killed by White men who were later acquitted by an all-White jury. Carolyn Bryant Donham and Marsha Bryant said they were really impressed by Tyson's work on the book about that killing and wanted to talk with Tyson about working on Carolyn's book.

A short draft of her manuscript already had been developed—only about twenty or thirty pages—but the two recorded interviews Tyson did with Carolyn helped Marsha expand it to a hundred pages. We were told that Tyson did some light editing on the longer draft of the manuscript. His editing and comments are documented on the manuscript pages we reviewed through tracked changes and comments.

They confirmed once again that, in the formal interview with the FBI on February 21, 2017, Marsha and Carolyn told Special Agent

Shannon Wright that Carolyn had not recanted, as Tyson had written in his book. In fact, Marsha said she had known Carolyn for forty years and that Carolyn had always said Emmett Till grabbed her in the store. Marsha said that she and her husband, Tom (Carolyn's son), were both there with Carolyn during the interviews with Tyson, adding that Tyson turned on his recorder immediately when Tyson began talking. The Bryants had gotten copies of the transcripts, but not the audio recordings. Marsha also told the FBI that there was no written agreement with Tyson for his editing work on the manuscript, or for archiving the interview transcripts, the recordings, or the manuscript. Special Agent Wright was told that no one gave Tyson or anyone else permission to publish the Carolyn Bryant Donham story or use her material to write a book. Marsha Bryant said she only found out that Tyson had written and published another book when a writer for *Vanity Fair* came to her house to interview her about it. It also seemed like Tyson was writing his own interpretation of whatever had been said, according to Marsha and Carolyn. In fact, Carolyn claimed that Tyson often took her words out of context and she would have to correct him.

All this was interesting because their version of the story contradicted what Tyson had been saying about how he produced his book and about the cooperation he had gotten from Marsha Bryant and Carolyn Bryant Donham. Of course, Marsha and Carolyn would have every reason to deny that Carolyn had confessed if they thought that admission might open her up to legal jeopardy and possible prison time for lying to the FBI when she said that everything she claimed about Bobo *was* true, and denied that she had recanted in her interview with Tyson. But it was the information the authorities shared with us about the audio recording that shifted the focus back to Tyson in what was beginning to look like a Ping-Pong match. Who was telling the truth? Who was not? We had to keep our eyes on the ball as it kept bouncing from one side to the other.

In his first conversation with the FBI more than a year before, in February 2017, Tyson had implied that the Carolyn Bryant Donham quote in question—the recantation, the confession—had been recorded. When he was putting together the materials under the North Carolina grand jury subpoena in September 2017, Tyson said he couldn't locate the other recording, suggesting once again that something important—you know, like that critical quote—had been included there on that recording. The one he couldn't find. In other words, it had been recorded, but was missing. That was the interpretation by the FBI. Tyson claimed that his assistant, Melody Ivins, had lost it. So, of course, the FBI contacted the assistant, Ivins, to verify, and maybe even help the agents track down the lost material. Ivins told them that she "vividly recalled" hearing the quote as she was transcribing the recording. She said that she and Tyson knew it was important. Okay, that was a good start. That meant the quote had to have been recorded somewhere. But where? She remembered that the quote was on the first recorded interview, and that she and Tyson only discovered it was missing when the Tyson book went to press. They tried to find it, she said, and couldn't.

For his part, Tyson said the audio was on a recorder that belonged to Duke University and that it was erased after he returned it. Wiped clean. Then Ivins told the FBI that she believed the quote also was on her laptop. Okay, good. The recorder had been erased, but before Tyson turned it in, he and Ivins had downloaded everything from the recorder to the computer so Ivins could transcribe it all. Everything. But then she revealed that her laptop had crashed and she could no longer access the interview. So now it was gone—no longer on a recorder, and no longer available on a computer file. I felt like I was getting whiplash, and, it seemed, the FBI was getting the runaround. But here's where it got even more interesting. The FBI asked if Ivins would voluntarily lend them the laptop. "Voluntarily," as in they wouldn't have to take a whole lot of time to get another subpoena, which, of course, they could if they had to in the event she refused to do it, voluntarily. She agreed, voluntarily. Now, remember, we're talking about the FBI. They know a thing or two about finding stuff. It's what they do. Right? From airplane crashes to computer crashes. So, after getting the laptop from Ivins, they sent the hard drive to the lab at FBI headquarters in Washington. The recording of the interview was restored. The infamous quote was not. There was nothing there that even came close to Carolyn Bryant Donham saying the words that were published in the Tyson book. It simply was not recorded. When Ivins was told all this, she said, basically, maybe Tyson just *told* her about the quote and she only *thought* she heard it on the recording. The recording with the quote she had remembered "vividly" in the earlier meeting with the FBI, the one she and Tyson had searched for just before the book was published, because they knew it was important and they knew they had it—somewhere.

After Tyson's book was published and publicized, Marsha Bryant said she saw Tyson being interviewed on television about words she claimed she never heard Carolyn Bryant Donham speak. Marsha contacted Tyson. "Why are you lying on Carolyn?" According to the FBI, Tyson replied, "I have tape and notes of all quoted material." As the FBI showed, there was no evidence of a recording of the quote, and there was only one handwritten note about it. That note was scribbled onto a yellow Staples legal pad. We were shown a photo reproduction of that single sheet provided by Tyson. Not an original, mind you, but a reproduction of the original. It read: "That pt wasn't true . . . 50 yrs ago I just don't remember . . . Nothing that boy ever did cd justify what happened to him." This was Tyson's only handwritten notation about Carolyn Bryant Donham's remarks contained with the documents from those two recorded interviews.

According to the FBI, Tyson had never mentioned the handwritten note when he implied in his earlier conversation with agents that Carolyn's quote had been recorded. He certainly didn't mention that this handwritten note was the only record of the comment.

Marsha Bryant told the FBI that her family never formally ended the relationship with Tyson. They just stopped communicating. Marsha and Carolyn took the position that there were no agreements permitting Tyson to do any of the things he wound up doing with the Carolyn Bryant Donham interviews. Not sending it to the archives at a university and definitely not writing a book.

After providing a summary for us, the authorities in Chicago moved several stacks of documents to our side of the conference table. We had been eager to see what these documents might reveal. But now that they were right there in front of us, there was a bit of hesitation for the same reason—because of what they might reveal. Were we ready for that? After the long buildup, the anticipation, the requests, no, the demands, here we were. It wasn't something we said, not a question we uttered aloud. There were no words spoken at all in that moment. But after we each took a deep breath, Marvel, Chris, and I began turning the pages in front of us. One would read a document, and then pass it down to another on our side of the long table. We started with the transcripts of the interviews.

They were not marked or numbered the way court exhibits might be, and the pages within each set were not numbered, either, which apparently was how they had been received. One of the first things we all noticed in one set of the transcripts was that it began with a series of 1s and dashes, just that, 1-1-1-1-1-1 repeated for entire lines, nine entire lines at the top of the first page. Strange, and no one would be able to figure out what that meant.

In what appeared to be the partial transcript of the first interview, Tyson checked his equipment to make sure he was recording. It is referred to in the transcript:

TYSON: "Well, I'm curious."
CAROLYN: "Well, do you want me to tell that first? Want me to go ahead and tell it?"

[Interlude—making sure the equipment works.][1]

We all made a mental note of that. In the conversation that followed that "interlude," there was some discussion about race, mostly Donham's connection to it as she was growing up in the Delta. She told Tyson about her early experience with her father when the two of them attended service in a Black church. She expressed wanting to return to the church because "they were dancing" during the service.

Judging from the back-and-forth of the conversation, it looked like Tyson was trying to humanize her, maybe show that she was not one-dimensional, not a racist. That conclusion was reinforced later when we read her manuscript with his notations urging that kind of personal narrative. It was clear from the conversations documented in the transcripts that Tyson knows something about narrative and about fully developed character, as he tried to help Carolyn do more for her book image than she had done in real life. So it looked like he was trying to bring to life the cardboard cutout of a character Carolyn and her daughter-in-law had produced for their first draft. That twenty- or thirty-page draft. That hardly-even-a-college-term-paper draft. Tyson got her to talk about a Black playmate she had as a youngster. This was not so unusual in the South, when very young Black and White kids might play together for a little while growing up. Of course, that would last only until the White kids got old enough to learn about their place in society—their place and ours. That's when everything would change and they'd start demanding their *former* Black friends call them "sir" or "ma'am." That's when they'd start feeling entitled to call their former Black friends the most degrading form of "Black" just to make sure they made the point, set the social boundaries.

Beyond her childhood associates and her family housekeeper, Donham discussed another connection to Black people she had as she was coming up—through her father. It wasn't in a Black church, either, a Black church where everybody was dancing. Her father worked at Parchman Farm. I recalled what I'd grown up knowing about Parchman. Though it was a prison, formally named the Mississippi State Penitentiary, everybody referred to it as a farm, most likely because that's the way it operated and "farm" probably sounded better than calling it a plantation, which is what it actually was. Parchman was a brutal place meant to continue the enslavement of Black people, who, in addition to working the prison fields, might be leased out to private plantations and worked to death. Literally.[2] After all, inmates had even less value than enslaved people because the inmates were cheaper to replace—just go out and arrest some more Black folks on minor offenses like vagrancy. At Parchman, White men worked as "drivers" on horseback or muleback—very much like the antebellum overseers—and regularly whipped the inmates. Carolyn's father was a driver. But, she said, he never whipped the inmates.

Here she was, talking with Tyson about how much her father was in demand as a driver because of how well he did the work—basically, the work of an overseer. But the work included taking part in brutal "whipping nights." That's what it took to be a good driver. Even though it was expected, it was part of the culture, Carolyn said her father never took part in it. Anything is possible. But knowing what I did about the terror of Parchman—how the threat of being sent there for no good reason drove so many families away from the Delta and made many more of us wary of *any* contact with White folks—I had serious doubts about what Carolyn had said about her father. If this man was good at his job as a driver, and a key part of a driver's job was to take part in the abuse of the inmates—to make a point about White power over the Black body—well, then it might be possible, but not exactly probable that he sat it out and never abused Black inmates.

As I reviewed her words, talking about her father, I understood in a different light all I'd read through the years about how she talked about Roy Bryant, his family, the lynch mob that tortured Bobo. To me, it sounded like a fantasy, a recasting of what her father did, just like her fantasy claims about what happened in the store.

Basically, after childhood, living partly at plantation prisons—Parchman wasn't the only one it seemed—Carolyn said she didn't have much contact with Black people until she married Roy Bryant. His family owned small stores in the Delta that catered to Black sharecroppers, and she said his family's racism was "such a shock" to her with, among other things, use of "the N-word all the time."[3] I remarked to Marvel how this transcript reflected a more polite Carolyn Bryant Donham than a much earlier transcript had revealed. The Carolyn Bryant who testified in that Mississippi courtroom in 1955 freely said "nigger" when describing Bobo in front of the judge, attorneys, and spectators. In the conversation with Tyson, Carolyn described a Milam/Bryant clan whose members were often brutal, violently arguing among themselves, often drinking alcohol first thing upon waking up in the morning. And, of course, all of them carried guns. Though at times during the interview she claimed to be naïve about guns and reluctant ever to use one, she basically justified White people carrying them for the kind of reasons you would expect a family like that to give. "The thing about the pistol," she said, "is that from the time this country was settled, people kept guns for protection."[4] This was a classic colonial perspective on the need for "protection" from a threatening "other." And the "other" was usually anybody who was not White. So these settlers "kept guns" to take whatever they wanted. And dare somebody to say something about it—dare someone to question their right to have it, land, labor, *lives*.

Even though these Milams and Bryants were rowdy and loud and violent, they also were a close-knit family, according to Carolyn. Family meals were like banquets "most every weekend . . ." And after these festive meals, the men would play poker and the women would clean the kitchen. The women knew their place because they were reminded constantly in every way. And those reminders weren't confined to the home. The first time Carolyn was old enough to vote, she found out that J. W. Milam already had cast her vote in her stead.[5]

I watched Marvel's face, doing what she does when she's sickened by something she's seen or heard. According to Carolyn, he'd cast her ballot because the Milams and Bryants were politically connected, at least at the local level. She said that the family was "in close with" Tallahatchie County Sheriff H. C. Strider, a man she described as "like the Godfather in Mississippi." Strider was widely recognized as a plantation owner. And he was widely recognized partly because he was so wide in body. You couldn't miss him, even from up in the sky. He'd arranged the houses for the sharecroppers on his property with letters on their roofs to spell out his name S-T-R-I-D-E-R to be seen by plane pilots. Their relationship with Strider gave the Milam/Bryant family a "lot of clout," leading them to believe "they were a little above everybody else," and could get away with whatever they wanted to do, Carolyn said.[6]

Marsha: "So they were above the law."

Carolyn: "Yeah."[7]

Of course, "above the law" is just another way of saying "lawless." And if the Milam/Bryant men had no respect for women's rights—to the point of casting their votes for them without their say-so—and if they saw that the proper place for their women was in the protected space of the kitchen while the men smoked cigars, drank whiskey, and fought over card games in another room, then you can only imagine how they felt about the place reserved for Black folks in this family's way of life, and the strong belief they held that Black folks had no rights they were bound to respect.

Although Carolyn said she and her husband "were good" to the mostly Black clientele at their store, and "they were good to us," that goodwill obviously only lasted as long as Black folks knew where they stood and stayed there with their heads hung low and their eyes diverted. This family was quick-tempered and just as quick to remind Black folks of their place—in the most violent ways.

One example was during a Christmas-season gathering at the store owned by the family matriarch, Eula Lee Bryant. The large number of family members present included Roy Bryant's sister Mary Louise and her husband, Melvin Campbell, who was known to have a short fuse, according to Carolyn. When a Black man in the store neglected to say "yes, sir" or "no, sir" to Campbell, the fuse was lit. Campbell hit the man over the head with his pistol. All at once, the gun went off and blood spurted out of the man's head. Everybody saw the blood all over the blouse of Mary Louise and panicked. As it turned out, she had not been hit by the bullet. She was not wounded. The blood had splattered from the Black customer, whose head was grazed by the bullet. Everybody started laughing at the incident as the Black customer stood there bleeding. Yeah, that was real funny. I certainly wasn't laughing as I read this; I knew it was lucky the man hadn't been killed. He would have been if he had complained about the incident. According to Carolyn, Roy Bryant stepped forward and washed the man's wound with turpentine, then drove the man away—whether to the man's home or to the hospital was unclear, since Carolyn had told this story a couple of different ways at different points in time. But in every telling, she always made Roy Bryant the compassionate man of the family, her man.

Reading about these incidents and the way these people basically saw no value in Black life just reminded me once again of all the lessons I learned in my first seven years growing up in the Delta—all the things I learned to avoid. Moving to Chicago was a way for my family to assert our value, making a statement that there was a better life for us out there and we deserved it. Reading the stories of this Milam/Bryant clan also made me think of Bobo again. The brutality he experienced at the hands of people who probably didn't even see him as human. How could he have understood what he was walking into during his visit to the Delta? He had lived among people who valued him highly and thought him worthy of status in our society. There is no way he could have grasped the depravity of this group. He was expendable. In fact, Carolyn quoted the Milam/Bryant matriarch, Eula Lee Bryant, as saying that it was too bad Carolyn had left her gun outside the store under the car seat when Bobo whistled at her. If she had it with her in the store, she could have "saved us all a lot of trouble." What she meant was that Carolyn could have just shot Bobo on the spot. As chilling as that comment was, the real point of it was even worse. The family would have avoided the arrest, indictment, and trial of Eula Lee Bryant's sons. Same outcome, just a lot sooner.

Carolyn's attempts to use her voice to rehabilitate her husband continued for years after he took part in one of the most brutal lynchings on record. Roy Bryant is portrayed in Carolyn's words as having "some feelings. He wasn't all hard." Even Marsha Bryant joined in on Carolyn's comments on the transcript, saying that even though Roy Bryant "didn't talk much about the Emmett Till mess," he said enough, she claimed, to indicate a personal feeling that has not really been supported by anything anywhere in the public record. "He told me that if there was one day he could change in his life it would be that day," the day he and others beat and bludgeoned and cut and stomped and blinded Bobo, and ultimately shot him and dumped his body into twenty or thirty feet of river water. "And that is something I would like the public to know about my father-in-law, about Tom's daddy, Carolyn's husband, that he wasn't a horrible ruthless monster."[8]

Donham chimed in. "Oh, and he was good to his customers . . ." giving them credit. She described him as "free-hearted" with "a good work ethic . . . always trying to make a dime." Including off the Emmett Till tragedy, it seems.

"Everybody has made money off this thing but me," Marsha Bryant recalled him saying once. "I have never made a nickel. So if some reporter wants to come talk to me, he better bring a train load of money."

As painful as it was for me to read all this, it would get worse.

Carolyn claimed her husband and brother-in-law brought Bobo to the store for her to identify. And, according to this version of the story, she denied that he was the one they were looking for, but claimed Bobo smiled and said that he was the one.[9] Then her assertions go all over the place. At one point, maybe she urged the men to take Bobo back home and believed that if her husband had been alone, he would have taken him back unharmed. At another point, maybe after Bobo was beaten savagely, her husband wanted to take him to the hospital in Charleston "where our doctor was, and leave him at the emergency room," but the others didn't want to let him have the truck to do it. Marsha seemed to co-sign all this, affirming that Roy Bryant was not bloody or bruised when he finally got home early the next morning after the lynch mob had done its bloody job. She said she believed Roy Bryant would have taken Bobo back home, if he had been alone. He would have taken him to the hospital if he had been allowed.[10]

That's not what Roy Bryant said. Years after Bobo was lynched, the "free-hearted" Roy Bryant freely offered to a friend a story that was much different from the one Carolyn Bryant Donham and Marsha Bryant want us to believe.

The FBI investigation led by Supervisory Special Agent Dale Killinger between 2004 and 2006 uncovered an audio recording by an informant whose name was kept out of the report. In a conversation recorded in 1985 as they were driving around the Delta, the informant asked Bryant if he and J. W. Milam had been drinking the night of Bobo's murder. "Yeah, hell yeah we was drinkin'," Bryant said. He went on to show just how little he cared about getting medical treatment for Bobo. "Well, we done whopped the son of a b——, and I backed out of killin' the motherf—— . . ."

Then, ". . . and we gonna take him to the hospital. But we done whopped the son of a b——. I mean, it was, the, carryin' him to the hospital wouldn't have done him no good (laughs)."

Finally, after considering dumping Bobo's body in the Mississippi River, they "put his ass in the Tallahatchie River."[11]

Carolyn Bryant Donham said she had read that FBI report. Maybe she skipped the part that included the quotes by Roy Bryant. Maybe she just believed we would never see that passage when she and Marsha Bryant talked with Timothy Tyson. For the historical record.

MARSHA BRYANT: "Roy wasn't as harsh as the media has portrayed him."

CAROLYN BRYANT DONHAM: "No, he wasn't. He had lots of good qualities."[12]

Right, like his sense of humor, his ability to laugh in a "freehearted" way about beating a fourteen-year-old kid beyond recognition, beyond all hope that a hospital could ever save him. "Good qualities."

WHAT HAS BEEN missing from the stories about the lynching of Emmett Till has been Carolyn Bryant Donham's story, Tyson suggested in his comments to Carolyn and Marsha. How he could suggest this was beyond me. Who exactly was missing the story of the White woman in lynching narratives? Could a historian—a historian of the American South, no less!—truly believe we missed how "White women have sort of been used" by White men who are protecting "sacred White womanhood . . ." through violence? But in these documents, he seemed to go pretty far in this direction, expressing this in what seemed like sympathy for Carolyn Bryant Donham, as if she was a victim. He told Carolyn that the value of her book would be in filling in that gap, the story that has not been told by the White woman. "We don't have the account, in her own voice, never. And certainly not in this case, but also in general. So that's exciting . . ."

It was hard to tell whether he was expressing his sincere feeling or just playing her. Either way, it was almost impossible to bear. To think that what he felt has been missing from public understanding of horrible racist violence committed against Black men has been the story of how the White women accusers are the real victims—well, that really was hard to stomach. In defaulting to this White male savior mindset, Tyson completely ignored the White woman's power in lynching cases: the power to condemn without conscience. Carolyn's defense of Roy Bryant only seemed to reinforce this conclusion. But we all had to press through each awful word and despicable exchange, keep reading between the lines—reading between the lies—in order to find anything that could result in justice for Bobo.

And if it was for me, and for Chris, I knew this was unbearable for my wife, Marvel. We all found it revolting, especially when reading Carolyn's words when she expressed sympathy for Mamie.

"I don't know how she went through the trial the way she did. I really don't," she said.

Marsha picked up on the point. "I think she was a really brave woman."

"She had to be," said Carolyn, who claimed her "heart went out" to Mamie.[13]

Whatever she might've been saying here, she didn't do what a true heart should have led a compassionate person, a responsible person, an accountable person to do when she still could have made a difference: Tell the truth. Instead, she admittedly was preoccupied.

Not with the horrific loss of another mother's son, but with the potential loss of her own husband, one of the men responsible for such terrible grief. "I was thinking, I had all these things going through my mind, my husband's going to the penitentiary, maybe for life, I have children to support." In other words, it was all about her. Which is why she was overjoyed on hearing the "not guilty" verdict, when the only thought she had was "Oh, thank God . . ."[14]

They had gotten away with it. Her ordeal was over. And she believed she would get on with her life.

"But it wasn't over," Marsha noted.[15]

"It will never be over. That's the thing," Carolyn responded, most likely not reflecting a lifetime of regret for Bobo's death. No, most likely reflecting a lifetime of anxiety that she one day might have to answer for it.

EARLY IN THIS phase of the investigation, back at that first meeting in Oxford, Chris had asked if we would be able to interview Carolyn Bryant Donham and Timothy Tyson ourselves. The authorities had no objection. While they awaited the right time to pursue that, there was another opportunity before us. About halfway through our review of the documents, the authorities excused Marvel and Chris from the conference room at the FBI offices. They wanted me to listen to a portion of one of Tyson's recorded interviews of Carolyn. The only recording they had.

It was chilling. Even after reading all the dialogue in the transcripts. I realized when I started listening that I had never heard her voice before. Not even when I went into the store that fateful August 24, 1955. I mean, I couldn't recall her saying anything that day and never really thought about that until the moment they started that audio recording. So it was chilling to sit there and listen for the first time to a voice I had never really heard, but had heard so much about. As I listened, I thought about how that voice and language might have changed over time. For one thing, now she called Bobo by his name, Emmett, like she really knew him, knew him as a human being. In court back in 1955, on the stand, under oath, in front of a white-hot crowd of White people, that lynch mob of townsfolk and hill country people, back there, back then, Bobo was not human. He was a Black beast. Not Emmett, a just-turned-fourteen-year-old boy. No. In her description, in her sworn testimony, he was a "nigger man." How else had things changed? How had her voice changed? The tone of it. Had it softened? Or hardened? I had no basis for comparison, so I just listened for anything I might recognize. Not the way you recognize some*one* you know. But the way you might recognize some-*thing* you know, something about anybody. I listened for humanity. I listened for remorse. I listened closely. Was hers the voice of compassion, sympathy, empathy? Was there any eagerness, or even willingness to confess? Recant? Apologize? Or was I hearing the voice of indifference? Maybe there had been no change at all. Maybe *we* had changed. Maybe it was that now we were seeing it all more clearly. What once looked like hate really only covered over her desperation—desperation to hold on to something that was slipping away. The desperation of White supremacy and the fear of losing a grip on power. The power to put us in our place by defining us, degrading us, dehumanizing us, and the power to enforce that place through violence. In that normal-sounding voice, maybe she was expressing something even more frightening than what she had said under oath on the stand. Maybe she was using Emmett's name now to conceal the fact that she still saw him as a "nigger man."

Maybe—just maybe—this was the same voice Papa heard that night in the blackness, the dark-as-a-thousand-midnights blackness, that voice in that darkness on that night and so many nights after that one, the voice that haunted and tormented as it kept rising in Papa's memory, rising from the front seat of the truck, from the shadowy figure in that seat in that truck, the "light" voice, the voice of a woman who pronounced the indictment, the verdict, the death sentence when asked if Bobo was the one: "Yes."

11

Alternative Facts

I F IT WAS difficult to hear Carolyn Bryant Donham's recorded voice, and "listen in" (by way of the transcripts) on the conversations that unfolded among Carolyn, her daughter-in-law Marsha Bryant, and Timothy Tyson in the two interviews, it was nothing compared with the painful experience of reading the manuscript Carolyn and Marsha had written. But I read through it during our two days of meetings with the authorities at the FBI Chicago field office, because I had to—not just to answer questions for the FBI and the DOJ and the DA, all the representatives of justice watching over me from across the conference table and gauging my reaction. No, I had to read the manuscript to see if any truth could be found there. Not so much in the words that were written, but rather to find the truth of moments recounted or reworked, truth that possibly could be found *between* those words. What was Carolyn revealing without even knowing that she was? What was she telling me without really meaning to?

Knowing what I do about Bobo's encounter at Bryant's Grocery and Meat Market on August 24, 1955, the "alternative facts" presented in the Donham book read more like passages of a novel—a work of fiction—than any honest account. Carolyn was trying (unsuccessfully) to prove a point in that self-absorbed Southern Gothic. Clearly, she still wanted to humanize Roy Bryant, maybe even absolve him, but she failed to persuade. She wanted to be sympathetic, portray herself as a victim, but she was not convincing. I still knew her as the woman who lied in open court, and to the FBI, and probably even to the husband she was trying to rehabilitate. The words I read looked like all she had learned over the years was how to do a better job of masking, concealing, and hiding from the truth. Nothing I read in her story, as polished by her daughter-in-law Marsha, could amount to clearing the record. None of her words revealed any sense of wrongdoing on her part, no honest reckoning, no atonement for her sins.

She makes that point clear right up front in her preface where she states she had no awareness of what was "planned or carried out concerning Emmett."[1]

With that, she apparently felt free to blame everybody else. She blamed Bobo, of course, basically for being there, in her store. She blamed Papa for not getting Bobo out of town after that fateful moment at her store. She blamed the lynch mob that destroyed Bobo. And she played the helpless victim—weak and powerless—a lot in her manuscript. We can only speculate on whether she played that same helpless role when she said whatever she said to her husband about Bobo and what she claimed had happened in the store.

Speculation aside, we can be sure of one thing: She did not recant in her manuscript. She did not take responsibility. And clearly Timothy Tyson knew that, given that his fingerprints are all over this material, starting with his notes on the first page of the copy we reviewed, a draft dated 2008 and titled *I Am More Than a Wolf Whistle: The Story of Carolyn Bryant Donham as Written by Marsha Bryant*.

Tyson's note to Marsha Bryant confirmed that he had "finished the revisions" and made a number of editorial suggestions. He advised Marsha to urge Carolyn "to tell all she knows about the murder," which he considered to be "a key selling point," though he clarified that he didn't mean that "in a commercial sense."[2] Not sure exactly what other sense that could make. Even if he meant completing the narrative from her perspective—selling her story—that would be a "commercial sense." But there was a whole lot more to consider beyond that.

Tyson also seemed to be nudging her away from her notions about the focus of the book, stressing that "this *is* necessarily a book about race to some extent. Emmett Till died in part because of his race, because what he did was considered a much greater offense due to his race."[3]

That was a point we agreed on. Many of us—family, friends, activists, and scholars—consistently argue that this story *is* about race and *not* "to some extent," but overwhelmingly. It is about race and power and the way they are connected. Bobo died *only* because of his race and the need that the lynch mob had to exert their power over him. It doesn't seem that anyone even would be interested in Carolyn's story otherwise.

Referring to the Emmett Till story as one of this country's "most notorious race stories," Tyson insisted that Carolyn "must tell it all, and never appear to be holding back. She knows more than she is telling here. She can no longer be part of a conspiracy to obscure the truth . . ."[4] As he ended his editor's note to Marsha, Tyson expressed the anxiety we all have felt for so many years. "The truth as Carolyn knows it should not depart this world with her."[5]

We certainly did not want her to "depart this world" without fessing up. But we recognized that the "truth as Carolyn knows it" and the actual truth might have been two different things. The "truth as Carolyn knows it" might only have been what she had convinced herself over the years was the truth—her truth—because she either couldn't own up to her responsibility in setting things in motion, or didn't want to have to account for it all in the legal system. So Marvel, Chris, and I began turning the pages to see what would be revealed, to find out how much of the *absolute* truth she would tell, as opposed to the "truth as Carolyn knows it." The truth we know she knows, the truth we only want everyone else to know now: that we are the ones who have been speaking the truth all along, not her.

The promise that she might tell the truth in the manuscript was made in the opening lines of the "dedication" as Carolyn and Marsha wrote, "Finally, the time was right for me to speak." They went on to say that "peace" came with the "flow" of words.[6] That said, Carolyn never explained what made 2008 the right time. It was just three years after FBI Special Agent Dale Killinger interviewed her—several times—in his search for the truth, the whole truth, nothing but the truth.

Whatever she had expressed in those 2005 FBI interviews—the ones conducted under penalty of felony conviction for giving false statements—apparently, something was left out. Most likely, there had been quite a bit left out. Enough, apparently, to fill a book manuscript. But she didn't offer anything more on that, and Tyson, the researcher, the documentarian, the historian, never asked for an explanation. Never followed up. Never tried to clarify. In the end, I found that the promise Carolyn appeared to make in that dedication was broken. There would be no admission about Bobo, no truth, only more lies. Not that I was surprised.

Carolyn's reasons for working on a book were set out from the start. "This is all about her," Marvel said softly in disbelief, almost to herself, as she read with me, by my side. It certainly was not about race, the compelling issue wrapped around it all, as Tyson had suggested. She paid lip service to the full impact of this story on "the history of the nation,"[7] but she never elaborated on that history and that impact. It is doubtful that she even understands what the lynching of Emmett Till means in our national story. She was more concerned with her own image—making sure people knew she was more than a moment in time, that moment at the store. As her title sets out, she wanted people to know that she was more than that event, that prank by Bobo that set everything in motion. She didn't want that moment to define her. But what else is there about her that really is even worth knowing? Maybe the moment when she told her husband whatever she told him to set him off? Or maybe the moment when she lied in court? Or the moments when she couldn't remember so many things Special Agent Killinger was asking? Which of *those* moments should define her more than the one she wanted us all to forget?

A lot of Carolyn's manuscript presented a rather mundane narrative about her life, including events like eloping with Roy Bryant when she was a teenager, starting a family, setting up their store together, family day at Six Flags, a fender bender, that sort of thing. She never really foreshadowed the horror that was in store. She never revealed the evil that lay deep in the heart and soul of Roy Bryant and J. W. Milam.

For a good part of her story, she focused on the everyday life of a Delta Ozzie and Harriet. More than half of the forty-two chapters are about her personal life, quite apart from the murder of Emmett Till, with such titles as "I Fall in Love," "Our Second Son Is Born," "Our Dream Dies" (which originally was "Our First Business"), "We Own a Store in Money," "My Life Changes," "Move to Mama's," "Carol-ann Is Born," "Back to Louisiana," "We Leave Louisiana," "A New Life," "Move to Brookhaven."

The chapters connected to Bobo only pop up like an interruption in the Bryants' happily-ever-after. And even those still tend to be focused on her: "My Life Changes," "We Are Shuffled" (about how the Milam/Bryant clan moved her around from one family home to another to keep her from being found and giving up any information or, it seems, being arrested), "A Visit to Jail" (gushing over seeing her husband again), and "I Testify" (which doesn't include one single word of the lies she told in the witness chair).

Carolyn's tendency to want to focus on the everyday makes the story all the more horrifying—evil masquerading as normal. Somehow in the balance of her presentation, everything seemed to be given equal weight. So racism is as routine as morning sickness on a bus ride from North Carolina to Mississippi, or a gravel-hauling business, or a son's first haircut, or picking out the "perfect ring" for a later engagement. Or, this too, a teenage boyfriend taking her out to the lynching tree where a frayed rope fragment was still tied to a limb, hanging to the memory of racial atrocities.

She did allow that it made her sick to think about the people who celebrated the lynchings at that site. She referred to this moment as a "rude awakening" to racial hatred and claimed to reject it all.[8] It came across as if she felt she *had* to say something like that; as if such a statement would be expected of any human being who was *not* a central character in a gruesome tragedy. But she was just that. Central to everything that happened to Bobo. Maybe, responding to Tyson's coaching on character development, she included this episode as something of a turning point. She "wanted no part of" that world of violence. But then, if that honestly was a turning point, it seems she turned back around again. She married Roy Bryant, married into a lynch mob. A family of racists, she told Tyson. Yet and still, a family she loved.

Even after the gang torture, disfigurement, murder of Bobo, she was all too happy to visit Roy Bryant in jail awaiting trial for all that, and professed her continued love for him, despite the brutal crime he had committed.[9] There was no expression of anger or remorse, or even a recognition of the horror of it all, just joy at seeing her husband, the killer, freely seated outside his cell.

Roy Bryant and J. W. Milam weren't just allowed to walk freely around the county jailhouse during family visits. They also were permitted to leave jail altogether—no bail, no problem—to have a supper with the family. The very large clan came together on the Sturdivant Plantation in Sunflower County at the home of plantation manager Leslie Milam, the brother of J. W., half brother of Roy Bryant. Carolyn described a mixture of anger and affection when she was surprised to see her husband walk in. There are places in the manuscript where she expressed a few moments of anger, but, again, it always seemed like something she felt she was supposed to express, something expected of her, something she had to do for readers, for the public, to connect and to be more sympathetic. Playing the role. But it never really rose to the level of credibility, let alone absolute truth, since she mostly was supportive of her man, her defender, the murderer. Her manuscript was full of contradictions.

The dinner scene is just one example. She described the dinner conversation as nothing unusual, but it was a time when life was nothing *but* unusual, a time when two family men at the table were facing a murder trial and the threat of a later kidnapping grand jury. It was like they already knew it was over before it even got started. There was laughing and joking and horseplay with the little boys throughout the night, as Carolyn recalled it. The only thing that came close to a discussion of the murder, arrest, indictment, and possible conviction was Roy Bryant talking about the jailer's wife, who cooked supper for them every night. That was it. Nothing about the seriousness of it all, or the consequences—just dinner from the jailer's wife. And Roy Bryant said he liked her cooking. Why would Carolyn assume anyone would care about such a thing? On that night, the night of the festive family feast, the killers were allowed to stay with their folks until two in the morning.

As I read the scene, I could practically hear the laughing and joking Carolyn described in the manuscript, echoes of the laughter and the goodbye hugs and kisses in the lane at the house as two murderers got in the car that would chauffeur them back to Tallahatchie County to sleep in unlocked jail cells with guns that were provided for their protection. Like *they* were the ones in danger. In my mind, the laughter of this family gathering seemed to drift into echoes of the moans, screams, cries for help, pleas for God and for Mama rising from a different gathering of some members of the Milam/Bryant clan just a couple of weeks before this one, as they came together in another family ritual, beating Bobo mercilessly in the shed, the seed barn there just a few hundred yards from the house where they had enjoyed their supper and their fellowship and where the women cleaned up after their men. As was their custom.

It is all so depraved. There was no recognition of Bobo's humanity. Only weeks after the grisly crime, this monstrous group already had moved on. And, as mentioned, Carolyn still considers herself a victim. She complained in the manuscript about being "hounded" by the press on anniversaries of Bobo's lynching. She expressed concern about retaliation against her and her family. And she felt she was a pawn in a political struggle, serving "as a silent symbol of someone else's cause."[10] It was not clear whose cause she was considering in that passage, whether it was the cause of White supremacy or the cause of those who opposed it. But it was yet another piece of her helpless-victim narrative, one that Tyson appeared to feed when he said in one of the interviews that "White women have sort of been used" in such political projects. Carolyn claimed the lawyers told her to smile for the cameras and to hug and kiss her husband. But then she also wrote in her manuscript that she was overjoyed by Roy Bryant's acquittal for murder.[11] So was she acting for the cameras the same way she had acted during her testimony? Or was her on-camera affection for a murderous husband the one honest moment in this whole ordeal? We all have seen the photos of her loving gazes at her husband, as if admiring her hero, and, of course, their hugs and the victory kiss after the verdict. Was this all just a cover story? This just did not seem credible.

She went even further in the manuscript—further than any reasonable reader could stomach. "I always felt like a victim as well as Emmett," she wrote. After once again setting out the unproven claim that Bobo touched her, she made a dreadfully offensive and insensitive observation. "He paid dearly with his life. I paid dearly with an altered life."[12] At this point, as Chris was reading, he dropped his pencil on the table and put his hand to his forehead. We all were disgusted. How could she possibly think there was a comparison to be made? This was beyond tone-deaf. An "altered life" is not a butchered life. It is not a life cut painfully short.

Her sickening comparisons didn't stop there. She also suggested she understood Mamie's suffering, given her own loss of a son who died of complications from a lung disorder. Even though she wrote that she was not comparing her pain of loss to Mamie's, that is exactly what she was doing in even bringing it up, discussing the medical condition that cost her son his life in the same paragraph she expressed a commonality with Mamie in the loss of her son to a pitiless act of racial violence.[13] She expressed no such recognition of Mamie's grievous loss—empathizing with the loss of another mother—at a time when it might have mattered on both legal and personal levels.

Years later, after Mamie's death, Carolyn was writing in her manuscript that she wished she "could have contacted" Mamie. She claimed that she just wanted "to say how sorry I was for all the pain that Roy and others" had caused her.[14] It was one of several half-baked apologies we found in the manuscript, the book she wrote to set the record straight. You see, she didn't contact Mamie. But what would she have said if she *had* contacted her? Sorry for what "Roy and the others" did? What about what *she* did—her own contribution to Mamie's pain, and the pain we all have felt over the years while the truth has been covered up?

Carolyn did give up some interesting points in the manuscript. One is confirmation that J. W. Milam and Bryant did not act alone in what she referred to as an "unjust and gruesome murder." Yes, we know the murder of Emmett Till was "unjust," and photographs of his remains show the "gruesome" nature of his killing. This acknowledgment feels like her attempt to play to the court of public opinion, just as she had done in that Tallahatchie County courtroom back in September 1955—though with opposite effect in a different time in history. To me, it reads like a self-conscious effort to appear more compassionate than she was back in the day. Maybe even to this day. In 1955, the crowd in that Sumner courthouse expected her to talk about the threat of the "Black beast." Today, the public would expect more compassion. It seems she consistently plays to the crowd of the moment.

Carolyn further revealed that the hair-trigger brother-in-law Melvin Campbell—the guy who battered the Black man in the store with his pistol—was the person who put the bullet in Bobo's head. That wasn't newsworthy; it was included in the 2006 FBI report. And, of course, we'd known from the 1955 testimony of the late Willie Reed that there was a group of men involved in Bobo's beating at the Sturdivant Plantation barn in Sunflower County near Drew. But Willie was an eighteen-year-old Black sharecropper, and his testimony had been discounted by the White defense lawyers and jurors. Willie

Reed also had been largely ignored by so many journalists who for years had taken the William Bradford Huie magazine article as the official story on the lynching of Emmett Till—a murder Huie told everyone was committed only by J. W. Milam and Roy Bryant. How ironic that the truth-tellers here were assumed to be the liars and the liars were assumed to be telling the truth, only because of their race.

But Carolyn's continued protection of Roy Bryant in her writings suggests she really didn't care about Bobo or Mamie or anybody but herself, her husband, their children. She wrote that Roy Bryant and J. W. Milam brought Bobo to the store to have her identify him. She claimed that she refused to do that, that she denied he was the one, even though she begged them to take him back to Papa's house, which is kind of an identification. She claimed that Roy Bryant would have taken Bobo back home if the others had let him. And despite his own words to the contrary, she still claimed that Roy Bryant would have taken Bobo to the hospital after the beating started if the others had let him.

She clearly tried to paint a sympathetic picture of Roy Bryant, as Marsha Bryant said in one of the Tyson interviews, to make sure the public would believe "that he wasn't a horrible ruthless monster." Carolyn suggested he would have taken back the day he participated in the lynching of Emmett Till, if only he could. "It affected him all his life." Later, even after their marriage had dissolved, she wrote, she still had a strong emotional reaction to Roy Bryant's death from cancer in September 1996. She had visited him in the hospital and described how painful it was to see him on his deathbed. She wanted to forgive him for the wrongs he committed and to ask his forgiveness. Following Roy's death, Carolyn was grateful that he was able to see his children before he died.[15]

If only Mamie had been blessed with the vision of her own son and her own grandchildren before she died in January 2003.

In the end, Carolyn's non-apology apologies left me cold. In the preface, she wrote that she was sorry for Bobo's "tragic and uncalled for" death. It is passive—pretty much the way her life appears to have been lived. "I was the excuse for murder and lies to defend that murder."[16]

In fact, it's the words she left out that speak the loudest. She never took responsibility, which, to me, means she can't really be sorry. In all her giddy discussion about the moments of everyday life she went on to enjoy with her hardhearted, homicidal husband, she never once admitted what Timothy Tyson wrote that she admitted, the statement he reinforced in numerous interviews about his book: "That part's not true." She did take one more stab at an apology, one more shot at the very end of her manuscript after summarizing once again what Professor Davis Houck has identified as the "justification defense" for the lynching of Emmett Till. Even while appearing to condemn the murder, she wrote that Bobo "came in our store and put his hands on me with no provocation" before adding that he should not "have been killed for doing that." And then, "I am truly sorry for the pain his family was caused."[17] Not the way that sentence should have been written. Not "Sorry for the pain I caused his family."

In effect, it was no apology at all. It was no recantation. It was a restatement of her lie.

As we approached the end of our two days going through the investigation files at the FBI Chicago field office, I wanted to share something with the authorities—something personal, something happy to push aside all the pain we had been focusing on. I wanted them to see our neighborhood, our community, our home: Summit, the place we always called Argo. The place where Bobo and I had the most special time together as boys. Even with all the details these officials had combed through, all the records they had reviewed, all the testimony they had collected, this was a part of the story they needed to experience in order to know what we once had with Bobo in our lives. They wanted this experience, and I was very happy to make it possible for them.

I never grow tired of playing tour guide, as I often do in the Mississippi Delta with people who take part in the programs of Delta State or the Mississippi Center for Justice, and as I do in a heartbeat when people visit Summit. No doubt, these two spaces provide con-

trasting scenes and experiences and narratives. There is the suste-
nance of life in Summit and the tragic end of it in Mississippi. As I
pointed out the places in Summit where Bobo, the neighborhood
boys, and I would play war games, the once-upon-a-time field that
now is the parking lot for the Emmett Till Memorial Center, and the
school we once attended, and the vacant lot where Bobo's house once
stood next to the one where my family once lived, something occurred
to me. In making our way along this path around corners and down
streets as well as back in time, I realized why I have stayed in Summit
most of my life. Yes, I pastor a church in this community, for some a
central part of this community and its history, a place where once
upon a time, we didn't even lock the doors to our homes, never locked
our car doors either, and only rolled up the car windows in the summer when it looked like rain. We might wake up to find homeless
people asleep across the seats of those cars. But that was all right.
This was just that kind of welcoming place. Yes, my wife and I helped
to strengthen the community through development. Yes, this place
always will feel like home to me because it always will be home to
me. But more than all of these things, I realize that in reliving long-
ago experiences with Bobo for visitors I have found an everlasting
comfort in this place, a place once called Argo—a place that exists
now only in the memories of a carefree boyhood.

These are the memories I have wanted to hold on to forever with
the hope that one day they just might overtake the ones I desperately
have wanted to lose.

WITHIN A FEW days of the two-day review session with the government authorities in August 2018, we were back at it again. In our own
private meeting, Marvel, Chris, and I gathered to talk more about our
takeaway from the documents we read. It was striking to see how
much Carolyn Bryant Donham's stories had grown over the years.
Especially the ones about her brief encounter with Bobo. They hadn't
grown in the direction of recalling facts and correcting the record.
Instead, they had moved deeper into embellishing her story, as if she

had been rehearsing it and rewriting it and refining it. Her claims about interacting with Bobo in the store already were revolting back when she originally told them in 1955. We never imagined they could get worse than the lies she had sworn to in court. They did.

In her manuscript, for the first time ever, Carolyn used the word "molest" to describe the scene. She "thought" Bobo "was going to molest me or worse. I was afraid for myself, and my babies." But it got worse still because of Tyson's edit. According to the tracked change on this passage, he substituted the word "feared" for the word "thought," as if he and Carolyn were playing a game of one-upmanship to see who could do the most to heighten the imaginary threat posed by a fourteen-year-old kid. She went on to claim that Bobo "grinned at me as I jerked my hand free from his . . ." which painted him as even more sinister—the Black beast—than she ever had before.[18]

None of those words appeared in her September 2, 1955, statement, given to Sidney Carlton, one of the five lawyers who eventually would defend J. W. Milam and Roy Bryant. That was just five days after Bobo was taken. According to Carlton's notes summarized in the *Mississippi Clarion-Ledger*, a "boy" with a "Northern brogue" came into the store, went to the candy counter, made his selection, and, when she held out her hand for the money, "he grabbed my hand & said how about a date and I walked away from him and he said, 'What's the matter Baby can't you take it?'" She claimed Bobo said "Goodbye," and left with another boy, then whistled when she went outside to get her gun. She told Carlton, "I reported the incident to my husband when he came in about 4:30 A.M. Friday."[19]

None of those words appeared in her testimony weeks later. As she sat in the witness chair, under oath, she told Carlton on direct examination that it was a "nigger man," not a boy she encountered in the store. She repeated her claim that he grabbed her hand, but in this version, he held it tightly and it was with "much difficulty" that she freed herself. As she tried to get away, she said he grabbed her around the waist and he told her she "needn't be afraid," that he had sex with White girls before, suggesting a word for sex that she couldn't repeat in court. (She did spell it out in her book, though.) In court, she also was asked whether Bobo had "any speech defect." She said no. When asked whether she had any trouble understanding him, she said no.[20] In her manuscript, she wrote that she didn't recall whether Bobo "stuttered or stammered," but did recall that he "spoke in a clear voice" as if she was answering a question that hadn't been asked.[21]

By the time the manuscript was written, she must have learned that Bobo had such a pronounced stutter that it not only could be hard to understand him when he spoke at times, but that he couldn't have said all the things she said he did. It would have been next to impossible for him to get all those words out. There is no way she wouldn't have noticed that. Everybody else did.

Distressed as we were by Carolyn's insistence on keeping the lie alive—and even compounding it with layers of new lies—we were even more upset by Tyson's comments and edits. Not only did he change the word "thought" to "feared," but his notes seemed to encourage her to play to racial narratives, to flesh out what she saw as the threatening circumstances she lived under, to get her to restate the reasons White men in her town gave for always wanting to know where their women were. "This does not seem irrelevant to what happens," he wrote.[22] And he seems to have accepted her claims about the encounter in the store, perhaps even suggesting that White fear of a Black threat was relevant to her story.

It was very distressing to us. We kept talking about the question that was too obvious to ignore. Why would Tyson help her establish credibility, give a sense of reasonableness to her claims, if he really believed she had recanted in their very first interview? We kept coming up empty—unless he had deliberately misinterpreted something. He seemed to be coaxing her into reinforcing the opposite of what he claimed to have taken from their interview. He had written to Marsha about a "selling point" for Carolyn's book, so he was aware of the market value of a revelation. If it had happened the way he said it did and she just blurted out her recantation, it seemed he was taking away her chance to put that in her book (keeping it for his own book). Then again, maybe it never happened in the first place.

It was not as if he didn't feel he should correct or guide or even change the references in the manuscript. He did it in some cases, like the repeated references to Roy Bryant. We talked about his notes in the manuscript, notes about how she seemed to be "making excuses" for her husband's bad behavior in their marriage as well as his role in a murder "he didn't mean to have happen. The reader is going to be unsympathetic," Tyson wrote.[23]

"The account that we get in this book seems to be still protecting people. I don't think that is the right posture and readers surely will have no sympathy for it," he wrote, adding that Carolyn seemed to be "bending over backwards to diminish Roy's role" in Bobo's death.

"The reader will have a hard time swallowing this. There seems to be more sympathy for Roy than for Emmett and Mamie, and so it comes off badly."[24]

To his credit, Tyson raised questions in a number of places throughout the manuscript where Carolyn was inconsistent. In the chapter titled "I Testify," there are barely more than three hundred words—the entire chapter—and she never even recounted her testimony. The entire four paragraphs in this chapter focused pretty much on how nervous she was. Tyson suggested that she return to the trial transcript.[25] Surely twenty pages of her testimony and lawyer arguments could yield something worth writing about.

Likewise, he did offer comments on one of the most offensive passages of the book—where she claimed that she told Milam and Bryant that Bobo wasn't the person and then pleaded with them to return him to where they found him. And it went on like that for a couple of paragraphs in which she claimed to be "terrified for his safety," as her heart raced and her legs weakened.[26]

Tyson wrote that this was "just not credible . . . The boy ended up dead. This kind of special pleading will make many readers suspicious of the entire book."[27]

To say the least.

Worse still—and here is where it really gets outrageous—was what she wrote about the reaction to it all by Bobo, who was not harmed, she claimed. "To my utter disbelief, the young man flashed me a strange smile and said, 'Yes, it was me,'" and he didn't seem "scared in the least,"[28] an echo of the lies William Bradford Huie wrote in his January 24, 1956, *Look* magazine article. That was pretty much the way J. W. Milam described Bobo just before he said he shot him.

Tyson found these passages about Bobo in Donham's book "implausible," in that it made it look like Bobo was "committing suicide"[29] by being so antagonistic, so belligerent, so cocky. It was interesting that Tyson would raise this issue with Carolyn and Marsha in his comments on the manuscript, since he failed to raise the issue with the Huie characterization when writing his own book about ten years later. Since he had told Carolyn and Marsha in one of their interviews that he "wouldn't trust William Bradford Huie as far as I could throw him," calling the writer "sort of a yarn-spinner,"[30] Tyson could have clarified for his readers his critique of Huie's account, which he interpreted as Bobo "virtually committ[ing] suicide" by "taunting" J. W. Milam and Roy Bryant at the riverside.[31] Even a brief review of the record produced by the FBI back in 2006 would show that Emmett Till was in no condition to say or do the things Huie wrote that he said and did at the river. He already was dead when his murderers and their accomplices carried him to that place. It would seem that if Tyson was a careful historian, truly committed to the full truth of this story, he would have intentionally clarified this point, too.

There was yet another reason for Tyson to recognize Carolyn's inconsistency. In the notes he took of his September 2, 1955, conversation with Carolyn, defense attorney Carlton wrote that she said: "Negro was scared but hadn't been harmed. He didn't say anything."[32] If he was "scared" and "didn't say anything," then how was Bobo defiant? And why didn't Tyson point this out in his story, since he had gotten the Carlton notes from reporter Jerry Mitchell? So many unanswered questions. So many discrepancies.

Tyson submitted the Carolyn Bryant Donham–Marsha Bryant

manuscript to the Southern Collection at the Chapel Hill library to be kept under wraps until 2038 when future researchers would have access. The record of the archive does not reveal any explanatory note by Tyson, clarifying that there was a discrepancy between what she was writing and what she had told him. So, again, if he believed she had recanted, why would he allow future scholars, journalists, and biographers to be misled by putting his stamp of approval on the documents archived in his name?

IN A WAY, most of what Carolyn and her daughter-in-law wrote about Emmett Till failed to check out, just based on how her story seemed to grow, according to the review by the FBI. As discussed earlier, in 2017 Supervisory Special Agent Dale Killinger was brought in to review the manuscript. Since he led the FBI investigation between 2004 and 2006, he was able to spot the contradictions between what Carolyn was claiming in her manuscript and what she had told him in several interviews. In quite a few cases in his December 22, 2017, report after reviewing and reprinting passages in the manuscript, Killinger wrote in an understated FBI just-the-facts-ma'am kind of way: "The statement above differs from the statements made by DONHAM in the past in that it is the most complete recounting of the events DONHAM has made regarding what took place in Bryant's Grocery and Meat Market on August 24, 1955."[33]

In one example, the manuscript described in great detail an incident in the store on Saturday, August 27, 1955, when Roy Bryant confronted a Black teenager with his mother questioning the boy and demanding that the boy say "Yes, Sir" or "No, Sir." Carolyn wrote that she insisted to her husband that that boy was not the one.[34]

As she tells it, this was her first indication that Roy must have heard something. The implication, of course, is that he didn't hear it from her.[35]

In an October 2, 2005, interview, Agent Killinger asked her about that incident.

"I vaguely, remember something happening in the store with the young black boy and, and his mother, but I don't remember the details of it," she said then.[36]

Again, on October 19, 2005, Agent Killinger followed up with her about the incident.

"Seem like it was like mid-afternoon or something like that," she said then. "And I, I don't know what happened. I can't remember what was said or what, uh, anything, I just remember that they did come in."[37]

It goes on like that. But the really distressing lie is the one about J. W. Milam and Roy Bryant bringing Bobo back to the store to have Carolyn identify him when, to her "utter disbelief," Bobo gave her a sinister smile and said he was the one.[38] In the October 19, 2005, interview with Agent Killinger, Carolyn said: "I think they probably asked me who, if that was him and I probably told 'em no. I believe."[39]

Later in that interview:

KILLINGER: "Did the boy say anything?"
DONHAM: "I think he did say something, but I can't remember."[40]

Again, in her September 2, 1955, interview with attorney Sidney Carlton, she recalled that Bobo didn't speak. With Special Agent Killinger in 2005, he might have said something. In her manuscript just a couple of years after talking with Killinger, she remembered Bobo speaking defiantly.

As Marvel pointed out during our review, Carolyn Bryant Donham seemed to remember quite a bit in writing a book beginning in 2006 after forgetting so much during her interviews with the FBI ending in 2005.

Because of his editorial guidance, his comments and tracked changes, it would seem that Timothy Tyson has to take responsibility, too, for what is written in the Carolyn Bryant Donham manuscript, even the things he let slide. The authorities left Chicago committed to determining whether Tyson actually did lose the most important documentation of his career—a recording or some other reliable or credible evidence that Carolyn recanted—or whether there was some other explanation. We looked forward to learning whether he would take responsibility for the lies in the manuscript, or whether he'd simply wanted to exploit them to sell his book.

CAROLYN BRYANT DONHAM began her manuscript noting that she finally was able to tell her story, "to illuminate my small part in this tragedy" for "the first time in more than fifty years..."[41] A "small part"? Seriously? And what did she tell us that was new? The stories about Bobo? If "new" means exaggerated, or embellished, or excessive, or just plain lying, then maybe. There were new lies to be sure, built on the foundation of old lies. Things that just didn't add up.

As for the personal glimpses of a killer's family life, the only reason we might care is if that family life shed light on the only thing that ever gave it meaning. An atrocity. Carolyn wrote that the lynching of Emmett Till changed "both my life and my country forever."[42] Not Bobo's country, mind you, not even our country, but hers. That says a lot, as far as I'm concerned—a lot about how self-absorbed she appears to be, how incapable of critical self-examination. Even while she claimed ownership of *her* country, she never once expressed an understanding of just what that country stands for and how much the lynching of Emmett Till actually did change things—the loss of all that could be contributed by such a bright light, such an energetic and industrious kid. For Carolyn's part, it is as if she has only heard the words about change and repeated them without knowing the real meaning. Without really even trying to understand. They sound good. They reverberate. But only the way empty words can sound when they echo.

In setting us up for her story, Carolyn stated the obvious. Understated it, really. Grossly understated it. "His death was tragic and uncalled for beyond all doubt. For that, I am truly sorry. If it had been within my power to change his fate, I would have done so."[43] Actually, there was something she could have done back then. If she really is sorry, then there is something she still could have done most recently. Something within her power.

Tell the truth.

12

Monuments, Memorials, Memories

ONE OF THE cruel things White people do to Black people is to give us hope—promising what we never are allowed to obtain. If we just believe in a system of merit and fair play, a system that they designed to benefit them, they promise social progress. If we ignore the setbacks, the disappointments along the way, if we just wait our turn, we won't get left behind again by others who seem never to have to wait. They promise equal justice if we ignore the imbalance, that thumb on the scale that winds up tipping toward racial profiling and mass incarceration and, yes, unresolved hate crimes. Like the lynching of Emmett Till. Be patient, remain hopeful, they tell us, and for centuries, we have. We have been blessed and cursed by hope. Blessed because it propels our determined move forward. Cursed because that forward march seems endless, fulfillment too often just one step beyond our exhaustion. And because of that, just as often, hope is all we are allowed to have as we are left on the side of the road, blistered by the steps we have taken.

Even as we saw the evidence of Timothy Tyson's revelation—the hope for resolution—begin to evaporate during our two days reviewing Carolyn Bryant Donham's manuscript with federal and Mississippi state authorities in Chicago, we held on to our hope that something still would come of the effort to find that proof. The people we were working with at ground level—the FBI, the DOJ, the DA—impressed us with their commitment to reaching a just outcome. That never was questioned. But we were not so sure what the people at the top—the political people like Attorney General Jeff Sessions and, yes, even the president, Donald Trump himself, the people with the ultimate power over this investigation—would do to serve their own ends, a political agenda that encouraged and exploited racial division. The Trump administration was stained by racist claims practically right out of the gate, following the president's apparent support of the White supremacists at the Charlottesville "Unite the Right" confrontation. And Sessions? Civil rights groups had opposed his nomination as attorney general, even citing a nine-page letter written in 1986 by the late Coretta Scott King arguing against his rise to the federal bench at that time. His "reprehensible conduct" on voting rights, she wrote, showed that Sessions lacked "the temperament, fairness and judgment to be a federal judge," leaving so many to challenge his ability to be the country's chief law enforcement officer now as attorney general.

So, what would this administration do to this case if the top political people asserted their power to be the final authority on releasing a record and a recommendation for the State of Mississippi to indict Carolyn Bryant Donham? Would they sympathize with the White woman, pick up on her lie about Bobo, and reinforce the myth about Black male sexual violence? Would they seek political points, playing to White supremacists—once again—by sending a signal that the racists had a friend in, well, in the *White* House, as well as the Department of Justice? Would they perpetuate the myth of Emmett Till as a symbol of Black threat?

We wanted to believe our contacts—the government agents and lawyers working the case—would be able to keep their promises to us: to keep us in the loop about new developments, inform us before anything went public, and prevent others from taking control of the narrative. And, despite our suspicions, we also wanted to believe that the powers would not choose to sweep under the rug all things pertaining to the investigation. We didn't want to consider the possibility—the risk—that our promise to quietly wait for justice might be seen as complicity in their ultimate cover-up. The political climate of this period added a whole new level of stress for our family. But even before we could sort it all, a breaking news story seemed to confirm our worst fears.

On August 21, 2018, just one week after we met with the officials in the FBI Chicago Field Office, a story appeared in the *Mississippi Clarion-Ledger* under the headline: "Bombshell Quote Missing from Emmett Till Tape. So Did Carolyn Bryant Donham Really Recant?"[1] The story was written by Jerry Mitchell, the award-winning investigative reporter for the *Clarion-Ledger* who had spent years reporting on Emmett Till and other civil rights cases. He had talked with me a few times, and we had a very friendly relationship. This latest story came as a shock to us, as well as to the public, but for different reasons. Before this report, the public really had no idea of what had just been revealed to us at the FBI Chicago field office: the lack of a recording of Carolyn's quote; the lack of even a transcript of a recorded quote; the lack of a believable explanation as to why there was no recording, why there was no transcript. So the only thing widely known was that Timothy Tyson had written a book that included that quote, that recantation, that confession. But what had been revealed to us (and not to the public) was supposed to have been kept confidential, away from public disclosure until the investigation was completed. So we were shocked to think that someone possibly had breached all that and leaked the information. But what would the purpose have been? And what did it indicate about how much we should rely on anything the government promised us? We jumped on it right away.

Chris contacted Special Agent Henry. While the timing was curious, Henry assured that the information had not come from the FBI, DOJ, or the Mississippi DA. As we talked it through, another scenario began to emerge: Instead of a leak from an investigator, this information may have been revealed by one of the sources of the investigation itself.

Faith, belief in the possibility of things unseen, like justice, was at the core of our family and we became members of the Argo Temple Church of God in Christ immediately after arriving in Argo in 1947. Pictured: Wheeler, at age 12, is at the center of the congregation on the church steps. *Wheeler and Marvel Parker Collection*

We always have been a close-knit family. My mother, Hallie, and father, Wheeler Sr., had six children. Pictured: Wheeler; brothers William and Milton; and father, Wheeler, Sr. *Wheeler and Marvel Parker Collection*

I met my cousin Bobo after we moved to Argo, when he was five going on six and I was seven going on eight. From that moment in 1947, we were inseparable, until the night he was taken from us. Pictured: Emmett, Wheeler, Joe B. Williams. *Wheeler and Marvel Parker Collection*

After his family moved to Argo, following the murder trial, my little twelve-year-old uncle, Simeon, became my part-time responsibility. As his babysitter, I even had to discipline Simmie when he got out of line. *Wheeler and Marvel Parker Collection*

It was 1962 and I got drafted. I would see another face of racism in the military and the aftermath of what it had done to a whole society when I served in Germany. *Wheeler and Marvel Parker Collection*

Mamie Till-Mobley always wanted the truth to be told about the death of her son—what it meant, what it still means. She had passed the baton to Uncle Simmie and me. *Wheeler and Marvel Parker Collection*

Marvel and I had no idea what lay ahead of us in March 2017, when we traveled to Oxford, Mississippi, to meet with the FBI and other government officials. *Christopher Benson*

Special Agent Walter Henry met us at the hotel the night before our big meeting in Oxford and began to prepare us for the twists and turns we were about to experience in the investigation. Pictured, from left: Wheeler, FBI Special Agent Walter Henry. *Christopher Benson*

On the steps of the Ethridge Professional Building, the headquarters of the U.S. attorney for the Northern District of Mississippi, we stood at the threshold of a nearly four-year journey of revelations. *Christopher Benson*

The Tallahatchie River, as seen from the Tallahatchie Bridge, the one immortalized by singer Bobbie Gentry. Her song "Ode to Billie Joe" reportedly was inspired in part by the Emmett Till story. Pictured, from left: Wheeler, Christopher Benson. *Christopher Benson*

As we entered and left the courthouse during the two-day trial reenactment in April 2017, we were confronted by that Confederate statue that still stands guard over the Summit town square and stands as a reminder of the struggle for justice that played out inside. *Christopher Benson*

I never grow tired of playing tour guide, as I often do in the Mississippi Delta with people who take part in the programs of Delta State or the Mississippi Center for Justice. Pictured, from left: attorney Kimberly Merchant, Wheeler, Marvel. *Christopher Benson*

A sign of the times, as people keep punctuating historical markers with bullets, trying to kill the story of Emmett Till so many years after he was lynched. We made sure the complete story—even the attempts to silence it—would be told as an exhibition in the Smithsonian's National Museum of American History. *Wheeler and Marvel Parker Collection*

In reliving long-ago experiences with Bobo for visitors, I have found an everlasting comfort in this place, a place once called Argo—a place that exists now only in the memories of a carefree boyhood. Pictured, from left: Chris Benson, Wheeler. *Christopher Benson*

It was a special day to give praise. Over the course of this Sunday service, I began to see this recognition of my life as an example of what life can be, what it should mean. *Wheeler and Marvel Parker Collection*

Chris joined with Marvel, Ollie, and Perri Irmer, president of the DuSable Museum of African American History, to produce a special commemorative program in the museum's theater on what would have been the eightieth birthday of Emmett Till. *Courtesy of Perri Irmer*

There was a Sunday church service at Argo Temple in honor of what would have been Bobo's eightieth birthday, with a dedication of a plaque, a historical marker, on the residential lot where Mamie and Bobo's original home once stood across the street from the church. *Constantinos Isaias*

It was great to see Joe B. Williams again at the dedication and commemoration of Bobo's eightieth. He is our childhood friend, the one seated on the crossbar of my bicycle in the cover photograph. *Constantinos Isaias*

The meeting finally was set. And the day of revelation, the day of reckoning, finally had come: December 6, 2021. Pictured, front row, from left: Kristen Clarke, Assistant Attorney General for Civil Rights; Thelma Wright Edwards; Dr. Marvel Parker; Annie Wright (Simmie's wife); Ollie Gordon; Barbara Kay Bosserman, DOJ Deputy Chief of the Cold Case Unit. Second row, from left: Rev. Wheeler Parker, Jr.; Dewayne Richardson, District Attorney for the Fourth Circuit Court of Mississippi; Chris Benson; Clay Joyner, acting U.S. Attorney, Northern District of Mississippi; Jerrica Watson, Victim Specialist, Department of Justice; and Walter Henry, former Special Agent, FBI. *Courtesy of the Office of the Assistant Attorney General for Civil Rights, U.S. Department of Justice*

"Today is a day we'll never forget," I said at the news conference we held to announce the Department of Justice decision to close the case. "Officially, the Emmett Till case has been closed after sixty-six years." *Tyler LaRiviere, Chicago Sun-Times, Associated Press*

"I'm not surprised, but my heart is broken," my Aunt Thelma Wright Edwards said at the news conference at Northwestern University. She expressed what we all were feeling at the time. *Tyler LaRiviere, Chicago Sun-Times, Associate Press*

ABC producer Fatima Curry had waited patiently for nearly two years to lock up the documentary *Let the World See*, which would air with the *Women of the Movement* series. She had helped to bring us into conversation with producers Aaron Kaplan (Kapital Entertainment), Jay Brown (Jay-Z's Roc Nation), and James Lassiter (Will Smith's Overbrook Entertainment). Finally, we would be able to tell the story to the widest possible audience. No longer on standby, ready to roll. *Christopher Benson*

Christopher Benson

At the Hollywood premiere of the *Women of the Movement* TV series with actors. Pictured, from left: Wheeler; Ollie Gordon; Julia McDermott (Carolyn Bryant); Ray Fisher (Gene Mobley); Tonya Perkins (Alma); Marvel; Cedric Joe (Emmett); Tony Award winner Adrienne Warren (Mamie); Carter Jenkins (Roy Bryant); Chris Coy (J. W. Milam); and showrunner Marissa Jo Cerar (*The Handmaid's Tale*). *Wheeler and Marvel Parker Collection*

Actor Joshua Caleb Johnson, who portrayed me at age sixteen, actually carried me back in time, as I once again rode the train down to Mississippi with Bobo, and we hung out together in Greenwood earlier the night that ended in terror. *Wheeler and Marvel Parker Collection*

With the Rose Garden signing of the Emmett Till Antilynching Act, the federal government has made sure that Bobo's name will continue to be invoked whenever justice is served in racial hate crimes, making a vital national statement. *White House*

THE WHITE HOUSE
WASHINGTON

April 14, 2022

The Reverend Wheeler Parker Jr.
Summit, Illinois

Dear Reverend Parker,

I was honored to speak with you at the White House when I signed the Emmett Till Antilynching Act into law. Thank you for everything you and your family have done to fight for justice. Your ability to turn pain into purpose has inspired so many, including me, and I am grateful for your continuing efforts to advocate for what is right and good.

This law not only honors your beloved cousin Emmett—it also honors every other victim of racial hatred in our Nation's history. We still have a lot of work to do, but I will never give up. I know you won't either. God bless you.

Sincerely,

Wheeler and Marvel Parker Collection

A major part of our work in moving forward is establishing a non-contiguous national historical park in honor of Emmett Till and Mamie Till-Mobley in Mississippi and Chicago, where Robert's Temple Church of God in Christ will become a central landmark in the national honor. We accompanied Secretary of the Interior Deb Haaland during meetings in the Mississippi Delta on a tour of significant sites along the Emmett Till trail, and here at the Department of the Interior. She was quite moved and very supportive. *Wheeler and Marvel Parker Collection*

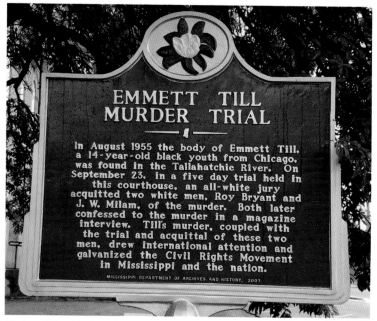

Wheeler and Marvel Parker Collection

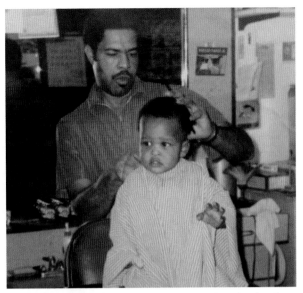

The barbershop business was so successful that even when the shop burned down shortly after Marvel and I got engaged, my customers stuck with me as I continued cutting hair in my parents' basement. Most likely, that is because, like a town square, the barbershop is a center of the Black community, especially in a community like Argo, "Little Mississippi." *Lynn Davis*

Much of what I am, I owe to the strong role models in my family. My father, Wheeler Parker, Sr., moved his family out of Mississippi for a better life in the Promised Land. And his brothers, my Uncle Elbert Parker and Uncle William Parker, helped me escape Mississippi the day after Bobo was taken. *Wheeler and Marvel Parker Collection*

Finally, on August 4, 2022, we would have our day in court, so to speak. The district attorney would tell the story to the Leflore County grand jury in Greenwood. *Wheeler and Marvel Parker Collection*

It was over. We had done all we could do to seek justice and Carolyn Bryant Donham's fate would be in the hands of the grand jury. *Wheeler and Marvel Parker Collection*

Much of the credit for the success of my life and my life's work is due to my wife of more than fifty-five years, Dr. Marvel Parker. *Wheeler and Marvel Parker Collection*

Jerry Mitchell's *Clarion-Ledger* article featured direct quotes from both Marsha Bryant, Carolyn's daughter-in-law, and Timothy Tyson. Marsha told Jerry that she was present during the two recorded interviews with Tyson, as we already had learned, and that Carolyn "never recanted."[2] For his part, Tyson admitted what we and the FBI, DOJ, and DA had only speculated based on the evidence we saw, or all that we never saw. The quote Tyson published never had been recorded. We were stunned by this frank admission, made to a reporter at that. "It is true that that part is not on tape because I was setting up the tape recorder," Tyson told Jerry Mitchell.[3] It was outrageous. Even if that wound up being the truth, "setting up the tape recorder" was not what he had told the FBI. He had told the authorities that he grabbed his legal pad to note the words Carolyn was speaking *just in case* the recorder failed him—the recorder that was supposed to be recording, not the recorder that had not been turned on yet. Beyond that, in explaining to the FBI, Tyson had suggested not only that the recorded *quote* was lost, but that the entire *recording* was lost. His assistant said pretty much the same thing—that they had heard the quote but the recorder was erased and the computer with the downloaded interview had crashed. Now the story was that the recording never even existed and the only proof of anything Carolyn might have said was set out in Tyson's handwritten notes. Actually, the only thing anybody saw was a *photo* or *photocopy* of handwritten notes—not the original notes—and every pen mark on that copy was beginning to look contrived, concocted, and just a little too convenient. As a result, it was more than a little concerning.

Still, we were not ready to reach a conclusion—about the words or the way this whole thing went public. In any event, we were convinced that nothing had leaked from the government, and that gave us a little bit of peace.

In the *Clarion-Ledger* story, Marsha repeated to Jerry some of what we already had gotten from the FBI. Her family had not agreed to send Carolyn's manuscript to the UNC archives, as Tyson had told investigators, nor were they aware of Tyson's plan to write his own book using material from their interviews and draft manuscript. She also said Tyson had been her editor in writing Carolyn's book. Tyson had denied this in his published interview with Jerry, claiming that he had only given "garden-variety" advice on getting published. Tyson also claimed he had mentioned to Marsha and Carolyn that he planned to write a book.[4]

It was a hot mess, but it left us with even more questions for Timothy Tyson—questions the FBI was determined to have answered, although there was one obstacle, created years prior by Eric Holder, President Barack Obama's attorney general. Holder had issued an internal memorandum designed to protect journalists from harassment by FBI investigators. That memo set limitations on interrogating journalists about their reporting and their sources of information, a good thing on one level.[5] But in our case, it looked like Special Agent Henry might need special permission to continue to interview Tyson about anything beyond the materials Tyson already had produced under the subpoena. And that meant setting everything out for the political people at the top back in Washington, calling their attention to the investigation that so far seemed to be flying below their radar.

Before we even had a chance to sort that issue, a new one came up based on yet another story in the *Mississippi Clarion-Ledger*. This one also was written by Jerry Mitchell and was published on August 27, just six days after the first and one day before the sixty-third anniversary of Bobo's lynching. This piece was titled "Emmett Till Mystery: Who Is the White Girl in His Photo?"[6] The story presented seventy-six-year-old Joan Brody of Illinois as the White girl whose photo was rumored to have been in Bobo's wallet. It was as outrageous as it was incredible. There was no evidence—apart from Brody's comments—to support what Jerry set out in the article. As Brody told the story, she was in summer school with Bobo in Chicago just before he left with Papa and me for Mississippi. She said they had become friendly, playing around in class. She also said that a class photo was taken when the summer program ended.[7] The suggestion was that this was the photo that, according to way too many false reports, Bobo carried in his wallet and showed off in the Delta. The photo his killers said they found.

Even though there are several photos of Emmett and various school classes in Mamie's collection, no one ever saw a summer school photo like the one mentioned in the *Clarion-Ledger* article. It also would have been unusual for a summer school class photo to have been taken and for such a large photo—a group shot, after all—to have fit into Bobo's wallet. How fast could such a photo have been processed between the end of the summer term and the beginning of our trip to Mississippi? But those are details. The point is that this story fit into a rumor that had been circulating for years. It started with the story about a photo of a White girl that first was told by William Bradford Huie in his 1956 *Look* magazine article, a story that has been discredited. It had been told by our cousin Curtis Jones, who recanted, knowing what we all knew: that he wasn't even there in Mississippi when we were all at the Bryant store that fateful Wednesday evening. If there was any photo at all, it was the photo that came with the wallet.[8] Curtis later apologized to Mamie for telling that false story in the 1987 *Eyes on the Prize* documentary, admitting that he didn't know anything about everything he said he knew.

We have known Jerry Mitchell for some time and both supported and respected his work. So we were very upset that he would write such a piece. Marvel made sure he knew it, too, in an email she sent to him referring to his story as a "National Enquirer article" and noting that Jerry's long relationship with me should have prevented him "from validating this lie."[9] Jerry responded citing a few other articles he had written on Emmett Till and explaining that he believed the Brody story clarified that she was not Bobo's girlfriend, just a classmate for the summer. The story about the White girl in the photo had been retold a number of times over the years, and he believed the added material in his article would help to clarify some of the misrepresentation.[10] Fair, and we accepted that this is what he intended. But it seemed that his piece had just the opposite effect, confirming the rumor, as suggested by some of the headlines of stories that picked up on his piece. An August 28, 2018, story in the *New York Daily News* titled "Emmett Till's 'Girlfriend' Discusses His Murder for the First Time" started off: "A decades-old mystery surrounding the photo of a white woman linked to the Emmett Till case and his racially charged murder has been solved."[11] Had it, really? In Cleveland, WKYC posted an August 28 story with the headline, "Did Emmett Till Have a 'White Girlfriend'? Yes, and She's Been Found."[12] As far away as London, the August 28 *Daily Mail* headline included, "White 'Girl-friend' of Emmett Till Speaks Out for the First Time" and opened with "More than 60 years after 14-year-old Emmett Till was savagely beaten to death in segregated Mississippi for 'boasting of having a white girl', his 'girlfriend' has finally spoken out."[13] His "*girlfriend*."

Clearly, the damage had been done and the rumors had been revived and ratified without any solid evidence. Maybe Joan Brody has her own copy of that class photo with Emmett Till, if it ever existed at all. But it apparently was not sent to Jerry Mitchell, and it does not appear it was shared with anyone else.

We saw in just a couple of days how the media could begin to pass along a story that it seemed nobody ever checked out, but that every-one might believe regardless—amplifying the false information. There was a valuable lesson for me in all this. For some time, I had been saying that setting the record straight was one big part of our pursuit of justice in the case of Emmett Till. Now I could see very clearly how disinformation and misinformation were two sides of the same coin—public understanding.

The disinformation was put out there by people like William Bradford Huie and Carolyn Bryant Donham, people who seemed to be intentionally distorting the record for their own purposes. For Huie, it was about selling a story. For Carolyn, it was about selling her image, the innocent bystander, the victim, targeted by Black men and objectified by White men. On the other side of the coin, the mis-information was put out there by people who were too willing to echo the disinformation, willing to accept some things without question:

the reliability of a fellow journalist's work, or the truth of a White woman's allegations, or the belief that a Black kid did something wrong, with nothing more to hang it on than a White woman's claim.

With that in mind, a big part of justice for Emmett Till would involve exposing the most significant lies—the ones proving responsibility for a crime—in an attempt to preserve an accurate record of the truth. Even if memorializing the truth in every way possible was the only thing we accomplished, it would be a big deal because of the way things had gotten so distorted over time. So I chose to spend my time trying to identify the woman in the truck, while reporters seemed to want to spend their time trying to identify a girl in a photograph. Even assuming that both are real, one of them definitely is worth our time, while the other seems to be a waste of our time. You see, at the end of the day, only one is responsible for the death of Emmett Till. The only one we need to identify and hold to account.

WHITE PEOPLE WANT to move on. It's a privilege, I guess, to be able to do that. Just move on. Bygones. Water under the bridge. All that. Not so easy to do when you've been a victim of racial violence or racial injustice. But they can choose to let a Delta store disappear in disrepair, reclaimed by the land as Bryant's Grocery and Meat Market has been, or throw away a gin fan—key historical evidence—as one Sumner lawyer reportedly did, or kill a historical marker with gunfire as people repeatedly have tried to do at the site of the river where they reportedly brought Bobo's body up. They don't want to be reminded. They don't want to be responsible. They don't want to be accountable. Just forget about it.

They erected Confederate statues to intimidate us but also to convince themselves that their power to intimidate, and humiliate, and decimate was justified. The statues have served as monuments to "heroes" who protected White supremacy, and as inspiration to new generations to do the same under their rock-solid guardianship. To be convincing, these White folks have had to make sure there was no counternarrative. That means they have needed to erase a big part of history so they could rewrite it on a clean slate, a blank screen, a legal pad, a block of stone—chiseled with no respect for the truth.

Bobo won't let them do that. His historical markers won't let them do that. And that is why they have to kill him all over again, by wiping out his memory, destroying the markers that stand at the side of the road like so many stop signs, blocking their way down a guilt-free path.

Reckoning with our past is the important first step in reconciling for the future. Sadly, it seems like too many people desperately have been trying to avoid racial reckoning by rubbing out the reasons for it, like so many words on a whiteboard. By 2018, we were well on our way to making sure that our story would live on, that Emmett Till's story would live on, which is what we had set out to do on multiple levels more than ten years earlier.

TUESDAY, OCTOBER 2, 2007. "We the citizens of Tallahatchie County believe that racial reconciliation begins with telling the truth. We call on the state of Mississippi, all of its citizens in every county, to begin an honest investigation into our history."[14] We couldn't have said it better ourselves and we definitely were pleased to hear those words, the first words of the proclamation issued by the Emmett Till Memorial Commission of the Tallahatchie County Board of Supervisors. They were read from all those gathered in front of the Tallahatchie County Courthouse—the courthouse where two of Bobo's confessed killers, J. W. Milam and Roy Bryant, had been acquitted. How much things had changed.

At this point in the early Delta fall, the time to harvest what has been sown, the county board was headed by Jerome Little, the board's first Black president. Simmie and I were there, along with other family members. We were grateful for this important statement. An apology, after all, is a recognition that a wrong has been done. And we appreciated the historical marker that was placed in front of the courthouse summarizing the injustice that had been done inside that building, in a county where justice was denied, in a state where lawmakers made sure it would happen just that way. Yet, even while we listened to the words being read in a state that over time had elected more Black officials than any other state in the country, a shadow was cast over the whole event by the Confederate statue that still stood there out front protecting, preserving the history of the place—the dominant White narrative.

"We want to thank you all today for what you are doing here. You are doing what you could. If you could do more, you would," Simmie told the crowd of dignitaries there.[15]

Apart from all the comments made, the ceremonial activities that took place, the important, dedicated people we met that day, for me there was one encounter that stood out for significant reasons that would matter in the years to follow.

Patrick Weems introduced himself to me and expressed his commitment to preserving the Emmett Till story. Everybody was saying nice things like that, so I was polite, too, but as I learned more about him, I took note of the meaning of it all. Patrick was beginning that work I talked about, work that would lead to the Emmett Till Memorial Commission restoration of the county courthouse and the establishment of the Emmett Till Interpretive Center, a small museum that would be located on the Sumner town square directly across from the courthouse. Patrick would serve as the founding executive director. He would seem to be an unlikely Emmett Till advocate, but not just because he is White. You see, his father was the longtime head of the Republican Party in Madison County, one of the most conservative counties in Mississippi. Patrick also was a self-described conservative Republican for quite a while before he had some experiences that caused him to change his views. The first was his introduction to the Emmett Till story by a progressive teacher in a private high school he attended. He was moved by it. "You get to a point in high school where you think you know everything in the world," he told me. "How did I not know *this*? It's atrocious that this story had been hidden from me for eighteen years." Later, as a student at the University of Mississippi, he interned for the progressive William

Winter Institute for Racial Reconciliation and strengthened his commitment to social justice, learning how to write grant proposals to get progressive projects funded. When Barack Obama later was elected president in 2008, Patrick would change his political affiliation.

The reason this meeting at the county courthouse site was so memorable for me was not just because we would strike up a relationship that would last, but because of what Patrick represents: the power of the Emmett Till story and the reason we must preserve it accurately, share it widely. After all, it was the story of Emmett Till that opened Patrick's eyes and caused him to see the world differently, realizing the unifying themes of the story, a story that can bring us all together—across political and racial lines—in our commitment to shared values. Eventually Patrick would bring Marvel and me into the projects he had under way, including the smartphone app that was being developed by Professor Dave Tell at the University of Kansas, guiding visitors along the many sites of the Emmett Till narrative in the Delta and eventually Chicago. That Emmett Till Memory Project work, which we and Patrick advised Dave on, also involved Patrick's success in establishing Emmett Till historical markers—eleven of them across the Delta. A significant part of that effort increasingly would require him to replace the narrative signs destroyed by racists intent on making their mark on the story of Emmett Till—punctuating it with bullets.

OCTOBER 2, 2018. I never thought I "oughta be in pictures," as the song goes. Like Mamie, making a movie about Emmett Till was not nearly as important to me as writing a book to make sure that the story would be told truthfully and that it would live on. That is why it was so easy for Marvel and me to walk away from any possible involvement with the folks who were turning Devery Anderson's book into a motion picture, or series. That meeting not quite a year earlier just didn't feel right. We weren't sure where the Serendipity Group producers were coming from, starting with the place we were coming to meet with them: the Nixon Library. Besides, Chris Benson told us people already were talking to him about eventually doing something with television or movie theaters or streaming services for our story. So we didn't really feel an urgent need to talk to anybody about making movies, if ever.

But the Devery project kept following us for some reason we really didn't understand. In one of his many conversations with Chris, our dear friend Alvin Sykes began talking up the project. According to Alvin, who, like us, had a friendly relationship with Devery, the production group was not making much progress on developing a limited series with HBO and, as a result, they were making moves to strike a deal with another network. Over several conversations, Alvin convinced Chris that the time was right to open up a new conversation with the producers. Devery's book had a lot of facts, but not enough feeling, he believed. Alvin said they needed an authentic voice for the production and that my experience, my story offered that possibility. Chris was lukewarm to the idea, and Marvel and I were even cooler about it all when we finally were told about it.

We had heard that our cousin Airickca Gordon-Taylor had been in touch with someone connected to the production, although we never found out who that was. Airickca was Mamie's goddaughter and had lived with Mamie for a while as she was growing up. She established the Mamie Till Mobley Memorial Foundation to pick up the work that had been done by Mamie providing educational opportunities for young people. An activist, Airickca also had organized public events for mothers of Black victims of racial violence, speaking out the way Mamie had during her life. Who better to tell the story of the pain of loss than the families of victims of racial violence? So Airickca felt our family at least should have been consulted in connection with the development of an Emmett Till television series. As I learned, the person she talked with in connection with the production thanked her for her offer of engagement before basically dismissing her. It was a *don't-call-us-we'll-call-you* kind of thing.

Even with that on our minds, we were convinced that maybe something had changed and that there was nothing wrong with at least listening to see if we could have some impact on the way the story was told. Actually, we felt we had an obligation to do so. Once again, it seemed like an opportunity to make sure the truth came to light. And that truth could not be anything even close to Richard Nixon as a champion of civil rights. No way. So we authorized Chris to reach out to Devery to let him know we would be open to listening to what his team had to say about their project, even though we had rejected that possibility the year before.

To say the least, Devery's October 18 email response was disappointing. He wrote that he was not actively involved in the production, although Alvin had told us that he was. He basically made it clear that we would have to ask the producers for a meeting. We had been under the impression that the production team was interested in talking to us, that *they* were the ones who wanted a meeting. So our reaction essentially was "never mind." As Marvel, Chris, and I discussed it again, we didn't believe we would have been in a position to positively impact the project after all; instead of what Alvin had insisted, the more likely scenario would be the kind of brush-off we'd seen with our cousin Airickca. Devery's response cooled our interest in participating. We never responded to his email.

NOVEMBER 7, 2018. The day after the midterm elections, Jeff Sessions was forced to resign as attorney general.[16] There were so many reasons we might have been pleased with this development, given everything we had come to believe about Sessions and his lack of support for racial equality and criminal justice reform. But we had no idea what might come next. At least we knew where Sessions was coming from. The only thing we knew about Matthew Whitaker, the person who had served as Sessions's chief of staff and now was going to take his job as acting attorney general, was that he was loyal to the president. And Donald Trump had made no secret of his desire to control the Department of Justice. The question now was how far that need to control might go in appealing to White supremacists who probably would not look too kindly on an investigation focusing on the White woman who set the lynching of Emmett Till in motion. After all, look at what they were doing to the historical markers. Our discomfort only intensified knowing that the investigators might have to go to Main Justice for permission to talk to Timothy Tyson again. That would only draw more attention to the case, and attention from people at the top of that administration was one thing we did not want.

FEBRUARY 22, 2019. Tensions were mounting at the University of Mississippi after the first of the year. A group that supported Confederate statues—like the one that stood in the circle of the Oxford campus—demonstrated on campus, while counterprotesters tried to shout them down. Many of the folks who supported leaving the campus statue in a central place were not even students at the school, while just about all of the folks who opposed the statue were students.[17] Eight members of the school's basketball team even took a stand by taking a knee during the national anthem at a game against Georgia in solidarity with the protesters.[18] In the end, the University of Mississippi students would carry the day when the faculty senate followed the lead of a unanimous student senate vote on March 5, 2019, and also voted unanimously to move the Confederate monument from its central campus location to the Confederate cemetery on campus.[19] Obviously, that decision did not sit well with some people.

Later that month, Special Agent Walter Henry received a copy of an Instagram photo of three White fraternity members posing in front of a bullet-riddled Emmett Till historical marker—one of the markers established by Patrick Weems and the Emmett Till Memorial Commission, the one at Graball Landing, where Bobo's mutilated body was believed to have been pulled from the Tallahatchie River, the sign that already had been replaced two times. The frat members—students at the University of Mississippi—were photographed holding long guns, which suggested that they were the ones who had shot up the sign. After Agent Henry reviewed the matter, he determined that there might have been a crime committed if it could be proven that the students in the photo vandalized the sign, but it would not have been a federal offense; at best it would have been a state crime, or possibly just a matter for university discipline. The photo was sent to the University of Mississippi for appropriate action. Patrick Weems had the sign removed and placed on display at the Emmett Till Interpretive Center in Summit. Even as he tried to figure out the next move, his museum would leave the bullet-riddled sign on display, exposing the underlying message of this latest act of vandalism.

MARCH 2019. "WHEELER, do you want to start us off?" Patrick invited me to open a meeting with officials of the National Park Service in Washington, DC. We had been invited to travel to Washington for the ongoing discussions Patrick had started with the National Park Service, the National Parks Conservancy, and the National Trust to dedicate a non-contiguous national historical park in honor of Mamie Till-Mobley and Emmett Till. Patrick had gotten us involved in this effort a couple of years earlier. It was a very ambitious plan, but it seemed to be moving forward, and it promised to move the Emmett Till story forward. You see, there are national parks like Yellowstone and then there are national historical parks like the Martin Luther King, Jr. National Historical Park. That thirty-five-acre site in Atlanta includes Dr. King's birth home, as well as Ebenezer Baptist Church, which he pastored, and a visitor center with a museum dedicated to the Civil Rights Movement just across Auburn Avenue from the church and the Martin Luther King Jr. Center for Nonviolent Social Change.[20] We had a similar vision and were discussing with the National Park Service the feasibility of a national historical park in Mississippi dedicated to civil rights. We saw the Emmett Till story as central to that effort and began discussing sites in the Mississippi Delta, and later expanding to include sites in Chicago that would tell various aspects of the Emmett Till narrative as it connected to the beginning of the Civil Rights Movement.

That's why Patrick wanted me to start the discussion. I was there as the authentic voice on the story. I could talk about the various geographic spaces that could add a powerful dimension. While a list of places had been reviewed, the people at the meeting that day had not heard from an eyewitness talking about those places, bringing them to life. Places like the store in Money, the barn where Bobo was beaten, Graball Landing, the Tallahatchie County Courthouse, and, of course, Roberts Temple Church of God in Christ, where the funeral took place, and where future civil rights activists got religion.

There would be practical concerns. One of the main ones was how we might acquire the property—especially in the Delta—to establish the historical space. Bryant's Grocery and Meat Market looked to be the biggest problem. Over the years it had been acquired by the late Ray Tribble, one of the jurors who acquitted Milam and Bryant back in 1955. He had stood by that denial of justice, commenting in a later interview that the verdict was the right decision. So it was really hard to consider paying for that store. But that wasn't the worst of it. Tribble had left the property to his descendants. They wanted $4 million for the store and the adjoining property that included a pecan grove. Obviously, that was far more than the fair market value for the place— which was collapsing into the ground—and we had been deeply offended by what clearly was an attempt to extort, to profit from the death of Emmett Till, the way George Zimmerman had profited a few years earlier when he sold the gun he used to kill Trayvon Martin for $250,000.[21]

Clearly, this was a moral dilemma. As with any moral dilemma, you have to weigh the benefit on the one hand against the harm on the other. Certainly, there was the benefit from having the park service own the store in order to teach the public about Emmett Till and the history of race relations and power and the violent enforcement of power. Still, what is the message that would be sent if we were to allow these people to reap such a huge profit off the blood of Emmett Till? That would amount to one injustice on top of another. But then, what if someone else bought the property and used it to advance a different take on the narrative? After all, the store represents two sides of the same story—Black oppression and White supremacy. Was the purchase of the store worth a premium price just to keep it from falling into the hands of someone bent on distorting the narrative, justifying the crime that was set in motion there?

This was an issue we knew we were going to struggle with for some time, even as we worked with the National Park Service on the very concept of a national historical park, let alone acquiring the land it would occupy. At the time of our Washington meeting, I pointed out that we had been waiting more than sixty years. "We can continue to wait." After all, there was some split within the Tribble family and we would see how that played out, hoping that the price tag would not keep increasing even while the value of the collapsing store kept decreasing. In any event, we were not about to pay $4 million for the raggedy remains of a store.

Special Agent Henry believed he was getting close to clearing the way to revisit Timothy Tyson and interview him about all the questions that had arisen over the last year and a half. The FBI needed to connect up the dots on what had happened to the missing recording, why there was no evidence of the quote on the transcripts, and why the explanation of all this from Tyson and his assistant did not match up. Even more important, it looked like there was an alternative to going all the way up to the deputy attorney general for approval to do a follow-up interview, despite the DOJ memo that had been issued by former Attorney General Eric Holder. There were a few technicalities being explored. First, the FBI already had authorization to interview Tyson based on the grand jury subpoena that had been issued for production of the documents. So the follow-up would not be a new interview but a continuation. Second, there was a compelling need for the information the government was seeking from Tyson since it might amount to evidence that Carolyn Bryant Donham had lied to the FBI when she said she had not recanted. That would be a federal offense, and there might be no other evidence available to prove it. Third, and this was the weakest consideration, the Holder memo was issued to avoid potential harassment of journalists. Tyson was not a journalist. Like I said, this was the weakest rationale and we definitely did not want to set a precedent that would allow the FBI to exploit a loophole to drag journalists or historians in for questioning. But there would be no need to try that one if the first two rationales worked.

We would remain on standby, awaiting the final decision.

MARCH 17, 2019. It was a special day to give praise. A Sunday, and ordinarily that would have been enough of a reason for reflection and gratitude. But this day also was a moment of convergence. Marvel saw to it. This Sunday was organized around my eightieth birthday, our fifty-second wedding anniversary, and my twenty-five years as pastor of the Argo Temple Church of God in Christ. Marvel's first idea had been to organize a big celebration at a banquet hall with all our family, friends, church members, her local political colleagues— even the mayor of Summit—but she knew I wouldn't go for that. I've never been one to call attention to myself at all. But she knew if she centered everything on Sunday service, there would be no way for me to avoid my weekly appointment to praise the Lord. Not that there wasn't some to-and-fro on the whole thing. "Twenty-five years of service," she reminded me. "You have to let us do something." But I was determined to have the final say. As I told the congregation that Sunday when it finally was happening, "After fifty years of marriage, you learn how to have the last word: 'Yes, dear.'"

I have to admit, this was a special moment. Not so much because people wanted to celebrate me. But more because that recognition was a reminder of something I never had spent quite enough time considering: just how much each one of us can make a difference in the lives of so many others. Over the course of this Sunday service, I began to reframe it all, and to see this recognition of my life as an example of what life can be, what it should mean. And I said as much to the congregation.

"God woke us up for a purpose. To serve humanity."

One form of that service was introduced that day by Marvel, who reminded the congregation that, while she and I never had any biological children, we had "a whole community of children." And they stepped up that day to share their appreciation.

"We called him señor," said Dr. Antonio Mister, now an obstetrician-gynecologist. "He was a father figure for so many fatherless boys," he told the congregation in sharing that I always was "so accessible and so giving."

"There were certain things I didn't get into because of the teachings of Pastor Parker. He taught us how to go someplace. He taught us how to be real men," said Torrence Anderson, before adding the all-important point of it all. At least the point that meant the most to me. "I'm not praising the man, but praising the God within the man."

It is the God within us who points the way. Once we have opened up to that guidance, there really is no other way. I know. I made that promise to God on a night of terror and acted like I didn't remember it. Until I was reminded—in 1961 six years after Bobo was taken and I nearly went to jail for gambling, and then again in 1977 when I was directed to the ministry, and again in 1993, when I was blessed to pastor the church that Emmett Till's grandmother Alma Carthan helped to build in 1926, the church my family had joined shortly after we arrived from Mississippi in 1947. That guidance hasn't stopped there, either, as I was directed to follow the path to Belmopan, Belize, where, in 1979, Marvel and I inherited land to build another church.

Even though Marvel has been by my side on that righteous path since we married in 1967, it really seems as if the road map for that journey had been charted even before we connected in person.

IT WAS 1965 when we first met. Marvel was visiting my younger sister Elayne. She was so petite at first I thought she was a little girl. "She needs to be at home with her mother" is what I thought at the time. I was twenty-six and she was seven years younger. Even now, she doesn't look her age. But I couldn't get that "little girl" out of my head. One day, a friend of Elayne invited me to visit her friend Marvel McCain. The McCains had moved to the Chicago area from Mississippi, too, before Marvel was born, but lived in Robbins, far south of our "Little Mississippi" community in Summit. While we might have lived about fifteen miles apart up north, we found out our families had lived pretty close to each other back in the Delta. The McCains had come up from Teoc, just across the levy from Money. Even though our immediate families didn't know each other, they shared mutual friends. And I found out she had been thinking about me, too. Apparently, we Parker boys were considered a "catch." We were all gainfully employed for one thing. In fact, I was running my own barbershop by this time. We also had been pretty popular tall basketball players as we were coming up. So, Marvel and I struck up a friendship and even exchanged letters after she moved to California for a while. When she returned to Chicago during the great snowstorm of January 1967, and I couldn't get out of my garage to go see her, I realized this was more than friendship. I was smitten, eager and impatient, waiting for the snow to clear enough for us to reconnect. Only twenty-nine days later, I asked her to marry me. She did not have to think about it. She later told me God had given her the answer she gave to me: yes. It was meant to be. Our families had moved so far from our Mississippi homes, yet we still found each other in the Promised Land. We married on July 23, 1967—two days before what would have been Bobo's twenty-sixth birthday.

Each set of parents gave us $100 as wedding gifts, which was a lot of money back in 1967—especially to us, especially under the circumstances. Although I had been working full-time in the barbershop, my shop had just burned down. Talk about a way out of no way, I cut hair in my parents' basement for the next three years and we kept moving forward, eventually getting a new shop.

Marvel and I have been blessed to have discovered our connection and to have strengthened it over the years. In a way, a very deep way, our relationship serves as an example of connections we all have, rooted in the uniquely American story. "Little Mississippi" represents the story, the struggle of Black migrants who picked up every-thing and traveled to a new life up north. It is a complicated American story, to say the least. There is no better example of this than Mar-vel's family history. I met her relatives down in that tiny town of Teoc, where her very large family reunions would be held every couple of years. Over time, Marvel's Mississippi relatives started referring to themselves as the "Black McCains," to identify themselves in a curi-ous way—curious because all the McCains I met at these reunions were Black. But I learned that "Black McCains" was a way of con-necting and disconnecting all at the same time. They were connect-ing themselves to the "White McCains," while distinguishing themselves from those *other* folks, those members of, well, their "extended" family.

There were some notable members of that side. The White McCains. The acclaimed southern author Elizabeth Spencer was one of those members. We met her during one of the gatherings and she was delightful, even though she was considered something of a rebel in a family of plantation-owning ancestors. That was her story. And, of course, it was Marvel's story, descended from people who were con-sidered part of the property owned by those plantation-owning ances-tors.

The McCain family members—the White McCains—were enslavers. There were fifty-two enslaved persons listed on their "schedules" at the two-thousand-acre family plantation in Carroll County, Mississippi. Spencer's grandfather John S. McCain had man-aged that plantation before he later became an admiral in the US Navy, followed in the navy by his son Admiral John S. McCain Jr. and later still by his grandson and Spencer's cousin Navy Captain John S. McCain III, the late Republican senator from Arizona, presidential candidate. Marvel's cousin.

Over time, the "other" side of the family, the side that included the decorated naval officers, an author, a politician, and, well, the *property* owners, deeded a parcel of their Mississippi land to their darker cousins. It was land Marvel's ancestors had cultivated, developed up to their deaths—land that continued to be nurtured by their remains buried there. Finally free. A cemetery of Black McCains was included in that deeded parcel. Given her expertise, Marvel is helping to manage that property on behalf of the family.

We never met Senator McCain at any of those family reunions. He was busy running for higher office. Other members of his side of the family did attend and they have embraced the connection. John McCain's brother Joe brought the senator's flight jacket once to share with us the story of a war hero. My hope is that Senator John McCain—Marvel's cousin—can live on in our memory as a representation of more than just personal heroism and accomplishment, but as an example of what we can become when our worlds coincide rather than collide, and why it is important to recognize even the difficult parts of our history rather than erase them.

In the end, Marvel was right—once again—in organizing that March 2019 moment to celebrate my eightieth birthday, our anniversary, and my pastorate. I realized that there was nothing wrong with taking such a moment. Not self-indulgent or egocentric—it was a moment to reflect and rededicate. And to do it to an uplifting spiritual soundtrack. You see, in the church there is no hiding, no holding back. Just can't help it, can't stop the feeling, whether you're singing praises from the pews or literally moving into song—stepping to the mic without introduction. A guest singer might start out a cappella. And the organist always catches up, doesn't need sheet music to hit the right notes, either. In the church, the organist has perfect pitch. After all, we sing in the key of God, the key to everything.

It was wonderful to be able to enjoy this day in fellowship. Among so many others, my cousin, retired major Sheila Chamberlain, the army's first Black combat intelligence pilot, who insisted that I write a book and share my lifetime journey to justice. Airickca was there, too, with her mother, Ollie Gordon. It was good to see them, especially since Airickca had not been well, following two kidney transplants—one from Ollie. Someone was missing, though: Alvin

Sykes had not made it in, even though he had promised to be there. It was only later when we discovered that Alvin had an accident on his way. Sheila got the call and the details. He was running to catch the train to Chicago from Kansas City. He tripped over an obstruction, took a terrible fall, and badly hurt his head. He had to be hospitalized and wound up being partially paralyzed. As he would tell us later, the horrible pain of his injuries was only made worse by the longing to be there with us as he had been on so many special occasions.

APRIL 29, 2019. A breakthrough: Special Agent Walter Henry had reasoned out a justification for talking with Timothy Tyson again without requiring approval from the higher-ups at the Department of Justice. First, Tyson would not be asked to reveal any sources or methods of his work, which is what the Holder memorandum was designed to protect. The investigators only wanted him to show credible evidence of the quote by Carolyn Bryant Donham, the one he had included in his book. Second, and related to the first rationale, the questions investigators wanted to ask only followed up on the documents Tyson had produced under the grand jury subpoena. So a further contact would only be an effort to complete the unfinished file. This was enough justification for the folks at the mid-level DOJ offices in Washington to approve.

It was good that this question did not have to go higher, to the level of the new attorney general, William Barr, who—according to wide opinion—considered himself to be Donald Trump's man, the president's personal lawyer, not the chief law enforcement officer of the people. If Barr took a close look at this matter, there was no telling whether he would feel the need to brief the president on it. If that happened, there was no telling how Trump would feel about it. Again, we considered how he just might want to protect Carolyn if only to score points with his supporters—people who might seize the opportunity to demonize Bobo all over again.

*　*　*

JULY 25, 2019. The story about those University of Mississippi fraternity members broke in Jerry Mitchell's Mississippi Center for Investigative Reporting journal. Jerry's article carried the Instagram photograph that Walter Henry had reviewed back in March, the one with the three White students posing in front of the bullet-riddled Emmett Till historical marker, two of them holding long guns.[22] According to the story, the Instagram posting resulted in a complaint filed with the University of Mississippi Office of Student Conduct. "The photo is on Instagram with hundreds of 'likes,' and no one said a thing," the complaint reported.[23] Alvin Sykes, bedridden, still recovering from his fall, told Jerry that the shot-up sign should not be replaced as the others had been. It should just be stood up again, bullet holes and all. "The sign going back up is a sign of progress," he said. "The bullets are showing how much further we need to go."[24] University of Kansas Professor Dave Tell took that public education idea a step further. He later would urge that the shot-up sign be placed in a museum to help tell the story of American racism.[25]

Patrick Weems decided to replace the historical marker, this time with a bulletproof sign. In fact, he had gotten word of the vandalized sign before it was publicized and already had started a fundraising campaign for the replacement. He also invited Marvel, Chris, and me to meet with officials at the University of Mississippi to talk about ongoing programs to address bias, prompted by the national publicity the university had gotten from this incident. We agreed to do it.

AUGUST 5, 2019. Disney/ABC announced that it had "greenlit" a series of civil rights presentations focusing on "Women of the Movement." The first installment was going to be a six-episode series on Mamie and Bobo executive-produced by Jay-Z and Will Smith, among others.[26] This is the series that those other producers had discussed with Marvel and me during the Nixon Library event—the one Alvin Sykes thought should involve me in some way, the one based on the book written by Devery Anderson. But now it had a sharper focus, which we found curious and concerning. How could a television series presenting a more intimate story about Mamie and Bobo be based on a book written by someone who never knew either of them?

SEPTEMBER 2019. NOT long after we got the news about the ABC limited series, I was contacted by an ABC documentary producer. As with all the calls like this, Marvel and I referred the caller to Chris Benson to screen for us and advise on whether to take it seriously . . . or take it at all. We did. On September 20, 2019, Marvel and Chris met with Fatima Curry. We had learned that she was an award-winning producer who had an impressive list of credits. Among other things, she had served as a producer of John Ridley's *Let It Fall* about the 1992 Rodney King riots in Los Angeles, and she was a producer of the six-part documentary *1969* that included coverage of assassinated Black Panther Party leader Fred Hampton. It was that last connection, she said, that had led her to us. Our cousin Airickca was friends with the family of Fred Hampton, and Fatima met her through that connection. Of course, Airickca, an Emmett Till activist with a national reputation, told Fatima enough about the Emmett Till narrative to arouse her interest in producing the story. Fatima arranged to have dinner with Marvel and Chris in Chicago. They told her that we were involved in the government investigation, since the news of that probe already had been publicized. She was intrigued. But they told her we would not divulge any information about the investigation until it was concluded, per our agreement with the FBI. She agreed to wait if she could get an exclusive on that story for a documentary. Marvel and Chris agreed, but before the handshake, there was one more thing. Since she was producing for ABC, they told her they would have to have a guarantee that there would be a firewall between her production on the news side and the production associated with the scripted project on the entertainment side of ABC. She assured them that this was the policy at Disney/ABC and there would be no problem. Great, but wait, before the handshake, now *she* had one more thing. Fatima wanted to sign a non-disclosure agreement so she could take a first look at this book before it was released to the public. That's when Chris hit the pause button.

At long last, it was going to happen. We got word that the meeting with Timothy Tyson and the government authorities had been arranged for the following month, October. Even with the news of this progress we would have a new reason to race the clock—Special Agent Henry was being forced to retire, given his years of service. The timeframe now was even more compelling and there still were questions taunting us. What would come of this session with Tyson? Would it finally reveal the evidence—the proof—that *we* had been telling the truth all along, and that Carolyn had been telling a lie for years? She had made it up. Bobo never laid a hand on her and never threatened her. Would Tyson be able to produce evidence of the truth about the lie? Would we be able to see this through with Special Agent Henry?

The one thing we held on to with these developments was the only thing we had left, a cruel thing leading us on . . . hope.

Saturday, October 19, 2019. It was a solemn occasion at the riverside—the kind of place we might consider for a baptism, a rebirth. In a way, that is what the site represents. Graball Landing, not far from Glendora in Tallahatchie County, had been cleared by enslaved people to serve as a steamboat landing in 1840. It was near the spot where Emmett Till rose again, three days after his death. On Wednesday, August 31, 1955, his battered body reportedly was pulled from the Tallahatchie River at this place marking a moment the Reverend Jesse Jackson described as the "big bang" of the Civil Rights Movement when he eulogized Mamie Till-Mobley on January 11, 2003.[27]

On this sunny harvest season day, we had returned to this place to dedicate a sign and with that, to rededicate our commitment to keeping alive the story told by that sign—the fourth historical marker to stand in this place, five hundred pounds strong, bulletproof. A beacon

OF RACIAL PROGRESS AND A TRENCHANT REMINDER OF THE PROGRESS YET TO BE MADE, read the words on the marker written by Professor Tell. There was the story told by those words. And there was the story told by the very fact that this was the fourth marker to be planted in this place. The *fourth*. "That makes a statement in itself," I said to the family, friends, politicians, and activists who had traveled to this place. "Vandalism is a hate crime," Airickca said, revealing the real meaning behind the efforts to destroy a narrative.[28]

This was the third day of a series of events hosted by the University of Mississippi—events that included the screening of Stanley Nelson's award-winning documentary on Emmett Till, and a panel discussion on "Race, Memory and Responsibility" that featured Airickca, along with Jessie Jaynes-Diming, board member of the Emmett Till Memorial Commission; Dave Tell, whose book, *Remembering Emmett Till,* had been published a few months earlier; and Dr. Shennette Garrett-Scott, associate professor of history and African American studies at the University of Mississippi. Fatima Curry was there to cover the event for her proposed documentary. We had agreed to cooperate with her as much as possible, short of breaching our agreement with the government or releasing the manuscript for this book too far in advance.

"Of course, we are here because of the legacy of Emmett Till," I told those gathered at the river site, even while expressing disappointment that Mamie was not there to share her feelings, knowing that I was only there to speak for her, and for Bobo. "We are here because Emmett Till speaks."

It was my intention to make sure he would continue to speak and be heard. To be remembered. To be memorialized.

As a people whose story had been distorted in a twisted attempt over the years to discredit and diminish and dismiss us, we knew it was vital that we protect that story. Preserve it as something—maybe the only thing—that shows we have existed, that our existence has mattered. The marker set down in this place and fortified against the assaults by people desperately trying to blot us out—in a very important way that marker documents our truth, the truth of our lives, the lives to be memorialized. In the coming years, the effort to erase and replace our story, our memory, would intensify with the banning of books and with censorship, criminalizing the truth while commemorating lies. Imposing penalties for people who might dare to break new laws against teaching history. Our story. And by "our story," I mean the story of all of us. That's the thing. What these history vandals don't seem to realize is that our story and theirs are one and the same. In erasing "our" story, they, in fact, are erasing their own. We couldn't let that happen and stay true to Emmett Till. So we were not about to let it happen. For that reason, and in that frame of mind, with this historical sign carrying both a legend and a promise, we were planting a bulletproof intention, laying down a marker to show what we were fully prepared to do. Fight back.

13

House of Mirrors

THE MAN IS full of charm. Easygoing. Gracious. That's how his visitors found him on October 25, 2019, when he greeted them and welcomed them into his Raleigh, North Carolina, home. A professor's home. As the visitors would discover, this house, this professor's home, was exactly the representation Timothy Tyson might have wanted to make to the world—distinguished, dignified—but not at all like the person who would be revealed that day. After all, this house, this professor's home, was orderly, organized, nothing out of place.

With the extensive briefing I would get later, well, I felt like I had been a fly on the wall to observe, to listen, to analyze the details. Everything from the information that was discussed to the manner of the man presenting it. And that manner, that personality, set up an important framework for the information he provided. It all started there. Timothy Tyson's charm. It seemed cultivated—one part southern gentleman, one part absentminded professor. Senior research scholar at Chapel Hill, adjunct at Duke, where his wife, Dr. Perri Anne Morgan, is professor of family medicine and community health. So it seemed so natural at first, coming from this native North Carolinian, a historian lost in time. But his visitors on this day would leave after two hours, twenty-four minutes, and fifty-six seconds of their interview considering that charm—that *aw-shucks* ease and rumpled coziness—as not so much natural as affected, purposeful in a to-and-fro Q and A, but not so much weapon as shield. In the end, it just might have been his most effective defense in a free-flowing session with government officials. No need for a subpoena, no need even for legal representation—just southern hospitality. Where you might expect to disarm with pound cake, coffee, that sort of thing.

The visitors—Special FBI Agent Walter Henry, Mississippi District Attorney Dewayne Richardson, and his district manager Tamicko Fair—asked Tyson how he wanted to be addressed in their report. Doctor? Professor? Either would be fine, he told them, but today, they could just call him "Tim." Charming.

There was a bit of small talk . . . at first. Southern food, customs, the North, the South, the differences, the similarities—stuff like that. It just might have been tactical, this small talk—loosen things up a might the way Tyson would reveal he softens up a source, the way the FBI might soften up a target. They all seemed to be playing the same game—at first. But the conversation would get serious, real serious, real fast.

The officials wanted to talk about Carolyn Bryant Donham, her quote in Tyson's book. The quote, "That part's not true." So why was it in his book, but not hers?

They had reviewed her manuscript and there was nothing in it that even came close to what he said she said. Nothing in the interview transcripts, either. Tyson began with yet another mention of the pound cake with Carolyn, and the disarming conversation when she "started muttering about" something he never quite finished saying in this conversation with the authorities. He explained his practice of refraining from turning on a recorder too early in an interview session because "you don't want it to dominate the, what goes on between you."[1] So it wasn't until after all of that—after she'd apparently said, "That part isn't true"—he said, "So the tape starts . . ."

Tyson took Special Agent Henry through the whole narrative, though, beginning with the call he received from Marsha Bryant and his early interest in having a conversation with Carolyn. While the Emmett Till story had been "told and retold," her story had never been published. So he agreed to sit down with her and talk. Why wouldn't he?

There had been a question about the precise time of Tyson's two interviews with Carolyn. After quite a little to-and-fro with the authorities on this, he revealed that both interviews occurred in 2008.[2] That would mean only three years after Carolyn told a different story to the FBI during its initial investigation into Emmett Till's lynching between 2004 and 2006. And that would mean that, if Tyson really had a confession from Carolyn, he also would have had evidence of a criminal offense by her—that she lied to federal investigators—well within the five-year federal statute of limitations on making false statements to the FBI. But Tyson seemed to be waffling pretty early in his conversation with the officials at his home over even the smallest matters. For example, he said Carolyn and Marsha showed him a copy of the transcript of the Bryant and Milam murder trial. But Marsha had told the FBI in an earlier interview that they did not have one in the first place, and Carolyn even mentions that during one of the interviews with Tyson. When confronted with this contradiction, Tyson said, "I thought I saw it. But, you know, I probably—I wouldn't bet, bet the farm on it. That's my memory."[3]

They redirected their questions back to examining Carolyn's alleged confession, how she said it, and how Tyson documented it. Responding to a question by Special Agent Henry, Tyson said he believed she made the statement during the first of their two interviews, but couldn't really recall. "For a historian I don't have a very good memory sometimes. And those two interviews kind of blur together for me. But, I'm pretty sure, 'cause I remember my jaw hit the table."[4] Even so, he didn't say he asked any kind of follow-up question or pursue this jaw-dropping, history-making line any further.

He said he was "messing with the machine," although earlier he had said that it hadn't started yet since he didn't want the recorder to dominate. You know, part of that softening-up thing. But then he said,

"The tape starts." So, wait a minute, did he record her comment, or not? Tyson gave a long, rambling response that included mentions of technical problems he had with his first book, *Blood Done Sign My Name*. "But, uh, I was, I've lost interviews just because I, you know, I thought the red light meant it was recording and it, the red light meant I was on pause or whatever. And, I was, that's, uh, something I'm always, I'm not very good with, uh, technology. I'm always trying to make sure the recorder is going. But, um, and I didn't like the recorder I was using. I didn't really know how to use it very well. The, but it did, it did work. So, I don't know if, uh ... anyway, I don't know ... I'm not sure at what point the recorder kicked in."[5]

Apparently, at this moment in his interview with Carolyn, thinking he might need backup, Tyson said he began writing notes down. "So I just kind of reached over without hiding it. But, I didn't wanna make it, it's, 'cause I didn't wanna forget what she had said if it wasn't on the tape. So, I must've thought that at least there was some danger it wasn't on the tape."[6] The tape that wasn't recording—couldn't have been—because he said earlier that he hadn't turned it on, that is, before he said, "the tape starts."

Then it got even more confusing because he suggested that he didn't worry about the recorder and seemed to suggest that he heard something on the recording later, after the interviews. "But, uh, but I know from listening to the tape that, uh, uh, nothing that boy did could ever, uh, deserve what happened to him, could never justify what happened to him. And, um, uh, she was talking about her testimony and said, 'Well, you know, that part is not true.'"[7]

On follow-up questioning, though, he admitted that he didn't listen to the recorder right away. "Um ... I think it was a good while because I, uh, I had been worried that I didn't catch it so that's why I took the written notes." And even though he was worried that he hadn't recorded the quote he went on to completely turn the whole thing around in terms of the significance of it all. "I didn't really think that her lying at the, at the trial was like, that wasn't like the morning news to me. I never thought she was telling the truth."[8]

Wait, what? He said earlier in this session that Carolyn's comment about lying in court was a jaw-dropping moment. Then he said he really didn't think it was all that important—"not like the morning news to me"—because he always knew she was lying. He said earlier that he was worried he had not recorded, so he grabbed his notepad to make sure he would remember a very short and simple sentence: "That part's not true." He wanted to make sure he got it down in case the recorder didn't record it, because, we can only assume, he thought it was important. But when asked at this point, he said, "I just didn't think it was that significant."[9]

"It's perjury, which you know is not arson or murder. So, you're not gonna . . . I just didn't think it was that significant. Uh, it ended up being significant in the marketing of the book."[10] Well, yeah, there is that. But, even if it only was perjury, then it was perjury *about a murder*. And Marvel, Chris, and I were infuriated that he could consider this to be insignificant. This was about the taking of Bobo's *life* and the accountability for that. I was glad to have not been literally in the room with Tyson in this moment. It would have been too upsetting.

Whatever Tyson might have thought was important or not, he didn't think anything on the recorder was important enough to check promptly. He said he didn't transcribe right away.[11]

He went on to say that he reviewed the notes defense attorney Sidney Carlton took during his interview with Carolyn Bryant on September 2, 1955, about her encounter with Bobo in the store, when "she said he insulted me. She never said anything about him putting my, his hands on me."[12] So it seemed like he might have been putting together different pieces of the record in his book, to conclude for his readers that she was lying. But that would be circumstantial evidence—which is fine if he could support it and, of course, tell the world in his book that that's what he was doing. After all, there was no record of her admitting she was lying, except for notes scribbled onto Tyson's legal pad—the only notes, it seems, he *ever* made on his legal pad during these interviews.

It was pretty clear by this time in the session with the authorities that there was no actual documentation of Carolyn's quote, apart from Tyson's handwritten notes. But they had to be absolutely sure because the story kept shifting: *Maybe* there had been a recording, or then again, maybe not.

On further questioning by Tamicko Fair, Tyson was not able to say when he realized he did not have Carolyn's admission on his recorder. "I just don't remember, honestly."[13] He went on to admit that he knew he did not have the recording when he completed his book, when it went to press and finally was released on January 31, 2017. "But, you know, uh, historians wrote books before there were recorders."[14] The visitors overlooked that bit of sarcasm and just kept pressing on.

According to Tyson, no one besides Carolyn was in the room at the time he says she made her admission, even though Marsha had said she was always in the room. It was interesting to see how much of this narrative Tyson continued to develop in his conversation with the authorities. He was quoted by Jerry Mitchell in the *Mississippi Clarion-Ledger* story admitting that he never had a recording of Carolyn admitting what he wrote. "It is true that part is not on tape because I was setting up the tape recorder."[15]

It is not completely clear from the way he talked during the interview when he realized that he did not have a second audio recording; he had acknowledged in an earlier email that he couldn't find the second one when he checked to respond to the FBI requests starting after the book was published in February 2017.[16] But even if he had provided a second audio recording, it is not likely it would have answered the critical question that sparked this phase of the investigation. Tyson had said in an early part of the interview that he realized he had no recording of Carolyn's quote when he was preparing to publish, even though, again, he was quoted in the newspaper saying he hadn't even started recording, meaning there never was a recording he needed to check. It was all very confusing. The bottom line was that the quote was not heard on the one recording the FBI had gotten from Tyson, it was not included in the transcripts of that recording or of the other one, the recording that had disappeared.

Even so, Tyson's assistant, Melody Ivins, "made the representation that she heard it in one of the recordings and she thought she had transcribed it," Henry said. Tyson's response was really kind of strange. "Well it's possible, but you guys got the recording correct?"[17] This was going in circles.

As the frustrated authorities tried to nail down whether there was or was not a recording of Carolyn uttering the words that were published in Tyson's book, what followed was almost impossible for anybody else to follow without a road map, or GPS!

HENRY: "But you're saying that wouldn't . . . you're certain that it wasn't, so if she made a representation that she heard it on . . ."

TYSON: "well . . ."

HENRY: ". . . a recording that . . . Now I'm not saying that it is . . ."

FAIR: "Did you ever hear it on a recording?"

TYSON: "I did make notes . . ."

FAIR: "Yeah. Did you ever hear it on a recording? I guess a better question is, did you ever hear it."

TYSON: "Yeah, that is a better question . . . um, I don't think so, I don't think so . . . uh, but it was a while before I listened to it, and I just don't know. It would have been I imagined, well, so what I do is make, I go through primary documents interviews whatever and I make four-by-six note cards of like quotations and the meat of what that sort of fact and uh, or idea but, and I put the uh citation like the source and everything on the upgrade like it was a letter and a return address what it was uh and then that's what I work with so I've got a bazillion, you know . . ."

FAIR: "Uh huh."[18]

It was clear that the government team just wanted to get back to the relevant facts. So Tyson was asked about the transcript of one of the recorded sessions, the transcript that started off with nine lines of the number "one" repeated and typed a total of 578 times.

TYSON: "So . . . my memory would be that this would be where the uh quote of confession where she . . ."

HENRY interrupted: "Where all the ones are displayed?"

TYSON: "Where she . . . yeah. I don't know why those ones are there, I don't know, uh, I know ones and zeroes some kind of digital I don't know digital squat, and I don't know what that . . . I can't imagine she'd type in that many lines."

HENRY: "So uh . . ."

TYSON: "So maybe she's right?"

HENRY: "But you didn't hear it? You don't recall?"

TYSON: "I'm not positive but . . . I remember being not that happy that I didn't have it on the recording but I knew at the time of the recording that I might not have it."[19]

"Might not have it," because, well, he hadn't turned the recorder on, right? Isn't that what he had said only minutes before?

The passage following the "ones" on the transcript does suggest at least a paragraph of conversation had been taking place with Carolyn, preceding the first quote you can read on the first page of text in the transcript. But whether those ones were purposely obscuring the quote or just some kind of technical error could not be known. The transcript opens with Carolyn apparently responding to a question, an answer that comes right after the ones. "Oh, well, I tell you what, I have just thought and thought and thought about everything about the Till, the killing and the trial, telling who did what to whom, well, you know, I really don't know who did what to whom."[20]

At this point in the interview with Tyson, Special Agent Henry asked one of several critical questions. If Tyson wasn't sure he had recorded the quote, "why didn't you follow up, once you're sure that the recording is going and say ok, you've said this before, I just want to make sure?"

"I just didn't think, I didn't think to do that," Tyson said.

I found that shocking, but even more disappointing is what followed in his lengthy and meandering explanation that "I, I wouldn't, you don't want, uh, you don't want to step on the interview and create evidence, you know . . . and you also don't want to panic the interviewee you uh you know you don't want 'holy Hell, that's perjury,' when she . . ." might realize that she had admitted something important.[21]

So he didn't want to "step on the interview" by verifying the one thing that made the interview valuable, worthwhile: potentially the most critical revelation in the history of this case. He didn't want to get clarity because he didn't want to spook Carolyn? What could have been more important than confirming the confession of a lie and documenting the reason behind the lies she had told under oath in court? Was he documenting history in a case of a lynching that sprang from a lie, or protecting Carolyn Bryant Donham, the person he quoted in his book as telling the lie?

Tyson didn't seem to remember much during his interview with authorities. Starting with those "ones."[22] In fact, he didn't recall even seeing them until they were called to his attention by the authorities. But they were so unusual, how could he really forget them? Especially if the transcript was important to the book he was producing and the most important quote of the book just might be buried under those ones. The point is that the quote was not there. It couldn't have been if Tyson had not turned on the recorder. The question still was whether the quote existed anywhere and whether Tyson's handwritten notes were valid. He didn't recall whether he made any other handwritten notes, apart from the abbreviated notation scribbled onto the single sheet of a legal pad—the only notes he took during two lengthy interviews.[23] And there was no context for the notes, nothing to indicate what was said before or after. Later, though, he suggested that he might have copied the notes over and just might have other notes.[24] But they were not produced, despite a request by Henry that he look for more.[25] So there was no telling if the notes were edited, expanded, or reduced. And, if he copied them over, what was the reason for the transfer, or change, if any?

Putting aside the notes, Tyson told the authorities during the meeting that day that he had a precise recall of the Carolyn quote, but his only explanation of what the quote was referring to was "sorta" connected in his mind to Carolyn's testimony.[26] It was his memory of the context for the quote that he was relying on, the memory he has admitted is not very reliable. "Bumbling," is how he described himself. Not such a good quality for a historian.

Despite the fact that he included the confessional quote by Carolyn in his book, Tyson admitted that, "in her memoir, she tells more or less what she told in court."[27] Actually, it was not "more or less" what she said in court; the description in the book definitely was more, and it was helped along with an important edit by him. Again, he changed her text to read she "feared" Bobo was going to molest her. It was the first time she ever used the word "molest" and he jacked it up to "feared" to replace the word "thought" that she and Marsha wrote in the draft. And the authorities at Tyson's home that October day wanted to know why. If he edited her manuscript in 2008, and she stuck with the lie she told in her 1955 courtroom testimony, why didn't he ask about that contradiction between what's in the manuscript and what he said she told him—"That part's not true"—before he edited the manuscript and increased the level of perceived threat with his editing?

Carolyn had been interviewed by Special Agent Dale Killinger several times late into 2005. In those 2005 interviews, "she said she didn't remember but based on reading the transcripts and her memoir, she had a pretty good memory, three years later," Special Agent Henry noted. "A quite detailed memory."[28] And if she had perjured herself, the authorities would have had an interest in knowing that. "So you have this information and you have this confession or retraction of information, here it is 2008 and we just had the presentation of this case in the grand jury," Henry said. "So the question for you will be did you think about providing this information to law enforcement; did it cross your mind . . . ?"[29]

"I'm thinking as a historian, I didn't think that changed the story. It just didn't strike me as, you know, that I know that's weird to different kinds of folks who, you know, but, I'm not following the People's magazine story of Emmett Till, you know it's, I'm not, I just, you know, for a historian to hold a press conference or something on his unpublished research is pretty weird [laughs] in my world so I, it never even occurred to me.

"And I didn't think anybody believed it anyway, I mean, I just didn't, I didn't go through my mind and go should I tell somebody this? No, it doesn't really change the story but my assumption was uh, it was significant that she said it but I didn't think it was, changed the story. I still, if I thought it did change the story I probably wouldn't have uh, uh, done anything with law enforcement about it because my understanding was that that, I thought that was closed to tell you the truth. It's my, I got the perhaps misinformed but I thought the [unintelligible] was opened in 2004/2005 and went for a couple more years uh and then was closed with no prosecutable stuff . . ."[30]

Closed or not, he did recognize there might be a legal question. "I did know that this was perjury, but . . ."[31]

He never really answered the question, though, about how he could resolve the contradiction between what Carolyn and Marsha were writing (and he was "lightly" editing) with what he ultimately wrote in his book. He never addressed the huge gap between her writing about Bobo in an even more frightening and threatening way than she ever had before, and him writing that she said the frightening, threatening parts she had just written were "not true." What he did say really didn't make sense. "I did a little editing on it then I realized that it was unpublishable and furthermore that any further help from me would entail, uh, changing her, prettying up her story. Like I didn't think I could go on and edit this because I realized I didn't want my name on Carolyn Bryant's, I didn't want to be as told by Tim Tyson, I didn't want anything to do with that . . . I had talked to my agent at the time, too. She's just my guiding angel for me but, uh, and I just she's like no, no, no, no, no because I was trying to pass her along to my agent to see if my agent would have any advice for her on how to publish it, um, but I came to the conclusion that the only publication this was going to see would be archival if you pub-lish it as a book it's not a, it's not very long either. Like, it's not really long enough to be a book and it's not close to being long enough to be a book and then it's full of stuff that is only useful as archival mate-rial."[32]

What deeply concerned me was his seeming lack of concern about everything. I would find this particularly disturbing when I learned about it later. He was sitting there talking to a special agent of the FBI, a Mississippi district attorney, and the DA's district manager who focused on victim's rights and reconciliation—a conversation where there could be consequences for not telling the truth. That didn't seem to matter. The news media, social activists, and the public—unforgiving stakeholders—had celebrated his award-winning book, based on content that now appeared to be in doubt. That didn't seem to matter. At the very least, his admittedly sloppy record keeping was a poor reflection on his reputation as a scholar and author, and could prove embarrassing to any academic colleagues who cited his work and his publisher who distributed it. That didn't seem to matter. And then there were those of us who had lived with all the lies over the years, those of us who survived the trauma of haunting memories of a denial of justice, those of us who survived on the hope that one day the truth would be revealed, those of us who saw in Tyson's book the fulfillment of hope. It truly is one of the cruel things White people do to Black people, giving us hope and then dashing it. Tyson didn't seem to care about that, either.

He didn't seem to care about us. Otherwise, he would have reached out to us as he was putting together his book. Like William Bradford Huie, Timothy Tyson had relied on a White version of the Emmett Till story. Even while he rejected the value of talking to any of us as he was putting together his book, Tyson also expressed a harsh view of Carolyn in his interview with the government officials. He said after doing what he called "a little editing" and what we saw as a little more than a little editing, he saw her racism coming through in their conversation. "I wouldn't say viciously racist, but just her

White supremacy was underneath her assumptions about everything when she would just say things that you can't, you know, you can't say in a book and publish it in 2010 and not just get run over by a tractor trailer . . ."[33]

He said there were "overt expressions of white supremacy." But in his book he quotes Carolyn in a way that separates her from all that. "They were racists, the whole family," he wrote, publishing a quote from their interviews, adding that she was "implicitly exempting herself."[34] He never bothered to come back and present evidence of what he set out for the authorities in the October 2019 session. His express references to "white supremacy" in his book really never characterized Carolyn. On page 49, he refers to defense attorney J. J. Breland in this connection. On page 79, it is US Senator James O. Eastland. On page 80, he refers to civil rights activist Amzie Moore's awareness of White supremacy. On page 81, Moore again making the same point. On page 93, it is in connection with the segregationist Judge Thomas P. Brady attacking *Brown v. Board of Education.* On page 97, it is the segregationist Citizens' Councils. On page 200, he discusses the concept generally. On page 201, there is a discussion of northern hypocrisy. On page 206, the term is used in connection with the savagery of Emmett's beating, as an illustration and in support of Carolyn's comment that he "didn't deserve what happened to him . . ." On page 213, it is referenced as a factor in the ongoing attacks against young Black men. On page 214, the term is used in connection with the horrific mass shooting at Mother Emanuel AME Church on June 17, 2015. Finally, the term is used on pages 215–217 as a general reference. If he really believed Carolyn to be a White supremacist—and I don't doubt that she is—then why didn't he deal with it, write about it, show evidence of it, in connection with making the case that she might have participated in Bobo's kidnapping and death, or that she might have done something to set it all in motion, or cover it up, or obstruct justice?

This all ties to questions about his true assessment of Carolyn.

On February 13, 2014, author Devery Anderson began a corre-

use of Carolyn's interview material in his book and the archiving of the book at UNC. After struggling to pin down a clear answer, Special Agent Henry asked point-blank, "Was there an agreement that you could use the information for your book?" Tyson responded, "Yeah, I mean they, they knew I was working on the book. They assumed it before I was working on the book. They never really came up to that I wasn't working on a book or would not work on a book at some point. Um, yeah that would, uh, my memory is that they were . . ."[39]

The curious thing about all this is that it appears that Tyson only interviewed Carolyn to help flesh out her memoir, not to collect information for his own book. At least that's what it seemed she would have understood from the transcribed conversations we read. There is no record that Tyson conducted separate interviews for a book of his own. And he never asserted that he did. In fact, there are many areas of the interviews that are reserved only for her manuscript. Yet he clearly used some of the material from the Carolyn/Marsha manuscript for his own work. There was nothing in the record we saw that proved he had permission to do that. "They were sure I was going to work on a book," Tyson insisted to the authorities.[40] But the only references to publishing anything appear in a conversation among Tyson, Carolyn, and Marsha focusing on how he was going to help get literary representation for them, to advise them on getting published.[41] If he was interviewing Carolyn "like as a historian," for his own purposes, why did he promise to submit the interview transcripts to the archives along with Carolyn's manuscript? That appears to have been the understanding—that he was delivering the materials to the archives and not appropriating them for his own purposes. This is not to speak up for the legal rights of Carolyn Bryant Donham and Marsha Bryant, but only to raise questions about how much credit we should give to all the explanations Tyson was offering. They just don't seem to add up. If he said he had an agreement and he didn't, well, maybe he also said he had a quote and he didn't. If it can be reasonably concluded that he is not being straight on his understanding with Carolyn and Marsha, how can we trust that he is being straight on anything? And "anything" would include everything, like the Carolyn quote that set all this in motion—got us involved, raised my hope that she finally was telling the truth. The truth about her lies.

IF YOU TRAVEL through the South, you're bound to run across a shotgun house. More likely, you'll see a bunch of them. Shotgun houses, Black folks' houses, started springing up in southern cities a couple hundred years ago. If you haven't seen one, a shotgun house is straight-ahead, narrow, one room right behind the other so that, if you opened the front door and fired a shotgun, the pellets would go straight through the back door without hitting anything else. When we started out with the FBI and the DOJ and the DA in March 2017, I kind of thought this leg of the investigation would be pretty much like a shotgun house: straightforward, just walk on through it, beginning to end. Either Carolyn said what Tyson wrote in his book, or she didn't.

That's not how it was turning out. There were no straight lines. No persuasive evidence, no recording, proof beyond a reasonable doubt. Not open and shut, like the front door and the back door of a shotgun house. No. Just a bunch of curves and digressions and twists and turns. More like a house of mirrors. Each time we thought we were seeing straight ahead, a path forward, clear-eyed answers, it seemed like we were just reflecting back on ourselves, bumping up against ourselves, trapped by a maze of speculation and theories of the case and answers to questions that just curved back on themselves and took us back with them, back where we started from.

Was Tyson doing this on purpose, playing us with this *absentminded-professor* thing? Or was he really so bumbling that he didn't keep records of the most important thing he had claimed in his book? Had he just grossly misunderstood something that really was said? Did he misinterpret and then discover his mistake later, after it was too late to walk it back? Too late because he had committed to the mistaken thing, committed to his agent, to his book editor, to the public. Or had he just made up the whole thing? We weren't quite ready to reach that last conclusion.

But one thing was certain as we reflected on all this, reflected from all angles, all points of view, as you can do in a house of mirrors just before you realize that you really are looking in the right direction after all, at the actual thing itself. The one true thing.

There was no credible evidence that Carolyn Bryant Donham had ever confessed her lie to Timothy Tyson.

14

Appropriation

Octover 31, 2019. The Judiciary Committee of the House of Representatives approved the Emmett Till antilynching bill, introduced by Congressman Bobby Rush, who represented Mamie in life, and in a very important way still represented her so many years after her passing. There had been nearly 120 years of failed attempts to pass such a law. Now this bill clearly was making a powerful statement during a difficult time. The powerful statement was that Black lives do matter, racial violence was not going to be tolerated, and the bill's enhanced penalties for hate crimes—up to thirty years—punctuated that statement. The difficult time was painfully obvious with what seemed like too many officials letting too many White supremacists get away with too many racial crimes of violence. The Rush bill was expected to pass in the majority-Democratic House after the first of the year, but it was uncertain what might happen in the Senate, where Republicans still were in control. Then there was no telling what might happen if it actually reached the desk of Donald Trump, who just two years earlier had spoken approvingly of those White supremacists in Charlottesville.

December 11, 2019. It was late afternoon when Marvel, Chris, and I arrived at Central Station in Memphis, Tennessee. Central Station is a Hilton Curio hotel on South Main Street, but its past as a train station is still evident, with tracks right there alongside still in operation. Central Station is listed on the National Register of Historic Places and there definitely is quite a lot of history in the place, in the heart of Memphis's artistic district and within sight of the Mississippi River. Once known as the Grand Central Station of Memphis, this has been for more than a hundred years an important stop on a line traveling from New Orleans, through Mississippi, and up to Chicago—the final destination. This station often served as a rest stop for the City of New Orleans train that carried so many Black folks away from the racial atrocities of the South to freedom in the North.

Music played constantly through the lower-level bar and up through the converted lobby during our stay there. The iconic "sound of Memphis" from the hotel's curated list of local vinyl all-stars even piped into the guest rooms. This resurrected and restored building stands as a reminder of how much we can gain by creating something new and progressive out of something old and deteriorating, even while preserving the basic value of it all—the value and the values. Ideas and policies and relationships, as much as communities and train stations.

Even though we would be in Memphis a very short time—just one day—we planned to cover a lot of ground, at least in terms of information sharing. Patrick Weems had arranged a meeting with administrators from the University of Mississippi, following that Instagram posting showing the university's students with their long guns in front of the bullet-riddled historical marker we had replaced just about two months earlier. That meeting would take place the next morning, Thursday, December 12. After that, in the early afternoon, we would meet with Special FBI Agent Walter Henry and Special FBI Agent Shannon Wright. But we were not even going to wait until morning to get started. Henry was driving up from Oxford, Mississippi, to meet us over dinner that evening and offer us an informal briefing on his October interview with Timothy Tyson. We were eager to get the details on what Henry already had teased out.

He picked us up to take us to dinner at Central BBQ. Seemed like "Central" was the focus in this area, where they were trying to balance old and new: our hotel, Central Station, this popular restaurant, Central BBQ, and even Central Gardens, a trendy neighborhood with roots in the 1850s, when the city of Memphis developed. The city where Nathan Bedford Forrest made a fortune selling human beings—Africans smuggled into the country against the law—before he went on to become a Confederate general and later the first grand wizard of the Ku Klux Klan.[1]

It was a bit of a challenge to work around our Memphis Q and fries to make it through the briefing. While the food was enjoyable, the briefing was enough to give us indigestion. We learned more about the contradictions in Tyson's meeting with Henry, Dewayne Richardson, and Tamicko Fair. Henry talked about the conflicts among what Tyson was saying at this point, what he'd said in earlier interviews, and what he'd written in his book. Their latest meeting still left open questions about whether Carolyn's confession of a quote was recorded or not. Early on—like two years earlier—Tyson had indicated that it was. He and his assistant, Melody Ivins, also had indicated that the quote was transcribed and then lost. In our review at the FBI Chicago field office a year earlier, the missing recording had been discussed, but we all still held out hope that there would be some reasonable explanation. Hope—such a cruel thing, right?

As we were briefed, I recalled how Tyson actually told Jerry Mitchell at the *Mississippi Clarion-Ledger* that he had not turned on the recorder when he claimed Carolyn spoke the words that launched all the news stories starting in 2017. He said he only had the notation on a page from a legal pad, and had only produced a photo of that note page, not the original sheet of notepaper. Tyson's responses in the recent interview raised even more questions about a lack of consistency since, in the course of only two and a half hours, he said he did not recall whether the quote was recorded, but hoped it was. He also said he wrote the book knowing that the quote was not recorded, and blamed the transcript "omission" on his trusted assistant.[2]

The real head-scratcher was confirming that Tyson attached no real importance to the quote by Carolyn, a quote that everybody else considered the most important thing in his book. He said as much to the authorities in the October interview—that he didn't think that "jaw-dropping" quote was all that important—and he also had written something like that in his February 21, 2017, email to Brandis Friedman, the anchor and reporter for *Chicago Tonight*, on WTTW, Chicago's PBS station. Marvel and I couldn't help but recall that email, where he cast blame on the "sensationalist media" reporting on the quote, trying to distance interest "in titillating stories that focus on the drama of the white conscience," from any "historical interest" in his book.[3] Marvel just sighed, knowing it was the only thing of value in the entire book, as it seemed like practically everything else was his own interpretation of things that other people already had written about, or at least documented. I have to say I was surprised that he was sticking to that line, especially since he was the one person who benefited from the headline-grabbing attention he got from it.

While Tyson might be dismissing the importance of the Carolyn quote now that the authorities were pressing him to prove he had heard it—maybe *only* because of that—this was a dramatically different position from one he had taken years before the book's release, and years before he was questioned by the FBI about it, pressed to prove it. In that seven-month-long email correspondence Tyson had with Devery Anderson in 2014, he wrote about just how important such a quote by Carolyn would be in marketing his book. It seemed that the only reason he even was chatting with Devery about it was because he had gotten outed.

In a March 31, 2014, email sent at 12:32 P.M., Devery asked about the quote he had seen online.[4] According to Devery's email, he had found a passage attributed to Carolyn that was included in a Timothy Tyson online posting for one of his courses:

"You tell these stories for so long that they seem true, but that part is not true. I wish I could tell you the truth, I really do. Honestly, I just don't remember. It was fifty years ago. I am not sure what is true. But nothing that boy did could ever justify what happened to him. —Carolyn Bryant, 2010."[5]

Devery went on to ask whether the quote really was reported by Tyson and whether its posting online was "unauthorized."[6]

Tyson responded almost immediately at 1:17 P.M. that day, confirming that the quote was reported by him, but that the posting was not authorized.[7]

"Bad news if Carolyn hears of it," Tyson wrote, in what I interpreted as an expression of sympathy for her. "She is not well in body but also not well in her mind and spirit, and cries incessantly at any mention of the case." Finally, he wrote, "I agree with all you said about her," referring to all that Devery had expressed about how unfairly he felt Carolyn had been treated by people who wanted her "burning in hell . . ."[8]

To this day, it makes me uncomfortable to reflect on this exchange, two White men expressing sympathy for the White woman who set in motion the events leading to the death of Emmett Till—the story they published in books that likely earned them some money and certainly earned them some notoriety. This exchange between these two guys practically echoed the words of Carolyn's manuscript that she felt she was a victim just like Emmett Till.

In a July 25, 2014, email, Devery asked again about the online reference, which he had confirmed had been included in materials for a course Tyson taught titled "The South in Black and White." Devery wanted to review Tyson's notes to support the writing of his own book, since that quotation by Carolyn had never been reported on before then.[9] Tyson responded to Devery by email the following day, writing that a teaching assistant had posted the paper mistakenly, when he was only supposed to distribute hard copies to the seminar students. Tyson had the materials taken down from the internet.[10] But the FBI was able to get the entire document anyway. That's what they do.

The paper, titled "Emmett Till Case and Montgomery Bus

Boycott 1955–56," included some of the narrative Tyson eventually would include in his book about how he came to meet Carolyn and Marsha. He expressed his surprise that Carolyn seemed to him like a "beloved aunt," as she was cutting him a slice of pound cake, part of the reason, he wrote, that he was "surprised to find her a sympathetic character."[11] Perhaps that gentle perception led to Tyson writing in this paper that, based on his assessment of her truthfulness, "her revelations in our interview" were "sometimes slightly at odds with the stories in her memoir . . ." Seriously? Now that we'd been able to read her memoir, we knew her claim and his quotation were not *slightly* at odds." They were completely opposite. And we were further disturbed by his reference to her as "a captive witness at the 1955 murder trial, her testimony contrived by her husband's family and their lawyers."[12] Even if you were going to give her the benefit of the doubt and assume she was under some kind of pressure from her husband and others back in 1955—a benefit Devery Anderson and Timothy Tyson seemed quite eager to give and one I definitely was not going along with—in 2008, years after the deaths of J. W. Milam and Roy Bryant, there was nobody standing over her, or twisting her arm, or doing anything to pressure her to repeat the lies or, worse, expand on them with the outrageous claims she wrote in her manuscript. And with Tyson's help! Beyond the courtroom fantasies, she and Tyson wrote in her book that she "feared" Bobo was going to "molest" her. She had never said anything like that before and Tyson knew it.[13]

Over the course of a couple of months, Devery Anderson continued to ask Tyson whether he could use the quoted material or refer to it in some way the two of them could agree on—even offering several items of his own research for use in Tyson's book. But Tyson held out. In his July 26, 2014, email to Devery, Tyson expressed concern that Devery's book on Emmett Till and one that Loyola University professor Elliott Gorn was writing would come out before his book. "I am all but certain that I am going to be third in this lineup, so I need to have a little something new to say, which my editor has made emphatically clear." Apart from his original interview with Carolyn, he wrote, much of his research was from "newspapers and all of the many secondary sources."[14] In other words, the only thing new in Tyson's book would be the material from Carolyn. Again in an August 14, 2014, email to Devery, Tyson wrote that his editor was "emphatic that I hang on tight to the only two new things that my book will have, the documents and interviews with Carolyn, and their insights."[15]

Then there was an earlier email exchange with David Beito, at that time a professor of history at the University of Alabama–Tuscaloosa, who, with his wife, Professor Linda Royster Beito, then chair of the department of social sciences at nearby Stillman College, was an expert on the Emmett Till story through their research and book on Mississippi activist Dr. T.R.M. Howard. In that email exchange, it was clear that Tyson recognized the value of what he claimed to be getting from Carolyn, even though the precise headline-producing quote did not appear to be part of it. "I interviewed Carolyn Bryant," Tyson wrote to David Beito.* "She sang like a canary."[16] Beito wrote back. "Are you serious about Bryant?!" As a matter of history, Beito wrote, that would be the "coup of the decade." Beito asked some pointed questions about what Tyson had gotten and Tyson was quite open with him—colleague to colleague, historian to historian.[17] Tyson responded, "Yes, indeed, I am serious about Bryant and will make the interview available to everyone as soon as I possibly can." He went on to summarize what he had gotten. "Her testimony at the trial about what Till did and said is the same one, more or less, that she gives now. She did acknowledge that it has been fifty some years and her memory may not be the fact of the matter." He went on to write in detail the account Carolyn has been giving most

---

* Tyson's footnotes in *The Blood of Emmett Till* list a single interview with Carolyn Bryant as having taken place in September 2008. However, this email exchange with Beito, which includes the line, "I interviewed Carolyn Bryant *on Sunday*" (emphasis added), is date-stamped July 9, 2009, and July 15, 2009. That Sunday would have been July 5, 2009.

recently about how Milam and Bryant brought Bobo to the store for her to identify, "and she told them it was not the right one and that they should take him back where they got him, but that they did not believe her, possibly, and left with him, promising to take him home. And we know more or less what happened after that." Tyson wrote that Carolyn had given him "great characterizations and stories about" the Milam-Bryant family and quoted her saying, "They all killed him, all of them killed him."[18]

This email exchange seems to show a few things. First, Tyson does not even come close to suggesting that Carolyn had recanted. In fact, he wrote quite clearly that her story had not changed since her 1955 testimony, and his two interviews with her had concluded by this time. For the record, though, her story had changed a bit—for the worse—with enhancements that he either approved or had a hand in changing. But there was nothing in the interview transcripts or in Carolyn's manuscript to suggest a recantation. There would be no more meetings with her after this email exchange, no more chances to get the quote that really would have become the historical "coup of the decade." Also, Tyson appeared to be accepting the continued lie that Carolyn tells about how Milam and Bryant brought Bobo to the store and how she urged them to take him home, even though she said *he* (not "it" as Tyson wrote) was not the one. Second, he was gushing about the specifics he had gotten from her about family characterizations and that killer quote about how they all were responsible for Bobo's death. A quote, by the way, that like the widely reported quote does not appear in the transcripts of his two interviews with Carolyn and was not scribbled onto that one sheet of legal pad he photocopied for the FBI.

Finally, it is clear that any reasonable historian would recognize the significance of the Carolyn interview, which, again, Beito, a tenured professor of history, described as the "coup of the decade." And Tyson clearly respects Beito's judgment. "When I get a draft together, I would be glad to show it to you. You'd be about the best reader one could hope for," he wrote in his July 15 email.[19] Yet and still, he wrote to Brandis Friedman nearly eight years later in February 2017 that the Carolyn material was not significant. It was "not even in the top ten sources" among the "thousands" of sources he claimed to have reviewed.[20]

We know better than to accept that source count of his. We checked the cited sources. None of this seemed to add up.

IT WAS ABOUT nine that night when we got back to our hotel following dinner with Walter Henry. We were too worked up to even think about going to bed, despite a demanding schedule the next day— from an 8:30 A.M. breakfast with the officials from the University of Mississippi through the afternoon meeting with Agents Henry and Wright. But Marvel, Chris, and I needed to keep talking about the briefing we had gotten over dinner. We needed to process it all so that we could provide the responses we were expected to give the FBI agents the next day.

That dinner with Agent Henry confirmed for us, finally, that in the interview the federal and state officials had conducted with Timothy Tyson, the truth had been revealed: There was nothing to prove that Tyson ever had heard the words from Carolyn Bryant Donham, the words that he had included in his book. The words that had arrested national attention, raised expectations, and reignited the passions of so many people who believed we finally might see someone held accountable in the lynching of Emmett Till. The words that moved the FBI to continue its investigation. The words Tyson scribbled onto a legal pad and reproduced and sent to the government investigators as proof of the truth of the words he had published.

Words. Everything started with them. There were the words that had been written down by the defense lawyers, probably on another legal pad. The words that translated Carolyn's words, sharpening them as weapons in preparation for the battle, the trial that would win freedom for Milam and Bryant. The new words that shifted and morphed in her memory between her recitation to her husband and that to a lawyer in court under oath. The words of accusation, claiming Bobo had assaulted her. Now there were new words that contradicted the other words, the ugly words that had led to Bobo's grisly murder.

After all of that, it was looking like Tyson had no proof that Carolyn Bryant Donham had ever spoken those words, as he had claimed. "That part's not true" might as well have been the words Carolyn was speaking about Tyson's book.

We sat at a long table in the lobby of the Central Station hotel going over it all while Chris typed notes into his laptop. The music was blaring from the lower-level bar—the sound of Memphis: "Hold On, I'm Coming."

It was about ten o'clock when Chris looked up from the computer, gazed out over my shoulder through the wall of windows behind me, and blurted out what I had been confirming for him ever since we checked in earlier that evening—almost like our running joke.

"Wow," he said. "This really *is* still a train station."

"That's what I've been telling you," I said with a laugh.

"No, really," he said, pointing out at the tracks behind me. "And there's a train."

I turned around to see what he saw. About a hundred yards away on the platform, a train had pulled into the south of the Central Station hotel, headed north, passengers getting off onto the platform, headed our way.

"Wait," Chris said, "that's the City of New Orleans train."

It took a moment for me to process it. The City of New Orleans train—the train that carried me back to Chicago after Bobo was taken. As if in a trance, drawn to the bright headlamp of the engine, I slowly rose from the table, walked across the lobby closer to that wall of windows, and gazed out at the train. It almost seemed to be exhaling, breathing as heavily as a long-distance runner might in the cold December air. Even though it was facing north preparing for the rest of its trip, I felt like it was carrying me back south, back across the Mississippi River, to the edge of the Delta and the moment I desperately wanted to escape sixty-four years earlier and ever since. As I felt the weight of the baggage I had been carrying all that distance, and over all that time, it began to come back to me. The memory of a threat so vivid that it made the threat so real. Still.

IT WAS EARLY that Sunday morning, August 28, 1955, only a few hours and a lifetime after those men had taken Bobo, when we hooked up with my uncle Elbert Parker. He was my father's brother and had a reputation for being bad and not taking stuff off White folks. He's the one who got into it with the boss man over his cotton tally. The one the boss man threatened. The one who nearly lost his tongue for talking back, complaining. That was Uncle Elbert. Never hesitated to stand up for his rights. But this was different, so, taking no chances, he grabbed his gun that morning when he also was armed with instructions from my parents: Get me over to my uncle William Parker's place in Duck Hill. Uncle William would then put me on the next train at the Winona station five miles from his house. Everything had been planned out very quickly, but very carefully, except for one thing. Uncle Elbert didn't own a car. So he walked to us and then my uncle Maurice drove us all in Papa's sputtering car, the one with the stripped gears that we had driven Uptown to Money the night Bobo had whistled at Carolyn, and then piled in to make our getaway from that scare, chugging down Darfield or Dark Ferry or Dark Fear Road. The same car we had driven over to Greenwood the night before. Hit up shots of 'shine. Hit that dog on the way back. Made Bobo cry. This would be my last ride in that old car—past Carter Plantation, the next one over, where Uncle Elbert lived, and then over to Duck Hill where Uncle William lived with his family.

Curtis Jones rolled with us. Just in case. He had been talking kind of wild, about getting a gun and going after the kidnappers. But he had not been through what I had been through. I had been up all night after the kidnappers left. Simmie, too, sitting there in the dark—terrified. My imagination had been running like crazy, wondering what would happen when those men came back, wondering what would have happened if that gun had gone off in my face, agonizing over how I didn't want to stay there and find out if they did come back. I was in Mississippi. How was I going to get out of there, get back home? All that had been running through my head while Curtis had slept through it all. Now he was talking big talk about shooting up some people and all I wanted was just to get out of there.

And I did.

Uncle Maurice got me to Duck Hill, and I stayed over that Sunday with Uncle William, Aunt Hester, and their daughters: Gladiola, Charlestine, Jewel, and Joy. I had gotten away from the house of terror, but I really didn't get away from the terror itself. That's how terror works. That's how it works you. So, that night in the dark, the horror set in again. Someone had said the kidnappers were going to come after me. I couldn't escape that thought. It stalked me. Had I gotten far enough away? Had somebody seen me being driven over here? Were they waiting for the right moment to come after me in the pitch black with flashlights and guns like the night before, terrifying my family in this house the way they had done with my family in the other house? I walked the floor all that night looking out the window so I could see them before they could see me. I don't know what good it would have done to see them first, but it was the only thing I could do. That's how terror works. That's how it works you—lurking out there in the dark, waiting for the moment you let your guard down and close your eyes and think it's safe to sleep once again. Terror is about the fear that a thing is going to happen more than the fear of the thing itself.

Uncle William planned to put me on the train in Winona the next day for the short trip up through the Delta, across the Mississippi River, to connect with the City of New Orleans train passing through Memphis on the way back home to Chicago. That was the plan. But my uncle had the train times mixed up. Maybe he was nervous, too—in as much of a hurry to get me on that train as I was to get on it and get away. On our first trip to the station we found out the train was not due in until much later than he thought. Thank God he didn't leave me there. Seemed like it took another week to get to the train departure time that night.

When I finally made it aboard, I still was unsettled. Was I really safe? I worked up the nerve to take in the rest of the car, the passengers I hadn't really noticed when I jumped into my seat. For the first time I realized everybody else was in uniform. They were soldiers, African American soldiers. This was a troop train. And I was relieved. Something about those uniforms made me feel like I had my own personal military escort. I had no idea whether they really would protect me, but I was pretty sure they would not shoot me.

Even so, I kept looking around—across from me, in front of me, behind me. Through the window, I could see the end of the train as the tracks curved. For some reason, I kept staring at the end of the train. Not really sure why. Crazy as it seems, it might have been to make sure no one was following us, like that night in the car on Dark Fear Road. After Bobo whistled.

When we crossed over the Mississippi River and pulled into Memphis—the big city—I figured I was home free. Or at least free, if not home yet. After all, I had escaped from Mississippi and the nightmare of a night I had endured. Getting off the train, I felt comfortable enough to race across the huge waiting room of Central Station. It had been a short ride from Winona, but just long enough. And I was so nervous. I needed to use the restroom. That's when it happened.

"Hey. You. Stop." It was a man's voice yelling out to me.

My fear had been realized. Somebody had followed me all the way to Memphis!

"You can't go in there, boy."

I looked up and realized that in my haste and with no sleep, I was about to stumble into the "Whites Only" restroom. The man who was yelling at me was not one of the kidnappers. He was reminding me of my place. Memphis might have been the big city compared with Money, it might have been on the other side of the Mississippi River, I even might have been north of Mississippi itself, but I was still in the South. At least the man who caught me didn't try to hurt me. Even so, there would be no peace right then, or for some time. It was going to be a long wait for the City of New Orleans train and a long ride home as I would think about place and the power of some White man I didn't even know to keep me there.

When I finally got to Chicago, I made it straight to Mamie's house on South St. Lawrence Avenue on Chicago's Southside, a two-flat building her family owned. It seemed like everybody was there when I walked into the room. Mamie. Her mother, Alma. My parents. Other family members. Neighbors. Church people. Union people. Everybody. It was strange in that room—so many people there, nobody saying anything. *Please, somebody say something so I don't have to stand here trying to figure out what everybody's thinking, nobody's saying.*

Mamie broke the silence and told me to go over and hug my mother. After I did, the room was kind of hushed again. Mamie and I didn't say anything more to each other. I kept thinking there was something I was supposed to say, but I couldn't figure out what that was. In a way, I wanted to say something hopeful, to be of comfort. But that would have been dishonest since hope wasn't what I was feeling in my heart. It definitely wasn't what I was feeling in that room with all those folks who seemed to be waiting for confirmation more than news. It had been over twenty-four hours since the kidnapping and no word. No word seemed to say so much more than any word could express at that moment. These were my people and my people had come from Mississippi and people who come from Mississippi—Black people—know what happens when White people come for you in the night. So everybody just waited quietly as if they already knew much more than anybody wanted to express at that moment.

I was waiting, too. In a way, I was waiting for Mamie to say more and, I guess, she was waiting for me to say something. And we wound up just letting the moment pass until it was too late to say anything at all. In a way, that said everything. I had made it out of Mississippi. I had made it home. Her son hadn't made it back. I was his older cousin, but in a way, he was my younger brother. So that quiet space created enough room to rethink, relive that moment of horror as those racists took Bobo away. Was there something I could have done to stop it? Should I have stayed to help find Bobo? If I had stayed behind, could I have done more than others who stayed behind? Then, at least, I would have something to talk about with Mamie, something to report, instead of saying simply that I had gotten out of there as fast as I could. As I sorted it all, I remembered how those men threatened Papa, warned him to keep his mouth shut, ordered my grandmother back to bed after my grandparents had pleaded, even offered money. I remembered the look on Bobo's face. It was a look I could never describe to Mamie. How could I tell her that her son was afraid, that he looked to us for an answer as well as help? What was happening? He had no idea what was about to happen. But he must have been filling in the blank space of "no idea" with some pretty bad notions. And even these ideas could not match the reality in store for him. How could I tell Mamie that there was nothing we could do to comfort him, to say more on his behalf, to save him? How could I describe the emptiness, the dead silence after that word— "Yes"—was spoken at the truck identifying Bobo as the one? That voice that was lighter than a man's voice. A woman's voice.

After that for an eternal moment, just like the people in the room at Mamie's place, no one at the Wright home that night said a word.

As I STARED through that wall of windows at Central Station terminal and hotel that December night in 2019, it all came back to me: my sixty-four-year-long journey that began with the City of New Orleans train, carrying Bobo and me down to Mississippi, carrying me back home alone, and ultimately carrying back Bobo's remains to be identified, memorialized, buried.

My two uncles had been my saviors that day when they helped me escape. As it turns out, I wasn't the only one who didn't sleep that night before Uncle William put me on the train. My cousin Gladiola would tell me years later that no one in the house could sleep that

night. Could have been their own fear. Then again, she said, it probably was the sound of me walking the floor all night—creaking like a
ghost in the darkness to gaze out the window. She also shared that my
aunt Hester had not wanted Uncle Elbert to bring me there to her
home in the first place, afraid for her family. But I was the oldest child
of Uncle William's baby brother, Wheeler Sr. So, despite the fact that
I was carrying with me the dread of what had happened in the Wright
home the night before, and bringing it into their home that day, there
was no way Uncle William could refuse.

It seems Aunt Hester had good reason to be afraid for me to be
there. Almost fifty years later, Uncle William told me what he had
never wanted to tell me sooner than that. Sure enough, shortly after I
had gotten safely away, two White men had come up to Uncle William in the cotton field and asked him if the boy from Chicago was
there. He played dumb. Playing dumb is how we outsmarted White
folks. So he acted like he didn't know what they were talking about.
But he knew, all right. Of course he knew. He knew that someone
had given him up, told these men about his connection to me. But he
knew better than to let on that he knew. That's because he knew
what to not know. Most of the time the best way to survive in that
hateful place was to not know.

It all rushed over me in my stare-down with that train, just like the
voice of that man who caught me before I nearly crossed the line and
stepped into the Whites Only restroom, echoing in that vast space of
the Central Station hotel lobby and terminal—just how close I had
come, how narrowly I had escaped. That man calling me back. Sam
and Dave calling me forward. "Hold On, I'm Coming." And I felt
haunted by one more thing. The thing I had agonized over in the
eternal silence between Mamie and me and all the years since: I had
left my cousin behind.

DECEMBER 12, 2019. Chris and I were seated at the head of a horse-
shoe of conference tables. That was when I learned that we were
expected to lead the conversation among the impressive group of

University of Mississippi representatives. Dr. Katrina Caldwell, vice chancellor for diversity and community engagement, had organized the meeting with Patrick Weems. The university provost, Dr. Noel Wilkin, was there, too. So were Dr. Shawnboda Mead, assistant vice chancellor for diversity; Dr. Cade Smith, assistant vice chancellor for community engagement; Dr. Arthur Doctor, director of fraternal leadership and learning; Dr. E. J. Edney, director of inclusion and cross-cultural engagement; and Tracy Murry, director of conflict resolution and student conduct. These were the people who would have a voice in the campus-wide conversation about a long-standing problem at the University of Mississippi. It was a problem that had been well publicized starting in 1962 when race riots broke out over the integration of the school by James Meredith and then again in 2014 when White students hung a noose around the statue of Meredith.[21] Even the nickname of the school had become problematic, causing tension in recent years as people discovered in the university archives that Ole Miss was how—and this is actually in writing—"old 'darkies' on southern plantations" addressed the White plantation mistress.[22] Our meeting, of course, was prompted by the latest incidents following the protests over the Confederate statue on campus and the fraternity students posing in front of the bullet-riddled Emmett Till sign. There also was a national search going on for an executive director to lead a new racial reconciliation institute that was under consideration. Patrick was on that committee and used that connection to these folks to suggest that the Mississippi administrators talk to us about a possible way forward.

We had gone into the belly of the beast and figured it was a good chance to have an open discussion that might lead to some positive change. Picking up on a stated mission of the university to "transform communities," we presented an informal outline of a comprehensive program of possibilities focusing on building new scholarship on racial reconciliation and social justice. Among other things, the plan we proposed included a yearlong symposium on racial hierarchy with monthly lectures by prominent national figures; development of special-topics courses; joint digital investigative projects with the Knight Lab at Northwestern University's Medill School of Journalism; and a residency for me to engage students on a regular basis—humanizing the narratives they would engage in the other areas.

The group seemed to appreciate our suggestions and wanted to continue the planning. We were encouraged by this group's assurance that there would continue to be significant dialogue on the ideas we had discussed as we moved forward. We left the meeting feeling as if we at least had stimulated some progressive thought, even if the conservative higher administration and trustees might wind up taking a view that was different from this group's.

There was an even more important takeaway from this meeting, which would endure no matter what happened (or what didn't happen) later in connection with the University of Mississippi. In preparing for that meeting, we had sharpened our view of what justice for Emmett Till might include. Education on multiple levels would be key. Civic engagement would flow from that education. Participation in elections and social justice activism would be critical parts of that engagement. The common consideration in all of this was a focus on young people: cultivating the emerging generations of national leadership. Nothing could do more honor to the legacy of Emmett Till and Mamie Till-Mobley than that.

Before we could move forward with such considerations, though, we had to resolve the lingering issues with Timothy Tyson and Carolyn Bryant Donham. And that looked as challenging at that moment—after two and a half years of investigation—as it had been in the very beginning.

THAT AFTERNOON, WE had our follow-up meeting at the Central Station hotel with Special Agent Walter Henry and Special Agent Shannon Wright before heading back to the airport. For the record, they wanted to get my reaction. Of course, I was deeply disappointed by what we had learned from Henry the night before and what we discussed further during this meeting. We had hoped that the truth about Emmett Till finally would be validated. Instead, the lies continued. What was being revealed about Tyson reminded me so much of William Bradford Huie, who wrote the *Look* magazine article that people cited for years. Except for the admission of murder by Milam and Bryant, that article was a pack of lies and was written from the perspective of two of the White killers. Even though Tyson was critical of Huie and his methods, he still insisted on repeating the Huie version of events in putting his own book together. Again, Tyson never talked with any of us and arrogantly said he didn't think he needed to. If he had, he might have learned that there were comments and quotes reported in the media back in the 1950s that were incorrect.

Words were put in my mouth by some reporters—words I never would speak, and even words that might have been spoken by my father, Wheeler Parker Sr. There were articles that quoted me and were written by reporters who never even met me. One example of this is a story published in the *Clarion-Ledger* on September 2, 1955.[23] The quotes don't even sound like the way I spoke back then. Any reasonable person would know this. Michael Randolph Oby recognized it and wrote about it in his 2007 master's degree thesis at Georgia State University. He cited passages from that story that just didn't ring true to his ear. "The article also quoted Parker as saying 'I guess Emmett was killed because of the 'wolf' call he whistled at a pretty 27-year-old white lady in a store last Wednesday.' Parker was raised in rural Mississippi so the dialectical tone of the quote is questionable."[24] Oby concluded that these and other facts he listed "raise suspicion as to the validity of the quote."[25] Well, he sure got that right. For one thing, I never referred to Bobo as Emmett Till. Even now, I have trouble referring to him by his full formal name, because that is not the way I knew him. He was Bobo to me and everybody who was close to him. Also, I never thought of Carolyn as "pretty," and I had no idea how old she was.

Even the celebrated late journalist David Halberstam made a serious mistake. He wrote that Emmett Till and Curtis Jones drove to Mississippi together. That was wrong on multiple levels, and Halberstam should have known better. As a young reporter, he covered the murder trial of Milam and Bryant, and everyone knew we'd traveled down by train—at the very least.

Devery Anderson wound up doing something similar to what Tyson had. While Devery did spend some time interviewing Simmie and me, it seemed that he spent even more time raising questions about our memory of the things we lived through. The federal investigators showed me examples of how Devery substituted his own research for the truth of events, even while reporting what we had told him. In other words, he left readers with the conclusion that he knew our story better than we did, instead of seriously questioning whether the White reporters of the news stories got it right.

And I let the agents in our meeting know how offensive it was for Timothy Tyson and Devery Anderson to try to take control of the story—appropriating it, trying to make it their own, dismissing the actual victims of the horrible crimes committed against Bobo, the crimes committed against our family.

One element of this can be seen in an exchange between Timothy Tyson and Devery Anderson about Dark Fear Road. Tyson questioned the accuracy of the name some folks used for the road that fronted Simmie's Delta home. He posed the question to Devery in a July 29, 2014, email at 8:04 A.M. "Despite Simeon Wright is otherwise a pretty good source, I have a hard time swallowing that the road they lived on was actually named 'Dark Fear Road,' as he claims in *Simeon's Story*"—Simmie's book. "I mean, *Dark Fear Road*? Do you believe it?"[26] He went on to write that the reference to Dark Fear Road "smelled to high heaven."

Devery answered, writing at 11:32 that same morning that Simmie had told him that the name he always had heard was "Darfield Road" but that it was "Dark Ferry Road" in the 2006 FBI report.[27] Devery referred to the name and the association Simmie made to lynchings, suggesting that either he or his co-author, journalist Herb Boyd, "clearly made that up" and he went on to refute other assertions in Simmie's book.[28]

Even I was surprised to learn that I was quoted in the FBI report referring to "Dark Ferry Road." But maybe that is just what people heard Black folks saying in what graduate student Oby called that "dialectical tone" that transformed Darfield into Dark Ferry and ultimately Dark Fear, just as Shurden became Sheridan and Schlater became Slaughter across generations. That was our truth. But it was like these White guys felt they knew more about us than we knew about ourselves and that we couldn't be telling the truth about our lived experiences. They could have asked Herb Boyd, as Chris Benson did in an interview. Boyd said that Simmie told him the name of the road was Dark Fear. Chris also had asked Simmie about it after reading his book, while interviewing him for a December 2009 article in *Chicago* magazine.[29] Simmie told him he only recently had heard the name as Dark Fear. As Black writers, both Herb Boyd and Chris Benson accepted the possibility of a slow drift on the name since they understood something about the Black voice, Black vernacular, and how Black lore in the Black voice can become what Simmie said it had become.

Apparently, neither of the White writers cared to really understand that possibility. They could have followed up with the Black people they were writing about to clarify. But they arrogantly preferred to talk to each other as the only credible sources to verify and validate and valorize.

Tyson's arrogance on this front wasn't limited to his correspondence with Devery, which we touched on with the FBI agents in the hotel meeting. Despite the kind words Tyson spoke about Mamie in his public interviews promoting his book, he took quite a different tone during his interview with Carolyn Bryant Donham. During one of the conversations with Carolyn and Marsha, they seem to be effectively demeaning Mamie by rejecting two of her stories. One is her version of Bobo's whistle. Mamie had said for years that she taught him to whistle to steady his stutter so that he could speak more clearly. "Oh, please!" Tyson said to Carolyn and Marsha as he dismissed Mamie's story. "But people just tsk tsk tsk cause it suits their purpose—"[30]

Now, I was at the store and I know that Bobo whistled as a prank and not to steady his voice. But while Tyson is sympathetic to Carolyn—who could have been like a "beloved aunt" in his family—he seemed to be laughing at Mamie. If he really cared about understanding Mamie, her humanity, her feelings, the way he appeared to do for Carolyn, he might have wanted to explore why a mother would naturally think about her son the way Mamie did—to believe that he had done nothing wrong. To convince herself of that. Tyson would have considered what it must have been like for a mother who had convinced herself that the one thing she felt she taught her son to have a better life just might have cost him his life. A mother who felt responsibility for the loss of her son and felt the need to punish herself with that narrative, not even realizing that she was doing so. Only a few months before her death, Mamie shared how she knew that in the last moments of his life, Bobo "must have cried out. Two names. 'God and Mama.' And no one answered the call."[31] What does that say about her truth?

Devery was just as willing to see Carolyn as a sympathetic character, as discussed earlier in the email exchange with Tyson. But he also made some assumptions about her and her motivations that were teased out in his February 3, 2017, review of Tyson's book on the Amazon.com site. Among other things, he defended Carolyn against the beliefs that have existed for years among so many of us. "To declare that Carolyn's lies led to Emmett's death is simply not true."[32] Really? Then what else? How do you explain the killers Milam and Bryant showing up at Papa's house asking for the boy from Chicago who did the talking? There had been no talking by Bobo at the store, so right there is evidence of a lie that set Bobo's kidnapping and murder in motion. Even the earliest version of the lie she told to Sidney

Carlton the defense attorney amounted to enough for racists to want to kill Bobo to assert their White power.

In addition to the examples cited earlier in the conversation among Tyson, Carolyn, and Marsha, there also was the earlier email exchange between Devery and Tyson about whether Bobo should have known about racism because of the racism that existed in Chicago. Devery echoes that point in his February 2017 Amazon.com review, calling Tyson's treatment of this topic "One of the strongest parts of the book, to me . . ."[33] Devery endorses Tyson's description of Chicago "as anything but a paradise for its black citizens," writing that Tyson "paints a vivid picture of racism in the windy city that rivaled the South, except for its de facto nature. In other words, Emmett Till should have entered Mississippi with enough experience with racism to have already learned a lesson or two on his own."[34] This sounds a whole lot like blaming the victim. But there's even more here that reflects White assumptions about the Black experience than any real evidence these two guys bothered to produce.

Now, I came from Mississippi, and I lived in the Chicago area. I know both places, and because I do, I know the difference and know for a fact that racial discrimination in Chicago—which has existed for years—does not and did not rival the racial violence that threatened Black folks in the South. Devery's point comes across as a contradiction of Mamie, who wrote that Bobo did not have the same experience of the rest of us who had lived it in Mississippi. I know as a fact that what she said about Bobo is right. He did not know what we knew. If he did, he never would have pulled the prank that led to his death. People in Chicago might have been aware of racial discrimination, but we lived in such insulated, self-contained, tightly segregated communities back in the day that we really didn't experience it on a daily basis the way you did in the South, and certainly not as intensely. Besides, Mamie talked about discrimination in Chicago and, among other things, the fact that she had to shop in the basement at Marshall Field's department store with all the other Black customers, and the fact that her first date with Louis Till involved a racial incident with a drugstore owner that they were able to overcome.

The point is not just that Timothy Tyson and Devery Anderson don't understand the full scope of what they are talking about when it comes to Black folks, but that they don't seem to know what they don't know. And because of that, they conclude that it's the Black folks who got it wrong. We got it wrong about Carolyn Bryant Donham. We got it wrong about the consequences of a mother's grief. We even got it wrong about our own communities—communities these guys never really experienced.

When Black folks complain about White folks appropriating our stories, we tend to be dismissed as unreasonable. I would never argue that the tragedy of Emmett Till cannot be considered and written about by anyone. What I will say is that we should recognize the limitations of some storytellers. It's what leads to skepticism about whether Black storytelling is factual, and the assumption that White storytelling can be accepted at *face* value. What caused me to just shake my head in disappointment was seeing examples of suspicion, of distrust that Timothy Tyson and Devery Anderson brought to their evaluation of Black narratives and their willingness to accept so much of what White sources said without verification. How can they be honest in rendering stories if they are not honest in recognizing their preconceptions, their assumptions that can color their reality?

There is another aspect of this issue of appropriation. One thing I have learned is that it is not just something that only White people do. When it comes to Emmett Till, especially, it seems like everybody wants to own a piece of the story. Without question, it is a story that connects with everyone. But connection to a story as an emotional trigger or even as a cultural or national unifier is one thing. It's quite another to assert ownership of pieces of the story—whether it's reusing iconic photo images taken from Mamie's personal collection without proper attribution, or misusing the Emmett Till name for distasteful comparisons.

Over the years, Airickca Gordon-Taylor was vigilant in policing the misuses of the name of Emmett Till, which is why she intervened on behalf of the Till family to stop the use of Bobo's name in the Lil Wayne rap on "Karate Chop" in 2013. The rap artist wound up apologizing for the lyric comparing the beating of Bobo to an offensive sex act, and his sponsor, PepsiCo, dropped him as an endorser for Mountain Dew, even after the lyric was changed.[35]

There also are concerns when people use the name Emmett Till in fundraising efforts, as some have done, promising to seek justice for Bobo when personal enrichment really seems to be their goal. Mamie was confronted with this reality very early when she began making public appearances following Bobo's death in 1955. One example is recounted in her book. She had completed an appearance in a Detroit church where a couple of collections had been taken up for the NAACP and she wanted to thank the pastor for his support, only to discover the pastor, a noted minister and father of a world-famous R&B recording artist, in the private office stuffing money from the collection plates into his briefcase.[36] This was one of a few incidents that led to Mamie's long-standing practice of making sure she had a clear legal understanding with anyone who wanted her to appear at fundraisers or wanted to use her name, her likeness, or images of Bobo in any moneymaking effort. As family members often would joke, Mamie was all about the money. In fact, she was all about avoiding being exploited, or having her son exploited.

As in life, Emmett Till has been magnetic over so many years of his afterlife. Just as he always had a way of pulling people close to him during the years I knew him, so his story continues to pull people closer to him. I thought about this after we ended our meeting with Special Agent Henry and Special Agent Wright in Memphis, considering what to take away at the end of our analysis of Timothy Tyson's work against the backdrop of others who have attempted to represent the story of Emmett Till. While we can appreciate the lessons people might learn about systemic racism from Bobo's story, it seems too many people miss the point about the challenge of Bobo—the challenge to understand the impact of systemic racism and our duty to work for social change. It seems people simply want to control Bobo's story as a way of elevating themselves. They want to be seen as heroes if only because they are telling the story, or their version of the story, or because they present something they say is more authoritative than the last thing that was said about the story, or because they claim to have found something new about the story. And if they are elevated by all this, it is because the public celebrates them for all this. For standing up for something we all believe in. Justice.

I am not a hero. I don't want to be seen as a hero. I am a survivor. And I am dedicated to the truth about Emmett Till and how that truth can lead us forward. Survivors all. Of the challenges that lie in wait.

15

Ghost Skins

WE BEGAN THE year 2020 with a mixture of anticipation and dread. Two meetings that past December left us with both optimism and skepticism; the extremes had given us double vision. The meeting with the University of Mississippi officials was uplifting. The meeting with Special Agents Henry and Shannon later that day was disappointing. Bobo was the one common theme in both settings. He represented the denial of justice on the one hand, and on the other, the promise of building something positive, something inspiring on the foundation of that disappointment. Just as Mamie had mined her grief for a mission in life—a mission as an activist—I would now need to look beyond charges, indictments, convictions for new answers to the question that had motivated us down the path we had been traveling since March 2017: What does justice look like?

The investigation was pretty much drawing to a close. We were not certain how long it would take for the Department of Justice to process all the information, reach a conclusion, issue a report to close the matter, or whether they would have enough information to justify Mississippi District Attorney Dewayne Richardson convening a new grand jury. At least Special Agent Walter Henry would continue on the case no matter what. Chris had written a note to DOJ officials expressing our wish that Henry continue since he was familiar with the matter and we trusted him, had confidence in his work and his dedication to the case. Even though his retirement was mandatory, Henry would be allowed to continue working on the matter in a special status. That was especially important now because DOJ civil rights attorney Dana Mulhauser was leaving. She had taken a position as the founding chief of the Conviction and Incident Review Unit at the St. Louis County Prosecuting Attorney's Office in Missouri. That unit had been started up as a result of the August 2014 police shooting death of Michael Brown. Her deep commitment to justice in our matter continued to show even on her way out the door. Before she left, she spent a considerable amount of time writing a detailed summary for her successor, DOJ attorney Angela Miller.

Still, we kept weighing it all, what justice would look like. That was what we were left with following our trip to Memphis. Our course of action was clear: Keep building. Keep moving forward. Keep the legacy of Emmett Till and Mamie Till-Mobley alive.

ON FEBRUARY 26, 2020, the House of Representatives voted to approve Representative Bobby Rush's Emmett Till antilynching bill by an overwhelming vote of 410 to 4.[1] Airickca Gordon-Taylor and her mother, Ollie Gordon, had traveled to Washington as the bill was scheduled to come to the floor. They wanted to be on hand as part of an eleventh-hour push for passage. Obviously, their presence helped, reminding lawmakers of the lack of justice in the lynching of Emmett Till and the need for a federal law to address this continuing problem.

Sadly, though, Airickca did not live to see the measure go further. She died on March 22, 2020. She had suffered kidney failure, a recurring problem most of her life. Even with one of her mother's kidneys, she finally gave up her valiant struggle, not only to live on, but to do so through lawmakers' commitment to a progressive agenda in honor of Mamie and Bobo.

There was quite a bit of press coverage of Airickca's transition. An announcement even was published by the Lawyers' Committee for

Civil Rights Under Law that had been associated with the work of Airickca's Mamie Till Mobley Memorial Foundation.[2]

"Airickca dedicated her life's work to lifting up the legacy of her cousin, Emmett Till, and she stood in solidarity with other families who had lost loved ones to racial violence in our country. She fought for truth and justice, and worked tirelessly to promote racial healing," wrote Kristen Clarke, president and executive director of the Lawyers' Committee. The statement included a photograph from happier times, including Director Clarke standing behind Airickca, who was seated next to Ollie. Director Clarke's hands rested on Airickca's shoulders—in a way, embracing her mission as well as her body.[3]

WE REMAINED IN constant contact with Special Agent Henry and periodic contact with DOJ attorney Angela Miller during this time. Their reports back were pretty much always the same. The file was being reviewed and a draft report would be forthcoming. That draft would be sent to Mississippi District Attorney Dewayne Richardson for his input and then returned to the DOJ for more tweaking. It would ping-pong like that until everything had been perfected. We tried to analyze each phone conversation for slight changes in the language of the updates, reading between the lines, looking for nuance, any indication that the government was leaning one way or another. The government wasn't giving up anything in these conversations, although we took it as a positive sign that they kept in touch. Their regular contact signaled to us that no final answers to their questions had been determined. But was anything discovered in the ongoing probe? Anything beyond what we had seen? Was there anything new that would lead to a murder or manslaughter indictment of Carolyn Bryant Donham? Was there anything new that would lead to an indictment on those charges against anyone else who was still alive? Was there any credible evidence that Carolyn had lied to the FBI in February 2017 when she denied making the statement to Timothy Tyson that he included in his book? There would be different jurisdiction depending on whether anything came of any of this.

Murder in this case would be a state offense, so DA Richardson would take over. Lying to federal authorities would mean the DOJ would take it up. The clock was ticking on that one. The statute of limitations was five years from the meeting between Carolyn and the FBI. That meant that the federal government would have only until February 2022 to charge her with making a false statement to the FBI. But since there is no statute of limitations on murder, the state would have time, as long as any perpetrators were still alive—including Carolyn Bryant Donham.

The clock was ticking for us, too. It did not seem that time was on our side. We were getting anxious all over again about whether the clock would just run out. This was an election year, and in the months that followed with nothing new on the investigation, we began to wonder whether someone at the top had given orders to slow-walk this case, hold it until after the November presidential election. We were disappointed that Attorney General William Barr had announced the summer before that there would be no new federal charges in the choke-hold death of Eric Garner.[4] Special Agent Henry was especially disappointed since he had worked the case and, like others at DOJ, believed there was enough evidence to bring a case of federal civil rights violation. What would happen to our case? Couldn't say one way or the other about that. But one thing was certain. People in power at the White House and at the top of the Department of Justice seemed to be getting even more hostile to people of color, more friendly with people who were hostile to people of color, more willing to support the use of raw power—including police power—against people of color, and much more comfortable demonstrating all of that. Three cases that year raised the tension and reinforced our anxiety—not just about the tragic occurrences of the events themselves, but also about the official responses.

On February 23, Ahmaud Arbery was hunted down by three White assailants and shot to death while he jogged through their neighborhood in Brunswick, Georgia. He was twenty-five years old.[5] On

March 13, Breonna Taylor, asleep in her bedroom, was shot to death by White police officers who were executing a no-knock warrant targeting the wrong residence in Louisville. She was twenty-six.[6] On May 25, George Floyd was killed by police officer Derek Chauvin, who restrained Floyd by kneeling on his neck for nine minutes and twenty-nine seconds, causing Floyd to suffocate—slowly—while handcuffed, head pressed against the pavement, crying out "I can't breathe" at least twenty-seven times.[7]

These cases of unwarranted force—brutality—only confirmed what African Americans have been pleading with everyone else to recognize. We are unfairly treated by the criminal justice system on multiple levels. Subject to extreme force and subject to a lack of accountability for wrongdoing by authorities, or people acting with authority they believe they have as a birthright.

None of the police officers were charged in the death of Breonna Taylor. Only one of the officers was indicted on a charge of reckless endangerment, not for shooting at her, but for shooting the wall in her bedroom—a bullet that entered the apartment of her neighbors.[8]

The killers of Arbery were not even arrested until after a video surfaced and went viral. Police and prosecutors first decided that the civilian killers were protected under Georgia's citizen's arrest law. It was pretty much the same with the Floyd case in terms of the lack of accountability, as the initial police report indicated only that Floyd expired during arrest. That was before the video by seventeen-year-old Darnella Frazier went viral.[9]

I've often wondered how different things might have been if there only had been a video in Bobo's case. Would the lies have continued for so long? Would people have believed Simmie and me when we told them over and over and over again that Carolyn lied? Would authorities still have given her the benefit of the doubt for so long? Of course, even when there is video evidence, justice is not a sure thing for Black victims. Defendants—the killers—often want the jury and the public at large to consider what happened *before* the video. Use your imagination. Fill in the blank spaces where racism—

even unconscious bias—can color and distort an encounter and escalate the confrontation before the video recording.

This year would be different. You might call it "2020 vision" that was sharpened across the country by social media images. People started standing up, stepping out, staking a claim on racial justice. Insisting on it.

There was an interesting takeaway from this moment. The name Emmett Till was on the lips of so many protestors who urged everyone to "say their names" and humanize the victims of racial atrocity, so we can appreciate much more fully what is lost with these deaths, as we have with Bobo. But so much of the connection to Bobo was superficial. Crimes against Black people, victims, in which White people, perpetrators, too often are set free. Yes, that is part of it. But the multiracial demonstrations in 2020 reminded us of the demonstrations that began in 1955 and continued on into the 1960s as a mass movement developed. "Black Lives Matter" was the battle cry during this recent time. But Emmett Till was the first Black Lives Matter story. The late John Lewis would say it in a different way in that essay published in *The New York Times* following his death the next year. "Emmett Till was my George Floyd."[10]

There was pushback. In a throwback to the 1950s when civil rights activists—including Mamie—were painted as Communists by FBI Director J. Edgar Hoover, protestors and activists in 2020 were painted as "anarchists" by Attorney General William Barr, the very person who might have the final word on the investigation into Bobo's murder.[11] Would he see it the way Hoover had?

All of this was set against the backdrop of a virus—fear. As in 1955 when change was in the air and equal rights were being supported by the Supreme Court, in 2020 many people were looking out at the horizon with anxiety about the changing complexion of America, a country where White people no longer were going to be in the majority. And, yes, there was COVID, too. COVID, especially. Inconvenient at one extreme, deadly at the other. We were on lockdown, which not only slowed our movement but also transformed our interactions. At a time when we needed to come together as a nation, we were isolating. Pulling apart, with so many people becoming victims of their own unchallenged thoughts and beliefs and conspiracy theories spreading like a virus. People were suffering from a widespread sense of threat on multiple levels.

AFTER THE MURDER of George Floyd, Senators Cory Booker and Kamala Harris reintroduced their antilynching bill in the Senate. That billed failed to pass, and the senators prepared to fight again another day. But, of course, there were bigger things in store for Senator Harris, who was nominated to be Joe Biden's vice president and was elected with Biden—the first woman and the first person of color ever elected as vice president. As we all know, though, that wasn't exactly the happy ending Biden-Harris supporters had hoped for, since a movement was growing among people who didn't want to accept a new day and a new way forward.

Change doesn't come easy.

While the January 6, 2021, Capitol insurrection—the riot and near takedown of the Congress by supporters of Donald Trump who wanted to oppose change, to block the certification of the election of Joe Biden and Kamala Harris—while that was frightening enough, there was something else. This particular threat has existed for quite a number of years—White nationalists, White supremacists in uniform, in the military and law enforcement departments. This dark moment highlighted people who were more dedicated to fighting for the *right* than they were to fighting for rights. Some were former skinheads, less recognizable in their uniforms, but even more threatening—armed and fully trained to be dangerous.[12]

They are called Ghost Skins.

IT WAS 1963 and I got drafted. At first the army stationed me in Texas at Fort Hood—named after Confederate General John Bell Hood—and then at Fort Sam Houston. For years, the army had a practice of sending Black GIs to the South for their first posting, for training, because they believed White southerners—officers—knew how to handle Black people, "train" us in that delicate balance, staying in our place even while we were killing people. Powerless and powerful all at the same time. I was pretty clear on my place in that place, so I really didn't need any reminders and tried to be very careful. I didn't want to wind up being one of those "*friendly*-fire accidents" we read about.

This was only the second time I had been South since Bobo was lynched. In 1959, I had traveled to Atlanta, Texas, for a funeral with Joe B. Williams, a preacher from our church. What I remembered most about that trip was that we were driving in a new car, which always made Black folks a target of jealous White folks in the South, and Joe kept insisting on being served food from the front of diners— "If I have to pay in front, then I want to eat in front"—which meant we didn't eat much at all on the road back then.

When my draft number was called, I petitioned for conscientious objector status, like Papa, a minister, had done before me. I refused to train while awaiting the decision on my status and was thrown into the stockade for that act of defiance. By this time, I had kept my promise to God, turned my life around, and was deeply religious. I intended to uphold the commandment "Thou shalt not kill," demonstrating that God had taken charge of my soul. But, of course, the army had control over my body. I became a medic once they released me from the stockade so I would not have to take up arms—saving life instead of ending it.

Although I had told the army that I wanted to be stationed in Chicago close to home—I mean, they did ask—they wound up sending me to Nuremberg for my permanent posting, as far away from home as I could be, maybe just *because* I had asked for Chicago. As it turned out, Germany was a much better assignment, teaching me something I would need for the rest of my life. In Germany, not all that long after the end of World War II, I could still observe some of the scars left by an authoritarian regime. As a result, I was able to put my experience with oppression in perspective and I began to see where my own country could be headed if we didn't do something about the kind of intense racism and lust for power that had led to genocide and massive destruction in Europe. I saw it in ways I never could have appreciated as much in books or even movies, or in a Chicago posting, for that matter. I visited Hitler's bunker and reflected on the insanity of White supremacy. You could still feel it in that place: the desperate need to massacre an entire population, millions of people you don't even know, not only because you are repulsed by the idea of their existence—their coexistence—but also because you see power in stoking mass hatred against them.

People have said for years that the things I saw in Europe, mostly in my mind's eye—in a sense, the smoldering remains of fascist atrocities—never could happen in America. I wasn't so sure then and haven't been convinced by anything I've seen in real life since then that we are safe and secure in the values we say hold us together.

The army had only been desegregated for about fifteen years when I was inducted. But, as I always say, you can change the law, but not people's hearts. Many of the enlisted persons were White southerners. And while the service provided a kind of close contact I'd never before experienced with them, these soldiers were quick to remind me that I was Black and still supposed to yield to them at all times.

They would test me in small ways, starting back in Texas. In church one Sunday, they talked about how interracial union was forbidden by the Bible. After the service, some White GIs asked what I thought about interracial marriage. I knew it was a trick question. I replied, "Marriage is hard enough when you marry in your own race." But they wanted more than that. They always want more.

As there was a White woman in our congregation down there, they didn't just want to know how I might behave in a particular situation. They wanted to know that I had a whole belief system that would never allow me to step out of line in *any* situation. Although I'd added, "I would never marry a White woman because of all the trouble it would cause," their stares and scowls let me know they wanted assurance that I knew better, that I would never try to talk to her, and that I would agree with their depraved justification for hatred in a book that teaches love.

The Civil Rights Movement was in full swing by this time, and I'd also heard so much disdain from White GIs, raging on about how unreasonable the civil rights activists were, breaking the law with sit-ins and boycotts. I never said a thing—despite knowing how the murder of my beloved cousin had sparked so much of this rightful protest. Obviously, I never mentioned my relationship to Bobo in those tight quarters with folks like those who well could have taken part in taking him from us, if given a chance. I simply listened, and recognized just how much they were proving the righteousness of the movement in everything they said against it.

Whatever I experienced in the army, though, was nothing by comparison. The injustice that so many Black troops had experienced in the past—long before my induction—shows that the issue of Ghost Skins is not a new thing at all.

LOUIS TILL's DEATH by hanging on July 2, 1945, at the end of World War II, puts a few contemporary issues in perspective. Louis Till, Bobo's father, was court-martialed, sentenced, and executed in Italy for the rape of two women and the murder of a third.[13] But the circumstances surrounding his execution have been called into question. Did he really do it? Was he framed? After reading the court-martial transcript and talking with someone who served with Louis Till in Italy, I believe those questions are well founded. Louis Till suffered the same end as many thousands of other Black men: at the end of a rope. And his case might serve as an illustration of much larger problems: the way Black GIs were treated generally during the war, and especially the way hundreds were criminalized even while putting their lives on the line for a country that denied them the full and equal rights they were protecting for everybody else.[14] Before the question of Louis Till's guilt or innocence can be answered, it is important to consider the context.

A report had been put together by the US Army War College after World War I—a terrible document that concluded that Black men were mentally inferior to White men; that we were superstitious; afraid of the dark; lazy; lacked initiative; had no leadership qualities; and had weak character.

> His ideas with relation to honor and sex relations are not on the same plane as those of our white population. Petty thieving, lying, and promiscuity are much more common among negroes than among whites. Atrocities connected with white women have been the cause of considerable trouble among negroes.[15]

Black GIs were seen as "unmoral," according to White standards, but we still were needed to bolster US troop strength. All the falsehoods written about Black troops in this report, including that we had not "progressed" as far as others in the "human family" in "the process of evolution," justified the practice of Black GIs being used only for labor and "never . . . assigned to White units."[16]

So, in a way, the case against Louis Till started back on October 30, 1925, when this report of the Army War College issued the manual on "Negroes"—some twenty years before twenty-three-year-old Louis Till was executed. His execution and the execution of many other Black troops can be seen as proof of the report's deeply flawed concept. Among other things, there is evidence that Louis Till did not have good counsel—no apparent fight against the inadequate evidence leading to his charge and conviction. The surviving victims could not even identify Louis Till as one of the persons who attacked them, and stories of other witnesses changed over time, and appeared coaxed and coached.[17]

The treatment of Louis Till seems to fit a pattern. Mary Louise Roberts, a distinguished history professor at the University of Wisconsin–Madison, has written extensively about how White officers "scapegoated African American soldiers for sexual crimes abroad, used false stories about rape to justify racial segregation at home and ignored sexual crimes committed by white GIs." Because they knew Black soldiers would not be believed, according to Professor Roberts, White soldiers who had raped women overseas could accuse Black soldiers of the offenses and get away with them.

There also was just plain old-fashioned fraternization going on— relations with much more severe consequences for Black GIs. Just like White enlisted men, Black GIs had consensual relations with European women. But White southern commanding officers and NCOs did *not* consent to Black men and White women having anything to do with each other. So, as far as they were concerned, no consent—that is, consent from them—meant rape. Racially constructed rape.

The Reverend Wealthy Mobley, Mamie's brother-in-law, saw it firsthand, up close. And Mamie quoted him in her book. "[Reverend Mobley] had served in Europe and recalled how black soldiers would get roused at three in the morning. Military police would look over the black soldiers in formation. The MPs would bring in local women who would point out someone in the line," but because of the language barrier, he said, these women thought they were just pointing to men they had dated. "Black soldiers who were pointed out at three in the morning were taken away. They were not brought back."[18]

That could be what happened to Louis Till, who wound up buried in a grave marked only with the number 73 in disgraced Plot E, stripped of his identity and set apart from all the military graves of distinction at the Oise-Aisne American Cemetery, Seringes-et-Nesles, France. Plot E is the resting place for people who had been dishonorably discharged and executed by the army. As partial evidence of racial discrimination in the execution of military justice, and a sort of coda on the racist narrative set out in that 1925 Army War College report, the one that basically cautioned army officers to watch out for oversexed Black men who lusted after White women, of the ninety-six bodies in Plot E, eighty-three are people of color—more than 86 percent of the convicted criminals in this cemetery, but only 10 percent of the military population overall.

Interestingly, while the Louis Till court-martial transcript was leaked to the southern press in 1955, the stage might have been set for that drama ten years earlier, when Senator James O. Eastland came back to the United States following a trip to Europe. Eastland had been overseas just two months before Louis Till's execution in 1945 gathering information on Germany's wartime destruction. Among other things, he brought back with him outrageous claims of sexual assaults by Black GIs. He used these allegations in a filibuster against continuing the Fair Employment Practices Committee.[19] One thing clearly had nothing to do with the other, except in appealing to racism for political gain, kind of like the authoritarians the Allies had just defeated in the war. As it turns out, claims of Black sexual violence were part of Eastland's political project to push back against equal rights and equal justice for years before he reportedly used Louis Till's court-martial to serve that hideous agenda.

Many years after completing my tour of duty, I visited Lemorse Mallory, "Sergeant Mallory," as Aunt Alma always called him. He was Mamie's second husband, the first one I ever knew personally. But Mamie never talked about him after their marriage ended, maybe because of the way it ended—with his infidelity. Anyway, for the first time ever, I asked him about Louis Till. He had been there, serving in the same unit, and said Louis made a terrible mistake. But it wasn't rape and murder, he said. Apparently, Louis had a relationship with a White woman in Italy. His misfortune was that his White commanding officer knew about it. Worse, not only was Louis violating the racist code, but the officer had lusted after the same woman. That's what Lemorse told me. And there was something else. As he awaited the hangman's noose, Louis asked Lemorse to do him a favor. He wanted to make sure Lemorse would return to Argo/Summit and look after Mamie and Emmett. Obviously, Lemorse kept the promise, granting the last wish of a dying man who wanted to provide for his estranged wife and the son he would never know, the son who would know him only through a ring, a ring it seems they each wore when they were lynched—ten years apart.

This is not meant to be a defense of Louis Till. If he committed a horrible crime, then a just system provides for a penalty and the entitlement to due process before punishment. Rather, it is an indictment of a system that just might have presumed his guilt without feeling a need to prove it. Make no mistake about it. Louis Till was not really a good person. After all, he'd enlisted in the army because he had abused Mamie, and in a resulting trial, the judge gave him a choice between military service and a jail sentence. It's just that, in the end, he might not have been as bad as he was seen by White people who had the power to define him and judge him and use him to send a message to all those other Black men who might dare to think that wearing the same uniform as White men made them equal.

IF I COULD summarize the year 2021 with a single word, that word would be Zoom. The events of the year seemed to pass by just that quickly, and technology—videoconferencing—was the only way we could have made it through.

The year started off with a plan—a plan that would lead to a new organization and the beginning of special projects aimed at advancing the legacy of Mamie Till-Mobley and Emmett Till.

Over the preceding year, we had strengthened our association with Patrick Weems, who wound up bringing someone new into our conversation and our journey: Joseph Olchefske, a retired Seattle Public Schools superintendent. Patrick met Joseph in Mississippi in 2020 when Joseph, his wife Judy, and his daughter India made the trip by car because they wanted to see some of the important places in the Delta—the ones associated with the Emmett Till story, which they recently had read about. Joseph had been an investment banker prior to his position as schools superintendent and began talking with us about raising money to fund a national public school curriculum on the foundation of the Emmett Till story. Intrigued, we rolled up our sleeves and began planning what would become the Emmett Till and Mamie Till-Mobley Institute later in the year—starting with the curriculum.

Through Joseph's connections, we had begun a dialogue with people at the Chan Zuckerberg Initiative, which has a division focusing on education. Marvel, Patrick, Joseph, and I worked on a program plan to present to CZI. Chris's help was particularly critical here, as he recently had been named to the board of scholars of Facing History and Ourselves—a national organization that works with educators on introducing important diversity discussions in the classroom. The Holocaust and civil rights are two of the leading areas for the group's offerings, and Chris had presented on various Emmett Till themes at summer teacher institutes in Chicago for a number of years. And with his advocacy, Facing History agreed to partner up with us. Patrick brought in the William Winter Institute for Racial Reconciliation in Mississippi—another education-based organization—and together, we presented a complete pilot program designed to launch in select Mississippi schools. The proposal was a success, and CZI awarded us a grant for the program—a six-class curriculum that would become available on the Facing History website.

By the summer of 2021, we were able to add several members to our team. Earl Watkins, former superintendent of Jackson Mississippi Public Schools, Von Gordon, head of the Winter Institute, and Jay Rushing, youth coordinator for the Emmett Till Interpretive Center (ETIC), the group that would lead our student engagement effort in Mississippi—an effort that allowed us to recruit a blended group of twenty-four students, mostly from area high schools, with a few college students included. Elliot Long, also of the ETIC, began handling our business affairs. We also were able to recruit several of Chris's journalism grad students as Emmett Till Fellows for research. Debbra Lindo, former schools superintendent for the Emery Unified School District in California, was included to deal with assessment of our success for future funding. Mike Small would become a member of the Till Institute Board. Mike is an educator in the Chicago area and, with his wife, Tina, had been friends with Mamie for many years. Other members named to the Till Institute Board were Ollie Gordon as vice president, Patrick as treasurer, and Joseph as secretary; Marvel would become executive director, and Chris would become the president. We got to work right away bringing together the other projects we had under way, including a traveling exhibition developed by the Children's Museum of Indianapolis; the development of a national park; and the design of a national memorial, in partnership with the socially conscious MASS Design, the group that designed and developed The National Memorial for Peace and Justice (The National Lynching Memorial) for Bryan Stevenson's Equal Justice Initiative in Montgomery, Alabama.

We certainly were breathing a sigh of relief with the change in political power, if only because the new administration in Washington seemed committed to supporting racial justice. A new attorney general, Merrick Garland, spoke out against White supremacy. His new assistant attorney general for civil rights, Kristen Clarke, had done the same. That was a good thing for us. She was the person whose division presided over the Emmett Till investigation report and already had become familiar with the case as former director of the Lawyers' Committee for Civil Rights Under Law, the group that had supported Airickca's efforts. Even if Assistant Attorney General Clarke couldn't actively participate in the case, at least we could be sure she would not block any progress, as we had been afraid her predecessor might have done.

No matter what happened regarding legal justice for Bobo as a result of the ongoing federal investigation, we were determined to achieve social justice in his name, by preparing future generations of civic leadership through our educational initiatives to carry on the mission of Mamie Till-Mobley.

IT TOOK MARVEL and me a while to come around to the idea of buying a parcel of land in Drew, Mississippi, the property that included the barn where Bobo was beaten, tortured, and killed. Though I was eager to secure land for our proposed national park and memorial, it just didn't sit right with me, paying money for what had been the Sturdivant Plantation, the site of such horrific racial violence. And paying White people for it at that. But we kept talking it through with Patrick and finally decided that owning this significant property in Mississippi, a place so central to the Emmett Till story, would, if nothing else, keep it out of the hands of anyone else who might want to use it to develop a counternarrative and continue distorting Bobo's story. Besides, the current White owner of the property, a dentist, had no connection at all to the murder or its aftermath. He just owned some land that included the barn, which still was intact. And he had been allowing people to come to the property to observe, to meditate on its meaning. We decided that this could be at least one part of the non-contiguous national park we were planning, or the national memorial we had started discussing with MASS Design. So we agreed, but still had to raise the money. Lots of it.

In one conversation about the matter, Patrick mentioned to Chris in passing that we might have a donor who was willing to put up money to buy the land and barn near Drew. Patrick and the Emmett Till Interpretive Center had been assisting the production companies working on the ABC series on Mamie and Bobo. The location production office had been set up in the ETIC museum in Sumner, just across the town square from the Tallahatchie County Courthouse where the murder trial had taken place and where a good chunk of filming would take place. Patrick's staff members also were serving as guides to significant sites for the project's location scouts. And he had developed a pretty good relationship with one of the producers, Rosanna Grace, the person who had invited me to join Devery on the Nixon Library panel. At one point, Grace had told Patrick she might be able to deliver a $1 million contribution toward the purchase of the barn. Like I said, we needed lots of money to realize our vision of an Emmett Till memorial and a national park. Patrick told Chris the contribution would come from some guy involved in the production, some guy named "John," he said. This John was the son of the owner of a Pennsylvania sports team—football, he thought, maybe Pittsburgh. He also was a supporter of the Young Republicans.

Chris began to search for the identity of this John person, looking first at the Pittsburgh Steelers ownership and seeing no connection. Maybe Patrick got it wrong. Maybe it was baseball. Nothing in the Pirates ownership that connected, either. Maybe Patrick got the city wrong. Maybe Philadelphia. That's where the first part of the answer was revealed. The principal owner of the Philadelphia Phillies is a billionaire businessman and philanthropist. His son John Powers Middleton is a film producer and head of the Middleton Media Group, collaborating with Grace's Serendipity Group, and in partnership with actor/producer Casey Affleck in the Affleck/Middleton Project. Middleton's film credits include *The Lego Movie*, *Bates Motel*, and *Manchester by the Sea*. So far, no problem, nothing objectionable. But, then, beyond all that, we found that his partnership had contributed $5,000 to Donald Trump's Presidential Inaugural Committee, something that had shocked and concerned a business partner when it was reported in a Hollywood trade magazine, and it certainly raised our eyebrows when we saw it a couple of years after the fact.[20] That was one thing. But there was another: John Powers Middleton also reportedly had contributed $250,000 to the Committee to Restore America's Greatness, the Trump political action committee headed by longtime Trump supporter Roger Stone. Reportedly, that contribution accounted for 80 percent of the PAC's funding during 2016.[21]

Now that 2017 Nixon Library event seemed to be coming into focus. We remembered that one of the people on the panel with Devery Anderson and me was Alex Foster, an executive producer of the ABC-TV series and, we now learned, president of production for the Middleton Media Group—or at least he was at the time of the panel. I can't say for sure that there was a connection between the scheduling of that event and a significant Republican funder, but it was starting to look like quite a coincidence, at the very least.

We didn't have to think or talk about this connection very long at all. To accept a financial contribution aimed at preserving the vital legacy of Emmett Till from someone who also was supporting someone else who appeared in every way to be leading the effort to undermine that legacy—well, that would be to work against everything we have stood for, everything we have lived for. We didn't know anything about John Powers Middleton and made no moral judgment about him. This was not a personal or partisan consideration. We just could not bring ourselves to associate with someone who had associated with someone whose agenda we opposed. It just seemed to us that we would be giving cover to something we could never accept.

So we declined the offer and walked away from a million dollars on principle.

SOMEHOW DISNEY/ABC WAS ever-present in our lives. We had agreed to cooperate with Fatima Curry in her documentary production as soon as we could talk more freely—publicly—about our experience, as the FBI and DOJ investigations were finalized. That was our deal with the government. We were in fairly regular contact with her, sort of just checking in. During 2021, though, the TV series *Women of the Movement* came up again. The show runner—the chief writer—Marissa Jo Cerar contacted me to talk about my personal story in connection with the series. She certainly was a big deal since she had been the writer of the series *The Handmaid's Tale* and now wanted to build the ABC series with more of the intimate details that Devery Anderson's book apparently lacked, the details needed beyond what Devery had cited from Mamie's book.

Marvel and I turned to Chris again, and he contacted Cerar to hear what she had to say about the scope of her interest since she also was going to be credited as a producer of the series in addition to the writing credit she would earn. Chris told us that he had a delightful conversation with Cerar and believed that, as a woman of color, she had a genuine interest in crafting a story for television that was authentic. We remained concerned that the producers already were locked into the story they wanted to tell based on Devery's book, even though it appeared that Devery's book was insufficient as the basis for the more intimate story about Mamie and Emmett that had evolved. And even though Devery had told Chris he had nothing to do with the television production, we'd learned he was quietly reaching out to at least one distant Till family member to get background stories that could help build a character—Gene Mobley, Mamie's last husband. The more we thought about it, the more troubled we grew. So, following their discussion, Chris wrote an impassioned note on our behalf, expressing our appreciation for Cerar's interest, but also our deep concern that the production had not demonstrated a sincere interest in our involvement from the start—which appeared to have been five or six years earlier. We did not want to get involved as window dressing, just to provide credit to the production for including us and potentially appear to endorse something that might not turn out right and that we would have no power to correct, but responsibility to excuse. Nothing personal against her, but our answer regarding participation was essentially "thanks, but no, thanks."

MARCH 19, 2021. We got the sorrowful news that Alvin Sykes had died. He was sixty-four and had never recovered from that terrible fall he had taken while rushing to catch a train to take part in my eightieth birthday celebration the year before. Alvin truly was an amazing person. It wasn't just that he has to be credited with the history he made, causing the federal government to launch the 2004 investigation into Bobo's lynching, *and* helping pass the bipartisan Emmett Till Unsolved Civil Rights Crime Act, *and* contributing to the development of the antilynching legislation before Congress, *and* even working for the issuance of the Congressional Gold Medal in honor of Mamie and Emmett, co-sponsored by Democratic Senator Cory Booker (NJ) and Republican Senator Richard Burr (NC). He was still on his back in a hospital bed when he pulled that one off, assisted by longtime friend and aide Corey Weibel. It wasn't just all those things that he *helped* to make happen, but he was able to pull together people on opposite ends of political ideology to actually *make* it all happen. Alvin Sykes showed the kind of sophisticated political skill and deep intelligence of a person with much more formal education than he had as a high school dropout. I would say he was an unsung hero of the Civil Rights Movement, but that would not be accurate. It might recognize the fact that he didn't seek out the headlines that some people have lusted after, but it would ignore the people who stepped up to sing his praises, to pay tribute to him, a process that only began during the funeral on April 1 at the Metropolitan Missionary Baptist Church when Ronnique Hawkins stepped to the mic.

After reading a personal statement from Mike and Tina Small, Ronnique, like the Smalls a longtime friend of Alvin, delivered an unexpected revelation during her loving tribute to him. She talked about the film *The Untold Story of Emmett Louis Till*, produced by Keith Beauchamp, who for years was credited with causing the federal government to open its investigation into the Emmett Till lynching in 2004. Those of us who were close to the entire investigative process knew the truth. Ronnique was a producer on that documentary and had a personal relationship with Beauchamp. She also knew the truth. Clearly, she wanted to set the record straight, as we also had tried to do. "Alvin Sykes alone, *not* our film *The Untold Story of Emmett Louis Till*, should be credited for the Emmett Till case reopening," she declared. "This is something that should be corrected immediately. To the journalists from here on in, in the name of our friend Alvin, please give him the credit that he deserves. To continue to print or promote anything else is a discredit to Alvin's legacy, and the families deserve better."

The tributes would continue in the weeks and months to follow. On the Senate floor a couple of weeks after the funeral service, Senator Burr would read a statement into the *Congressional Record*. Referring to a famous quote by President Teddy Roosevelt, Burr said, "Alvin Sykes was the man in the arena. He was a man who knew great devotion, who dedicated himself to a worthy cause, and who helped move our Nation even closer to our founding promise of 'liberty and justice for all.'" He ended his remarks with a special sentiment. "Personally, I learned from Alvin Sykes. I admire Alvin Sykes. I mourn his passing. I pay tribute to him today and thank God that he created Alvin Sykes."[22]

Senator Booker would later record comments for a special event in honor of Emmett Till. "Alvin Sykes was a hero in this nation, a civil rights hero," Booker began, adding that Alvin effectively had been doing the Lord's work, remaining true to "our noble faith traditions . . . To be humble. To do kindness. And to always stand up for justice," he said. "May his legacy continue. May we not just remember him but let him inspire us in continuing his work."[23]

As Mamie had taught us all, we each have a purpose in life, something that sets us apart from every other person on the planet. The greatest joy we can experience is finding that purpose, living it. Alvin truly lived on purpose. And so have I, continuing Alvin's work, and Simmie's, and, of course, Mamie's.

Even so, I couldn't help but think during the course of the funeral and on so many days since then about the connection between Bobo and Alvin, something beyond the work that Alvin had done to achieve some measure of justice for Emmett Till, for us all. But there has been something. It is something rooted deep in my soul. Something I know I will bear for the rest of my life.

Bobo had run for a train to Mississippi to hang out with me, and Alvin had run for a train in Kansas City to celebrate with me. Death had tracked each of them. And it was all because of me. As a man of faith, as a pastor, I had forgiven so many people over the years. Now I clearly would face my biggest challenge yet. Forgiving myself.

SEVERAL MONTHS AFTER Chris wrote to Marissa Jo Cerar, the ABC television series producer, documentary producer Fatima Curry contacted us and asked for a meeting. We had kept in touch with Fatima and, by this time, even had begun cooperating with her doing preliminary background interviews that didn't touch on the FBI investigation. She wanted to talk about the *Women of the Movement* series on the entertainment side. That was a surprise since we had not thought about that production since Chris sent the letter, and because Fatima had assured us she would have nothing to do with the entertainment side. She was on the news side. There was a firewall, right? But we had developed a relationship of trust with her and expected her to be straight with us, as she had been all along, so we agreed that Marvel and Chris would meet with her. They would brief me later. They always liked to do it this way so they could process everything before bringing me into it. Make sure I didn't agree to anything too quickly.

So they got together with Fatima in a conference room at the Summit Public Library. Since Marvel is a member of the Summit Board of Trustees, the library staff was quite accommodating. Over lunch, Fatima laid it all out. Apparently, our note to Cerar had circulated and people associated with the production, including ABC executives, had discussed it on several levels. We had not threatened legal action or negative publicity—hadn't even suggested these things. We had said our piece and moved on. However, those other possibilities apparently had been considered by the folks who were on the hook for the production's success, and those who cared about doing good in the spirit of the production. At some point, we heard, Jay-Z got wind of what was going on and gave an instruction to everyone else. "Make it right." So, out of respect for that good-faith gesture, we reconsidered and ultimately agreed to meet with the scripted series producers.

Marvel and Chris made it clear to Fatima that we were going to meet in order to listen and discuss the basis for our concerns, but not to negotiate. We were not taking part in the discussion to become part of the production. That decision already had been made.

The plan was set in motion to meet in Los Angeles. But COVID was still running rampant with deadly consequences across the country and we were concerned about traveling. At one point, someone offered to send a private jet for us. Though that was tempting, we pushed for a Zoom session, which we would join from our Chicago home base. And we promptly turned our attention back to other matters.

THE PACE OF the year and everything along the way sped up even more by the time we got to summer. Everything but the conclusion of the Department of Justice investigation. Again, we had decided that, no matter what happened at the conclusion of that probe, we were committed to staying on the high road and moving the story of Emmett Till ahead on multiple levels of public education and social justice.

A weekend of activities was planned by Marvel and Dallis Anderson to commemorate what would have been the eightieth birthday of Emmett Till on July 25. Guests were invited to attend from all over the country. In connection with the commemoration, our nonprofit organization received a grant from the State of Illinois to purchase the property where the home of Emmett and Mamie once stood in Summit. A welcome reception was held Friday night at the Emmett Till Memorial Center in Summit for the out-of-town guests. We served breakfast on Saturday morning prior to a bus tour that included a visit to Roberts Temple Church of God in Christ, where Bobo's funeral was held, and continued on to Burr Oak Cemetery. We all gathered at Emmett Till's grave site, and then at the crypt of Mamie and her husband Gene Mobley, before a final stop at the grave site of Airickca Gordon-Taylor, where Ollie had organized a vigil for her daughter that included an address by Representative Bobby Rush.

Chris joined with Marvel, Ollie, and Perri Irmer, president of the DuSable Museum of African American History, to produce a special commemorative program in the museum's theater that Saturday night.

The DuSable event included video presentations by Lonnie Bunch, secretary of the Smithsonian Institution, and Senator Cory Booker; readings by Northwestern University Professor Natasha Trethewey, former U.S. poet laureate, Mississippi poet laureate, and Pulitzer Prize winner; and an in-person onstage conversation with Nikole Hannah-Jones, Pulitzer Prize–winning author of *The 1619 Project*. Ollie and I also presented onstage. That event felt like a family reunion since so many family members attended.

There was a Sunday church service at Argo Temple with a dedication of a plaque, a historical marker, on the property we had purchased—the residential lot where Mamie and Emmett's original home once stood across the street from the church. The weekend commemorative was quite a success. But we were heartened by the participation of so many honorary family members—people who just wanted to take part in the celebration of the life of Emmett Till, a life that has touched them so deeply and connected with them so lastingly.

ON AUGUST 13, we met with the ABC *Women of the Movement* producers. Fatima had arranged for Marvel, Ollie, Chris, and me to attend a screening and Zoom with the California producers at Soho House in Chicago; Fatima is a member of that international private club. She had organized this session in three parts. First, she talked with us about what we might expect and recommended that we give fair consideration to all that would be discussed later. We were prepared to do that. Second, we screened the first segment of the series in the impressive theater there at Soho House. We were moved by what we saw. The portrayal of Mamie by Tony Award–winning actor Adrienne Warren was respectful and dignified, true to Mamie's powerful character, and Bobo was humanized by young Cedric Joe, whose depiction came across as a pretty good treatment of the boy I knew and loved. I have to say, I even liked Joshua Caleb Johnson, who portrayed me at sixteen. The entire cast was good, and Melissa Jo Cerar's writing of this first segment was strong and tracked Mamie's memoir in significant ways, beginning with Bobo's breach birth, just as with the book. Marvel and Ollie were reduced to tears. I was touched, too, and transported back in time.

Finally, we sat for the Zoom video conference with Aaron Kaplan, president of Kapital Entertainment; James Lassiter, co-founder of Will Smith's Overbrook Entertainment and producer of Smith's movies; Jay Brown, chief executive officer of Jay-Z's Roc Nation; Jeanmarie Condon, Fatima's co-producer; and Sandra Ortiz, attorney and head of business affairs for Kapital. That meeting started off with apologies—first from Aaron Kaplan, expressing regret that we couldn't all meet in person. I thought again about that private jet. But we took that as an indication of respect and sincerity from Kaplan, who came across as quite gracious. He explained that a terrible mistake had been made. When his group—the group that included Smith and Jay-Z—approached HBO to produce a series on Emmett Till, they learned that HBO already had rights to a book, Devery Anderson's book, that they would have to use. We assumed that original deal had been made by Rosanna Grace's Serendipity Films. They were not represented at this meeting. James Lassiter pointed to the value of having so many women of color—particularly the show runner, Cerar, and directors Julie Dash, Kasi Lemmons, Gina Prince-Bythewood, and Tina Mabry—involved in the production. We agreed that that was a story in itself and made a powerful statement that would have made Mamie proud.

We were asked how we felt about what we had seen in the opening segment and we shared our compliments. Chris mentioned the strong similarities to Mamie's book, but let it go at that, since he figured that partly was because Devery's book had cited Mamie's. I expressed my appreciation for the integrity of the presentation, and I took the opportunity to call attention to a point that was significant to me. In one scene in the segment, Papa used a cussword in confronting Bobo, who was depicted sitting in the shade instead of picking cotton like everybody else. I mentioned that Papa would never talk like that.

The people on the Zoom expressed their deep understanding of all that we had experienced, particularly me as a survivor of a night of terror and the loss of my dear friend. They persuaded us that they respected this and wanted to honor it. In that connection, we were assured by everyone on the video call that they wanted to correct the initial mistake that had been made. They wanted to do the right thing. They wanted to have our voice included in the final production and active promotion to make sure that what they offered the public would be true to the story, but also true to our experience, our grief, our journey to justice, and would continue the public conversation about it all. Even though we had said we were not coming to this meeting to talk about a deal, we certainly were prepared to listen and the conversation seemed to be going in that direction. It also seemed that they were prepared for Chris's notes about similarities to Mamie's book because of what was about to happen. What convinced us to hear them out was what Kaplan said next. While we were discussing everything else, he had followed up on my note about Papa and the cussword. He said he had texted his production people, telling them to edit that word out of the presentation, and he was happy to report that it already had been done—before the end of the conversation. Just like that, he had demonstrated a responsiveness that validated everything else. That convinced us of the genuineness of this group in wanting to present a story with integrity and wanting to give us voice in that process. It felt right.

We authorized Chris to follow up with Kaplan, Ortiz, and Fatima in a separate call right then to hear what they had to say. Within the next twenty minutes, he had agreed to a deal that included the TV rights to Mamie's book (Ollie is a beneficiary of Mamie's estate) and our retention as consultants on the project.

As important as anything was the feeling we experienced during this session. We had moved from suspicion to trust over a nearly three-year period based on that strongly positive feeling we had with this group. Yes, this was a business meeting, but what was clear to us was that the people on the Zoom call actually cared about the integrity of the Emmett Till story. After all the distortions we had seen over the years, this was as reassuring as it was refreshing.

If there was not going to be a happy ending on the Emmett Till story, at least there could be one on the story behind the story.

AS WE APPROACHED the month of November, we began planning how we would commemorate what would have been Mamie Till-Mobley's one hundredth birthday on November 23. We decided we would use that occasion to announce an entire year of programs and activities in honor of Mamie's legacy. There would be the traveling museum exhibition and, of course, the Emmett Till curriculum in partnership with Facing History and the Winter Institute. The discussion regarding a memorial and national park also would continue in what we were planning to launch as the Mamie Till-Mobley Centennial Initiative. All this was set against the backdrop of the airing of the ABC series *Women of the Movement* and the companion documentary with Fatima Curry and Jeanmarie Condon, titled *Let the World See*. The ABC promotional machine was in full swing and we appreciated all the careful thought that had been put into the planning of a major rollout with social media and television. We participated in Zoom sessions with more than thirty people at a time. And it seemed like nearly every one of them had a piece of the presentation. As impressive as anything else, everybody who spoke had an intimate understanding of the facts of the Mamie Till-Mobley and Emmett Till story, but also its national significance. It was truly amazing. Among other things, the first major trailer for television would air on November 23 as a special tribute to Mamie on her hundredth birthday. There were plans for panel discussions in several cities. There also were plans for special screenings in New York, Chicago, and a red-carpet event in Los Angeles. Marvel, Ollie, and I would take part in all of them. The six-part series would be broadcast with two segments on each night over three weeks. The documentary had grown from thirty minutes to ninety minutes and would air in thirty-minute segments following each presentation of the scripted series over the three-week run.

It would all begin on January 6, 2022—the nineteenth anniversary of Mamie's death.

FINALLY. THE MOMENT was near. The DOJ had completed its evaluation of all the evidence and its report after a couple of drafts that went back and forth between Washington and Mississippi. They were ready to meet with us, as we had planned nearly four years earlier.

The schedulers for the DOJ wanted to set the meeting for November 23. Schedulers only think about dates and times and the convenience of the officials they represent. The November date fit everyone's timetable—everyone they represented, all the people who would have to travel from Washington and Mississippi to Chicago to meet with us there. Kristen Clarke was especially important; the assistant attorney general for civil rights wanted to be there with the family because of her strong interest in the case. Even so, Chris pushed back. Based on the tidbits he had gotten and interpreted in his conversations with government officials, he knew the report could go either way. One possibility was that the investigators had found something they had not shared with us, something they could use to empanel a grand jury to consider indictments. Maybe they had come up with a fresh look at the evidence we already had seen that would allow the legal process to go forward. But the other very real possibility was that there would be nothing—no indictments, after nearly four years of probing. Whatever the outcome, he knew we would not want any headlines coming out of the DOJ final report to rob Mamie Till-Mobley of her moment of recognition, of commemoration. And he decided not to share any of these concerns with me. Understanding our resistance, the government schedulers set a new date.

EVEN AS WE planned for the enriching educational projects in the year ahead, we had to consider the challenges we would face in accomplishing some parts of our agenda. Especially the curriculum. Not that it wouldn't be very good—we knew it would be. Our partnership with Facing History and Ourselves and the William Winter Institute ensured that we would develop a stellar course of study, one that would inspire civic engagement and provide the preparation to get there. But, ironically, our potential success was exactly the problem. The far right had come up with a new way to erase our story—much more sophisticated than shooting up historical markers. They had developed a very effective propaganda campaign against Critical Race Theory—the law school framework they were claiming was a threat to students in grade school and high school, where it wasn't even taught. Anything promoting a critical evaluation of history, and particularly American race relations, was being labeled as CRT and thereby a threat to the sensibilities and the well-being of students—that is, White students. The idea of White students being made to feel guilty, or responsible for the sins of their ancestors, was at the heart of the campaign, framed as "parental rights," a smokescreen, a cover for the far-right politicians. Not unlike the cover of the Ghost Skins in the military and on the police forces.

Ghost Skins. The ultimate undercover operators hiding in plain sight—military personnel, law enforcement officers, apparently even elected officials. They used to wear hoods to hide their identity. Now they simply can wear a uniform, or take an oath of office and take cover, swearing their allegiance to something other than the unifying values of American democracy—justice, equality, fairness.

We knew what we were up against and knew we were up to the challenge, just as Mamie had been. We knew it would be Ghost Skins—political vigilantes hiding behind laws wrapped in propaganda. In a way, their agenda is the same as that of the people who carry guns. And it's the same now as it was in 1955, and 1877 for that matter. Whatever you call it, it basically all comes down to White supremacy: the power to control everything, starting with the narrative that justifies controlling everything.

I thought about that as I looked back and looked ahead, like the African Sankofa bird. I couldn't speak when I first saw Mamie after my escape from Mississippi back in 1955. Didn't know what I could say that would make a difference, give her comfort. My only hope now was that she might be comforted by all the ways we were speaking up and would continue to do so—speaking up through action, preserving her legacy, breathing new life into it, ensuring that her son, Emmett Till, would continue to live.

16

Reckoning with the Consequences

THE MEETING FINALLY was set. And the day of revelation, the day of reckoning finally had come. The plan for this day, December 6, 2021, had been outlined a little more than three years earlier, long before we even knew what day it would be, what time we would have to meet, or where we would have to be. We planned the rest of it, agreed on it all at the very place where we now were headed—the FBI Chicago field office on Roosevelt Road—for a 1 P.M. meeting. This was the place where Marvel, Chris Benson, and I had met with the Department of Justice, the FBI, and the Mississippi district attorney, Fourth Circuit, in August 2018. This was the place where we had reviewed all the documents collected by the FBI up to that point, analyzed it all, talked about it all, and committed it all to memory—not allowed to take anything out of the room. It was the place where we had agreed with the FBI and the DOJ and the Mississippi DA to the terms of that review. We promised that we would not reveal anything that we had seen in those documents until the investigation was closed. And in exchange for that agreement, we were promised time to process the outcome and issue statements before the government released its final report, officially making it public.

This was the deal Chris had negotiated back in 2018. He had

checked in again with the DOJ and Mississippi officials following the 2020 presidential election to make sure that nothing would slip through the cracks with an incoming administration—new people who might not have been told about the deal. He was assured the deal was still good. He had asked for a week's advance notice. The government agreed to a couple of days. With the passage of time, that couple of days shrank to a couple of hours.

We had asked whether the government was going to hold a news conference to announce the findings. They decided not to hold one, so we organized one ourselves through the media relations office of Northwestern University, where Chris is a journalism professor. The meeting with government officials was in two parts, with the first set to start at 1 P.M. and the second to begin at 2 P.M. The news conference was scheduled for 4 P.M. across town. The final report would be released at 5 P.M. We would have to move quickly from the briefing to the press event, with the clock ticking as we processed whatever would be revealed to us.

Fatima Curry, the ABC documentarian, had booked a car to pick us up at our home in Summit. She had worked it all out, which was as good for her as it was for us. This way she would keep track of our schedule, our movements, so she could lock in another piece of her exclusive, have her crew there to video record us leaving our house to go to the meeting, and then again as we arrived at the FBI field office. We arranged to have Ollie Gordon, Annie Wright, and Thelma Wright Edwards—who had flown in from Florida—meet us at our home to ride with us. Emmett's cousin Bertha Thomas would meet us at the field office. So would Chris.

Although we really didn't talk in the car about what was ahead, it seemed everyone had a feeling about it. It was sort of floating there between the lines of the small talk. But Marvel and I were the only ones in that car who had seen the evidence. We had known for more than a year what was adding up and what wasn't. Though we still didn't say a word, we saw the government decision to pass on the news conference as something of a "tell," the way poker players give up what they think they've been holding close to the vest. I grew up in a gambling town. I know how to read these things. A lean in can mean one thing, a slump back, something else. Whenever the government was going forward with a prosecution, they set up a news conference—leaning in. When they were going to decline prosecution, they sent out a news release—slumping back. Either way, a tell.

Even so, as we read the signs, interpreted the signals, there were some things we couldn't predict. For one thing, now there was a completely different kind of presidential administration in Washington than the one that had taken office just before this phase of the investigation started back in 2017. More committed to protecting rights, more vigilant in pursuing wrongs. If they were not going to push for an indictment, then at least there might be some powerful statements made. That would mean something. We were encouraged by the fact that Assistant Attorney General Kristen Clarke was coming in from Washington, along with her long, distinguished list of accomplishments in civil rights, the kind of experience you can draw on in moments like the one we were headed for, moments when strong statements and context were important. Barbara Bosserman, the deputy chief of the DOJ Cold Case Unit, was coming, too—also committed to justice. So was DA Dewayne Richardson, as well as Clay Joyner, the acting US attorney for the Northern District of Mississippi. They all were coming, and that meant something very important. But what cards would they lay on the table? Time would tell. One thing for certain: We might not have known just where they were taking this, but it seemed pretty clear from this lineup that they were taking it seriously.

SECURITY WAS HEAVY when we drove up. Fatima and her camera guy were chased off the FBI parking lot. She couldn't get into the lobby, let alone the briefing room. She did ask, though, for both. That's what she does. The COVID screening to get into the field office seemed as stringent as the general security protocols for this fortress of a building. We moved from one locked space into another, like decompression chambers, where it seemed like even our innermost thoughts were being scanned: temperature checks, mandatory masks, no electronics. We had wondered whether we even would be allowed to take handwritten notes. Chris was always taking notes—lots of notes. No one ever stopped him. Better to ask for forgiveness, he would say, than to ask for permission. He never asked for either.

Almost as soon as we all had assembled in a very large conference room Chris was called out to another meeting room, a smaller one, for a preliminary talk with the officials. They presented him with an envelope addressed to me. It contained a letter summarizing the investigation and its findings. It also included a redacted final report. There had been two drafts of that report circulated confidentially among officials a year earlier before they finally settled on this one. The officials reconfirmed the afternoon schedule with Chris: the 1 P.M. meeting with only me, Marvel, and Chris, and the 2 P.M. meeting with the three of us in addition to the rest of the family members present. Once again, the officials noted that the government would not sponsor a press conference. As he listened, Chris envisioned the activity already set in motion five miles away at Northwestern's downtown facilities—the press conference we had arranged. It was all coming together: the chairs, the cameras, the podium, the mics, one for the room, one for Zoom, all those remote journalists who had responded to some two thousand media advisories that had been sent out just that morning by Erin Karter, managing editor for media relations at Northwestern. As Chris confirmed our agreement to the terms going forward and once again accepted the decision on the press conference, he didn't mention the one we had set up. Better to ask for forgiveness.

Next, Marvel and I were ushered into the room with the officials and Chris. After introductions were made all around, Assistant Attorney General Kristen Clarke spoke first, addressing me as a victim, a survivor, a witness to a night of terror some sixty-six years earlier. "Racial violence, hate crime is a stain on our nation's history," she said. And she assured me that she shared my desire to do everything possible "to hold perpetrators responsible for hate crimes," which she described as "a priority" at the Department of Justice. She said she was personally invested in that priority. We believed her. The reputation she brought with her earned her that faith in her honesty. We were moved by the sincere passion and unwavering dedication to justice we felt in the words she spoke. But her opening words and the general somber feeling in that room were something of a tell. It was confirmation of where we thought this would go.

Clarke talked about her commitment to "leaving no stone unturned" in her continued protection of civil rights at DOJ. And it certainly was meaningful that she even would come to Chicago to personally deliver the message to us. "I wanted to come here to indicate how important this work is to our mission at DOJ." She wanted to personally recognize me for what she saw as my "courage in continuing" that effort.

Acting US Attorney Clay Joyner followed her and expressed his "profound sense of responsibility for suffering and sacrifice caused by the horrific injustice sixty-six years ago." And, as a White Mississippian, he apologized for that miscarriage of justice in the acquittal of two of Bobo's killers and the failure to investigate more effectively at the time to bring others to justice. "We gave our word that we would get to the truth" in the current investigation, he said, and "conduct as comprehensive an investigation as possible." He believed they had done so.

DA Richardson joined in expressing condolences and regret "on behalf of the state of Mississippi and especially my district," for the injustice we suffered. Joining with Clarke, he pledged an "endless pursuit of justice," and would even "continue to pursue efforts" in this case, which told us pretty much where this all was going.

The rest of the story was laid out by former Special Agent Walter Henry, who summarized the investigation and findings, which were detailed in the report in my envelope. The horribly painful finality of it all had been teased out by the opening remarks of the government officials, but now was spelled out clearly in the very heading of the report, the letters and the words and the decision they expressed. "Civil Rights Division: Notice to Close File."

SOMETHING HAD SEEMED terribly wrong about the Timothy Tyson book from the very beginning. Just the fact that a person who held himself out as a scholar of history would not want to discover or even check the information he would write about, or even get fresh perspectives by talking with the surviving family of Emmett Till, was strange. It's not like he didn't think talking to people would be important. After all, he based the whole idea of publishing a book on what he claimed he talked about with Carolyn Bryant Donham. But he would cite sources, like Simmie's book and Mamie's book, without talking to people connected to those books, people who were still around at the time to talk about it all and give additional information. He never talked to me, he didn't check with any of us—those of us who were at the store the evening Bobo whistled—to get our story, to make sure he was balancing against the story he was depending on to drive the whole thing, the story of the White woman who became the center of his presentation. So there was concern from the very beginning about his methods, even as we were quick to accept the outcome, what we were led to believe was Carolyn's recantation, her confession of the truth. Although we saw it all unravel during the investigation as we were able to review the documents that were produced and hear the assessment by the investigators, even after all that, there still was the possibility that something might have turned up over the two years leading up to this last meeting, something that might have confirmed what Tyson had written and what we had believed. That's the way it usually goes in movies. At the eleventh hour when all seems lost, something turns up to turn it all around. But this was no movie. This was real life. No cavalry. No SWAT team. No superhero to save the day. No happy ending.

Both documents in my envelope from the government—the letter to me and the final report—summarized everything that had been considered over the nearly four years of this phase of the investigation, the part that, as we know, was triggered by the publication of Tyson's book. But the officials linked this part of the investigation to the opening of the probe way back in 2004. They made clear that this was a continuation of that investigation that—despite news reports—actually never had been formally closed. The whole point of this final phase was to see if anything in the Tyson book might lead to new evidence on whether anybody who had participated in the kidnapping and murder of Emmett Till was still alive and could be brought to justice on federal or state charges—charges that would have to be proved beyond a reasonable doubt. Of course, that inquiry included Carolyn. In fact, it focused mostly on her. "We took four years because there was the will to hold someone accountable," Clarke said. But, as Richardson pointed out, that would mean something new, something that wasn't already considered in the 2007 grand jury. Apparently, there was quite a lot that had been considered back then.

Chris asked what exactly had been reviewed for criminal charges against Carolyn Bryant Donham in that secret grand jury process?

"In 2007, the grand jury looked at conspiracy, kidnapping, various forms of manslaughter, murder, accessory after the fact," Richardson said. But nothing the grand jury examined amounted to enough for them to indict, as indicated by the no true bill they handed down. And nothing new had emerged this time around to take to a new grand jury. Now, as then, there were no eyewitnesses who could help piece together the tons of circumstantial evidence that had been collected.

So that was one part, the part that connected directly to Bobo's lynching. But the other part, the part that had driven so much public anger and discussion, was whether there was anything to support Tyson's claim that Carolyn had recanted. If she did recant, then that would mean she had lied earlier on several occasions that mattered. If she was found to have lied in court, in sworn testimony in 1955, as everyone believes she did, then it would have been under oath. But that still would not be enough to convict her now. Perjury in a Mississippi trial would have been a violation of Mississippi state law, not federal law, and the time to enforce Mississippi state law on perjury is limited to five years, the statute of limitations. The possibility for the State of Mississippi to issue that charge ran out in 1960.

Even later, if it was shown that she made a false statement to Special Agent Dale Killinger in his multiple interviews with her between 2004 and 2006, that surely would have amounted to a federal offense, but any chance to charge her with a violation of federal law in that case would have run out at the end of the five-year statute of limitations by 2011 at the latest. So the only chance to indict and prosecute Carolyn would have been on the basis of proof she had made a false statement to a federal agent in 2017 when she was interviewed by the FBI on the claim made by Tyson in his book. She was asked then if she had recanted in the Tyson interview. She denied it. Her daughter-in-law Marsha Bryant corroborated that denial. If her denial was a lie, the government would need evidence that she was lying, which brings us back to Tyson. If Tyson had credible evidence that she had made the statement he claimed she had made, then denying to federal authorities that she made the statement to Tyson would amount to making a false statement to the investigators—a lie in violation of federal law.

There was no such evidence. We reviewed the manuscript Carolyn and Marsha had written and Tyson had edited. We reviewed other documents, including the transcript of the Tyson interview with authorities. Nothing revealed any credible evidence produced by Tyson that could have supported a court case against Carolyn. What all these documents showed was a bunch of shifting stories even about the way things got started with Tyson's interviews with Carolyn, and what the terms of his connection might be, as well as what actually was revealed in these encounters. At first there was a recording. Then there wasn't. Then there might have been. But then again, well, maybe not.

Tyson's assistant, Melody Ivins, probably made matters worse since she stated she heard Carolyn's statement before stating she didn't. After all this to-and-fro, Tyson wound up pointing to what the

DOJ report referred to as his "sparse handwritten notes" that ultimately proved nothing. "The undated, handwritten notes Tyson provided to the FBI do not include a full quotation of the alleged recantation that Tyson described in his book. The notes include only four statements without context as to what subject had been under discussion when the statements were made or what questions had led to the statement."[1] The government pointed to the fact we also had observed, that Tyson had not taken any other notes during his two interviews with Carolyn[2] and Marsha told authorities that "she could not recall Tyson taking notes" at all during the interviews.[3] What's more, Tyson did not provide anything that could help anybody understand what was really going on when Carolyn allegedly made the comment, again, if she made it all. What would she have been responding to? Could have been anything, assuming, again, that she actually said anything like what was published.[4] "The statement 'that p[ar]t wasn't true' is contained in Tyson's notes. But the notes do not indicate exactly *what* [Carolyn Bryant-Donham] said was not true," according to the report.[5]

All this made Tyson's notes completely unreliable, if they even were believable to begin with.

That opinion was supported even more by what we all had seen in the documentation—the transcripts of the interviews, the manuscript that Carolyn and Marsha had written, which Tyson had edited, and finally Tyson's interview with the authorities. Any reasonable person would have felt the same way we did, and obviously the way the government did, in reading what Tyson claimed in his book that Carolyn said, and what she actually did express in the draft of her memoir. As the government set out in its letter to me, Tyson "failed to explain convincingly why, if Carolyn Bryant had recanted her testimony early in an interview, he did not closely question her about the recantation when she later reverted to her original version of events. Nor did he offer a sufficient explanation for why he had asked no question and offered no comments or corrections when he reviewed and edited her written account of events at the store, even though that account was consistent with her 1955 state hearing testimony and inconsistent with the alleged recantation. Although Professor Tyson made numerous other suggestions and edits to her memoir, he never suggested that she include an admission that her state court testimony was untruthful, nor did he challenge why her written account differed from her alleged recantation."[6]

The puzzle pieces just didn't fit together. "He was not acting as a person who heard the comment," Bosserman said during our briefing. "Why wouldn't he change that in her manuscript? He didn't stop her in telling the story in the interview."

He had every chance to do just that. As we had observed, Tyson's digital "fingerprints" were all over Carolyn's manuscript in the form of tracked changes and forty-nine numbered comments bearing Tyson's "TT" initials. Among other things, he offered compliments for what he considered to be well-crafted passages; he asked questions to clarify certain points; he moved a passage up higher in the manuscript for narrative flow; he suggested foreshadowing certain narrative points; he even suggested corrections; and he urged the naming of names of anonymous characters.[7] But just as important, when he disagreed with something that had been written, he wrote comments like "I find this hard to believe, honestly,"[8] and "I find this implausible,"[9] and "This is not credible,"[10] and "This stretches credibility."[11]

So, then, when Carolyn wrote in her manuscript about Emmett in the store, adding even more offensive and fantasized details than she had provided in the 1955 courtroom testimony, why didn't Tyson comment as he was reading it all that "I find this hard to believe, honestly," or "I find this implausible," or "This is not credible," or "This stretches credibility"? If he got that recantation before he ever read and edited anything in her manuscript, then repeating the kind of comments he had expressed for other doubtful passages Carolyn and Marsha had written would have been appropriate and consistently honest as an editor with integrity.

Just as we had seen in our meeting with Special Agent Henry back in Memphis, the government had found that there were "numerous inconsistencies in Tyson's account that raised questions about the credibility of his account of the interviews."[12] The reason he was there in the first place—whether he was editing Carolyn's book, or interviewing her for his book—and why he didn't have better documentation of it were all issues that still were up in the air, disputed, confusing, and basically seemed to leave everybody scratching their heads.

Henry addressed the obvious question even before we could ask it. "We can't say he lied, but we can't rely on his information. There's no validation."

"There is a lot of reason to be skeptical" about Carolyn's story about what she claimed happened at the store with Emmett Till, Bosserman said, with or without Tyson's book. "But to prosecute Carolyn Bryant, it would have to be beyond a reasonable doubt." And, as everybody could see, there certainly were doubts in that room in the believability of Carolyn's evolving story but also in Tyson's unsubstantiated one. "He would be our key witness against her," Henry said. And all things considered, Tyson's credibility was the most doubtful part of it all. In the end, it would be one of the key reasons the government decided to just close the case.

Even so, some of the government's conclusions were uplifting.

"Just because we can't prosecute Carolyn Bryant Donham doesn't mean we believe her," Bosserman told me during our briefing, echoing an important point made in their letter to me.

"By closing this matter without prosecution, the government does not take the position that Carolyn Bryant's state court testimony was truthful or accurate. There remains considerable doubt as to the truthfulness of Carolyn Bryant's 1955 state court testimony, which is contradicted not only by your account of events but by the state court testimony of others who were with you and Mr. Till that day."[13]

I found that last point especially gratifying. The truth of the testimony Simmie and I had been giving for years finally was being validated. There was no dare for Bobo "to enter the store and speak to or flirt with Bryant-Donham. Nor did Till have a photo of a white girl that he showed to the men standing outside the store. Rather Till bought some items and he and [Simeon] Wright left the store together, without incident." There was no "commotion inside the store." And finally, the report factually concluded something critical regarding Carolyn's frame of mind at the time. "Shortly after Till and Wright exited, Bryant-Donham came out of the store, unhurried and undisturbed."[14] That's when Bobo whistled, when Carolyn rushed to her car, and when we rushed to ours.

Although no one in that FBI conference room during our briefing would say outright that Carolyn lied, it seemed as though everyone seated around the table definitely believed that she had. "There is no evidence to credit her version," Richardson said.

Maybe it didn't matter that they didn't come right out and say she lied. They really didn't have to. The report said it all. She had told her story, we had told ours, and the two stories were in conflict—opposite, contradictory. And the language in the report concluded we had told the truth. But our truth was not the level of proof necessary for a criminal prosecution and conviction.

After weighing the points coming from the different voices in the room, I finally made a statement in the form of a question that was, in fact, a conclusion. "So, it's over?" The officials around the table nodded to confirm what I had said, what already had been headlined on the report. "Notice to Close File."

In the end, we had to set aside our need to process our deep disappointment. We had to attend the second briefing session.

Though we were running over our set time—an hour for each session—the officials were not rushing at all. They clearly wanted to take their time to inform us and help us work our way through. They even had a victim's advocate there to talk us through, if we needed that. But our timeline was driven by the need to make it to our own planned news conference on time.

The second meeting was pretty much like the first one, but with fewer specifics.

Bobo's murder was described in the report summarized for the other family members as "one of the most horrific examples" of racial violence. And the acquittal of J. W. Milam and Roy Bryant was described as a "systemic failure of institutions" that are established to protect us from such violence and hold perpetrators accountable.

We wrapped up the second briefing and took a little more time for a group photo and farewell pleasantries.

All of that, the farewells, the rush to the car, even the last words that were spoken and the promises that were exchanged, promises to keep in touch, all of that seemed to go into a soft background of sounds, pushed into a corner of my head by the echo of the words spoken during the first meeting, the words everyone around the table had agreed on, the words that kept sounding in my head through most of the second meeting, as if those words were punctuating every statement the officials made to the other family members in the second briefing, the inescapable concluding line to all this. It was over.

MARVEL HAD THE right idea. She usually does. But sometimes, well, okay, many times, it takes me a minute to realize that she is right. I had wanted to drive us all to the FBI field office for the meetings we just left and then from there over to the news conference we were on our way to hold. She talked me out of it. She had the right idea. And she was supported by Fatima and ABC, who had arranged for the driver, and now I was glad that had all been set up. I don't know how I would have been able to concentrate on the driving in heavy afternoon traffic with everything running through my mind right then.

Clearly, the government briefing was a big moment. But another one awaited us. We had promised Fatima and ABC an exclusive, so she had wanted us to cancel the news conference. Chris refused to do that since the government announcement was going to go out wide—news organizations, civil rights groups, social action groups—and then everybody would get the story in bits and pieces. Some would quote us. Some would quote anybody they could grab who might think they had something legitimate to say about the case. Chris wanted us out there to respond to everyone at once and then provide the exclusive follow-up for Fatima. With that in mind, there first would be what the TV people call a pull-aside right after the news conference. Ollie and I would be on *ABC News Live Prime with Linsey Davis* that night, doing the interview right there in the television studio at Northwestern's Medill School of Journalism, and then we would appear on *Good Morning America* the next day. I would do a final interview with Fatima for her documentary at noon that day. Ollie would be interviewed after me.

We would have to keep that all in balance against the weight of the moment—a moment whose heaviness hit me in waves. Julie Bosman, the Chicago bureau chief for *The New York Times*, had called Chris that morning to see if she could get any information beyond the intentionally vague reference in the media advisory that had just gone out from Northwestern. That alert had only announced that Emmett Till family members would join Professor Benson "to address the final investigative report in the 1955 lynching of 14-year-old Till in Mississippi." Bosman wanted to know what that would mean so she could decide whether the *Times* would cover it. Chris told her we had been doing a "ride-along" with the FBI and the DOJ on the murder investigation that was ending. The findings would be released later that day. We, the family, would respond.

"Oh, that's history," she said. "We'll be there."

History. Since this all had started back in 2017, I hadn't really had time to think about it that way. It all had been so personal to me, so painful. For me it had all been about Bobo and Simmie and Mamie. I was the last person left who could represent their suffering in what the government had described as a "horrific" tragedy. The last one representing them along this quest for justice. The last one to make sure we did everything we could do. I had been so absorbed in the details, the brushstrokes, that I had not taken in the big picture for a very long time. Yes, this was about Bobo. But it also was about his impact on history. The officials had said as much in that first briefing back at the FBI offices. Barbara Bosserman had said that the "Till death was one of the greatest unsolved crimes in American history." She went on to say that "It was the catalyst for hate crime legislation," laws on the books now that didn't exist when Bobo was killed. Clarke agreed, noting that the federal government's pursuit of the killers of Ahmaud Arbery was connected to the legacy of Emmett Till. "It doesn't give much comfort in talking about the work we are doing today. But Till's death gave rise to laws that help go after criminals," she said. "The seeds of what gave rise to this awful crime are still with us," she noted, pointing to the racism and racial violence that still threaten our national unity. The need for these laws and law enforcement was as important as it ever had been.

THE NEWS CONFERENCE finally got started at Northwestern under the klieg lights and in front of the TV cameras and over the mics on the podium connecting us to reporters in a number of cities outside Chicago, thirty minutes late, as Chris stepped up to read the DOJ decision from my letter. Then, after the brief introduction, he turned it over to us.

"Today is a day we'll never forget," I said. "Officially, the Emmett Till case has been closed after sixty-six years."

It was over.

Then, moving past the torment of the past sixty-six years and even this moment of recognition, I reflected on it all. "Pain is somewhat numbed, but it never really goes away."[15] It was clear we all needed more time to think about what had happened and what would happen next. "I did not expect that they would have found any new evidence," Ollie said at the podium. "I ask where do we go from here?"[16] Pointing to her special relationship with Bobo who "was like a brother to me," Thelma expressed what we all were feeling at the time. "I'm not surprised, but my heart is broken." Like Ollie, she had lived with Mamie and Emmett for a while during her school years. "I pinned diapers on Emmett," she recalled, expressing regret that "nothing was settled" following years of investigation. "The case is closed and we have to go on from here."[17] Marvel picked up on that theme, the moving-forward part, as she spoke the words of the very last public speech Mamie Till-Mobley had delivered in December 2002 just days before her death, giving thanks to God "for taking hatred out of my heart." So, as Marvel said, "we are disappointed that the murderers of Emmett Till were found not guilty in 1955 and later confessed to the murder. We are disappointed that no one has paid for the tragic brutal murder of a fourteen-year-old boy for whistling at a White woman. But there is no hatred in our hearts, either . . ."

THIS LEG OF my journey had begun in 2017 with headlines from a book release. It was ending now with more headlines from our news release. This book has been about the search for truth and justice in the lynching of Emmett Till. It wasn't intended as a critique of Timothy Tyson's work, but it was inevitable that it would be. Tyson offered us a revelation of something we had been awaiting for a very long time. In the end, we have been left trying to figure out whether the Carolyn Bryant Donham quote he published was true, misunderstood, imagined, or just an out-and-out hoax.

Tyson's interview with the authorities was surprising because he didn't have the goods to back up his claim. But what we saw in one of the interviews Tyson had with Carolyn Bryant Donham and Marsha Bryant was more than surprising. It was shocking for what it seemed to reveal. It was something that was not reflected in Supervisory Special FBI Agent Dale Killinger's December 2017 summary report of the contradictions in the Carolyn/Marsha manuscript, and something that wasn't even noted in Tyson's book. There was a moment—just a moment—during an interview session that appeared to shed light on the possible motivation for Carolyn's "forgetfulness" in her interviews with Killinger. Those memory lapses seemed to be more like tactics—defensive maneuvers—than the result of the mere passage of time or a series of senior moments. As a matter of fact, the moment that caught our attention just might have helped to expose everything we had been looking for during the four-year investigation, during my sixty-six-year journey to justice.

For years following Bobo's kidnapping, we believed the story Papa had told about hearing that voice from the cab of the truck. The "light" voice. He testified about it under oath in the courtroom during the murder trial. He even repeated it to reporters. Even before he testified and was interviewed, though, he reported the kidnapping to Leflore County Sheriff George Smith later on the same morning when Bobo was taken. Three days later, after Bobo's body was pulled from the river, Sheriff Smith told a reporter for the Memphis *Commercial Appeal* that Papa had told him two White men and a woman had taken Bobo from his home.[18] Even though this could have been the way Smith interpreted Papa's report, he was basing his comment on the report Papa had made to him right after the kidnapping when the details—the identity of that shadowy figure in the cab of the truck—would have been fresh in Papa's memory, and in the memory of Sheriff Smith when he commented to the reporter about the same time he issued a warrant for Carolyn Bryant's arrest.

This is the story we believed and wanted everyone else to believe. Not only that Papa heard what he would call later at trial the "light" voice, but that the voice—lighter than a man's voice, a woman's voice he also would tell Simmie close to the time of the kidnapping—that the voice he heard belonged to Carolyn Bryant. We just never had anything—no corroborating witness—that could verify what Papa swore he had heard. In reviewing the documents with the authorities at the FBI Chicago field office in August 2018, though, we saw what we hoped would amount to that corroboration. The transcripts featured an exchange between Marsha Bryant and Carolyn Bryant Donham during one of the Tyson interview sessions. It might have been a slip of the tongue when they were distracted in a way, trying to fix the time when Papa came to the store looking for Bobo after he had been taken. After daylight.

He knocked on the door. He felt the presence from inside. It was

Carolyn listening to a man's voice. "They're not here," he said to John Crawford before turning to leave.

MARSHA: "So it could have been after Till was gone for a long time after he'd come to pick you up and they were coming to look for him. Or it could have been . . ."

CAROLYN (interrupting): "Marsha, they didn't pick me up."

Then Marsha appeared to catch herself, and she revised the narrative.

MARSHA: "No, after they'd picked Till and brought him to the house and told you they were going off with him, it could have been that Mose Wright thought they'd been gone for a long enough time, and came to find, to see if he was at the house. So, it could have been either before or after."

CAROLYN: "I think it was before."

MARSHA: "So where do you think they went before? Because didn't . . ."

CAROLYN (breaking in, as if to cut this conversation short): "I don't have any idea."[19]

It is interesting that there is no other place in the transcripts of two recorded interviews where Carolyn interrupted to correct Marsha on anything. No other place. No other interruption. No other correction. There would be a good reason to stop this chatter if by "after he'd come to pick you up and they were coming to look for him" Marsha was referring to Roy Bryant (with J. W. Milam) coming to pick up Carolyn to go look for Bobo. We weren't the only ones to take note of this in our session at the FBI Chicago field office. It raised some eyebrows on the other side of the table, too, when we asked about it. But there was more.

In the 2006 FBI report focusing on activities earlier on the night of the kidnapping, J. W. Milam, Roy Bryant, and Melvin Campbell were playing cards and drinking moonshine when the subject of Bobo's whistle came up. According to an unnamed source in the report, they picked up somebody in Money, went to the Wright home, then went back to Money to drop off the person they had picked up.[20] Who else could it have been besides Carolyn? At one point in the Tyson interview, Carolyn suggested that the voice in the truck—what she called the "soft voice"—might have been her sister-in-law Juanita Milam.

"Well she's the only woman who could have identified him other than myself."[21]

That might tell us who was picked up and dropped off in Money the night of the crime. Except for one thing.

MARSHA (responding to Carolyn): "Oh, my. But she didn't see him, did she?"

CAROLYN: "Not that I know of, but she—"

TYSON: "Unless she's the soft voice in the truck."[22]

The only person who made sense in that conversation was Marsha Bryant. According to Carolyn's own account, Juanita Milam never laid eyes on Bobo. Carolyn claimed that her sister-in-law was in the back room with their kids. In various accounts, Carolyn said she either screamed for Juanita Milam, or called to her to watch the store when she ran out to get her gun from Juanita Milam's car, or told Juanita Milam about her encounter only after it was all over. Again, in none of these accounts did Juanita Milam ever see Bobo, and she actually never heard anything. She only listened to Carolyn's claims and was shocked to hear about it all. So said Carolyn. The reveal in that story, though, is how Carolyn was trying to explain a woman's voice in the truck. In effect, she was verifying Papa's account. He heard a woman's voice. And she seemed to be trying to explain how that really could have been the case. Instead of denying that there was or even could have been such a voice coming from the truck, she confirmed that possibility just by playing a guessing game to determine who it might have been.

Another problem with that moment is that at other times, Carolyn claimed that J. W. Milam and Roy Bryant had brought Bobo back to the store for her to identify him. She never mentioned that Juanita Milam was with them. Obviously, she wasn't. And, it seemed, Carolyn only made that suggestion to shift the gaze away from herself and to another possible light or soft voice of a woman.

There's more. As Marsha pointed out in the Tyson interview transcript, Juanita Milam had never seen Emmett Till alive. In fact, when she was interviewed by the FBI during the 2004–2006 investigation, Juanita Milam told a completely different story. She denied that she even was in the store the night Bobo walked in. "I thought I was in Greenville," visiting family, she said, and "would not have been babysittin' for her."[23] The fact that Juanita Milam's car was parked outside the store doesn't prove anything. Carolyn said she typically would drive that car even when Juanita Milam was not with her. That would explain why Carolyn left her gun under the front seat. She had been driving the car that day. So, if J. W. Milam and Roy Bryant were going to take anybody to the Wright family home to identify and take Emmett Till, why would they choose Juanita Milam? It is much more likely that they would have taken Carolyn. More than likely, we believe they did.

In her manuscript and in her interviews with Supervisory Special Agent Dale Killinger, Carolyn talked about a confrontation in the store between Roy Bryant and a young Black boy on Saturday, three days after our visit to the store when Bobo whistled. She claimed the boy didn't show enough respect when her husband was asking if he was the boy her husband had been looking for. She claimed that she intervened and told her husband that he wasn't the one. According to the FBI report of 2004–2006, there is another story that Carolyn never has told—not in her interviews with the FBI, her interviews with Tyson, or in her manuscript—and perhaps it is the story she had in mind when she told the one about the confrontation inside the store. This one occurred in the road outside the store. The FBI report has Roy Bryant, J. W. Milam, and a Black man, J. W. Washington (possibly Johnny Washington), driving around at dusk on Saturday, August 27—only hours before they came to Papa's for Bobo. It seems that they had been hunting for Bobo that day. There was another person in the truck when this group picked up a young Black boy who was walking home after buying some molasses and snuff. Roy Bryant ordered Washington to throw the boy in the back of the truck. That's when the other person jumped out of the cab and yelled at Roy Bryant, "That's not the nigger," in a voice that it seems was pretty convincing. It was a woman's voice. Not a light voice, not soft at all, at least not in this moment. But the voice of a woman, to be sure. A determined, insistent woman who was identified.

There are names that are redacted from the FBI report—people who were still alive between 2004 and 2006 when the FBI was investigating the case. Makes sense: protect the innocent, which in the case of the 2006 report would be pretty much anybody who hadn't been charged with a crime. The name of this person—the one who jumped out and yelled "Roy I keep telling ya that's not the one"—the name of that person with the voice more emphatic, more adamant than light or soft, that person's name is one of the redacted ones. But we were able to confirm the identity. It was Carolyn Bryant. After she convinced her husband that the boy they had picked up was not Emmett Till, Roy Bryant told J. W. Washington to throw the boy off the truck. Washington followed orders. The boy wound up with a busted lip and broken teeth.[24] And, as we know, the lynch mob continued the hunt.

If there was a woman in the truck when they came for Bobo, and Carolyn Bryant had been the woman in the truck just hours earlier in the evening when they were looking for Bobo, why shouldn't we assume the woman in the truck in the middle of the night also was Carolyn Bryant? Why shouldn't we conclude that the unnamed person who was picked up in Money that night on the way to abducting Bobo, according to the anonymous FBI witness, the person dropped off back in Money after Bobo was grabbed, pulled from the house, and identified at the truck, is the same person who identified Bobo at the truck in front of the house? Why shouldn't we conclude that this person with the woman's voice was Carolyn Bryant?

Sheriff Smith issued a warrant for Carolyn Bryant's arrest the day after he arrested her husband on August 28, 1955. That showed that Sheriff Smith thought there was probable cause to bring her in for the kidnapping. In her manuscript, Carolyn wrote that she only learned about the warrant during the FBI investigation of 2004–2006.[25] But she also wrote that the family kept moving her around from one house to another to keep her from being harassed.[26] Could it be they were really trying to keep her from being arrested, keep her from talking, giving up something about being in that truck, giving up evidence against her husband and brother-in-law? Seems like a pattern with this family. Make sure the weaker ones didn't bend under pressure. Roy Bryant was the first to be arrested. Then J. W. Milam went to see him in jail just so he could get arrested, too—on purpose ensuring his half brother didn't give up something, didn't talk too much, as he already had, implicating his wife.[27]

William Bradford Huie wrote in *Look* magazine that they didn't need to take Bobo to Carolyn because Bobo already had admitted he was the one they were looking for as he got dressed to be marched out of the house. This is a theme Carolyn picked up on when she said Bobo admitted—right in front of her—that he was the one. It is the theme of the defiant thuggish Black boy from Chicago, unafraid of anything.[28] But the stories don't match up among Huie and Carolyn and court testimony. Sheriff Smith testified that Roy Bryant told him he brought Bobo to the store to have Carolyn identify him. Deputy Ed Cothran testified that J. W. Milam also said they brought Bobo to Carolyn to have her identify him. But then they just let him go, they said, without even talking to her or having her look at Bobo.[29]

Whether to protect Carolyn from the authorities' interrogations or protect the men who murdered Bobo from what her untrained answers might reveal, clearly the family wanted to keep Carolyn under wraps. That's why they kept moving her around. In the end, they probably didn't have to worry about that. Sheriff Smith decided "we aren't going to bother the woman." As with so many others—like Tyson and Devery Anderson years later—the balance of sympathy seemed to tip in her favor even with Sheriff Smith. "She's got two small boys to take care of."[30]

Not everyone fell for the sympathetic role Carolyn played. "Her sister-in-law did not back up her story when she was interviewed by the FBI," DA Richardson reminded us during the first briefing. According to Juanita Milam, Carolyn just might have been making the whole thing up because, as Juanita Milam figured it, "she did not want to take care of the store. She thought this wild story would make Roy take care of the store instead of leaving her with the kids and the store."[31] She went on to say, "That is a female point of view," leading Loyola University (Chicago) history professor Elliott Gorn to an interesting analysis. That "female point of view" appears to mean a "White" woman's view. A White woman in the Mississippi Delta. When she was pressed on whether she thought Carolyn's story made sense, Juanita Milam said it didn't. "And then, seemingly unrelated, she started talking about how she had been around black people all her life, how she had good black help, how she never expected them to bow down to her, how she was not afraid of black people. The implication was clear: Carolyn Bryant made up her story about Emmett Till, worked a whistle or a wink into an accusation of sexual assault, to a near-rape, because she was scared to death of being alone with black men. From the 'female point of view,' they terrified Carolyn Bryant, and only her husband could protect her, take her away from this lonely store, rife with what young white Delta girls had been taught to fear more than anything."[32]

There is no record that Juanita Milam ever was asked about any of this, or offered an opinion about any of this at the time of the murder trial in September 1955. She was called to testify, but only asked to describe her husband and his military service, not about the events on August 24. She was a character witness.[33]

Even so, there was one remaining point that raised questions about everything Carolyn Bryant Donham has said. In her interviews with Timothy Tyson and in her manuscript, Carolyn insisted that she didn't tell her husband about any encounter in the store until he confronted her about it; that she never identified Bobo as a person who had insulted her; and that she begged her husband not to hurt Bobo and to take him home. Putting aside for a moment the question of whether begging her husband not to hurt Bobo and to take him back home was a form of identification of the person who "done her wrong," the whole thing looks like a lie that keeps growing, evolving. "We know from history that she did not tell the story the same way over time," DA Richardson noted during the first briefing. In her first interview with attorney Sidney Carlton, Carolyn said she told her husband the story as soon as he returned from Texas early Friday morning.[34]

Over so many years, it would seem that Carolyn kept adding to her story in order to cover up something she never can truly hide from herself, running away from something she never will be able to escape. Even if she has managed to escape a criminal indictment.

IN A WAY, this journey—this four-year investigation in a lifetime search for answers—this journey ended without a formal legal conclusion. Maybe I never should have expected one. After all, how can there be a happy ending to a tragic story that never should have begun? There can be no justice for Emmett Till. "Justice would have meant Emmett Till coming home from the State of Mississippi, alive," DA Richardson had said during the first briefing.

That's what justice would have meant for George Floyd, or Breonna Taylor, or Ahmaud Arbery, or Philando Castile, or Tamir Rice, or Sandra Bland, or Eric Garner, or Trayvon Martin, or so many others.

Still, there should be accountability. There should be consequences. We do right and we are rewarded. We do wrong and we are punished. When we are wronged, it should be made right. Without consequences, how do we ever learn the difference between right and wrong, good and bad? Moral choices are the foundation of a civil society.

In the end, there have been no consequences for those who tortured and lynched Emmett Till. If there are no consequences for taking Black lives, then people come to see Black life itself as inconsequential. They will conclude that Black life doesn't matter. In the end, everyone is diminished. And we—all of us, not just Black people, but all of us—have to reckon with the consequences of that or risk the death of a truly just society for all of us.

Epilogue

THE DAY AFTER our final meeting with the government officials at the FBI Chicago field office and our news conference, I was back at The Drake Hotel on Chicago's Gold Coast with ABC documentary producer/director Fatima Curry. We had promised to give Fatima an exclusive interview following the release of the government report and, as exhausted as I was, we were keeping that promise in the same place we had recorded our first interview for her documentary.

The ABC folks had reserved a private dining room at The Drake, a room behind the hotel's Palm Court—the Palm Court, where ladies enjoyed afternoon tea in personal teapots and were served finger sandwiches, scones and petits fours, chocolates, vanilla pods, preserves, and lemon curds on three-tiered tea trays. It was a world of contrasts as I walked through a maze of tables to get to the room behind this room. Cheerful women—White women—in this room, the brightly lit Palm Court, talking about things that mattered it seemed only to them, completely unaware of the darker room just beyond the double doors, the room with the klieg lights and the cameras and the monitors, where we would tell dramatically different stories. Stories that *should* matter to them but might never reach them. Stories they might never even care to hear, let alone share at teatime.

As I took my seat, I couldn't help but think about what looked like two distinct worlds we had come to occupy. The incredible brightness on their side. The dramatic darkness on ours. The darkness of indifference on their side. The light of wisdom on our side. At least that's how it seemed. We were totally aware of them and they appeared to be oblivious to us. How might we bring these two spaces together, not just here in The Drake Hotel, but out there in the world? That's what my journey had been about and what the ABC production was set to document.

The ABC crew went through their checklist and I sat in the reflective spotlight waiting for my cue, the slate for the take. For a moment before we started the interview, I was able to think back on all we had learned over the past four years and all that we had set in motion for so many years to come.

Dewayne Richardson's District Manager Tamicko Fair had put the question to us back in Oxford, Mississippi, when this whole thing got started in March 2017. "What does justice look like to you?" Simmie and I didn't exactly see eye-to-eye on the answer to that question, although we really weren't all that far apart in the end. It's just that he was more on the side of retribution at first and I was more on the side of reconciliation. In the end, we both wanted accountability, which could have included the arrest of Carolyn Bryant Donham. But would accountability amount to justice?

DA Richardson had suggested an answer in our briefing the day before this ABC session. Justice would have meant that Bobo had lived, grown up to do good works, contribute to society, had a family with kids who could be spoiled by their grandmother. That's the way I interpreted what he said.

While retribution might have been satisfying in an Old Testament kind of way, how would our family have moved forward from that? How could we have been restored by that? This does not mean that

I didn't want to see Carolyn Bryant Donham punished. I did and I do. After considering it over the course of the investigation, I figured that holding people accountable is a form of justice, and accountability demands the truth. That would seem to mean that truth itself is a form of justice. But I also recognize that even that would not have been enough.

So, even today, what does justice require in the lynching of Emmett Till? For one thing, in my view, justice should not just be about getting even. An eye for an eye only leaves everyone blind. We need to see clearly during these times—more clearly than ever before. I believe my vision is keen now. That's because I'm not trying to win.

For some, winning becomes justice. If you are accused and you are acquitted, then you've won your case, and you could see that as just. If you are a victim and the accused is found guilty, then *you* win, and you could see that as just. But so many innocent Black folks are wrongly convicted and so many guilty White folks—like Milam and Bryant—have gotten off and continue to get off. They win. So where is the justice in that? Justice can't be a zero sum game—I win only if you lose.

Maybe justice really is in reconciliation, and reconciliation only comes from a meeting of the minds, an agreement on the injustice in the justice system, a problem that is rooted in race and power. So how do we get there? How can we all win with a new level of understanding?

In a way, it seems Mamie Till-Mobley found the answer to that question many years ago. Yes, she wanted wrongdoers to be punished. We all do. But she wasn't going to sit back and simply wait for that to happen. She also wasn't going to spend all of her time and energy trying to make that happen. She recognized that the lack of a just outcome in the murder of her son should motivate people to get out and make sure justice is never denied again. She worked with young people teaching them history and civic duty. She traveled the country inspiring the public with a sense of social responsibility.

People like the late activist Alvin Sykes got the message. He grabbed the baton and ran with it, carrying on after Mamie's death in January 2003, convincing the Department of Justice to launch an investigation into Bobo's death in 2004 and even devising the legal justification and strategy for the government to open the case that year—taking government lawyers to school. And, as we have established, he didn't just settle for that. He worked with Democrats and Republicans in both houses of Congress to gain passage of the Emmett Till Unsolved Civil Rights Crime Act of 2008 and its reauthorization in 2016. And for that reason, he deserves credit even for the four-year Emmett Till investigation that just closed since it was made possible by that Till Act. The government officials had pointed to this law and other hate crime legislation as a critical part of Emmett Till's legacy.

For some time now, I also have followed Mamie's lead. At this writing, we are moving forward on the programs established through the Emmett Till and Mamie Till-Mobley Institute and the campaign throughout Mamie's centennial year. The Till Institute got to work right away, designing the national curriculum with Facing History and Ourselves, advising on the development of the traveling exhibition with the Children's Museum of Indianapolis, developing fundraising plans for a national park and memorial. And, of course, there is our participation in and support of the ABC limited television series and documentary. It all comes together as part of a narrative that will set the record straight and continue to inspire young people in developing a sense of their civic responsibility in this society.

I believe I have seen the truth now. Something, it seems, Carolyn Bryant Donham desperately has wanted to conceal. In the process, I have developed a new understanding of my own truth as a moral human being. That is why I will not sit in judgment of Carolyn. If there is no court of law that will render judgment, then we must leave her to an even higher authority. The highest, in fact. Her reckoning will be with God. I know the truth, she knows the truth, God knows the truth. In the end, the truth will come out. She will have to ask

God for forgiveness. But before she can be forgiven, she will have to confess her sins. I know everybody is going to receive their due. You reap what you sow. In the end, everybody pays. There are going to be some consequences.

There is a part of me that actually feels sorry for Carolyn because of the reckoning I believe she has anticipated for years. And, in expressing that sympathy, I feel like I'm flipping the script. In effect, what I am expressing is my superiority. Not in racial terms—this is not about Black supremacy replacing White supremacy. No, in feeling sorry for Carolyn Bryant Donham, I show my superiority as a human being. A spiritual being, one who baptized true believers in the River Jordan, a person who feels as if I have been baptized myself by fire, the burning memory of trauma and injustice seared into my consciousness, enabling me to empathize with others, irrespective of their transgressions.

I am forever faithful. Good comes to those who recognize good, live it, and express it. It is with that enlightened spirit—revealed to me over a lifetime and clarified during the past four years—that I forgive Carolyn.

You see, there is a power in forgiveness. It cleanses our souls. After all, hatred keeps us stuck in a moment; it holds us back, trapped in spirals of negativity. That's why people often advise us to forgive *and* forget. Obviously, if you don't forget, then you're remembering the bitterness that led to the need to forgive in the first place. If you're holding on to that memory, then you are not forgiving—not completely. When we talk about forgetting, though, it is important to note that we are not talking about forgetting the thing that happens. We want to learn from bad experiences. I was called upon to remember in the FBI investigation, as a witness. And I drilled down into the most painful depths of my memory, things I would have preferred to forget. So we can't forget the thing that happens. But we have to forget the bitterness that attaches to the thing that happens. We have to do that, detach from the rage and resentment, in order to be a clear-eyed witness. That's what justice requires.

As important as it has been to find forgiveness for Carolyn Bryant Donham, and even her husband, Roy Bryant, and his half brother J. W. Milam, there has been something even more important to me. It is something of a process that began with me back in Memphis as I stood there in Central Station gazing out at that train—the City of New Orleans train—and dug up those memories that had been buried for so long, and resurrected once again as we mourned the loss of Alvin Sykes. In the course of reliving this story, I realized that there was something I needed to do. Something I had needed to do for years in struggling with my sense of my own personal responsibility for the things that have happened during my lifetime. I finally started that process that led to true forgiveness. For myself.

That was such an important step, as I had taken responsibility for so many lives I had touched over the years—touched and affected in ways I saw as damaging. Bobo, of course. Alvin Sykes. Even my uncle Elbert Parker, my uncle William Parker, and their families back in the Delta. All this had come rushing up through me and out of me the previous time I sat in the darkened room at The Drake Hotel for an earlier interview for the ABC documentary. As I talked about what it took to get me out of Mississippi following Bobo's kidnapping, I just broke down and started crying. In that crying I knew that I had to deal with the pain of responsibility, as well as the trauma.

There were so many questions that we faced and so many we were able to answer, either directly through the investigation, or in another way through our speculation. But one question still stalks me and connects to that experience in the ABC interview. When will the crying stop?

People have described me as well adjusted, outgoing, always there with a ready smile when that fits the occasion, or a prayerful embrace when that is what is needed. All that surely is part of me. That is the part of me people see, the person who moves with ease in a crowd. Funny thing about a crowd. It's so much easier to hide there—to hide your true self, to hide your constant pain. No one but Marvel knows what it is like to be me when I am not onstage, at the podium, the pulpit, at a memorial or funeral, when I am away from the crowd, that convenient hiding place. In those all-alone times, there is no way to escape from me. And I cry. Every day. So when does that stop? Does it ever stop? Maybe not, maybe not even after I have forgiven myself.

Strange as it might seem, there was a part of me that didn't want it to be over—the investigation. After all, the questions would still linger, and the answers would always taunt us, just beyond reach. I had lived with this whole thing practically all my life. And just like that, it was done. There was no more investigation to wake up to. No more testimony to contribute to. No more digging to find pieces to fit into a probe that had held so much promise. At least I could tell the story now, publicly, with the confidence that my observations were not merely allegations that could be dismissed easily. Now they would carry the weight of federal government findings. The truth. The whole truth. Nothing but the truth.

There is some justice in that.

Still, although that day passed quickly—the day it was over, the day the case was closed, the day that ending was announced to the public, that day just before this day—although that day passed quickly, it will take me a much longer time to process. And, as I continue to process, I will do what I have done, it seems, every day for as far back as I can remember. I will break down and cry. And I will find some purpose, some reason, some clarity through the tears and in them—a cleansing of sorts, washing away my own forgiven sins, as I did for the faithful back in the River Jordan, a rebirth with each tearful moment, preparing for the challenging work ahead. I am thankful for those future challenges, thankful that the investigation was not the only thing that defined me.

There are those who will continue to push for an indictment, a trial, a conviction, as if that is the only path to justice and to some sense of heroism in the fight for justice, no matter how futile that might be. I am not a hero, nor did I ever try to be a hero. As I've said, I am a survivor. And, as a survivor, I feel the pain so many survivors have felt over time. The pain of a question that torments the survivor. Why me? Why have I continued to live when others haven't? Why was Bobo the one who was taken? The answer comes in the form of a test. I have to go out every day and prove myself worthy of the life I have been given. I owe that to Bobo, and to the people who left here without ever seeing justice for his murder. I owe it to Mamie, to Papa, to Simmie, to Alvin.

It is interesting and symbolic that everything seems to be coming together during the month of December as my reflection for this book is completed. It is the darkest time of the year, but the time when we begin to bring on the light. Daylight, as the night gets shorter and surrenders to a new dawn. The darkness that has engulfed our society also must give way to the light of wisdom. It is both actual and spiritual wisdom. The intelligence to see that our divisions are not working for us. The guiding hand that will show us these divisions never will work for us.

Now I only have a few days left, a few days on God's calendar. I've got to make them count. After all, we are only given a few days filled with the troubles God has given us to overcome. A few days, born into trouble, the trouble caused by earthly things, our desire for them, the preoccupation with them, the temptations that draw us to them. As set out in Job 14, we come here as imperfect beings, striving to perfect ourselves to be worthy of sitting at God's side. I have been reborn in God's way, reborn in that higher consciousness as we all must be to prove ourselves worthy of the blessing of everlasting spiritual life. I have been awakened to that new consciousness, that new sense of connection, that new sense of purpose, and I will continue to do God's work.

Marvel previewed the road ahead at that Northwestern news conference as she ended her remarks. "Our goal is to continue to promote the legacy of Emmett Till and Mamie Till-Mobley through positive activism, promoting cultural awareness, and education." Purpose. With a full agenda.

I'm here to serve people. I'm going to keep doing what I'm doing because I'm doing the right thing. I'm the happiest person because I'm doing what I'm supposed to do, and my life is perfect because of that.

FINALLY, IN THE private dining room at The Drake Hotel, the time had come to move forward with the interview. The final interview for the ABC documentary. Fatima was finishing her checklist and preparing for it all with new information, as I was going through my own checklist in my head preparing for the days ahead with a fresh perspective.

Sound. Check. Perfect hearing.

Lights. Check. Bright and illuminating.

Focus. Check. More clear than ever.

Okay. Slate the take. Ready to roll.

Afterword: "Persevere"

The Emmett Till case now is closed. But the story continues. One reason is that there never was a just outcome in the criminal case. With the death of Carolyn Bryant Donham on April 25, 2023, in West-lake, Louisiana, many believe we never can see *criminal* justice, justice under the law. Maybe, even if Carolyn had lived on, we still would not have seen justice handed down in a court of law—though not for lack of effort.

In the months leading up to Carolyn's death, even after the exhaustive FBI investigation, some people still were determined to keep pushing for a legal judgment, relentlessly searching for rationale and evidence to justify reopening the case, to have her indicted. As we saw in public urgings during the first half of 2022, sadly, the efforts in this regard continued to fail. Having been there, in the rooms where it happened, during the closing phases of the investigation and leading up to the December 2021 final report by the Department of Justice, I know why the case turned out the way it did, and why others should have understood the record made public.

We saw the headlines during the summer of 2022. Some advocates pointed to two documents they believed offered evidence of Carolyn's culpability in Emmett Till's killing. First was a newly uncovered arrest warrant for Emmett's kidnapping—the warrant we always knew existed, but never had found—naming "Mrs. Roy Bryant" along with Roy Bryant and J. W. Milam. The second document was the manuscript of her unpublished memoir, *I Am More Than a Wolf*

Whistle, which, though unseen by the public, Reverend Wheeler Parker, Dr. Marvel Parker, and I had seen and analyzed several years earlier.

Because of all we'd seen in years of carefully reviewing all things pertaining to the case, we believed the public discussion—though led by passionate advocacy—was incomplete and misled. The physical arrest warrant was quite a significant historical discovery. No question about that. But it was not evidence. As we have written, Leflore County Sheriff George Smith told reporters back in 1955 that a warrant for Carolyn's arrest had been issued. And, even though he served the warrant on the confessed kidnappers Roy Bryant and J. W. Milam, he decided not to serve Carolyn, saying he didn't want to inconvenience the young mother of two small children. He scribbled on the file copy of the warrant that she could not be found in the county.

Interestingly, under Mississippi law, since the warrant never had been executed or vacated, it still could have been served on Carolyn in 2005 when she was interviewed by former special agent Dale Killinger, or in 2017, when she was interviewed again during the last phase of the investigation. But we knew what advocates for her arrest should have known. Even if Carolyn were arrested, the case for kidnapping would be dead on arrival. While there is no statute of limitations on kidnapping in Mississippi today, there was a two-year statute of limitations in 1955. The time to arrest Carolyn for kidnapping expired in 1957.

Certainly, many of us wanted to see her arrested. No one should get away with the crime we believe she set in motion. The crime we believe she had a hand in carrying out. At least a voice in the matter, as we show in this book. Arguably, then, it might have been a fitting end to this story to see Carolyn doing the perp walk in handcuffs, oxygen tank and all. But, in the end, it would have been only for show. And it possibly could have backfired, arousing as much sympathy as enmity, and allowing her to have the last word in *Trumpian* fashion, asserting that she had been exonerated. Yet another in her lifetime of lies.

As for her manuscript, despite some of the outrageous passages we have highlighted—and despite how much we tried to find *some* rationale for charges against her—it seems that Carolyn Bryant Donham insulated herself from prosecution, wrapping herself in her own inconsistent statements. When the manuscript was compared to other statements Carolyn made, it was clear that she was all over the place with respect to what she told her husband and under what circumstances she told him. This is significant because, as some have argued, she should have known that inflammatory and false claims she made about Emmett would cause her volatile husband to resort to violence. If that could be shown, then she could be held responsible for that violent outcome and, possibly, convicted of some level of manslaughter. Unfortunately, though, she had told enough different versions of the story as to create reasonable doubt at trial. Enough to get her off.

And this all was summed up in a Leflore County grand jury decision on August 4, 2022. Reverend Wheeler Parker Jr. was there. Called to testify. He knows how determined District Attorney Dewayne Richardson was to present the case, if there was any chance of convincing the grand jury. Still, there would be no indictment of Carolyn Bryant Donham. At long last, there would be no accountability.

We don't know everything that was presented during the seven hours of grand jury review that summer, and Rev. Parker was not able to comment on the process under Mississippi law. But there are things we can understand based on what we saw leading up to the grand jury proceeding. We saw an unrelenting effort by all the authorities involved.

That is why I know that the harsh criticism leveled against District Attorney Richardson was as ironic as it was unfair. An African American lawyer, Richardson had his hands tied in 2022 by the White Mississippi power structure of 1955. Their actions back then "guaranteed those who killed Emmett Till could go unpunished, to this day," Rev. Parker expressed in a 2022 statement. As we have seen, there historically has been a corrupt hierarchy of racialized power with consequences that tragically still are having effect on the denial of criminal justice. Perhaps now public attention will turn to that structure of injustice—structural racism—more than the failure to convict Carolyn Bryant Donham.

There is a great deal of value, though, in that ongoing discourse, exploring the meaning of the tragedy of Emmett Till and the public challenge it continues to stir in the contemporary moment. Without question, each open conversation about Emmett has the potential to awaken the collective consciousness of the racial injustice Black Americans continue to experience today. And each retelling of the truth of Emmett's story has the potential to lead to another course of action—the one I have chosen to take, following in the righteous path of Rev. Parker.

THERE IS AN African proverb central to our mission. "Until the story of the hunt is told by the lion, the tale of the hunt will always glorify the hunter." Mamie Till-Mobley was a lion. She took control of the narrative on racial violence, on White supremacy, by fiercely directing our attention to its consequences. She opened that casket and opened our eyes. Rev. Parker is a lion. He staunchly is making sure we never again look away, never again allow our gaze to be diverted, as some are encouraging us to do.

The ABC telecast of the six-part *Women of the Movement* scripted series and three-part *Let the World See* companion documentary helped frame the narrative. The scripted series portrayed Mamie in a way I know would have made her proud—consistent with her book, a source relied on by the production team. "This really shows me coming into my own," Mamie gushed as I once read to her the outline of what would become the award-winning *Death of Innocence: The Story of the Hate Crime That Changed America*. Fatima Curry, another lion, even had the actor Nia Long read passages from Mamie's book to great effect in the ABC documentary she produced, a documentary Kimberly Godwin, the African American president of ABC News, made sure was greenlit, affirming it was too important a story not to be told. And the public supported it. The two series drew a combined audience of three million viewers, and Mamie's book shot to number one in several Amazon categories the weeks they were aired.

The Emmett Till story continues. Marion Brooks has continued to build on her comprehensive documentary series—three parts, including dramatic readings of trial transcripts—as the television anchor and investigative reporter for WMAQ NBC 5 produced the perfect bookend for the work of her NBC colleague Rich Samuels, the first journalist to produce a documentary on Emmett.

There is a connection among lions, the only big cats to be connected as a unit—a *pride*.

While TV network media can offer an unparalleled platform, we're heartened to see the conversation bear important fruit with the formation of the Emmett Till and Mamie Till-Mobley Institute, our nonprofit that, as Rev. Parker has explained, will build on a vision of community and economic development, civic engagement, and of course education. A formidable grant has enabled the Till Institute to work with organizations like the Boston, Massachusetts–based Facing History and Ourselves, Mississippi's Alluvial Collective (formerly the William Winter Institute for Racial Reconciliation), and the Emmett Till Interpretive Center to develop a high school curriculum built on the Emmett Till story. It is so gratifying to see high school student co-creators—in just a few months of discourse—come to understand the meaningful context of the story. For one thing, they know that the Emmett Till story is about more than a single kid taken from us too soon. They know it is about more than racism. They are coming to appreciate—as we hope students around the country will learn—that the first step in combating racial violence is to recognize that racial violence is only the penultimate issue. The ultimate issue is a struggle for power—the power to assign identity and to use that identity to justify the allocation of place in our society and then to enforce it through violence. In this light, racial violence, in fact racism itself, is seen as an element in the process, a tactic in the politics of place. Minority rule. Illiberalism. The slow-motion deconstruction of democracy.

"BECAUSE OF MANY years of investigating lynchings, mob violence, and various forms of terrorism in the country, I am able to spot signs that indicate that we are on the verge of a dangerous racial conflagration in the Southern section of the country."[1]

He was right up to a point. Those words written by White House presidential aide E. Frederic Morrow on November 22, 1955, were prescient, though limited in scope. While the racial violence throughout the South he predicted has been well documented—televised, even—Morrow did not foresee the racial violence in places like Chicago, Boston, Washington, DC, Detroit, Los Angeles, and so many others during the 1960s. So many more places in the twenty-first century. Still. As Malcolm X would observe in multiple ways on multiple occasions, when it comes to racism, the Mason-Dixon line is the Canadian border. But racism is not just an attitude problem of dysfunctional individuals. It is structural and, more important, it is purposeful. "I thought in difficult times that this too shall pass. I'm not too sure anymore. I'm really not," Representative James Clyburn (D-SC) noted in an interview with *The Washington Post*.[2] "The country is in danger of imploding. Democracy is in danger of disintegrating . . . [M]aybe autocracy is the future of the country."[3] In making these remarks, Clyburn has both echoed the distant concerns of Morrow and expanded on them in a prophetic way. In fact, he has gone to the very heart of the matter that Morrow could not have foreseen.

In a way, the late Congressman John Lewis—Clyburn's close friend—recognized it, too, in his posthumously published essay in *The New York Times*, when he wrote that Emmett Till was his George Floyd.[4] There is a parallel between that period of the 1950s and the contemporary moment; between the "conflagration" back in the 1950s following the Supreme Court's *Brown v. Board of Education* decision and the growing hostility today as we stand on the cusp of a new demographic reality; between the end of American apartheid back then and the anticipation of a truly inclusive plural society on the horizon today.

Think about it. Connect the dots. On August 28, 1955, Emmett Till was brutally lynched when only a small deranged, bloodthirsty mob was watching in a secluded Delta barn. On August 28, 1963, Dr. Martin Luther King Jr. delivered his "I Have a Dream" speech as 250,000 people watched on the grounds of the Lincoln Memorial. On August 28, 2008, Barack Obama delivered his speech accepting the Democratic nomination for president of the United States as millions watched across the planet. From one August to another and yet another. From a time when people knew they could get away with dehumanizing, degrading, and destroying the Black body, to a time when a minister-prophet shared with us his vision of a new day and a new way, to a time when millions stood poised to realize the vision.

In the years since, we have watched the dream recast as a nightmare in the minds of those who believe the inclusion of Black and Brown bodies in the halls of power will force them out.

We have seen several historical moments when people became afraid of losing out. One was the flourishing of the Ku Klux Klan and other White supremacist groups during periods when democratic progress threatened power elites. The Klan was born during the rise to political power and prosperity of the formerly enslaved during Reconstruction. There was a resurgence of the Klan in the early twentieth century—probably their most powerful period when even a future Supreme Court justice, Hugo Black, was a member—following the influx of Catholic and Jewish immigrants. Then the movement for civil rights in the 1950s drawing the ire of people like Roy Bryant and J. W. Milam, mere enforcers of a power hierarchy that ultimately would have excluded them, too, because of their lower class. Something of a lesson for the working-class "Make America Great Again" masses who likely will never be invited to Mar-a-Lago.

Racial violence has always been about power. That was embedded in the message President Biden delivered when he signed the Emmett Till antilynching bill into law on March 29, 2022, pointing to the driving force behind the more than four thousand recorded lynchings of Black Americans. "Their crimes? Trying to vote. Trying to go to school. To try and own a business or preach the Gospel."[5]

Beyond his words, the president made an even more powerful statement through the very act of supporting and signing a federal anti-hate law. In so doing, he (and the legislators who brought the law into being) set out for the public what we stand for and what we stand against.

"You could feel it right away as he reaches out a hand to greet you," Rev. Parker commented after meeting President Biden in the Oval Office just before the Rose Garden signing ceremony. "It was clear that when he looked into your eyes, he was seeing more than just your eye color. He was seeing deep into your life and your soul. In a way, it seemed like he was seeing himself."

Empathy.

Clearly, we must recognize our commonality. Interior Secretary Deb Haaland did during meetings with Wheeler Parker and Marvel Parker in the Mississippi Delta, as they considered plans for a national historical park in honor of Emmett Till and Mamie Till-Mobley. That effort took a huge step forward on July 25, 2023—Emmett's birthday—when President Biden dedicated the Emmett Till and Mamie Till-Mobley National Monument at three sites in Mississippi and Chicago. Over an earlier dinner, Secretary Haaland leaned in to Marvel and said softly that, as an indigenous woman, she felt an affinity with the African American struggle. A commonality among people in a country built on stolen land by stolen labor.

Empathy. Connections. Based on a dedication to freedom, justice, and equality, and on the belief that shared power makes us stronger, not weaker.

This is where it begins. Seeing ourselves in others prevents us from seeing others as enemies. We have to recognize that the erosion of rights for one identifiable group diminishes the rights of everyone.

For example, voter suppression isn't just a Black problem; it is an American problem. Suppression of votes in Pennsylvania or Michigan subverts the electoral power of people in California and Illinois in a presidential election cycle, diminishing a candidate vote count total in the Electoral College, and thus devaluing rights of the American majority, not just people of color.

With this understanding, it is not enough to try to establish racist intent among political leaders. It might surprise people to learn that a number of these so-called leaders are not racist at all, despite the race cards they play in a zero-sum game. In a way, they're worse than racists. At least racists are honest. One doesn't have to be a racist to recognize the *utility* of race in manipulating the masses, sowing division in ways that can preserve one's grasp on power—political power, economic power, social and cultural power. The power to shape the narrative. To lionize the hunter.

Ironically, focusing our attention on racism takes our attention away from that ultimate goal of rising above it. Directing our gaze toward *White* supremacy diverts our focus from *right* supremacy. The political project of the ideological right. And the agenda of *right* supremacists has led a growing number of observers to point to a certain "democratic backsliding" and "creeping authoritarianism," the kind of thing journalists recognized—at least to an extent—when they began covering the fledgling Civil Rights Movement triggered by Emmett's lynching, after so many of them had fought against authoritarianism overseas during World War II. It is the kind of dynamic process of democratic drift that Representative Clyburn lamented in his interview with *The Washington Post*.

That is the story that must be told. That Black people are the canaries in the coal mine. Repressive policies and practices only start with us. If the late Pastor Martin Niemöller were to update his famous poem, it might begin with "First they came for people of color . . . and no one spoke out." That is the story of Emmett Till. Not just an African American story, but an American story. Indeed, this is Emmett's challenge to us all. To understand the full context of it all. That in a way his story is of a piece with that of Ketanji Brown Jackson, whose nomination to the Supreme Court subjected her to a different form of violent pushback. Violence of the word, as Republican senators subjected her to ugly attacks that were very much a part of the politics of place—questioning her qualification for elevated status—that historically led to the kind of physical violence suffered by so many others who dared to try to advance. Out of place. The same place that once welcomed a former Klansman into its ranks. The same place that now devalues the societal benefit of diversity in higher education.

One of the moving moments of Justice Jackson's Senate testimony was her explanation of how she withstood the harsh criticism and questions regarding her qualifications to serve on the high court, despite her stellar performance as a Harvard Law graduate. She told the story of her moment of self-doubt as a law student slowly crossing Harvard Yard, a despairing moment that apparently showed on her face. Another Black student, a woman, approached her and said simply, "Persevere."

In the time I have spent with the Reverend Wheeler Parker Jr. over the years, breaking bread, attending reunions, talking with him about Emmett Till, sharing the spotlight in public presentations, and now making this journey, doing our "ride-along" with the FBI during the last phase of the investigation, I have come to revere him. He is a man dedicated to the truth and to the justice that flows from it. Morally grounded. Spiritually driven. And because he is guided by a higher level of consciousness, he knows that at the end of the day, there never can be legal justice in the lynching of Emmett Till. There can only be accountability, and that accountability extends beyond Emmett's killers to all of the rest of us who now must take control of the narrative, and its challenge to make a difference.

That challenge is summed up in the direction of our Emmett Till and Mamie Till-Mobley Institute: "Memory, Meaning, Movement." We must preserve the memory of our common struggle for equality, especially during this current period of *erase-ism*. It is vital that we clarify the meaning of this history and the social structures that have maintained inequality. We must encourage the next generations of national leadership—young people, like Emmett Till—to move us forward, understanding their duty to become enlightened and engaged citizens in our democratic society.

IN EULOGIZING Mamie Till-Mobley in January 2003, Rev. Parker told the congregation that she died with her boots on. "How do you plan to die?" Now we well might consider how we plan to live. I have an answer to that question. I am a journalist and a lawyer, a writer and an advocate. There is purpose in my calling. I will live on purpose. A purpose that continues to remind me of my duty as I write this on the anniversary of the day in 1955 when Emmett rose again in the muddy Tallahatchie River. On the third day following his brutal lynching. And I will continue to remind myself. To meet head-on the challenges to our continued progress and to challenge those who stand in the way of that progress.

To persevere.

—CHRISTOPHER BENSON
Chicago, August 31, 2023

Questions for Discussion

1. First, a show of hands: Who among you already knew the story of Emmett Till before reading *A Few Days Full of Trouble*? How, if at all, did this book affect or alter your understanding of this dark chapter in American history?

2. Reverend Wheeler Parker was not only a family member of Emmett Till's; he was also his best friend. Did the events described in this book have a greater impact on you since they were told by someone who actually knew "Bobo" before his tragic death? And if so, how?

3. Take a moment to talk about how Reverend Parker's point of view shaped your reading experience—did it deepen your sense of identification, compassion, or empathy with Parker and Till's family? What stories about Bobo were most winning or troubling? Which characters or incidents in *A Few Days Full of Trouble* did you find to be the most memorable—or too devastating to forget?

4. Reverend Parker writes that "the story of Emmett Till is larger than Emmett Till himself. . . . It is the story of power, and the way that power is used to put Black people in our place in society." How is that power wielded in our world, even in the current era?

5. "The story of Emmett Till, today, is also about power over the story itself," writes Reverend Parker. "The way the story is told and who gets to tell it." What do you think the author is trying to convey about truth-telling and "alternative facts" in this book?

What is your take on American journalism and the justice system—how does one inform and/or challenge the other? Who are the "influencers" in the court of public opinion? Whose job is it to set the record straight?

6. How can a book such as *A Few Days Full of Trouble* help elevate the voices of Black Americans? Do you believe that books, in general, have the power to change the world? Talk about books that have made history or have made an impact in peoples' lives—even your own.

7. "To know Emmett Till is to know Trayvon Martin. And Breonna Taylor and George Floyd. . . ." In *A Few Days Full of Trouble*, Parker makes the case that Emmett Till was the first Black Lives Matter story. How, in your opinion, have we come so far only to end up (in 2023, with the publication of this book) fighting for racial justice—on the streets, in the classroom, at the polls—in America all over again?

8. Reverend Parker spent most of his life grappling with the tragic events of August 28, 1955—both personally/psychologically and on behalf of Emmett Till's whole family. *A Few Days Full of Trouble* is the culmination of sixty-seven years of the fight for, and the miscarriage of, justice. What lessons can be learned about Reverend Parker's journey through grief and healing? Did his struggles, as well as his beliefs, resonate with you? What does it mean to seek peace in the midst of chaos, or keep the faith when all hope seems lost?

9. Having read *A Few Days Full of Trouble*, do you feel more or less hopeful about the future for, as President Obama once put it—quoting the Preamble to the United States Constitution in his famous 2008 speech on racial justice—a "more perfect union" in America?

10. The search for justice is a theme driving this story. What does justice mean to you and what does it require in a case such as that of Emmett Till?

11. Talk about "white lies," the small lies we are taught to believe

are harmless, and "White Lies," the big ones that do nothing short of support Whiteness, as an identity supposedly deserving of its place, privilege, and power in the socio-political hierarchy. What does Reverend Parker intend to illustrate about this misconception of these two terms? Do you believe there's a difference between the two? Why or why not? And how can we do a better job of telling the whole truth, Black and White, for future generations?

12. In what ways has this story awakened or reawakened in you a sense of civic responsibility—to do something, anything to make a difference?

Acknowledgments

For practically all my life, I have survived by the grace of God and the love of family. Together, we have helped one another work our way through a horrific tragedy and its enduring pain. I have been blessed to have found a purpose in it all—a purpose that has been clarified by my immediate family, my extended family, and, indeed, the family we call the Black community.

There would be no book had it not been for my cousin, Dr. Shelia Chamberlain, who worried me to no end about writing my story. She had the tenacity like no other. My wife, Marvel, went to great lengths to help me tell my story. She even bought me a computer that I could talk to, but that didn't set well with me. Finally, she had to interpret my tiny writing and put my writing into paragraphs, pages, and chapters. That is why she is on the copyright.

To my brothers: Milton and William, who drove me hundreds of miles to my speaking engagements. My sisters: Pat, Elayne, and Alma, who always supported me, thanks much. Can't forget my niece, Lori, who is my right hand at the church. My mother, Hallie Wright Parker, and my dad, Wheeler Parker, Sr., who taught me to save my money as a paper boy, and taught me to cut hair at 14, which led me to the family's great friend, Joe B. Williams, who became my business partner, along with Johnny Jackson and Felix Lewis. They helped shape my career as a lifetime barber. Later, after the partnership dissolved due to a fire, Mr. Marvin Jarvis, a great man, became my partner. We had a wonderful run together. I am still in touch with his lovely wife Minnie and family. These are exceptional people.

Elder J. B. Williams became my spiritual mentor. Bishop G. E. Goodwin, my pastor and role model in the spiritual world, gave me the opportunity to serve at Argo Temple Church of God in Christ. He told me I would pastor after him. He was a man of high integrity. My church has been a great support in many ways: few in number but powerful—and I am thankful to the staff.

My aunt Thelma has been a great support throughout my life, a real jewel. She lived with Mamie and Aunt Alma when Emmett was born. There is a book in her also. Aunt Alma Spearman, Mamie's mother, helped our family leave the South. My youngest sister, Alma, was named after her—God rest her soul.

Mamie Till Mobley, Emmett's mother, took to me very early in life, to be Emmett's companion on fishing trips and picnics. We became inseparable. In 2002, not long before she died, she visited the church for the last time, the church that started in her mother's home. She also visited the Community Center, which we named after her son, the Emmett Till Memorial Center in Summit. It was during this visit when she asked for me and Marvel to carry on the work she had begun in preserving the legacy of her son.

Other family members have contributed to so many aspects of Mamie's life's work and, thus, to my story—a story of social and spiritual commitment. Ollie Gordon and her late daughter, Airickca, have contributed on the national scene, bringing together the mothers of other slain Black boys and men, demonstrating our commonality.

Much love to Dallis and Therese Anderson, who shared so much of this journey with us and lent their support in ways that are far too numerous to list. We are grateful for the blessings of you.

Alvin Sykes was something of an honorary family member. He was an unsung hero in the story of Emmett Till, and brought me along with him as he worked brilliantly to get the federal government to open an investigation, and to get laws passed in the name of

Emmett Till. His impact, on this story and our story, is incalculable. Thanks, too, to Ronnique Hawkins for being a friend and true believer, as well as a truth-teller and fellow traveler. To Mike Small, an educator and longtime family friend, who continues to teach young people the importance of this story, and Tina Small, who is there with you every step of the way.

Other historians, journalists, and storytellers were so generous in sharing their findings with us, even as they built their own narratives. David Beito, Linda Royster Beito, Elliott Gorn, and Dave Tell each brought details of this story based on their unique and insightful perspectives. Fatima Curry, who moved mountains to "network" us, and Marion Brooks, whose enterprise led her deep into video archives. Rich Samuels, who created those NBC archives, thirty years after Bobo's death, when he interviewed me for the first time, changed history, causing a renewed interest in this story.

Patrick Weems and Wright Thompson were among the people who have kept this impacting and transformative story alive. And, of course, the filmmakers who have carried this story to a much wider audience, Stanley Nelson, Aaron Kaplan, Jay Brown, and James Lassiter, truth-seekers all. To Vangela Wade and Reilly Morse, thank you for showing everyone that justice begins with a compelling narrative.

This is a story about a journey to justice that would have been a much shorter journey if not for the devotion that investigators and lawyers demonstrated along the way. Deep appreciation for that and for allowing us to do something of a "ride-along" in sharing so much sensitive material to shed light on the findings. Special Agent Walter Henry was extraordinary in processing the information collected by the FBI and sharing it with us. His dedication in the search for a just outcome was as moving as it was impressive. In fact, everyone associated with this investigation brought a high level of commitment to seeing it through. So, we also are grateful for the work of the Department of Justice, Kristin Clarke, Barbara Kay Bosserman, Dana Mulhauser, Chad Lamar, Clay Joyner, Shannon Wright, and, of course,

Dale Killinger, who produced so much for the historical record in the beginning. We also appreciate the work of Dewayne Richardson and Tamicko Fair.

Shout-out to Northwestern University and Charles Whitaker of the Medill School of Journalism, Media, Integrated Marketing Communications, for believing in this project and providing so much support. Thanks to Medill staff Hilary Hurd Anyaso, Erin Karter, and Sara Brazeal, Rafie Fields, Rachel Venegas, and Hector Palacios, and Medill graduate students, Matthew Ritchie, Kenyatta Coleman, Kinsey Crowley, and Hannah Shapiro for all their impressive work and valuable contributions.

To the stellar support team that helped translate the compelling Emmett Till story into a national curriculum: Brooke Harvey, Dr. Tanya Huelett, Maureen Loughnane, Denise Gelb, Dr. Earl Watkins, Von Gordon, Jay Rushing, Ashura Lewis, Germaine Hampton, and Dr. Debbra Lindo.

Deep appreciation to Robert Raben, founder and president of the Washington-based Raben Group, and a former assistant attorney general for legislative affairs, for superior strategic and media counsel, which we are confident will strengthen us in continuing to tell this story. And to Sarah Davey Wolman, a director at the Raben Group, for the highly successful media strategy in connection with our participation in the Emmett Till Antilynching Act signing, and so much more.

Gratitude to Facing History and Ourselves and the Children's Museum of Indianapolis for making sure this important story will reach and inspire new generations of leadership through curriculum development and a traveling exhibition. And to the National Park Service, the National Park Conservation Association, the National Trust for Historic Preservation, and MASS Design for our collaboration in translating the story of Emmett Till and Mamie Till-Mobley into a living experience for everyone. In this connection Secretary of the Interior Deb Haaland, for recognizing the connections of our stories, as well as Shannon Estenoz, Alan Spears, Jeff Sagansky, Michael

Murphy, Jha D Amazi, and Julie Rhoad. Special appreciation to Joseph Olchefske for raising the necessary money to get our Emmett Till and Mamie Till-Mobley Institute up and running—a fitting legacy to Mamie and Emmett. We also appreciate the support of the National Trust's Brett Leggs and Tiffany Tolbert. And Nikki Buffa and Peter Viola, Latham & Watkins, thank you for all your work on the parks initiative, balancing all the legal, political, and financial issues.

Obviously, this book would not exist without a dedicated publishing group. We couldn't have asked for a better team and we are proud for this work to live in the house that brought Mamie's book to the world. To Gina Centrello, thank you for your support and for making Random House the perfect choice for meaningful books such as this one. Chris Jackson, thank you for believing in this project so strongly and giving it a home. Thanks for all you do to make such an important difference. To our editor extraordinaire, Porscha Burke, whose vision has made this book a reality and an important voice in the Random House social justice narrative conversation. Thanks for your faith in the unseen and your unwavering dedication to preserving and sharing such a vital chapter in the American story. Your tireless support, as well as your diplomatic suggestions, and, of course, your patience as we awaited government developments were all indispensable, and your guidance can be felt in every line of this work. Thanks to Matthew Martin for the exceptionally careful prepublication review and for your balanced insights, making sure the substantive story and its significance would continue to live. Thanks to Benjamin Dreyer and Rebecca Berlant for keeping us on track and on time. And to Greg Mollica and Fritz Metsch for the dignified design this work deserves. We are indebted to Carla Bruce-Eddings and Lulu Martinez for their expertise in promoting this work.

Special appreciation to Kaye Benson, for all the tedious work on interview transcripts—bookmarked and searchable—helping us protect so much confidential and sensitive material.

I know I can't list everybody, but I must mention my wife's family, the McCains: Quitmon and Annie. Her parents were wonderful people. Sisters-in-law: Levorn and Quincie.

Argo High School, Mamie's alma mater, has commissioned a sculptor to create a sculpture of her and Emmett and has dedicated a section of the school campus, Mamie and Emmett Till Way.

I know I have left someone out—charge it to my head and not my heart. My life is filled with so many wonderful people, I could never name them all. Some special folks: Torrance Anderson, Bishop Gordon, Maurice Flowers, Allen Miggins, Carl Randle, Jimmy Daniels, Nathaniel Randle, Allen Dixon, Tommy Reed, Bishop James E. Washington.

There is a special place in my heart and mind and spirit for my Uncle Simeon Wright. He and I were bound by blood and tragedy, finding meaning in it all, and a lifelong purpose in seeking truth and justice. I continue to live that purpose in honor of Simmie in the hope that I can serve him proud.

Notes

INTRODUCTION:

1. Alan Blinder, "US Reopens Emmett Till Investigation, Almost 63 Years After His Murder," *New York Times*, July 12, 2018.
2. Richard Pérez-Peña, "Woman Linked to 1955 Emmett Till Murder Tells Historian Her Claims Were False," *New York Times*, January 27, 2017.
3. Kristine Phillips, Wesley Lowery, and Devlin Barrett, "New Details in Book About Emmett Till's Death Prompted Officials to Reopen Investigation," *Washington Post*, July 12, 2018.
4. "The Attorney General's Seventh Annual Report to Congress Pursuant to the Emmett Till Unsolved Civil Rights Crime Act of 2007 and First Annual Report to Congress Pursuant to the Emmett Till Unsolved Civil Rights Crime Reauthorization Act of 2016," Department of Justice, February 2018.
5. Anna North, "Amy Cooper's 911 Call Is Part of an All-Too-Familiar Pattern," *Vox*, May 26, 2020.
6. David K. Li, "Black Man Shot Dead While Jogging in Georgia, and Two Months Later, No Arrests," NBC News, April 30, 2020.
7. Minyvonne Burke, "Woman Shot and Killed by Kentucky Police in Botched Raid, Family Says," NBC News, May 13, 2020.
8. Jason Hanna, "Video: Boy with Air Gun Was Shot 2 Seconds After Cleveland Police Arrived," CNN, November 27, 2014.
9. Barbara Liston, "Family of Florida Boy Killed by Neighborhood Watch Seeks Arrest," Reuters, March 7, 2012.
10. Grace Hauck, "Emmett Till's Lynching Ignited a Civil Rights Movement. Historians Say George Floyd's Death Could Do the Same," *USA Today*, June 11, 2020.
11. John Lewis, "Together, You Can Redeem the Soul of Our Nation," *New York Times*, July 30, 2020.

1: WHITE LIES

1. Glenn Kessler, Salvador Rizzo, and Meg Kelly, "Trump's False or Misleading Claims Total 30,573 Over 4 Years," *Washington Post*, January 24, 2021.
2. Richard Pérez-Peña, "Woman Linked to 1955 Emmett Till Murder Tells Historian Her Claims Were False," *New York Times*, January 27, 2017; Timothy Tyson, *The Blood of Emmett Till* (New York: Simon & Schuster, 2017), 6.

3. Lilly Workneh, "Emmett Till's Accuser Admits She Lied About Claims That Led to His Murder," *Huffington Post*, January 30, 2017; "Emmett Till's Accuser Admits She Lied," Equal Justice Initiative, eji.org, January 31, 2017.

4. Tyson, *The Blood of Emmett Till*, 6.

5. Pérez-Peña, "Woman Linked to 1955 Emmett Till Murder."

6. Brandis Friedman, "Emmett Till's Family Reacts to Accuser's Confession, 60 Years Later," WTTW, February 23, 2017, news.wttw.com.

7. Friedman, "Emmett Till's Family Reacts to Accuser's Confession."

8. FBI Transcripts, Carolyn Bryant Donham interview, conducted by Supervisory Special Agent Dale R. Killinger, 2005.

9. Friedman, "Emmett Till's Family Reacts to Accuser's Confession."

10. Friedman, "Emmett Till's Family Reacts to Accuser's Confession."

11. Timothy Tyson, email to Brandis Friedman, February 21, 2017, 4:55 P.M.

12. Tyson, email to Friedman, February 21, 2017.

13. Tyson, email to Friedman, February 21, 2017.

14. Tyson, email to Friedman, February 21, 2017.

15. Matt Ford, "Trump's Press Secretary Falsely Claims: 'Largest Audience Ever to Witness an Inauguration, Period,'" *The Atlantic*, January 21, 2017.

16. Anna North, "Amy Cooper's 911 Call Is Part of an All-Too-Familiar Pattern," *Vox*, May 26, 2020.

2: WHAT IS LIFE?

1. Matt Apuzo, Adam Goldman, and William K. Rashbaum, "Justice Dept. Shakes Up Inquiry into Eric Garner Chokehold Case," *New York Times*, October 24, 2016.

2. Apuzo, Goldman, and Rashbaum, "Justice Dept. Shakes Up Inquiry."

3. Apuzo, Goldman, and Rashbaum, "Justice Dept. Shakes Up Inquiry."

4. Margaret M. Russell, "Reopening the Emmett Till Case: Lessons and Challenges for Critical Race Practice," *Fordham Law Review* 73, no. 2101 (2005).

5. "Justice Department to Investigate 1955 Emmett Till Murder," *Jet*, May 24, 2004.

6. "Justice Department to Investigate 1955 Emmett Till Murder," *Jet*.

7. "Justice Department to Investigate 1955 Emmett Till Murder: Federal-State Partnership to Develop Possible State Law Prosecution," Department of Justice Release, Monday, May 10, 2004; Representative Bobby Rush, "Department of Justice Investigation of the Murder of Emmett Till," Congressional Record H2820, May 12, 2004.

8. Seymour Hersh, "Torture at Abu Ghraib," *The New Yorker*, April 30, 2004; Susan Sontag, "Regarding the Torture of Others," *New York Times*, May 23, 2004; Staff, "The Murder of Emmett Till Justice May Be Delayed, But It Should Not Be Denied," *Buffalo News*, May 24, 2004.

9. Laura Ziegler, "The Life of Kansas City Civil Rights Activist Alvin Sykes," KCUR, *Morning Edition*, January 9, 2014; Monroe Dodd, "Pursuit of Truth: From Kansas City's Libraries, Alvin Sykes Plotted an Unlikely Course to Civil Rights History," Kansas City Public Library (library program about his work on the Steve Harvey case).

10. David T. Beito and Linda Royster Beito, *Black Maverick: T.R.M. Howard's Fight for Civil Rights and Economic Power* (Urbana and Chicago: University of Illinois Press, 2009).

11. Alvin Sykes and Monroe Dodd, *Show Me Justice,* unpublished manuscript, chapter 7, "In Memory of Emmett Till."

12. John W. Fountain, "Mamie Mobley, 81, Dies; Son, Emmett Till, Slain in 1955," *New York Times,* January 7, 2003.

13. Christopher Benson, "Scalia's Role in the Emmett Till Case," *Chicago Tribune,* February 19, 2016.

14. Benson, "Scalia's Role in the Emmett Till Case."

15. Benson, "Scalia's Role in the Emmett Till Case."

16. Benson, "Scalia's Role in the Emmett Till Case"; "Jurisdiction of the Department of Justice to Investigate the Assassination of President Kennedy," memorandum for Jack W. Fuller, special assistant to the attorney general, from Antonin Scalia, assistant attorney general, Office of Legal Counsel, July 28, 1976.

17. Benson, "Scalia's Role in the Emmett Till Case."

18. Benson, "Scalia's Role in the Emmett Till Case."

19. Benson, "Scalia's Role in the Emmett Till Case."

20. Benson, "Scalia's Role in the Emmett Till Case."

21. Benson, "Scalia's Role in the Emmett Till Case."

22. Benson, "Scalia's Role in the Emmett Till Case."

23. Benson, "Scalia's Role in the Emmett Till Case."

24. Christopher Benson, "Civil Rights Murders: The Till Bill Would Create Two Cold Case Squads to Reopen and Solve Dozens of Long-Forgotten Civil Rights Murders—if Congress Can Pay Attention Long Enough to Make It Law," *Chicago Sun-Times,* October 8, 2006.

25. Benson, "Civil Rights Murders."

26. Benson, "Civil Rights Murders."

27. Audie Cornish, "Mississippi DA Weighs Prosecution in Till Murder," *Morning Edition,* National Public Radio, May 8, 2006.

28. Christopher Metress, *The Lynching of Emmett Till: A Documentary Narrative* (Charlottesville and London: University of Virginia Press), 2002.

29. Prosecutive Report of Investigation Concerning [Carolyn Bryant Donham]; Roy Bryant—Deceased; John William Milam, also known as J. W. Milam—Deceased; Leslie F. Milam—Deceased; Melvin Campbell—Deceased; Elmer O. Kimbrell—Deceased; Hubert Clark—Deceased; Levi Collins, also known as Too Tight Collins—Deceased; Johnny B. Washington—Deceased; Otha Johnson Jr., also known as Oso—Deceased; [Henry Lee Loggins]; Emmett Louis Till—Deceased—Victim; Civil Rights–Conspiracy; Domestic Police Cooperation.

30. Transcript, Carolyn Bryant Donham interview, conducted by Supervisory Special Agent Dale R. Killinger, October 2, 2005.

31. Transcript, Carolyn Bryant Donham interview, conducted by Supervisory Special Agent Dale R. Killinger, October 19, 2005.

32. Ellen Barry, "Rumor of a Key Witness," *Los Angeles Times,* July 30, 2005.

33. Jerry Mitchell, "Reexamining Emmett Till Case Could Help Separate Fact, Fiction," *USA Today,* February 19, 2007; "Emmett Till Conspiracy Theory Debunked," History News Network, Columbian College of Arts and Sciences, The George Washington University, February 20, 2007.

3: "WHAT DOES JUSTICE LOOK LIKE?"

1. Elliott Gorn, "How America Remembers Emmett Till: 'Hatred Could Not Justify Child Murder, but Fear Could,'" Literary Hub, Oxford University Press, November 15, 2018.
2. Al Kuettner, "Ole Miss Enrolls Meredith After Riots Kill 2, Injure 75," UPI Archives, October 1, 1962; Debbie Elliott, "Integrating Ole Miss: A Transformative, Deadly Riot," WBEZ, National Public Radio, October 1, 2012.
3. The Daily Dish, "The Past Isn't Dead. It Isn't Even Past," *The Atlantic*, March 18, 2008.
4. Joel Schectman and Mark Hosenball, "Sessions Asks 46 Obama-Era US Attorneys to Resign," Reuters, March 10, 2017.
5. "President Obama Nominates Felicia C. Adams to Serve as US Attorney," The White House Press Office, March 2, 2011.

4: "INVESTIGATE AND LEGISLATE"

1. "Rush, Talent, Schumer & Rangel to Justice Department and State of Mississippi: Expedite Emmett Till Murder Case New Resolution Would Speed Inquiry to Bring Emmett Till's Murderers to Justice," Press Release, Office of Representative Bobby Rush, November 19, 2004.
2. "Rush, Talent, Schumer & Rangel to Justice Department and State of Mississippi."
3. "Rush, Talent, Schumer & Rangel to Justice Department and State of Mississippi."
4. "Rush, Talent, Schumer & Rangel to Justice Department and State of Mississippi."
5. "Rush, Talent, Schumer & Rangel to Justice Department and State of Mississippi."
6. Alvin Sykes and Monroe Dodd, *Show Me Justice*, unpublished manuscript, chapter 7, "In Memory of Emmett Till."
7. Sykes and Dodd, *Show Me Justice*.
8. Sykes and Dodd, *Show Me Justice*.
9. Sykes and Dodd, *Show Me Justice*.
10. "The Long Struggle for Representation: Oral Histories of African Americans in Congress," Office of the Historian, US House of Representatives, history.house .gov/Oral-History/Rainey/.
11. John Lewis and Michael D'Orso, *Walking with the Wind: A Memoir of the Movement* (New York: Simon & Schuster, 1998), 46–48; Elliott Gorn, *Let the People See: The Story of Emmett Till* (New York: Oxford University Press, 2018), 261.
12. "Unsolved Civil Rights Crime Act," S2679; Sykes and Dodd, *Show Me Justice*.
13. Sarah Lueck, "One-Man Gridlock: Meet Tom Coburn, Senate's 'Dr. No': Oklahoma Conservative Specializes in the 'Hold,' Stopping 90 Bills in 2007," *Wall Street Journal*, December 21, 2007.
14. Sykes and Dodd, *Show Me Justice;* Crosby Kemper III, "It Started at the Library: Tom Coburn, Civil Rights Ally and Friend," Institute of Museum and Library Services, March 2020.
15. Sykes and Dodd, *Show Me Justice*.
16. Sykes and Dodd, *Show Me Justice;* "ACLU Applauds Newly Enacted Emmett Till Unsolved Civil Rights Crimes Act," Press Release, American Civil Liberties Union, Washington, DC, October 8, 2008.

17. Sykes and Dodd, *Show Me Justice.*

18. Sykes and Dodd, *Show Me Justice.*

19. Lottie Joiner, "Inside the Effort to Solve Civil Rights Crimes Before It's Too Late," *Time*, October 15, 2015.

20. Robbie Brown, "45 Years Later, Apology and 6 Months," *New York Times*, November 15, 2010.

21. Brown, "45 Years Later, Apology and 6 Months."

22. "Former State Trooper, 77, Pleads Guilty in Civil Rights Case," CNN, November 15, 2010.

23. Brown, "45 Years Later, Apology and 6 Months."

24. "Four Senators, Two Reps Join John Lewis in Introducing Emmett Till Unsolved Civil Rights Crimes Reauthorization Act," Press Release, Georgiapol .com, April 28, 2016.

25. "Senator Burr Introduces Emmett Till Unsolved Civil Rights Crimes Reauthorization Act," Press Release, April 27, 2016.

26. Christopher Benson, "With a New Emmett Till Bill, Senate Says Black Lives Matter," *Huffington Post*, July 19, 2016.

27. "Conyers, Lewis and Sensenbrenner Applaud House Passage of Emmett Till Unsolved Civil Rights Crimes Reauthorization Act," Press Release, House Committee on the Judiciary, Chairman Jerrold Nadler, December 7, 2016.

28. "Obama Signs Bill to Review Civil Rights Era Killings," *PBS NewsHour*, December 16, 2016.

5: UNREASONABLE DOUBT

1. "The Murder of Emmett Till: Sheriff Clarence Strider," *American Experience*, PBS.

2. Simeon Booker, "A Negro Reporter at the Till Trial," *Nieman Reports*, January 1956; Dave Tell, *Remembering Emmett Till* (Chicago and London: University of Chicago Press, 2019), 41; Mamie Till-Mobley and Christopher Benson, *Death of Innocence: The Story of the Hate Crime That Changed America* (New York: Random House, 2003), 168–71.

3. Simeon Booker with Carol McCabe Booker, *Shocking the Conscience: A Reporter's Account of the Civil Rights Movement* (Jackson: University Press of Mississippi), 70–73; Elliott Gorn, *Let the People See: The Story of Emmett Till* (New York: Oxford University Press, 2018), 128–32.

4. Booker, "A Negro Reporter at the Till Trial"; Tell, *Remembering Emmett Till*, 46–47.

5. Testimony of Moses Wright, Trial Transcript, *State of Mississippi vs. J. W. Milam and Roy Bryant*, September Term, 1955 in Sumner, Mississippi, 258–77. As included in Prosecutive Report of Investigation, Federal Bureau of Investigation, February 2006, 8.

6. Testimony of Moses Wright, 8.

7. Testimony of Moses Wright, 9.

8. Till-Mobley and Benson, *Death of Innocence*, 174.

9. Testimony of Moses Wright, 16.

10. Testimony of Moses Wright, 12.

11. Testimony of Moses Wright, 19.

12. Testimony of Mamie Bradley, Trial Transcript, *State of Mississippi vs. J. W. Milam and Roy Bryant*, September Term, 1955 in Sumner, Mississippi, 183; Till-Mobley and Benson, *Death of Innocence*, 178.

13. Till-Mobley and Benson, *Death of Innocence*, 133–37.

14. Testimony of Willie Reed, Trial Transcript, *State of Mississippi vs. J.W. Milam and Roy Bryant*, September Term, 1955 in Sumner, Mississippi, 222; Till-Mobley and Benson, *Death of Innocence*, 182–83.

15. Testimony of Willie Reed, 221.

16. Testimony of Moses Wright, 9.

17. Testimony of Willie Reed, 238.

18. Testimony of Willie Reed, 228–29 and 244.

19. Testimony of Mamie Bradley, 187.

20. Testimony of Mamie Bradley, 192–95; Till-Mobley and Benson, *Death of Innocence*, 179–81.

21. "The Murder of Emmett Till: Sheriff Clarence Strider," *American Experience*, PBS.

22. Davis Houck, "Unique Defense Helped Emmett Till's Killers Get Away with Murder," *Mississippi Clarion-Ledger*, August 29, 2018; Tell, *Remembering Emmett Till*, 168; Davis W. Houck and Matthew A. Grindy, *Emmett Till and the Mississippi Press* (Jackson: University Press of Mississippi), 81.

23. Testimony of Carolyn Bryant, Trial Transcript, *State of Mississippi vs. J. W. Milam and Roy Bryant*, September Term, 1955 in Sumner, Mississippi, 258–77.

24. Hon. Robert B. Smith III, special assistant to the district attorney, Trial Transcript, *State of Mississippi vs. J. W. Milam and Roy Bryant*, September Term, 1955 in Sumner, Mississippi, 260.

25. Attorney J. J. Breland, Trial Transcript, *State of Mississippi vs. J. W. Milam and Roy Bryant*, September Term, 1955 in Sumner, Mississippi, 260; Houck, "Unique Defense Helped Emmett Till's Killers Get Away with Murder."

26. Attorney Sidney Carlton, Trial Transcript, *State of Mississippi vs. J. W. Milam and Roy Bryant*, September Term, 1955 in Sumner, Mississippi, 260.

27. Trial Transcript, *State of Mississippi vs. J. W. Milam and Roy Bryant*, September Term, 1955 in Sumner, Mississippi, 265.

28. Houck, "Unique Defense Helped Emmett Till's Killers Get Away With Murder."

29. Testimony of Tallahatchie County Sheriff H. C. Strider, Trial Transcript, *State of Mississippi vs. J. W. Milam and Roy Bryant*, September Term, 1955 in Sumner, Mississippi, 283.

30. Testimony of Tallahatchie County Sheriff H. C. Strider, 286.

31. Testimony of Tallahatchie County Sheriff H. C. Strider, 287.

32. Testimony of Tallahatchie County Sheriff H. C. Strider, 287.

33. Testimony of Tallahatchie County Sheriff H. C. Strider, 287.

34. Testimony of Tallahatchie County Sheriff H. C. Strider, 289.

35. Testimony of Tallahatchie County Sheriff H. C. Strider, 289.

36. Till-Mobley and Benson, *Death of Innocence*, 179.

37. Till-Mobley and Benson, *Death of Innocence*, 187.

38. Till-Mobley and Benson, *Death of Innocence*, 187; Testimony of Dr. L. B. Otken, Trial Transcript, *State of Mississippi vs. J. W. Milam and Roy Bryant*, September Term, 1955 in Sumner, Mississippi, 296

39. Testimony of Dr. L. B. Otken, 297.

40. Till-Mobley and Benson, *Death of Innocence*, 179; Testimony of H. D. Malone, Trial Transcript, *State of Mississippi vs. J. W. Milam and Roy Bryant*, September Term, 1955 in Sumner, Mississippi, 306.

41. Testimony of H. D. Malone, 310.

42. Testimony of H. D. Malone, 311–16.

43. Tell, *Remembering Emmett Till*, 151–52.

44. Sam Johnson, "Jury Hears Defense and Prosecution Arguments as Testimony Ends in Kednap-Claying Case," Associated Press, *Greenwood Commonwealth*, September 23, 1955, as published in Christopher Metress, *The Lynching of Emmett Till: A Documentary Narrative* (Charlottesville and London: University of Virginia Press, 2002), 100; Gorn, *Let the People See*, 164–66.

45. "Called Lynch-Murder, 'Morally, Legally' Wrong," *Cleveland Call and Post*, October 1, 1955, as published in Metress, *The Lynching of Emmett Till*, 101–02.

46. Richard Rubin, "The Ghosts of Emmett Till," *New York Times Magazine*, July 31, 2005.

47. Gorn, *Let the People See*, 168; Till-Mobley and Benson, *Death of Innocence*, 188.

48. Gorn, *Let the People See*, 168; Till-Mobley and Benson, *Death of Innocence*, 188.

49. Trial Transcript, 349.

50. Gorn, *Let the People See*, 168; Till-Mobley and Benson, *Death of Innocence*, 188.

6: A PLACE CALLED SLAUGHTER

1. Innocence Staff, "The Lasting Legacy of Parchman Farm; The Prison Modeled After a Slave Plantation," The Innocence Project, May 29, 2020; "Inside Mississippi's Notorious Parchman Farm," *NewsHour*, PBS, January 29, 2018.

2. Douglas Blackman, *Slavery by Another Name: The Re-Enslavement of Black Americans from the Civil War to World War II* (New York: Doubleday, 2008).

3. Michelle Alexander, *The New Jim Crow: Mass Incarceration in the Age of Colorblindness* (New York: The New Press, 2010), 31–32.

4. Innocence Staff, "The Lasting Legacy of Parchman Farm"; "Inside Mississippi's Notorious Parchman Farm," *NewsHour*.

7: BROKEN PROMISES

1. Testimony of Leflore County Sheriff George Smith, Trial Transcript, *State of Mississippi vs. J. W. Milam and Roy Bryant*, September Term, 1955 in Sumner, Mississippi, 91 and 119. As included in Prosecutive Report of Investigation, Federal Bureau of Investigation, February 2006.

2. Elliott Gorn, *Let the People See: The Story of Emmett Till* (New York: Oxford University Press, 2018), 113.

3. Testimony of Leflore County Sheriff George Smith, 91 and 119.

4. Testimony of Leflore County Deputy Sheriff John Ed Cothran, Trial Transcript, *State of Mississippi vs. J.W. Milam and Roy Bryant*, September Term, 1955 in Sumner, Mississippi, 136, 143, and 144; Testimony of Leflore County Sheriff George Smith, 119.

5. Simeon Booker, *Shocking the Conscience: A Reporter's Account of the Civil Rights Movement* (Jackson: University Press of Mississippi, 2013), 65; Mamie Till-Mobley and Christopher Benson, *Death of Innocence: The Story of the Hate Crime That Changed America* (New York: Random House, 2003), 166–67.

6. Simeon Wright, with Herb Boyd, *Simeon's Story: An Eyewitness Account of the Kidnapping of Emmett Till* (Chicago: Lawrence Hill Books, 2010), 70.

7. Till-Mobley and Benson, *Death of Innocence*, 130; Simeon Booker, *Shocking the Conscience*, 59.

8. Wright and Boyd, *Simeon's Story*, 81–84.

9. "Till's Dad Raped 2 Women, Murdered a Third in Italy," *Jackson Daily News*, October 14, 1955; "Till's Father Had Been Billed 'War Hero' During Fund Raising Drives," *Jackson Daily News*, October 15, 1955; Till-Mobley and Benson, *Death of Innocence*, 202–03; Davis W. Houck and Matthew A. Grindy, *Emmett Till and the Mississippi Press* (Jackson: University Press of Mississippi), 134; Gorn, *Let the People See*, 201–02.

10. Alice Kaplan, "A Hidden Memorial to the Worst Aspects of Our Jim Crow Army," *Chicago Tribune*, September 25, 2005; Latifah Muhammad, "The Disturbing Connection Between Emmett Till's Murder and His Father's Execution," *Vibe*, July 25, 2016; Till-Mobley and Benson, *Death of Innocence*, 202–03; Houck and Grindy, *Emmett Till and the Mississippi Press*, 134.

11. Timothy Tyson, *The Blood of Emmett Till* (New York: Simon & Schuster, 2017), 196–97.

12. Till-Mobley and Benson, *Death of Innocence*, 212–13.

13. Testimony of Leflore County Sheriff George Smith, 91 and 119; Testimony of Leflore County Deputy Sheriff John Ed Cothran, 136, 143, and 144.

14. William Bradford Huie, "The Shocking Story of Approved Killing in Mississippi," *Look*, January 24, 1956, as reprinted in Christopher Metress, *The Lynching of Emmett Till: A Documentary Narrative* (Charlottesville and London: University of Virginia Press, 2002), 206. (Note: This is the precise page number for the quoted material; the page numbers for the entire reprint are 200–08.)

15. Huie, "The Shocking Story of Approved Killing in Mississippi," as reprinted in Metress, *The Lynching of Emmett Till*, 204.

16. Huie, "The Shocking Story of Approved Killing in Mississippi," as reprinted in Metress, *The Lynching of Emmett Till*, 204.

17. Huie, "The Shocking Story of Approved Killing in Mississippi," as reprinted in Metress, *The Lynching of Emmett Till*, 204.

18. Huie, "The Shocking Story of Approved Killing in Mississippi," as reprinted in Metress, *The Lynching of Emmett Till*, 206.

19. Huie, "The Shocking Story of Approved Killing in Mississippi," as reprinted in Metress, *The Lynching of Emmett Till*, 202.

20. It was disappointing to see Timothy Tyson reiterate this in two passages in his book, repeating Huie's words that Bobo "taunted" Milam and Bryant with "stories of having sex with white girls."

21. Tyson, *The Blood of Emmett Till*, 197.

22. Till-Mobley and Benson, *Death of Innocence*, 214.

23. David Halberstam, *The Fifties* (New York: Villard, 1993), 431–32.

24. Halberstam, *The Fifties*, 437.

25. Wright and Boyd, *Simeon's Story*, 89 and 133–36.

26. Wright and Boyd, *Simeon's Story*, 86.

27. Wright and Boyd, *Simeon's Story*, 87.

28. Wright and Boyd, *Simeon's Story*, 87.

29. Wright and Boyd, *Simeon's Story*, 93.

30. William Bradford Huie, letter to Roy Wilkins, October 12, 1955, Ohio State University, Huie Papers, Box 39, File 353c; Gorn, *Let the People See*, 236.

31. Huie, letter to Wilkins, October 12, 1955; Gorn, *Let the People See*, 236.

32. William Bradford Huie, letter to Mr. Walters, October 18, 1955; Huie, letter to Wilkins, October 12, 1955; Huie, letter to Dan Mich, October 27, 1955, all in Ohio State University, Huie Papers, Box 39, File 353c; Gorn, *Let the People See*, 237–38.

33. William Bradford Huie, letter to Dan Mich, October 17, 1955; Huie, letter to

Mich, October 23, 1955, both in Ohio State University, Huie Papers, Box 39, File 353c; United Artists contract, re: The Emmett Till Story, February 9, 1956, in Ohio State University, Huie Papers, Box 85, File 353; publishing agreement with Simon & Schuster, in Ohio State University, Huie Papers, Box 85, File 353; Gorn, *Let the People See*, 239.

34. Huie, letter to Mich, October 17, 1955; Huie, letter to Mich, October 23, 1955; United Artists contract, re: The Emmett Till Story, February 9, 1956; publishing agreement with Simon & Schuster; Gorn, *Let the People See*, 239.

35. Metress, *The Lynching of Emmett Till*, 207.

36. Huie, letter to Roy Wilkins, October 12, 1955; Gorn, *Let the People See*, 236.

8: LAW AND ORDER

1. Jeremiah 1:5, King James Version.

2. Dan Baum, "Legalize It All," *Harper's Magazine*, April 2016.

3. Jeremy Meyer, "Nixon Rides the Backlash to Victory: Racial Politics in the 1968 Presidential Campaign," *The Historian* 64, no. 2 (2001), 351–66.

4. Gareth Davies, "Richard Nixon and the Desegregation of Southern Schools," *Journal of Policy History*, Cambridge University Press, 19, no. 4 (2007), 367–94; "Nixon, The Supreme Court, and Busing," Richard Nixon Foundation, April 2, 2015.

5. "Nixon and the Peaceful Desegregation of Southern Schools" (video), February 22, 2016, Richard Nixon Presidential Library and Museum, nixonfoundation.org.

6. "Nixon and the Peaceful Desegregation of Southern Schools."

7. E. Frederic Morrow, Memorandum for the Record, The White House, November 22, 1955; E. Frederic Morrow, *Black Man in the White House: A Revealing Diary of the Eisenhower Administration by the First Negro Presidential Aide in History* (New York: Coward-McCann, 1963), 28.

8. Morrow, *Black Man in the White House*, 82–84.

9. Milton S. Katz, "E. Frederic Morrow and Civil Rights in the Eisenhower Administration," *Phylon* 42, no. 2 (1981), 133; Peter Lyon, *Eisenhower: Portrait of a Hero* (Boston: Little, Brown, 1974), 555.

10. Morrow, *Black Man in the White House*, 18.

11. Morrow, *Black Man in the White House*, 28, 32, and 102; Katz, "E. Frederic Morrow and Civil Rights in the Eisenhower Administration," 142.

12. Mamie Bradley, telegram to President Dwight D. Eisenhower regarding Emmett Till case, September 2, 1955; "Till, Emmett," Alphabetical Files 1953–1961, Collection DDE-WHCF: White House Central Files (Eisenhower Administration), Dwight D. Eisenhower Library, Abilene, KS.

13. J. Edgar Hoover, director Federal Bureau of Investigation, personal and confidential letter regarding Emmett Till, to Dillon Anderson, special assistant to the president for national security, Collection DDE-1417, Eisenhower Administration, September 13, 1955.

14. J. Edgar Hoover, director Federal Bureau of Investigation, personal and confidential letter regarding Emmett Till, to Dillon Anderson, special assistant to the president for national security, Collection DDE-1417, Eisenhower Administration, November 22, 1955.

15. Morrow, *Black Man in the White House*, 48.

16. Morrow, *Black Man in the White House*, 48.

17. David T. Beito and Linda Royster Beito, *Black Maverick: T.R.M. Howard's Fight*

for Civil Rights and Economic Power (Urbana and Chicago: University of Illinois Press, 2009), 131.

18. Beito and Beito, *Black Maverick*, 135.
19. Beito and Beito, *Black Maverick*, 136.
20. Beito and Beito, *Black Maverick*, 139.
21. Jeffrey O. G. Ogbar, "The FBI's War on Civil Rights Leaders," *Daily Beast*, January 16, 2017.
22. Hoover, letter to Anderson, November 22, 1955.
23. "Racial Tension and Civil Rights," March 1, 1956, statement by J. Edgar Hoover, director Federal Bureau of Investigation, delivered to Eisenhower administration cabinet on March 8, 1956, 3.
24. "Racial Tension and Civil Rights," 4.
25. Maxwell Rabb, memo to White House Press Secretary James Hagerty, October 23, 1956.
26. Rabb, memo to Hagerty, October 23, 1956.
27. Katz, "E. Frederic Morrow and Civil Rights in the Eisenhower Administration," 136.
28. E. Frederic Morrow, Memorandum for Governor Adams, July 12, 1957, DDEL.
29. Allan Jalon, "1955 Killing Sparked Civil Rights Revolution: Emmett Till: South's Legend and Legacy," *Los Angeles Times*, October 7, 1985.
30. David A. Nichols, "Ike Liked Civil Rights," *New York Times*, September 12, 2007.
31. Steven Livingston, "John F. Kennedy, Martin Luther King Jr., and the Phone Call That Changed History," *Time*, June 20, 2017; Quin Hillyer, "On MLK Day, Remembering Calls from JFK and RFK," *Washington Examiner*, January 20, 2020.
32. Hugh Stephen Whitaker, "A Case Study in Southern Justice: The Murder and Trial of Emmett Till," *Rhetoric and Public Affairs* 8, no. 2 (2005), 220; Jalon, "1955 Killing Sparked Civil Rights Revolution."

9: TALE OF THE TAPE

1. "CDS Scholar Tim Tyson Wins Robert F. Kennedy Book Award for 'The Blood of Emmett Till,'" Center for Documentary Studies at Duke University.
2. Kristine Phillips, Wesley Lowery, and Devlin Barrett, "New Details in Book About Emmett Till's Death Prompted Officials to Reopen Investigation," *Washington Post*, July 12, 2018; Alan Blinder, "US Reopens Emmett Till Investigation Almost 63 Years After His Murder," *New York Times*, July 12, 2018.
3. Jay Reeves and Allan G. Breed, "Author of Emmett Till Book Gave FBI Interview Recordings," Associated Press, *Charlotte Observer*, July 13, 2018.
4. "Race in America: Justice Dept. Reopens Investigation Into Emmett Till Murder Case," MSNBC News, July 14, 2018.
5. "Race in America: Justice Dept. Reopens Investigation Into Emmett Till Murder Case."
6. The Reverend Al Sharpton, "The Case of Emmett Till," *Politics Nation*, MSNBC, July 15, 2018.
7. Timothy Tyson, email to Special FBI Agent Walter Henry re subpoenaed material in Emmett Till case, September 21, 2017, 2:16 A.M.

8. Jamiles Lartey, "'This Is Your Last Chance for Justice': Eric Garner's Family Wants NYPD Officers Fired," *Guardian*, July 18, 2018.

10: READING BETWEEN THE LIES

1. Undated, unpaginated interview transcript, Timothy Tyson, Carolyn Bryant Donham, and Marsha Bryant.
2. Innocence Staff, "The Lasting Legacy of Parchman Farm, The Prison Modeled After a Slave Plantation," The Innocence Project, May 29, 2020; "Inside Mississippi's Notorious Parchman Prison," *PBS NewsHour*, January 29, 2018.
3. Timothy Tyson, *The Blood of Emmett Till* (New York: Simon & Schuster, 2017), 44.
4. Tyson, *The Blood of Emmett Till*; undated, unpaginated interview transcript, Tyson, Bryant Donham, and Bryant.
5. Tyson, *The Blood of Emmett Till*, 49–50; undated, unpaginated interview transcript, Tyson, Bryant Donham, and Bryant.
6. Elliott Gorn, *Let the People See: The Story of Emmett Till* (New York: Oxford University Press 2018), 85; "The Murder of Emmett Till: Sheriff Clarence Strider," *American Experience*, PBS; Mamie Till-Mobley and Christopher Benson, *Death of Innocence: The Story of the Hate Crime That Changed America* (New York: Random House, 2003), 162.
7. Undated, unpaginated interview transcript, Tyson, Bryant Donham, and Bryant.
8. Undated, unpaginated interview transcript, Tyson, Bryant Donham, and Bryant.
9. Carolyn Bryant Donham and Marsha Bryant, *I Am More than a Wolf Whistle: The Story of Carolyn Bryant Donham as written by Marsha Bryant*, unpublished manuscript, 43.
10. Undated, unpaginated interview transcript, Tyson, Bryant Donham, and Bryant.
11. "Roy Bryant's Admission," Prosecutive Report of Investigation, Federal Bureau of Investigation, February 2006, 92.
12. Undated, unpaginated interview transcript, Tyson, Bryant Donham, and Bryant.
13. Undated, unpaginated interview transcript, Tyson, Bryant Donham, and Bryant.
14. Undated, unpaginated interview transcript, Tyson, Bryant Donham, and Bryant.
15. Undated, unpaginated interview transcript, Tyson, Bryant Donham, and Bryant.

11: ALTERNATIVE FACTS

1. Carolyn Bryant Donham and Marsha Bryant, *I Am More than a Wolf Whistle: The Story of Carolyn Bryant Donham as written by Marsha Bryant*, unpublished manuscript, 4.
2. Bryant Donham and Bryant, *I Am More than a Wolf Whistle*, 1–2.
3. Bryant Donham and Bryant, *I Am More than a Wolf Whistle*, 1.
4. Bryant Donham and Bryant, *I Am More than a Wolf Whistle*, 2.
5. Bryant Donham and Bryant, *I Am More than a Wolf Whistle*, 2.
6. Bryant Donham and Bryant, *I Am More than a Wolf Whistle*, 3.

7. Bryant Donham and Bryant, *I Am More than a Wolf Whistle*, 7.

8. Bryant Donham and Bryant, *I Am More than a Wolf Whistle*, 19.

9. Bryant Donham and Bryant, *I Am More than a Wolf Whistle*, 52.

10. Bryant Donham and Bryant, *I Am More than a Wolf Whistle*, 8.

11. Bryant Donham and Bryant, *I Am More than a Wolf Whistle*, 55–57.

12. Bryant Donham and Bryant, *I Am More than a Wolf Whistle*, 100.

13. Bryant Donham and Bryant, *I Am More than a Wolf Whistle*, 5.

14. Bryant Donham and Bryant, *I Am More than a Wolf Whistle*, 92.

15. Bryant Donham and Bryant, *I Am More than a Wolf Whistle*, 86–87.

16. Bryant Donham and Bryant, *I Am More than a Wolf Whistle*, 4.

17. Bryant Donham and Bryant, *I Am More than a Wolf Whistle*, 100.

18. Bryant Donham and Bryant, *I Am More than a Wolf Whistle*, 31.

19. Jerry Mitchell, "What Did Carolyn Bryant Say and When?" *Mississippi Clarion-Ledger*, August 24, 2018 (summarizing the notes taken by defense attorney Sidney Carlton during the initial interview with Carolyn Bryant, September 2, 1955).

20. Testimony of Carolyn Bryant, Trial Transcript, *State of Mississippi vs. J. W. Milam and Roy Bryant*, September Term, 1955 in Sumner, Mississippi, 258–77. As included in Prosecutive Report of Investigation, Federal Bureau of Investigation, February 2006.

21. Bryant Donham and Bryant, *I Am More than a Wolf Whistle*, 31.

22. Bryant Donham and Bryant, *I Am More than a Wolf Whistle*, 30, Timothy Tyson track changes comments 14, 15, 16.

23. Bryant Donham and Bryant, *I Am More than a Wolf Whistle*, 79, Timothy Tyson track changes comment 44.

24. Bryant Donham and Bryant, *I Am More than a Wolf Whistle*, 99, Timothy Tyson track changes comments 47, 48.

25. Bryant Donham and Bryant, *I Am More than a Wolf Whistle*, 56, Timothy Tyson track changes comment 36.

26. Bryant Donham and Bryant, *I Am More than a Wolf Whistle*, 43.

27. Bryant Donham and Bryant, *I Am More than a Wolf Whistle*, Timothy Tyson track changes comment 21.

28. Bryant Donham and Bryant, *I Am More than a Wolf Whistle*, 43.

29. Bryant Donham and Bryant, *I Am More than a Wolf Whistle*, Timothy Tyson track changes comment 20.

30. Undated, unpaginated interview transcript, Timothy Tyson, Carolyn Bryant Donham, and Marsha Bryant.

31. Timothy Tyson, *The Blood of Emmett Till* (New York: Simon & Schuster, 2017), 197.

32. Mitchell, "What Did Carolyn Bryant Say and When."

33. Review of "Till Material from Tim Tyson," completed by Supervisory Special Agent Dale R. Killinger for the purpose of identifying information regarding the murder and kidnapping of EMMETT TILL which may differ from information previously provided by CAROLYN BRYANT DONHAM. December 22, 2017. Review conducted as part of ongoing FBI investigation, 2017–21.

34. Bryant Donham and Bryant, *I Am More than a Wolf Whistle*, 37.

35. Bryant Donham and Bryant, *I Am More than a Wolf Whistle*, 37.

36. Transcript, Carolyn Bryant Donham interview, conducted by Supervisory Special Agent Dale R. Killinger, October 2, 2005.

37. Transcript, Carolyn Bryant Donham interview, conducted by Supervisory Special Agent Dale R. Killinger, October 19, 2005.

38. Bryant Donham and Bryant, *I Am More than a Wolf Whistle*, 43.

39. Transcript, Donham interview, Supervisory Special Agent Killinger, October 19, 2005.

40. Transcript, Donham interview, Supervisory Special Agent Killinger, October 19, 2005.

41. Bryant Donham and Bryant, *I Am More than a Wolf Whistle*, 4.

42. Bryant Donham and Bryant, *I Am More than a Wolf Whistle*, 4.

43. Bryant Donham and Bryant, *I Am More than a Wolf Whistle*, 5.

12: MONUMENTS, MEMORIALS, MEMORIES

1. Jerry Mitchell, "Bombshell Quote Missing from Emmett Till Tape. So Did Carolyn Bryant Donham Really Recant?" *Mississippi Clarion-Ledger*, August 21, 2018.

2. Mitchell, "Bombshell Quote Missing from Emmett Till Tape."

3. Mitchell, "Bombshell Quote Missing from Emmett Till Tape."

4. Mitchell, "Bombshell Quote Missing from Emmett Till Tape."

5. "Attorney General Holder Announces Updates to Justice Department Media Guidelines," Department of Justice, Office of Public Affairs, January 14, 2015; Attorney General Eric Holder, "Updated Policy Regarding Obtaining Information from, or Records of, Members of the News Media; and Regarding Questioning, Arresting, or Charging Member of the News Media," Memorandum to All Department Employees, January 14, 2015.

6. Jerry Mitchell, "Emmett Till Mystery: Who Is the White Girl in His Photo?," *Mississippi Clarion-Ledger*, August 27, 2018.

7. Mitchell, "Emmett Till Mystery."

8. "Sequence of Events," Prosecutive Report of Investigation, Federal Bureau of Investigation, February 2006, 44; Mamie Till-Mobley and Christopher Benson, *Death of Innocence: The Story of the Hate Crime That Changed America* (New York: Random House, 2003), 102.

9. Marvel Parker, email to Jerry Mitchell, August 29, 2018, 5:57 A.M.

10. Jerry Mitchell, email to Marvel Parker, August 29, 2018, 12:18 P.M.

11. Jessica Schladebeck, "Mysterious Woman Pictured in Old Photo, Described as Emmett Till's 'Girlfriend' Discusses Murder for First Time," *New York Daily News*, August 28, 2018.

12. "Did Emmett Till Have a White 'Girlfriend'? Yes, and She's Been Found," WKYC (reprinting Mitchell's *Clarion-Ledger* story), August 28, 2018.

13. Hannah Perry, "White 'Girlfriend' of Emmett Till Speaks Out for the First Time," *Daily Mail*, August 28, 2018.

14. Audie Cornish, "County Apologizes to Emmett Till Family," *All Things Considered*, National Public Radio, October 2, 2007; "The Apology: Resolution Presented to Emmett Till's Family," Emmett Till Interpretive Center, August 16, 2021, emmett-till.org.

15. Cornish, "County Apologizes to Emmett Till Family."

16. Peter Baker, Katie Benner, and Michael D. Shear, "Jeff Sessions Is Forced Out as Attorney General, as Trump Installs Loyalist," *New York Times*, November 7, 2018.

17. Emily S. Rued, "Ole Miss Students and Faculty Groups Vote Unanimously to Relocate Confederate Statue," *New York Times*, March 8, 2019.

18. Rued, "Ole Miss Students and Faculty Groups Vote Unanimously."

19. Rued, "Ole Miss Students and Faculty Groups Vote Unanimously."

20. "A Great Leader Is Born," Martin Luther King, Jr., National Historical Park Georgia, National Park Service, nps.gov.

21. Karen Brooks, "George Zimmerman Gun Sells for $250,000," *Huffington Post* (Reuters), May 20, 2016; "Gun That Killed Trayvon Martin 'Makes $250,000 for Zimmerman,'" BBC, May 22, 2016.

22. Jerry Mitchell, "We Found Photos of Ole Miss Students Posing with Guns in Front of a Shot-Up Emmett Till Memorial. Now They Face a Possible Civil Rights Investigation," ProPublica, Mississippi Center for Investigative Reporting, July 25, 2019; Neil Vigdor, "Emmett Till Sign Photo Leads Ole Miss Fraternity to Suspend Members," *New York Times*, July 25, 2019.

23. Jerry Mitchell, "A Year After an Instagram Photo of Ole Miss Frats Hoisting Guns in Front of a Bullet-Riddled Emmett Till Sign Went Viral, Questions Remain," Mississippi Center for Investigative Reporting, August 28, 2020.

24. Benjamin Fearnow, "Emmett Till Mississippi Memorial Sign Riddled with Bullets 35 Days After Being Replaced," *Newsweek*, August 15, 2018.

25. Dave Tell, "Put the Vandalized Emmett Till Signs in Museums," *New York Times*, November 14, 2019.

26. Michael Saponara, "Jay-Z & Will Smith to Executive Produce ABC Series Telling Emmett Till's Story from Mother's Perspective," *Billboard*, August 5, 2019.

27. The Reverend Jesse L. Jackson, Sr., Foreword, Mamie Till-Mobley and Christopher Benson, *Death of Innocence: The Story of the Hate Crime That Changed America* (New York: Random House, 2003), xii.

28. Aimee Ortiz, "Emmett Till Memorial Has a New Sign. This Time It's Bulletproof," *New York Times*, October 20, 2019.

13: HOUSE OF MIRRORS

1. Transcript, Timothy Tyson, FBI interview, October 25, 2019, 12.

2. Transcript, Tyson interview, 16.

3. Transcript, Tyson interview, 17–18.

4. Transcript, Tyson interview, 13.

5. Transcript, Tyson interview, 19.

6. Transcript, Tyson interview, 19.

7. Transcript, Tyson interview, 20.

8. Transcript, Tyson interview, 20.

9. Transcript, Tyson interview, 20.

10. Transcript, Tyson interview, 20.

11. Transcript, Tyson interview, 20.

12. Transcript, Tyson interview, 20.

13. Transcript, Tyson interview, 21.

14. Transcript, Tyson interview, 22.

15. Jerry Mitchell, "Bombshell Quote Missing from Emmett Till Tape. So Did Carolyn Bryant Donham Really Recant?" *Mississippi Clarion-Ledger*, August 21, 2018.

16. Transcript, Tyson interview, 28.

17. Transcript, Tyson interview, 30.

18. Transcript, Tyson interview, 31–32.
19. Transcript, Tyson interview, 33.
20. Undated, unpaginated interview transcript, Timothy Tyson, Carolyn Bryant Donham, and Marsha Bryant, first page.
21. Transcript, Tyson interview, 34.
22. Transcript, Tyson interview, 35.
23. Transcript, Tyson interview, 36.
24. Transcript, Tyson interview, 41.
25. Transcript, Tyson interview, 41.
26. Transcript, Tyson interview, 44.
27. Transcript, Tyson interview, 38.
28. Transcript, Tyson interview, 45.
29. Transcript, Tyson interview, 46.
30. Transcript, Tyson interview, 47.
31. Transcript, Tyson interview, 47.
32. Transcript, Tyson interview, 49.
33. Transcript, Tyson interview, 48–49.
34. Timothy Tyson, *The Blood of Emmett Till* (New York: Simon & Schuster, 2017), 44.
35. Timothy Tyson, email to Devery Anderson, March 31, 2014, 11:41 A.M.
36. Tyson, email to Anderson, March 31, 2014, 11:41 A.M.
37. Devery Anderson, email to Timothy Tyson, March 31, 2014, 12:32 P.M.
38. Anderson, email to Tyson, March 31, 2014, 12:32 P.M.
39. Transcript, Tyson interview, 56.
40. Transcript, Tyson interview, 57.
41. Undated, unpaginated interview transcript, Tyson, Bryant Donham, and Bryant.

14: APPROPRIATION

1. Hannah Baldwin, "Naming the Enslaved, Reconciling the Past in Memphis," Southern Poverty Law Center, October 19, 2018.
2. Transcript, Timothy Tyson, FBI interview, October 25, 2019, 28.
3. Timothy Tyson, email to Brandis Friedman, February 21, 2017, 4:55 P.M.
4. Devery Anderson, email to Timothy Tyson, March 31, 2014, 12:32 P.M.
5. Anderson, email to Tyson, March 31, 2014, 12:32 P.M.
6. Anderson, email to Tyson, March 31, 2014, 12:32 P.M.
7. Timothy Tyson, email to Devery Anderson, March 31, 2014, 1:17 P.M.
8. Tyson, email to Anderson, March 31, 2014, 1:17 P.M.; Anderson, email to Tyson, March 31, 2014, 12:32 P.M.
9. Devery Anderson, email to Timothy Tyson, July 25, 2014, 9:04 P.M.
10. Timothy Tyson, email to Devery Anderson, July 26, 2014, 10:48 A.M.
11. Timothy Tyson, "Emmett Till Case and Montgomery Bus Boycott 1955–56," online posting for "The South in Black and White," lecture and discussion course offering for "students at Durham Tech, NCCU, UNC, Duke, and to the larger community."
12. Tyson, "Emmett Till Case and Montgomery Bus Boycott 1955–56," 4–5.
13. Carolyn Bryant Donham and Marsha Bryant, *I Am More than a Wolf Whistle: The Story of Carolyn Bryant Donham as written by Marsha Bryant*, unpublished manuscript, 31.

14. Tyson, email to Anderson, July 26, 2014, 10:48 A.M.

15. Timothy Tyson, email to Devery Anderson, August 14, 2014, 6:28 A.M.

16. Timothy Tyson, email to David Beito, July 15, 2009, 1:31 P.M.

17. David Beito, email to Timothy Tyson, July 15, 2009, 4:59 P.M.

18. Timothy Tyson, email to David Beito, July 15, 2009, 5:26 P.M.

19. Tyson, email to Beito, July 15, 2009, 5:26 P.M.

20. Tyson, email to Friedman, February 21, 2017, 4:55 P.M.

21. "Ex–University of Mississippi Student Indicted for Noose on James Meredith Statue," NBC News, March 27, 2015.

22. Elliott McLaughlin, "The Battle Over Ole Miss: Why a Flagship University Has Stood Behind a Nickname with a Racist Past," CNN, July 27, 2020; Becca Andrews, "The Racism of 'Ole Miss' Is Hiding in Plain Sight," *Mother Jones*, July 1, 2020.

23. "Negro Describes Boy's Abduction; Implicates 3 Men, One White Woman," *Mississippi Clarion-Ledger*, September 2, 1955, 1.

24. Michael Randolph Oby, "Black Press Coverage of the Emmett Till Lynching as a Catalyst to the Civil Rights Movement," thesis, Georgia State University, 2007, 43.

25. Oby, "Black Press Coverage of the Emmett Till Lynching as a Catalyst," 43.

26. Timothy Tyson, email to Devery Anderson, July 29, 2014, 8:04 A.M.

27. Devery Anderson, email to Timothy Tyson, July 29, 2014, 11:32 A.M.

28. Devery Anderson, email to Timothy Tyson, July 29, 2014, 11:32 A.M.

29. Christopher Benson, "Eyewitness Account: Emmett Till's Cousin Simeon Wright Seeks to Set the Record Straight," *Chicago* (magazine), December 18, 2009.

30. Undated, unpaginated interview transcript, Timothy Tyson, Carolyn Bryant Donham, and Marsha Bryant.

31. Mamie Till-Mobley and Christopher Benson, *Death of Innocence: The Story of the Hate Crime That Changed America* (New York: Random House, 2003), 137.

32. Devery Anderson, "Significant Contribution and Worth the Read," Amazon.com, February 3, 2017.

33. Anderson, "Significant Contribution and Worth the Read."

34. Anderson, "Significant Contribution and Worth the Read."

35. R. J. Cubarrubia, "Lil Wayne Apologizes for 'Inappropriate' Emmett Till Lyric," *Rolling Stone*, May 1, 2013; "Emmett Till's Family Responds to Lil Wayne Lyric in New Open Letter," Black Voices, *Huffington Post*, February 21, 2013.

36. Till-Mobley and Benson, *Death of Innocence*, 193–94.

15: GHOST SKINS

1. Claudia Grisales, "'It's About Time': House Approves Historic Bill Making Lynching a Federal Crime," WBEZ, National Public Radio, February 26, 2020; Felicia Sonmez, "House Passes Historic Anti-Lynching Bill After Congress' Century of Failure," *Washington Post*, February 26, 2020.

2. Stanley Augustin, "Family Announcement Regarding the Passing of Mrs. Airickca Gordon Taylor, Cousin of Emmett Till," Press Release, Lawyers' Committee for Civil Rights Under Law, March 22, 2020.

3. Augustin, "Family Announcement Regarding the Passing of Mrs. Airickca Gordon Taylor."

4. Katie Benner, "Eric Garner's Death Will Not Lead to Federal Charges for NYPD Officer," *New York Times*, July 16, 2019; David Shortell, "Barr Sides Against Civil Rights Officials in Declining to Bring Charges Against NYPD Officer in Garner Case," CNN Politics, July 16, 2019.

5. "Ahmaud Arbery's Murderers Driven by 'Pent-Up Racial Anger,' Prosecutor Says," *Guardian*, February 22, 2022.

6. Alex Lubben, "Police Shot and Killed a 26-Year-Old EMT in Her Apartment While Looking for Someone Else Entirely," *Vice*, May 13, 2020, retrieved May 21, 2022.

7. Havovi Cooper and Austin Meyer, "Prosecutor Stresses That George Floyd Said 'I Can't Breathe' 27 Times While Derek Chauvin Kneeled on Him," *Business Insider*, May 10, 2021; Josh Marcus, "Derek Chauvin Trial: George Floyd Told Police 'I Can't Breathe' 27 Times as Defendant Accused of 'Betraying Badge,'" *Independent*, March 29, 2021.

8. Rukmini Callimachi, Nicholas Bogel-Burroughs, John Eligon, and Will Wright, "Fired Officer Is Indicted in Breonna Taylor Case; Protesters Wanted Stronger Charges," *New York Times*, December 29, 2020.

9. Eric Levenson, "How Minneapolis Police First Described the Murder of George Floyd and What We Know Now," CNN, April 21, 2021.

10. John Lewis, "Together, You Can Redeem the Soul of Our Nation," *New York Times*, July 30, 2020.

11. Sam Brodey and Spencer Ackerman, "AG Barr Calls Black Lives Matter Protests in Portland 'An Assault on US Government' in Testy Hearing," *Daily Beast*, July 28, 2020, retrieved May 21, 2022; Mary Clare Jalonick, Michael Balsamo, and Eric Tucker, "Barr Defends Aggressive Federal Response to Protests," Associated Press, PBS *NewsHour*, July 27, 2020, retrieved May 21, 2022.

12. Josh Margolin, "White Supremacists 'Seek Affiliation' with Law Enforcement to Further Their Goals, Internal FBI Report Warns," ABC News, March 8, 2021; Steve Volk, "The Enemy Within: White Supremacy in American Policing," *Rolling Stone*, May 12, 2021; Sara Kamali, "Ghost Skins: Military & Law Enforcement Members at the Insurrection," Rantt Media, February 12, 2021.

13. John Edgar Wideman, "A Black and White Case," *Esquire*, October 19, 2016; Pamela Newkirk, "Separate Deaths of Emmett Till and His Father Louis Suggest a Pattern of Injustice," *Washington Post*, December 2, 2016.

14. Elliott Gorn, *Let the People See: The Story of Emmett Till* (New York: Oxford University Press, 2018), 210; John Edgar Wideman, *Writing to Save a Life: The Louis Till File* (New York: Scribner, 2016), 112–19; Francis X. Clines, "When Black Soldiers Were Hanged: A War's Footnote," *New York Times*, February 7, 1993; Mary Louise Roberts, *What Soldiers Do: Sex and the American GI in World War II France* (Chicago: University of Chicago Press, 2013), 219.

15. H. E. Ely, Major General, USA Commandant, "The Use of Negro Man Power in War," memorandum for the chief of staff, Army War College Office of the Commandant, Washington Barracks, DC, October 30, 1925, 14.

16. Ely, "The Use of Negro Man Power in War," 6.

17. *Report, Board of Review, United States vs. Privates, Fred A. McMurray and Louis Till, Both of 177th Port Company, 379th Port Battalion, Transportation Corps, Peninsular Base Section, Mediterranean Theater of Operations, US Army, Branch Office of the Judge Advocate General with the Mediterranean Theater of Operations, U.S. Army*, 13 June 1945; Wideman, *Writing to Save a Life*, 112–19.

18. Mamie Till-Mobley and Christopher Benson, *Death of Innocence: The Story of the Hate Crime That Changed America* (New York: Random House, 2003), 203–04.

19. Roberts, *What Soldiers Do*, 235.

20. Yoselin Acevedo, "Casey Affleck Is 'Appalled' After Finding Out His Production Company Donated to Trump's Transition Team," *IndieWire*, February 27, 2017; Tolly Wright, "Casey Affleck Didn't Authorize Company's Trump Donation," Vulture.com, *New York* (magazine), February 26, 2017, retrieved May, 19, 2022.

21. Eric Hananoki, "Movie Producer and Son of Phillies Co-Owner Is the Big Donor Behind Roger Stone's Controversial Group," *MediaMatters*, April 20, 2016, retrieved May 19, 2022; "'Lego Movie' Producer Backs Roger Stone's Trump PAC," *Daily Beast*, April 20, 2016, retrieved May 19, 2022.

22. Senator Richard Burr, "Remembering Alvin Sykes," Congressional Record S1931, April 14, 2021.

23. Senator Cory Booker, "Emmett at 80: Memory, Meaning, Movement" (video tribute to Alvin Sykes), DuSable Museum of African American History, July 24, 2021.

16: RECKONING WITH THE CONSEQUENCES

1. Notice to Close File No. 144-40-1660, Re: Roy Bryant (Deceased); John William (J. W.) Milam (Deceased)—Subjects; Emmett Till (Deceased)—Victim; Civil Rights; US Department of Justice, Civil Rights Division, Chief Criminal Section, December 6, 2021, 11.

2. Notice to Close File No. 144-40-1660, 12.

3. Notice to Close File No. 144-40-1660, 12, footnote 22.

4. Notice to Close File No. 144-40-1660, 12.

5. Notice to Close File No. 144-40-1660, 13.

6. Letter to Reverend Wheeler Parker from Barbara K. Bosserman, Deputy Chief, Cold Case Unit, US Department of Justice, Civil Rights Division, Criminal Section, December 6, 2021, 4.

7. Bryant Donham and Bryant, *I Am More than a Wolf Whistle*, generally.

8. Bryant Donham and Bryant, *I Am More than a Wolf Whistle*, 32, Tyson track changes comment 17; Notice to Close File No. 144-40-1660, 16, footnote 34.

9. Bryant Donham and Bryant, *I Am More than a Wolf Whistle*, 43, Tyson track changes comment 20; Notice to Close File No. 144-40-1660, 16, footnote 34.

10. Bryant Donham and Bryant, *I Am More than a Wolf Whistle*, 43, Tyson track changes comment 21; Notice to Close File No. 144-40-1660, 16, footnote 34.

11. Bryant Donham and Bryant, *I Am More than a Wolf Whistle*, 46, Tyson track changes comment 23; Notice to Close File No. 144-40-1660, 16, footnote 34.

12. Notice to Close File No. 144-40-1660, 12.

13. Notice to Close File No. 144-40-1660, letter to Reverend Parker, 5, 14; Notice to Close File No. 144-40-1660, Section 3A, 4.

14. Notice to Close File No. 144-40-1660, Section 3A, 4.

15. Adia Robinson, "Family of Emmett Till Reacts to DOJ Closing Investigation into His Murder," ABC News, December 7, 2021, 9:46 A.M., retrieved December 7, 2021.

16. Audra D. S. Burch and Tariro Mzezewa, "Justice Department Closes Emmett Till Investigation Without Charges," *New York Times*, December 6, 2021, retrieved December 7, 2021.

17. Robinson, "Family of Emmett Till Reacts to DOJ Closing Investigation."

18. "Muddy River Gives Up Body of Brutally Slain Negro Boy," Memphis *Commercial Appeal*, September 1, 1955.

19. Undated, unpaginated interview transcript, Timothy Tyson, Carolyn Bryant Donham, and Marsha Bryant.

20. Prosecutive Report of Investigation, Federal Bureau of Investigation, February 2006, 90.

21. Undated, unpaginated interview transcript, Tyson, Bryant Donham, and Bryant.

22. Undated, unpaginated interview transcript, Tyson, Bryant Donham, and Bryant.

23. Prosecutive Report of Investigation, Federal Bureau of Investigation, February 2006, 46–48.

24. Prosecutive Report of Investigation, Federal Bureau of Investigation, February 2006, 46–48.

25. Bryant Donham and Bryant, *I Am More than a Wolf Whistle*, 47.

26. Bryant Donham and Bryant, *I Am More than a Wolf Whistle*, 48.

27. Undated, unpaginated interview transcript, Tyson, Bryant Donham, and Bryant.

28. Bryant Donham and Bryant, *I Am More than a Wolf Whistle*, 43.

29. Trial Transcript, *State of Mississippi vs. J. W. Milam and Roy Bryant*, September Term, 1955 in Sumner, Mississippi, 85–93, 134–178. As included in Prosecutive Report of Investigation, Federal Bureau of Investigation, February 2006.

30. Elliott Gorn, *Let the People See: The Story of Emmett Till* (New York: Oxford University Press), 76.

31. Prosecutive Report of Investigation, Federal Bureau of Investigation, February 2006, 42.

32. Gorn, *Let the People See*, 286.

33. Trial Transcript, *State of Mississippi vs. J. W. Milam and Roy Bryant*, September Term, 1955 in Sumner, Mississippi, 277–81.

34. Jerry Mitchell, "What Did Carolyn Bryant Say and When?" *Mississippi Clarion-Ledger*, August 24, 2018.

AFTERWORD: "PERSEVERE"

1. Morrow, *Black Man in the White House*, 28.

2. Leigh Ann Caldwell and Theodoric Meyer, "Clyburn: 'We Still Refuse to Admit that we Have a Race Problem in This Country,'" *The Washington Post*, May, 20, 2022.

3. Caldwell and Meyer, "Clyburn: 'We Still Refuse to Admit that we Have a Race Problem in This Country,'" *The Washington Post*, May, 20, 2022.

4. John Lewis, "Together, You Can Redeem the Soul of Our Nation," *The New York Times*, July 30, 2020.

5. Joseph R. Biden, "Remarks at Signing of H.R. 55, the 'Emmett Till Antilynching Act,'" March 29, 2022.

Bibliography

BOOKS

Alexander, Michelle. *The New Jim Crow: Mass Incarceration in the Age of Colorblindness*. New York: The New Press, 2010.

Anderson, Devery. *Emmett Till: The Murder That Shocked the World and Propelled the Civil Rights Movement*. Jackson: University Press of Mississippi, 2015.

Beito, David T., Linda Royster Beito. *Black Maverick: T.R.M. Howard's Fight for Civil Rights and Economic Power*. Urbana and Chicago: University of Illinois Press, 2009.

Blackmon, Douglas. *Slavery by Another Name: The Re-Enslavement of Black Americans From The Civil War to World War II*. New York: Doubleday, 2008.

Booker, Simeon, Carol McCabe Booker. *Shocking the Conscience: A Reporter's Account of the Civil Rights Movement*. Jackson, Mississippi: University Press of Mississippi, 2013.

Borstelmann, Thomas. *The Cold War and the Color Line: American Race Relations in the Global Arena*. Cambridge, Massachusetts: Harvard University Press, 2001.

German, Mike. *Disrupt, Discredit and Divide: How the New FBI Damages Democracy*. New York: The New Press, 2019.

Gorn, Elliott J. *Let the People See: The Story of Emmett Till*. New York: Oxford University Press, 2018.

Green, Adam. *Selling the Race: Culture, Community, and Black Chicago, 1940-1955*. Chicago: University of Chicago Press, 2007.

Halberstam, David. *The Fifties*. New York: Villard, 1993.

Houck, Davis W., Matthew A. Grindy. *Emmett Till and the Mississippi Press*. Jackson, Mississippi: University Press of Mississippi, 2008.

Lewis, John, Michael D'Orso. *Walking With the Wind: A Memoir of the Movement*. New York: Simon & Schuster, 1998.

Lyon, Peter. *Eisenhower: Portrait of a Hero*. Boston: Little Brown, 1974.

Metress, Christopher. *The Lynching of Emmett Till: A Documentary Narrative*. Charlottesville and London: University of Virginia Press, 2002.

Morrow, E. Frederic. *Black Man in the White House: A Revealing Diary of the Eisenhower Administration by the First Negro Presidential Aide in History*. New York: Coward-McCann, Inc, 1963.

Roberts, Mary Louise. *What Soldiers Do: Sex and the American GI in World War II France*. Chicago: University of Chicago Press, 2013.

Tell, Dave. *Remembering Emmett Till*. Chicago and London: University of Chicago Press, 2019.

Till-Mobley, Mamie, Christopher Benson. *Death of Innocence: The Story of the Hate Crime That Changed America*. New York: Random House, 2003.

Tyson, Timothy. *The Blood of Emmett Till*. New York: Simon & Schuster, 2017.

Wideman, John Edgar. *Writing to Save a Life: The Louis Till File*. New York: Scribner, 2016.

Wright, Simeon, Herb Boyd. *Simeon's Story: An Eyewitness Account of the Kidnapping of Emmett Till*. Chicago: Lawrence Hill Books, 2010.

ARTICLES

Acevedo, Yoselin, "Casey Affleck Is 'Appalled' After Finding Out His Production Company Donated to Trump's Transition Team," *IndieWire*, February 27, 2017.

Anderson, Devery, "Significant Contribution and Worth the Read," review of The Blood of Emmett Till, by Timothy B. Tyson, amazon.com, February 3, 2017.

Andrews, Becca, "The Racism of 'Ole Miss' Is Hiding in Plain Sight," *Mother Jones*, July 1, 2020.

Apuzo, Matt, Adam Goldman, William K. Rashbaum, "Justice Dept. Shakes Up Inquiry Into Eric Garner Chokehold Case," *The New York Times*, October 24, 2016.

Baker, Peter, Katie Benner, Michael D. Shear, "Jeff Sessions Is Forced Out as Attorney General, as Trump Installs Loyalist," *The New York Times*, November 7, 2018.

Baldwin, Hannah, "Naming the Enslaved, Reconciling the Past in Memphis," Southern Poverty Law Center, October 19, 2018.

Barry, Ellen, "Rumor of a Key Witness," *Los Angeles Times*, July 30, 2005.

Baum, Dan, "Legalize It All," *Harper's Magazine*, April 2016.

Benner, Katie, "Eric Garner's Death Will Not Lead to Federal Charges for NYPD Officer," *The New York Times*, July 16, 2019.

Benson, Christopher, "Civil Rights Murders: The Till Bill Would Create Two Cold Case Squads to Reopen and Solve Dozens of Long-Forgotten Civil Rights Murders—if Congress Can Pay Attention Long Enough to Make it Law," *Chicago Sun-Times*, October 8, 2006.

Benson, Christopher, "Eyewitness Account: Emmett Till's Cousin Simeon Wright Seeks to Set the Record Straight," *Chicago*, December 18, 2009.

Benson, Christopher, "Scalia's Role in the Emmett Till Case," *Chicago Tribune*, February 19, 2016.

Benson, Christopher, "With a New Emmett Till Bill, Senate Says Black Lives Matter," *Huffington Post*, July 19, 2016.

BET Staff, "Family of Emmett Till Urges Department of Justice to Reopen Investigation of 1955 Lynching," *BET*, March 14, 2022.

Blinder, Alan, "U.S. Reopens Emmett Till Investigation Almost 63 Years After His Murder," *The New York Times*, July 12, 2018.

Booker, Simeon, "A Negro Reporter at the Till Trial," *Nieman Reports*, January 1956.

Brodey, Sam, Spencer Ackerman, "AG Barr Calls Black Lives Matter Protests in Portland 'an Assault on U.S. Government' in Testy Hearing," *Daily Beast*, July 28, 2020.

Brooks, Karen, "George Zimmerman Gun Sells for $250,000," *Huffington Post*, May 20, 2016.

Brown, Robbie, "45 Years Later, Apology and 6 Months," *The New York Times*, November 15, 2010.

Burch, Audra D.S., Tariro Mzezewa, "Justice Department Closes Emmett Till Investigation Without Charges," *The New York Times*, December 6, 2021.

Burke, Minyvonne, "Woman Shot and Killed by Kentucky Police in Botched Raid, Family Says," NBC News, May 13, 2020.

Caldwell, Leigh Ann, Theodoric Meyer, "Clyburn: 'We Still Refuse to Admit That We Have a Race Problem in This Country,'" *The Washington Post*, May 20, 2022.

Callimachi, Rukimini, Nicholas Bogel-Burroughs, John Eligon, Will Wright, "Fired Officer Is Indicted in Breonna Taylor Case; Protestors Wanted Stronger Charges," *The New York Times*, December 29, 2020.

Clines, Francis X., "When Black Soldiers Were Hanged: A War's Footnote," *The New York Times*, February 7, 1993.

Cooper, Havovi, Austin Meyer, "Prosecutor Stresses That George Floyd Said 'I Can't Breathe' 27 Times While Derek Chauvin Kneeled on Him," *Business Insider*, May 10, 2021.

Cornish, Audie, "County Apologizes to Emmett Till Family," *All Things Considered*, National Public Radio, October 2, 2007.

Cubarrubia, RJ, "Lil Wayne Apologizes for 'Inappropriate' Emmett Till Lyric," *Rolling Stone*, May 1, 2013.

Davies, Gareth, "Richard Nixon and the Desegregation of Southern Schools," *Journal of Policy History*, Cambridge University Press, Vol. 19, No. 4, 367–394, 2007.

Dorfman, Ariel, "Will America Earn the Right to Survive? William Faulkner's Provocative Question From 1955 Echoes Loudly in 2016," *The Atlantic*, November 4, 2016.

Faulkner, William, "Can We Survive?" *New South*, September 1955.

Fearnow, Benjamin, "Emmett Till Mississippi Memorial Sign Riddled With Bullets 35 Days After Being Replaced," *Newsweek*, August 15, 2018.

Fountain, John W., "Mamie Mobley, 81, Dies; Son, Emmett Till, Slain in 1955," *The New York Times*, January 7, 2003.

Ford, Matt, "Trump's Press Secretary Falsely Claims: 'Largest Audience Ever to Witness an Inauguration, Period,'" *The Atlantic*, January 21, 2017.

Friedman, Brandis, "Emmett Till's Family Reacts to Accuser's Confession, 60 Years Later," WTTW, Public Broadcasting Service, February 23, 2017.

Gorn, Elliott, "How America Remembers Emmett Till: 'Hatred Could Not Justify Child Murder, but Fear Could,'" *The Literary Hub*, Oxford University Press, November 15, 2018.

Grabenstein, Hannah, "Inside Mississippi's Notorious Parchman Prison," *PBS NewsHour*, January 29, 2018.

Grisales, Claudia, "'It's About Time': House Approves Historic Bill Making Lynching A Federal Crime," WBEZ, National Public Radio, February 26, 2020.

Hananoki, Eric, "Movie Producer and Son of Phillies Co-Owner Is the Big Donor Behind Roger Stone's Controversial Group," *MediaMatters*, April 20, 2016.

Hanna, Jason, "Video: Boy With Air Gun Was Shot 2 Seconds After Cleveland Police Arrived," *CNN*, November 27, 2014.

Hauck, Grace, "Emmett Till's Lynching Ignited a Civil Rights Movement. Historians Say George Floyd's Death Could Do the Same," *USA Today*, June 11, 2020.

Hersh, Seymore, "Torture at Abu Ghraib," *The New Yorker*, April 30, 2004.

Hillyer, Quin, "On MLK Day, Remembering Calls From JFK and RFK," *Washington Examiner*, January 20, 2020.

Houck, Davis, "Unique Defense Helped Emmett Till's Killers Get Away With Murder," *Mississippi Clarion-Ledger*, August 29, 2018.

Innocence Staff, "The Lasting Legacy of Parchman Farm, the Prison Modeled After a Slave Plantation," The Innocence Project, May 29, 2020.

Jackson, Reverend Jesse L. Sr., "Foreword," in *Death of Innocence: The Story of the Hate Crime That Changed America*, by Mamie Till-Mobley and Christopher Benson. New York: Random House, 2003, xii.

Jalon, Allan, "1955 Killing Sparked Civil Rights Revolution: Emmett Till: South's Legend and Legacy," *Los Angeles Times*, October 7, 1985.

Jalonick, Mary Clare, Michael Balsamo, Eric Tucker, "Barr Defends Aggressive Federal Response to Protests," *PBS NewsHour*, July 27, 2020.

Joiner, Lottie, "Inside the Effort to Solve Civil Rights Crimes Before It's Too Late," *Time*, October 15, 2015.

Johnson, Sam, "Jury Hears Defense and Prosecution Arguments as Testimony Ends in Kidnap-Slaying Case," *Greenwood Commonwealth*, September 23, 1955.

Kamali, Sara, "Ghost Skins: Military & Law Enforcement Members at the Insurrection," *Rantt Media*, February 12, 2021.

Kaplan, Alice, "A Hidden Memorial To the Worst Aspects of Our Jim Crow Army," *Chicago Tribune*, September 25, 2005.

Katz, Milton S., "E. Frederic Morrow and Civil Rights in the Eisenhower Administration," *Phylon*, Vol. 42, No. 2, 1981.

Kemper III, Crosby, "It Started at the Library: Tom Coburn, Civil Rights Ally and Friend," Institute of Museum and Library Services, March 2020.

Kessler, Glenn, Salvador Rizzo, Megan Kelly, "Trump Has Made 18,000 False or Misleading Claims in 1,170 Days," *The Washington Post*, April 14, 2020.

Kuettner, Al, "Ole Miss Enrolls Meredith After Riots Kill 2, Injure 75," UPI Archives, October 1, 1962.

Lartey, Jamiles, "'This Is Your Last Chance for Justice': Eric Garner's Family Wants NYPD Officers Fired," *The Guardian*, July 18, 2018.

Levenson, Eric, "How Minneapolis Police First Described the Murder of George Floyd and What We Know Now," CNN, April 21, 2021.

Lewis, John, "Together, You Can Redeem the Soul of Our Nation," *The New York Times*, July 30, 2020.

Li, David K., "Black Man Shot Dead While Jogging in Georgia, and Two Months Later, No Arrests," *NBC News*, April 30, 2020.

Liston, Barbara, "Family of Florida Boy Killed by Neighborhood Watch Seeks Arrest," Reuters, March 7, 2012.

Livingston, Steven, "John F. Kennedy, Martin Luther King Jr., and the Phone Call That Changed History," *Time*, June 20, 2017.

Lubben, Alex, "Police Shot and Killed a 26-Year-Old EMT in Her Apartment While Looking for Someone Else Entirely," *VICE News*, May 13, 2020.

Lueck, Sarah, "One-Man Gridlock: Meet Tom Coburn, Senate's 'Dr. No': Oklahoma Conservative Specializes in the 'Hold,' Stopping 90 Bills in 2007," *The Wall Street Journal*, December 21, 2007.

Marcus, Josh, "Derek Chauvin Trial: George Floyd Told Police 'I Can't Breathe' 27 Times as Defendant Accused of 'Betraying Badge,'" *Independent*, March 29, 2021.

Margolin, Josh, "White Supremacists 'Seek Affiliation' With Law Enforcement To Further Their Goals, Internal FBI Report Warns," *ABC News*, March 8, 2021.

McLaughlin, Elliot, "The Battle Over Ole Miss: Why a Flagship University Has Stood Behind a Nickname With a Racist Past," CNN, July 27, 2020.

Meyer, Jeremy, "Nixon Rides the Backlash to Victory: Racial Politics in the 1968 Presidential Campaign," *The Historian*, Vol. 64, No. 2, p.351-366, 2001.

Mitchell, Jerry, "Bombshell Quote Missing From Emmett Till Tape. So Did Carolyn Bryant Donham Really Recant?" *Mississippi Clarion-Ledger*, August 21, 2018.

Mitchell, Jerry, "Emmett Till Mystery: Who Is the White Girl in His Photo?" *Mississippi Clarion-Ledger*, August 27, 2018.

Mitchell, Jerry, "Did Emmett Till Have a White 'Girlfriend'? Yes, and She's Been Found," *Mississippi Clarion-Ledger*, reprinted in WKYC, August 28, 2018.

Mitchell, Jerry, "Reexamining Emmett Till Case Could Help Separate Fact, Fiction," *USA Today*, February 19, 2007.

Mitchell, Jerry, "We Found Photos of Ole Miss Students Posing With Guns in Front of a Shot-Up Emmett Till Memorial. Now They Face a Possible Civil Rights Investigation," *ProPublica, Mississippi Center for Investigative Reporting*, July 25, 2019.

Mitchell, Jerry, "What Did Carolyn Bryant Say and When?" *Mississippi Clarion-Ledger*, August 24, 2018.

Muhammad, Latifah, "The Disturbing Connection Between Emmett Till's Murder and His Father's Execution," *Vibe*, July 25, 2016.

N.A., "A Great Leader Is Born," Martin Luther King, Jr. National Historical Park Georgia, National Park Service, nps.gov.

N.A., "Ahmaud Arbery's Murderers Driven by 'Pent-Up Racial Anger,' prosecutor says," *The Guardian*, February 22, 2022.

N.A., "Called Lynch-Murder, 'Morally, Legally' Wrong," *Cleveland Call and Post*, October 1, 1955.

N.A., "Emmett Till Conspiracy Theory Debunked," History News Network, Columbian College Arts and Sciences, The George Washington University, February 20, 2007.

N.A., "Emmett Till's Family Responds To Lil Wayne Lyric In New Open Letter," Black Voices, *Huffington Post*, February 21, 2013.

N.A., "Ex-University of Mississippi Student Indicted for Noose on James Meredith Statue," *NBC News*, March 27, 2015.

N.A., "Former State Trooper, 77, Pleads Guilty in Civil Rights Case," *CNN*, November 15, 2010.

N.A., "Just Permanent Interests," The Honorable Henry Lacy Clay Sr. "The Long Struggle for Representation: Oral Histories of African Americans in Congress," Office of the Historian, U.S. House of Representatives.

N.A., "Justice Department to Investigate 1955 Emmett Till Murder," *Jet Magazine*, May 24, 2004.

N.A., "'Lego Movie' Producer Backs Roger Stone's Trump PAC," *Daily Beast*, April 20, 2016.

N.A., "Muddy River Gives Up Body of Brutally Slain Negro Boy," *Memphis Commercial Appeal*, September 1, 1955.

N.A., "Negro Describes Boy's Abduction; Implicates 3 Men, One White Woman," *Clarion Ledger*, September 2, 1955.

N.A., "Nixon and the Peaceful Desegregation of Southern Schools," Video, Richard Nixon Presidential Library and Museum, nixonfoundation.org, February 22, 2016.

N.A., "Nixon, the Supreme Court, and Busing," Richard Nixon Foundation, April 2, 2015.

N.A., "Obama Signs Bill to Review Civil Rights Era Killings," *PBS NewsHour*, December 16, 2016.

N.A., "The Apology: Resolution Presented to Emmett Till's Family," Emmett Till Interpretive Center, emmtt-till.org, August 16, 2021.

N.A., "The Murder of Emmett Till: Sheriff Clarence Strider, Mississippi Sheriff Clarence Strider Became an Unforgettable Symbol of Southern Intransigence in the Emmett Till Case," *American Experience*, Public Broadcasting Service.

N.A., "Till's Dad Raped 2 Women, Murdered a Third in Italy," *Jackson Daily News*, October 14, 1955.

N.A., "Till's Father Had Been Billed 'War Hero' During Fund Raising Drives," *Jackson Daily News*, October 15, 1955.

Newkirk, Pamela, "Separate Deaths of Emmett Till and His Father Louis Suggest a Pattern of Injustice," *The Washington Post*, December 2, 2016.

Nichols, David A., "Ike Liked Civil Rights," *The New York Times*, September 12, 2007.

North, Anna, "Amy Cooper's 911 Call Is Part of an All-Too-Familiar Pattern," *Vox*, May 26, 2020.

Ogbar, Jeffery O.G., "The FBI's War on Civil Rights Leaders," *Daily Beast*, January 16, 2017.

Ortiz, Aimee, "Emmett Till Memorial Has a New Sign. This Time It's Bulletproof," *The New York Times*, October 20, 2019.

Perez-Peña, Richard, "Woman Linked to 1955 Emmett Till Murder Tells Historian Her Claims Were False," *The New York Times*, January 27, 2017.

Perry, Hannah, "White 'Girlfriend' of Emmett Till Speaks Out for the First Time," *Daily Mail*, August 28, 2018.

Phillips, Kristine, Wesley Lowery, Devlin Barrett, "New Details in Book About Emmett Till's Death Prompted Officials to Reopen Investigation," *The Washington Post*, July 12, 2018.

Robinson, Adia, "Family of Emmett Till Reacts to DOJ Closing Investigation Into His Murder," ABC News, December 7, 2021.

Rubin, Richard, "The Ghosts of Emmett Till," *New York Times Magazine*, July 31, 2005.

Rued, Emily S., "Ole Miss Students and Faculty Groups Vote Unanimously to Relocate Confederate Statue," *The New York Times*, March 8, 2019.

Russell, Margaret M., "Reopening the Emmett Till Case; Lessons and Challenges for Critical Race Practice," *Fordham Law Review*, Vol. 73, No. 5, 2005.

Saponara, Michael, "Jay-Z & Will Smith to Executive Produce ABC Series Telling Emmett Till's Story From Mother's Perspective," *Billboard*, August 5, 2019.

Schectman, Joel, Mark Hosenball, "Sessions Asks 46 Obama-Era U.S. Attorneys to Resign," Reuters, March 10, 2017.

Schladeback, Jessica, "Mysterious Woman Pictured in Old Photo, Described as Emmett Till's 'Girlfriend' Discusses Murder for First Time," *New York Daily News*, August 28, 2018.

Shortell, David, "Barr Sides Against Civil Rights Officials in Declining to Bring Charges Against NYPD Officer in Garner Case," *CNN Politics*, July 16, 2019.

Sonmez, Felicia, "House Passes Historic Anti-Lynching Bill After Congress' Century of Failure," *The Washington Post*, February 26, 2020.

Sontag, Susan, "Regarding the Torture of Others," *The New York Times*, May 23, 2004.

Staff, "The Murder of Emmett Till Justice May Be Delayed, But It Should Not Be Denied," *The Buffalo News*, May 24, 2004.

Swayer, Alex, "Ketanji Brown Jackson Gets Emotional, Tells Youth to 'Persevere,'" *Washington Times*, March 23, 2022.

Tell, Dave, "Put the Vandalized Emmett Till Signs in Museums," *The New York Times*, November 14, 2019.

The Daily Dish, "The Past Isn't Dead. It Isn't Even Past," *The Atlantic*, March 18, 2008.

Tyson, Timothy, "Emmett Till Case and Montgomery Bus Boycott 1955-56," online posting for "The South in Black and White," lecture and discussion course offering for "students at Durham Tech, NCCU, UNC, Duke, and to the larger community."

Vigdor, Neil, "Emmett Till Sign Photo Leads Ole Miss Fraternity to Suspend Members," *The New York Times*, July 25, 2019.

Volk, Steve, "The Enemy Within: White Supremacy in American Policing," *Rolling Stone*, May 12, 2021.

Whitaker, Hugh Stephen, "A Case Study in Southern Justice: The Murder and Trial of Emmett Till," Rhetoric and Public Affairs, Vol. 8, No. 2, p.220, 2005.

Wideman, John Edgar, "A Black and White Case," *Esquire Magazine*, October 19, 2016.

Wright, Tolly, "Casey Affleck Didn't Authorize Company's Trump Donation," *Vulture, New York Magazine*, February 26, 2017.

Yang, Maya, and agencies, "Ahmaud Arbery's Murderers Driven by 'Pent-Up Racial Anger,' Prosecutor Says," *The Guardian*, February 22, 2022.

UNPUBLISHED MANUSCRIPTS

Donham, Carolyn Bryant, Marsha Bryant. *I Am More Than a Wolf Whistle: The Story of Carolyn Bryant Donham as Written by Marsha Bryant.*

Sykes, Alvin, Monroe Dodd. *Show Me Justice.*

DOCUMENTARIES/TELEVISION/RADIO

Booker, Cory, "Emmett at 80: Memory, Meaning, Movement," Video, DuSable Museum of African American History, July 24, 2021.

Brooks, Marion, "The Lost Story of Emmett Till: Universal Child," WMAQ-TV, NBC Chicago, February 5, 2022.

Curry, Fatima, Jeanmarie Condon, "Let the World See," ABC, ABC News Studios, January 6-20, 2022.

"County Apologizes to Emmett Till Family," All Things Considered, with Audie Cornish, National Public Radio, October 2, 2007.

Dodd, Monroe, "Pursuit of Truth: From Kansas City's Libraries, Alvin Sykes Plotted an Unlikely Course to Civil Rights History," Kansas City Public Library, 2014.

"Eyes on the Prize; Interview With Curtis Jones," Film and Media Archive, Washington University in St. Louis, American Archive of Public Broadcasting, GBH and the Library of Congress, Boston, MA, and Washington, DC, November 12, 1985.

"Integrating Ole Miss: A Transformative, Deadly Riot," WBEZ, with Debbie Elliot, National Public Radio, October 1, 2012.

"'It's About Time': House Approves Historic Bill Making Lynching a Federal Crime," WBEZ, with Claudia Grisales, National Public Radio, February 26, 2020.

"Mississippi D.A. Weighs Prosecution in Till Murder." *Morning Edition*, with Audie Cornish, National Public Radio, May 8, 2006.

Nelson, Stanley, Jr., "The Murder of Emmett Till," *The American Experience*, Public Broadcasting Service, January 20, 2003.

Samuels, Rich, "Emmett Till: The Murder and the Movement," WMAQ-TV, NBC Chicago, 1985.

"The Case of Emmett Till", *Politics Nation*, with Reverend Al Sharpton, MSNBC, July 15, 2018.

DISSERTATION/THESES

Flournoy, Craig, "Reporting Movement in Black and White: The Emmett Till Lynching and the Montgomery Bus Boycott," Doctoral Dissertation, Louisiana State University, 2003.

Oby, Michael Randolph, "Black Press Coverage of the Emmett Till Lynching as a Catalyst to the Civil Rights Movement," Communications Thesis, Department of Communication, Georgia State University, May 2, 2007.

Whitaker, Hugh Stephen, "A Case Study in Southern Justice: The Emmett Till Case," Master's Thesis, Florida State University, 1963.

Whitten, Ellen, "Justice Unearthed: Revisiting the Murder of Emmett Till," Honor's Thesis, Rhodes College, 2005.

MEMORANDA/REPORTS

Memorandum, For All Department Employees From Attorney General Eric Holder, "Updated Policy Regarding Obtaining Information From, or Records of, Members of the News Media; and Regarding Questioning, Arresting, or Charging Member of the News Media," January 14, 2015.

Memorandum, For Jack W. Fuller, Special Assistant to the Attorney General, From Antonin Scalia, Assistant Attorney General, Office of Legal Counsel, "Jurisdiction of the Department of Justice to Investigate the Assassination of President Kennedy," July 28, 1976.

Memorandum, For the Chief of Staff, the Army War College Office of the Commandant, "The Use of Negro Man Power In War," From H. E. Ely, Major General, U.S.A. Commandant, Washington Barracks, D.C., October 30, 1925.

"Memorandum for the Record," From E. Frederic Morrow, The White House, eisenhowerlibrary.gov., November 22, 1955.

Memorandum Opinion for the Principal Associate Attorney General, From Beth Nolan, Deputy Assistant Attorney General, Office of Legal Counsel, "Possible Bases of Jurisdiction for the Department of Justice to Investigate Matters Relating to the Assassination of Martin Luther King, Jr.," April 20, 1998.

Memorandum, Review of "Till Material from Tim Tyson," completed by Supervisory Special Agent Dale R. Killinger, Review conducted as part of ongoing FBI investigation, 2017-21, December 22, 2017.

Notice to Close File No. 144-40-1660, Re: Roy Bryant (Deceased), John William (J. W.) Milam (Deceased)—Subjects, Emmett Till (Deceased)—Victim. Civil Rights, U.S. Department of Justice, Civil Rights Division, Chief Criminal Section, December 6, 2021.

"The Attorney General's Seventh Annual Report to Congress Pursuant to the Emmett Till Unsolved Civil Rights Crime Act of 2007 and First Annual Report to Congress Pursuant to the Emmett Till Unsolved Civil Rights Crime Reauthorization Act of 2016," Department of Justice, February 2018.

Prosecutive Report of Investigation, Emmett Till, Federal Bureau of Investigation, February 2006.

Statement by J. Edgar Hoover, Director Federal Bureau of Investigation, March 1, 1956, Delivered to Eisenhower Administration Cabinet, "Racial Tension and Civil Rights," March 8, 1956.

DOCUMENTS/TRANSCRIPTS

Contracts, William Bradford Huie, United Artists. re: The Emmett Till Story, Feb. 9, 1956; publishing agreement with Simon & Schuster. Ohio State University, William Bradford Huie Papers, box 85, file 353.

Transcript, Carolyn Bryant Donham Interview, conducted by Supervisory Special Agent Dale R. Killinger, October 2, 2005 (excerpted).

Transcript, Carolyn Bryant Donham Interview, conducted by Supervisory Special Agent Dale R. Killinger, October 19, 2005 (excerpted).

Transcript, Timothy Tyson Interview, Federal Bureau of Investigation, October 25, 2019.

Transcript, *State of Mississippi vs. J.W. Milam and Roy Bryant*, Trial, September 1955.

Transcript, *United States vs. Privates Fred A. McMurray and Louis Till,* Trial, January 16, 1945.

Transcript, Undated, Unpaginated Interview, Timothy Tyson, Carolyn Bryant Donham, Marsha Bryant "Unsolved Civil Rights Crime Act." S.2679.

CORRESPONDENCE

Email, David Beito to Timothy Tyson, July 15, 2009, 4:59 p.m.

Email, Devery Anderson to Timothy Tyson, March 31, 2014, 11:41 a.m.

Email, Devery Anderson to Timothy Tyson, March 31, 2014, 12:32 p.m.

Email, Devery Anderson to Timothy Tyson, March 31, 2014, 1:17 p.m.

Email, Devery Anderson to Timothy Tyson, July 25, 2014, 9:04 p.m.

Email, Devery Anderson to Timothy Tyson, July 29, 2014, 11:32 a.m.

Email, Jerry Mitchell to Marvel Parker, August 29, 2018, 12:18 p.m.

Email, Marvel Parker to Jerry Mitchell, August 29, 2018, 5:57 a.m.

Email, Timothy Tyson to Brandis Friedman, February 21, 2017, 4:55 p.m.

Email, Timothy Tyson, to David Beito, July 15, 2009, 1:31 p.m.

Email, Timothy Tyson to David Beito, July 15, 2009, 5:26 p.m.

Email, Timothy Tyson to Devery Anderson, March 31, 2014, 1:17 p.m.

Email, Timothy Tyson to Devery Anderson, July 26, 2014, 10:48 a.m.

Email, Timothy Tyson to Devery Anderson, July 29, 2014, 8:04 a.m.

Email, Timothy Tyson to Special FBI Agent Walter Henry, Re: subpoenaed material in Emmett Till case, 2:55 a.m.

Letter, Personal and Confidential regarding Emmett Till, J. Edgar Hoover, Director Federal Bureau of Investigation, to Dillon Anderson, Special Assistant to the President for National Security, Collection DDE-1417, Eisenhower Administration, September 13, 1955.

Letter, Personal and Confidential regarding Emmett Till, J. Edgar Hoover, Director Federal Bureau of Investigation, to Dillon Anderson, Special Assistant to the President for National Security, Collection DDE-1417, Eisenhower Administration, November 22, 1955.

Letter, Barbara K. Bosserman, Deputy Chief, Cold Case Unit, U.S. Department of Justice, Civil Rights Division, Criminal Section, to Reverend Wheeler Parker December 6, 2021.

Letter, William Bradford Huie to Roy Wilkins, Oct. 12, 1955; to Mr. Walters, Oct. 18, 1955; to Dan Mich, Oct 27, 1955; to Dan Mich, Oct. 17, 1955; to Dan Mich, Oct. 23, 1955. Ohio State University, William Bradford Huie Papers, box 39, file 353c.

Telegram, Mamie Bradley to President Dwight D. Eisenhower Regarding Emmett Till Case, Till, Emmett, Alphabetical Files 1953-1961; Collection DDE-WHCF: White House Central Files (Eisenhower Administration), Dwight D. Eisenhower Library, Abilene, KS, September 2, 1955.

PRESS RELEASES/STATEMENTS

"ACLU Applauds Newly Enacted Emmett Till Unsolved Civil Rights Crimes Act," Press Release, American Civil Liberties Union, Washington, D.C., October 8, 2008.

"Attorney General Holder Announces Updates to Justice Department Media Guidelines," Office of Public Affairs, Department of Justice, January 14, 2015.

Augustin, Stanley, "Family Announcement Regarding the Passing of Mrs. Airickca Gordon Taylor, Cousin of Emmett Till," Press Release, Lawyers' Committee for Civil Rights Under Law, March 22, 2020.

Burr, Richard, "Remembering Alvin Sykes," Congressional Record, S1931, Senate, April 14, 2021.

"CDS Scholar Tim Tyson Wins Robert F. Kennedy Book Award for 'The Blood of Emmett Till,'" Center for Documentary Studies, Duke University.

"Conyers, Lewis and Sensenbrenner Applaud House Passage of Emmett Till Unsolved Civil Rights Crimes Reauthorization Act," Press Release, House Committee on the Judiciary, Chairman Jerrold Nadler, December 7, 2016.

"Department of Justice Investigation Of The Murder of Emmett Till," Congressional Record, H2820, U.S. Rep. Bobby Rush, May 12, 2004.

"Four Senators, Two Reps Join John Lewis in Introducing Emmett Till Unsolved Civil Rights Crimes Reauthorization Act," Press Release, Georgiapol.com, April 28, 2016.

"Justice Department to Investigate 1955 Emmett Till Murder: Federal-State Partnership to Develop Possible State Law Prosecution," Press Release, Department of Justice, May 10, 2004.

"President Obama Nominates Felicia C. Adams to Serve as U.S. Attorney," The White House Press Office, March 2, 2011.

"Remarks by President Biden at Signing of H.R. 55, the 'Emmett Till Antilynching Act,'" The White House, March 29, 2022.

"Remembering Alvin Sykes," Congressional Record, S1931, Senate, April 14, 2021.

"Rush, Talent, Schumer & Rangel to Justice Department and State Of Mississippi: Expedite Emmett Till Murder Case New Resolution Would Speed Inquiry to Bring Emmett Till's Murderers to Justice," Press Release, Office of Rep. Bobby Rush, November 19, 2004.

"Senator Burr Introduces Emmett Till Unsolved Civil Rights Crimes Reauthorization Act," Press Release, Till Family and Alvin Sykes Release Statements, April 27, 2016.

NEWSPAPERS/PERIODICALS

Chicago Sun-Times
Chicago Tribune
Cleveland Call and Post
Daily Mail
The Greenwood Commonwealth
Jackson Daily News
Jet Magazine
Los Angeles Times
Memphis Commercial Appeal
Mississippi Clarion-Ledger
New York Daily News
The Buffalo News
The New Yorker
The New York Times
The Wall Street Journal
The Washington Post
Time Magazine

Index

MARVEL PARKER

THE REVEREND WHEELER PARKER JR. is Pastor of Argo Temple Church of God in Christ, in Summit, Illinois, and a Superintendent in the Church of God in Christ. In his quest for accountability in the 1955 lynching of Emmett Till, he has participated in the 2004 FBI investigation of the murder and the 2017 continuation, which resulted from the efforts of the late activist Alvin Sykes. Along with Sykes, he participated in the development of the Emmett Till Unsolved Civil Rights Crimes Act, which established a cold case unit at the Department of Justice, allowing the Department of Justice to reopen unsolved Civil Rights–era murders. As a public lecturer, Pastor Parker has presented in a variety of forums, including elementary, middle, and high schools and universities in the United States and Belize. He has led historical tours for social activists throughout the Mississippi Delta in connection with the Mississippi Center for Justice, and Delta State University. His journey to justice has included a relentless advocacy for truth, and he has carried this commitment with a message of love, forgiveness, and reconciliation.

JENNA BRAUNSTEIN

CHRISTOPHER BENSON, a Chicago-based journalist and lawyer, is an associate professor of journalism in the Medill School of Journalism, Media, Integrated Marketing Communications at Northwestern University. He has served as Washington editor of *Ebony* and *Jet* magazines, city hall reporter for WBMX-FM, and has contributed to *Chicago* magazine, *The Huffington Post, The New York Times, Chicago Tribune, Chicago Sun-Times, The Chicago Reporter, The Washington Post, The Crisis,* and *Savoy.* He was co-author with the late Mamie Till-Mobley of *Death of Innocence: The Story of the Hate Crime That Changed America,* winner of the 2004 Robert F. Kennedy Book Award, Special Recognition.

About the Type

This book was set in Caslon, a typeface first designed in 1722 by William Caslon (1692–1766). Its widespread use by most English printers in the early eighteenth century soon supplanted the Dutch typefaces that had formerly prevailed. The roman is considered a "work-horse" typeface due to its pleasant, open appearance, while the italic is exceedingly decorative.